Red Hat® Enterprise Linux For Dummies®

BESTSELLING BOOK SERIES

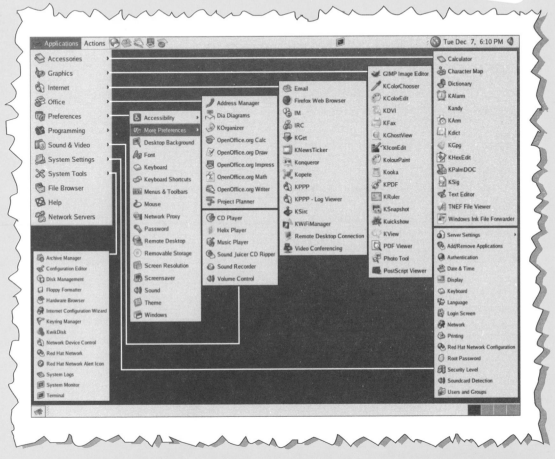

Copyright © 2005 Wiley Publishing, Inc. All rights reserved.

Item 7713-1.

For more information about Wiley Publishing, call 1-800-762-2974.

For Dummies: Bestselling Book Series for Beginners

Red Hat® Enterprise Linux® 4 For Dummies®

Cheat Sheet

Some Frequently Used Shell Commands

Here are some of the more frequently used shell commands listed for easy reference. Items shown in brackets indicate information you have to enter.

Command	Function
cd [directory]	Changes to another directory in the file system.
cat [options] [filename]	Displays the contents of a file to standard output.
chgrp [options] [directory or filename]	Changes the group rights to a file or directory.
chmod [options] [directory of filename]	Changes permissions to a file or directory.
chown [options] [directory or filename]	Changes the owner of a file or directory.
cp [source file] [destination file]	Copies a file.
date [options] [text string]	Displays the date and time (w/o text string) or set the date and time (with text string).
df [options]	Displays disk usage by device.
du [options]	Displays disk usage by directory.
echo [options] [text string]	Displays whatever is typed after the command.
find [path] [options] [filename]	Searches for files in the file system.
grep [options] [filename] [string]	Searches for the specified string and displays it on the screen.
less [options] [filename]	Displays a file to the screen one page at a time.
ln [options] [source file] [target file]	Links one file to another.
ls [options]	Lists the contents of the current directory.
more [options] [filename]	Displays a file to the screen one page at a time.
mkdir [options] [directory name]	Creates the specified directory.
mount [options] [device] [location]	Mounts a file system.
mv [options] [filename]	Moves or renames a file.
pwd [options]	Prints the working directory path to the screen.
rm [options] [filename]	Deletes the specified file.
rmdir [options] [directory name]	Removes the specified directory.
sort [options] [filename]	Sorts the lines in a text file.
umount [options] [location]	Unmounts a file system.
wc [options]	Counts the characters, words, and lines in a file.

Red Hat® Enterprise Linux® 4

FOR DUMMIES®

by Terry Collings

WILEY

Wiley Publishing, Inc.

Red Hat® Enterprise Linux® 4 For Dummies®

Published by
Wiley Publishing, Inc.
111 River Street
Hoboken, NJ 07030-5774

www.wiley.com

Copyright © 2005 by Wiley Publishing, Inc., Indianapolis, Indiana

Published by Wiley Publishing, Inc., Indianapolis, Indiana

Published simultaneously in Canada

For general information on our other products and services, please contact our Customer Care Department within the U.S. at 800-762-2974, outside the U.S. at 317-572-3993, or fax 317-572-4002.

For technical support, please visit www.wiley.com/techsupport.

Wiley also publishes its books in a variety of electronic formats. Some content that appears in print may not be available in electronic books.

Library of Congress Control Number: 2004117578

ISBN: 0-7645-7713-1

Manufactured in the United States of America

10 9 8 7 6 5 4 3 2 1

1O/SZ/QT/QV/IN

WILEY

About the Author

Terry Collings is the Instructional Technologist at Muhlenberg College in Allentown, PA where he is responsible for researching and implementing emerging technology in an educational environment. He is also the system administrator for Red Hat Linux servers on campus.

Terry is also an adjunct faculty at Lehigh Carbon Community College where he teaches A+ and Network+ certification courses. He has previously taught courses on Unix, Linux, TCP/IP, and Novell Netware.

Terry is the co-author of *Linux Bible* and *Red Hat Linux Networking and System Administration* (first and second editions) as well as a contributing writer to the Linux Weekend Crash Course. He was the technical editor for the *KDE Bible*, *The Samba Book*, *Unix Weekend Crash Course*, *Red Hat Linux 9 For Dummies*, *Solaris 9 For Dummies*, *Linux Timesaving Techniques,* and *Fedora Linux 2 For Dummies.*

Dedication

This book is dedicated to my lovely wife Nancy, who kept our toddler entertained so I could work on this project.

Author's Acknowledgments

I always have a hard time writing the acknowledgments for my books because there are so many people to recognize that I am always afraid that I'll miss someone. Well, here goes.

I would like to thank all the people at Wiley who worked on this book, especially Terri Varveris, my acquisitions editor, who finally convinced me to write a *For Dummies* book. I've known Terri for several years and have come to realize what a gem she is. Thanks to Chris Morris, my project editor, for keeping everything on track, and thanks to the technical and copy editors for putting their polish on the book. A special thank you goes to Doyle Smith who provided me with a few PCs so I could run all four versions of Enterprise Linux simultaneously.

And finally, I would like to thank my daughter Sabrina, whose early morning cries would wake me so I could do some work on this book. She was an essential part of its completion.

Publisher's Acknowledgments

We're proud of this book; please send us your comments through our online registration form located at www.dummies.com/register/.

Some of the people who helped bring this book to market include the following:

Acquisitions, Editorial, and Media Development

Project Editor: Christopher Morris

Acquisitions Editor: Terri Varveris

Sr. Copy Editor: Teresa Artman

Technical Editor: Susan Douglas

Editorial Manager: Kevin Kirschner

Media Development Manager: Laura VanWinkle

Media Development Supervisor: Richard Graves

Editorial Assistant: Amanda Foxworth

Cartoons: Rich Tennant (www.the5thwave.com)

Composition Services

Project Coordinator: Nancee Reeves, Emily Wichlinski

Layout and Graphics: Andrea Dahl, Lauren Goddard, Joyce Haughey, Stephanie D. Jumper, Melanee Prendergast, Jacque Roth, Ron Terry

Proofreaders: Leeann Harney, Joe Niesen, Carl Pierce, Dwight Ramsey, TECHBOOKS Production Services

Indexer: TECHBOOKS Production Services

Publishing and Editorial for Technology Dummies

Richard Swadley, Vice President and Executive Group Publisher

Andy Cummings, Vice President and Publisher

Mary Bednarek, Executive Acquisitions Director

Mary C. Corder, Editorial Director

Publishing for Consumer Dummies

Diane Graves Steele, Vice President and Publisher

Joyce Pepple, Acquisitions Director

Composition Services

Gerry Fahey, Vice President of Production Services

Debbie Stailey, Director of Composition Services

Contents at a Glance

Introduction 1

Part I: Becoming Familiar with Enterprise Linux 7
Chapter 1: Getting Acquainted with Enterprise Linux.............................9
Chapter 2: Exploring the Desktop 17
Chapter 3: Putting Your System to Work...41
Chapter 4: Exploring the File System and Command Shell......................61

Part II: Configuring Your Enterprise Linux Local
Area Network 83
Chapter 5: Configuring and Managing the X Window System 85
Chapter 6: Configuring and Managing Printers 97

Chapter 7: Configuring the Network...109
Chapter 8: The Network File System...123
Chapter 9: Connecting to Windows PCs Using Samba............................131

Part III: Securing Your Enterprise Linux System 141
Chapter 10: Security Basics 143
Chapter 11: Intrusion Detection and Prevention..................................161

Part IV: Configuring Your Enterprise Linux Internet
Services 179
Chapter 12: Configuring and Managing DNS Servers.............................181
Chapter 13: Configuring and Managing an E-Mail Server.......................203
Chapter 14: Configuring and Managing an FTP Server...........................221
Chapter 15: Serving Web Pages 235

Part V: Maintaining Your Enterprise Linux System.......251
Chapter 16: Maintaining Your System with the Red Hat Network...........253
Chapter 17: Administering Users and Groups 267
Chapter 18: Installing and Upgrading Software Packages 279
Chapter 19: Backing Up and Restoring Your Files.................................287

Part VI: The Part of Tens 311

Chapter 20: Ten Tips for Optimizing Your System 313
Chapter 21: Ten Troubleshooting and Problem-Solving Tips 329

Part VII: Appendixes 339

Appendix A: Installing Red Hat Enterprise Linux 341
Appendix B: What's on the CD-ROM? 361

Index 369

Table of Contents

Introduction 1

About This Book 1
How This Book Is Organized 2
    Part I: Becoming Familiar with Enterprise Linux 2
    Part II: Configuring Your Enterprise Linux Local Area Network 3
    Part III: Securing Your Enterprise Linux System 3
    Part IV: Configuring Your Enterprise Linux Internet Services 3
    Part V: Maintaining Your Enterprise Linux System 4
    Part VI: The Part of Tens 4
    Part VII: Appendixes 4
Icons Used in This Book 5
Typographical Roadsigns 5

Part 1: Becoming Familiar with Enterprise Linux 7

Chapter 1: Getting Acquainted with Enterprise Linux 9

Exploring the History of Enterprise Linux 9
Examining the Versions of Red Hat Enterprise 10
    Red Hat Enterprise AS 11
    Red Hat Enterprise ES 11
    Red Hat Enterprise WS 12
    Red Hat Desktop 12
Putting Enterprise Linux to Work 13
    Configuring your local network 13
    Using Enterprise Linux to maintain your system 14
    Securing your system 14
    Providing Internet services 15

Chapter 2: Exploring the Desktop 17

Examining the Graphical Login Screen 17
Logging In and Using the GNOME Desktop 19
    Playing with the panel 20
    Managing applets on the panel 21
    Choosing applications from the Applications menu 22
    Choosing actions from the Actions menu 24
Using the Nautilus File Manager 25
    Displaying your home folder 27
    Displaying the contents of a folder 27
    Opening files 27
    Accessing FTP sites 28

Using bookmarks 28
Managing your files and folders 29
Customizing the Nautilus File Manager 30
Editing File Manager preferences 31
Changing the File Manager background and icon emblems 32
Showing and hiding views 33
Configuring GNOME 33
Logging Out 34
Taking a Look at KDE 34
Managing applets 36
Choosing applications from the Applications menu 37
Using the Konqueror File Manager 39
Logging out 40

Chapter 3: Putting Your System to Work **41**
Getting Started 41
Browsing the Web 42
Changing Browser Preferences 44
Sending and Receiving E-mail 45
Receiving e-mail 48
Sending e-mail 48
Working at the Office 49
Writing with OpenOffice.org Writer 50
Calculating with OpenOffice.org Calc 52
Impressing with OpenOffice.org Impress 53
Configuring OpenOffice.org 54
Keeping Yourself Entertained 55
Configuring your sound card 55
Playing audio files 56
Playing video files 57
Working with Images 58

Chapter 4: Exploring the File System and Command Shell **61**
Examining the Enterprise Linux File System Structure 61
Commanding the Shell 64
Opening a terminal window 64
Shell command syntax 66
Frequently Used Shell Commands 68
Getting help 68
Working with files and directories 69
Gaining superuser (root) privileges 78
Changing your system path 78
Mounting and unmounting drives 79
Viewing and stopping processes 80
Checking disk space 80
Creating an alias 81
Writing Shell Scripts 82

Part II: Configuring Your Enterprise Linux Local Area Network 83

Chapter 5: Configuring and Managing the X Window System 85

Introducing the X Server 85
Configuring the X Server with the X Configuration Tool..........................86
 Changing the display resolution..86
 Changing the display color depth 87
 Changing monitor type settings 88
 Changing your video card type..89
 Configuring dual monitors..90
Manually Configuring Your X Server from the X Configuration File 91
 Device...91
 Direct Rendering Infrastructure..92
 Files 92
 InputDevice 93
 Module 93
 Monitor 93
 Screen 94
Restarting Your X Server 95
Disabling the X Server 95

Chapter 6: Configuring and Managing Printers 97

Starting the Printer Configuration Tool..98
 Configuring the print queue..100
 Selecting the print driver 104
Editing the Printer Configuration 105
 Deleting a printer...107
 Setting the default printer 107

Chapter 7: Configuring the Network 109

The Enterprise Linux Network Configuration Tool.................................109
 Adding an Ethernet device..110
 Adding a wireless NIC 113
 Adding a modem connection 115
Editing Your Network Configuration...117
 Removing a NIC..117
 Changing the NIC configuration 118
 Managing DNS settings 119
 Managing hosts..120
 Working with profiles 120

Chapter 8: The Network File System 123

Configuring and Managing an NFS Server...123
Adding Shares to Export 124
Editing and Deleting NFS Exported Shares 127

Command Line Configuration...128
Configuring an NFS Client 129
    Mounting an NFS directory 129
    Mounting NFS directories automatically at system start.............129

Chapter 9: Connecting to Windows PCs Using Samba 131

Installing Samba 131
Configuring the Samba Server...132
    Global...134
    Homes 135
    Printers..135
Creating Samba Users..136
Starting the Samba Server 136
Connecting to the Samba Server...137
Connecting to a Samba Client..138

Part III: Securing Your Enterprise Linux System . . . 141

Chapter 10: Security Basics 143

Developing a Security Policy 143
    Physical security 144
    Document security 144
    Network security 145
    Consequences for breaking security policy...............................145
    Responsibility 146
    Performing a security audit 146
Implementing Host Security 147
    System administrator security functions...................................147
    Keeping your system updated..152
Implementing Network Security..152
    Defining Internet services 152
    Disabling standalone servers 153
    Stopping services 155
    Disabling xinetd server services 155
Building a Firewall..156
    Configuring a simple firewall with the Security Level
        Configuration tool...157
    Configuring a simple firewall with the iptables command.............158

Chapter 11: Intrusion Detection and Prevention 161

Discovering the Types of Intrusion Detection.................................161
    Active detection 162
    Passive detection 162
Using Software Detection Tools to Test Your System Security.............163
    Scanning your network with nmap 163
    Using Tripwire to detect system changes 171

Part IV: Configuring Your Enterprise Linux Internet Services 179

Chapter 12: Configuring and Managing DNS Servers 181
Translating Web Names to IP Addresses 181
Types of DNS Servers 183
Examining the DNS Server Configuration Files 183
The named.conf file 185
Zone files 193
Configuring a Caching DNS Server 195
Configuring a Secondary Master DNS Server 196
Configuring a Primary Master Server 197
Checking Your Configuration 199
The host program 199
The dig program 199

Chapter 13: Configuring and Managing an E-Mail Server 203
How E-Mail Works 203
Mail User Agent (MUA) 204
The Ximian Evolution e-mail client 204
Mail Transfer Agent (MTA) 209
Local Delivery Agent (LDA) 209
Introducing SMTP 210
The Post Office Protocol (POP3) 210
The Internet Mail Access Protocol (IMAP4) 211
Using Sendmail 211
Checking that Sendmail is installed and running 211
Configuring Sendmail 212
The m4 macro processor 213
Managing the mail queue 214
Configuring POP3 215
Configuring IMAP4 216
Setting up aliases to make life easier 216
Maintaining E-Mail Security 217
Protecting against eavesdropping 218
Using encryption 218
Using a firewall 218
Don't get bombed, spammed, or spoofed 218
Some SMTP cautions 219

Chapter 14: Configuring and Managing an FTP Server 221
Installing an FTP Server 221
Configuring an FTP Server 222
Configuring the /etc/vsftpd/vsftpd.conf file 223
Configuring the /etc/vsftpd.ftpusers file 227
Configuring the /etc/vsftpd.user_list file 228

Starting the FTP Server 228
Testing the FTP Server 229
Logging In to FTP Servers 229
    Using gFTP for FTP access 230
    Accessing an FTP server with the command line FTP client........232

Chapter 15: Serving Web Pages **235**
Installing and Starting the Web Server......................................235
Configuring and Managing Your Web Server...........................238
Editing the Apache Configuration File Using the HTTP
   Configuration Tool...239
    Main tab..240
    Virtual Hosts tab...240
    Server tab 248
    Performance Tuning tab..249
Saving Your Settings and Restarting the Web Server.............250

Part V: Maintaining Your Enterprise Linux System *251*

**Chapter 16: Maintaining Your System
with the Red Hat Network** **253**
Registering Your System 253
Configuring the Up2date Agent 256
Using the Red Hat Enterprise Linux Up2date Agent..............259
Accessing the Red Hat Network with a Web Browser 262

Chapter 17: Administering Users and Groups **267**
Working with Users and Groups..267
    Adding a new user 269
    Adding a new group 270
    Changing user properties...271
    Changing group properties...272
    Removing a user 273
Restricting Disk Usage with Quotas..274
    Configuring disk quotas..274
    Obtaining disk quota statistics.......................................277

Chapter 18: Installing and Upgrading Software Packages **279**
Managing Packages with the Red Hat Package Manager 279
    Installing system packages...280
    Removing system packages 282
Managing Applications from Binary rpm Files.......................282
    Installing binary rpm files 283
    Finding installed package files...284
    Removing installed packages...285
Installing Applications from Compressed Zip Files 285

Chapter 19: Backing Up and Restoring Your Files 287

    Planning Your Backup Strategy 287
        Don't: Back up temp and cache files 287
        Maybe: Back up OS files 288
        Do: Back up database files and user files 288
    Selecting Your Backup Media 289
    Determining Your Backup Method 289
    Enterprise Linux Backup Tools 292
        Command line tools 292
        Advanced tools 300

Part VI: The Part of Tens 311

Chapter 20: Ten Tips for Optimizing Your System 313

    Optimizing the X Window System 313
    Optimizing NFS 315
    Optimizing Samba 316
    Optimizing DNS 317
    Optimizing Sendmail 318
    Optimizing FTP 320
    Optimizing Your Web Server 320
    Building a Custom Kernel 321
    Shutting Down Unused Services 322
    Administering Your System by Using Webmin .325

Chapter 21: Ten Troubleshooting and Problem-Solving Tips 329

    Unable to Log In 329
        Resetting a user's password 330
        Creating a user account 330
        Lost or forgotten root password 330
    CD-ROM Drive Not Detected During Installation 331
    CD-ROM Drive Does Not Mount After Installation 332
    Sound Does Not Work After Installation 332
    Unable to Unmount a Drive 333
    System Hangs During Boot 334
    Unable to Access Network Hosts 335
    Making an Emergency Boot Disk 336
    Shell Commands Don't Work 336
    Sources of Additional Information 337

Part VII: Appendixes *339*

Appendix A: Installing Red Hat Enterprise Linux **341**

Exploring Your PC's Components 341
Processor 342
Bus type 342
Memory 343
Video card and monitor 343
Hard drive 344
Floppy disk drive 344
Keyboard and mouse 344
SCSI controller 345
CD-ROM drive 345
Sound card 345
Network card 345
Checking for Supported Hardware 346
Starting the Red Hat Enterprise Linux Installation 346
Partitioning the Hard Disk for Red Hat Enterprise Linux 349
Configuring Red Hat Enterprise Linux Installation 351
Configuring the boot loader 352
Configuring the network 353
Configuring the firewall 354
Configuring additional languages 356
Setting the time zone 356
Setting the root password 357
Selecting the package groups to install 357
Completing the Installation 359

Appendix B: What's on the CD-ROM? **361**

Index *369*

Introduction

● ●

*W*elcome to *Red Hat Enterprise Linux 4 For Dummies.* RH Enterprise Linux 4 is the latest release of the OS intended for the business user. In this book, I introduce you to the four versions of Red Hat (RH) Enterprise Linux.

Two of the versions of Enterprise Linux, the AS and ES versions, are intended for systems that are used as servers. The other two versions, WS and Desktop, are intended to be used on standalone PCs.

This book is intended for network and system administrators who manage Red Hat Enterprise Linux systems running the AS or ES versions. For system administrators, this book shows you the steps required to successfully maintain or add to your systems. The book also helps those administrators who need to rapidly acquire knowledge of system administration and networking tasks for RH Enterprise Linux (RHEL). All tasks necessary to properly configure, maintain, and upgrade a Red Hat Enterprise Linux system are covered in this book.

If you are using the WS or Desktop versions of Enterprise Linux, don't worry — I didn't forget about you. Much of the information that is useful to system administrators is also useful to you. Some chapters are specifically intended for you and cover what you need to know to successfully use the WS or Desktop versions of Enterprise Linux.

About This Book

I have been told by several people whose opinions I value that my writing style is conversational and easy going. In fact, that was one of the selling points used by my acquisitions editor to convince me to do this book. Hopefully, I continue this style throughout this book, and you will enjoy reading it as you glean some valuable information about Enterprise Linux.

The book is primarily intended for new or less-experienced Red Hat Enterprise Linux administrators and users. The topics are explained in a concise, easy-to-follow style and will also be useful as a quick reference for more experienced readers. Some of the topics covered include

✔ Installing and configuring RHEL (printing, network services)

✔ Using the desktop

- ✔ Using shell scripting to manage an RHEL system
- ✔ Using system administration tools
- ✔ Using the Red Hat network service
- ✔ Installing and using security tools
- ✔ Optimizing system performance
- ✔ Using monitoring tools

It is critical for new and less-experienced users to rapidly acquaint them-selves with the details and functionality of Red Hat Enterprise Linux 4. This book provides these users with concise, step-by-step instructions of the key areas that will make them knowledgeable RH Enterprise Linux users. Users who buy this book can expect that they can read how to successfully admin-ister a RH Enterprise Linux system in a short time frame.

How This Book Is Organized

This book is divided into seven parts. The beginning parts give you an intro-duction to Enterprise Linux and progress through increasingly more complex topics. The middle parts get you started with system administration and security. The Part of Tens gives you some useful tips on optimizing your sys-tems as well as some solutions to common problems encountered by novice users. Finally, the appendixes offer installation instructions and also list what's on the book's companion CD material.

A nice thing about the book is that it is modular instead of linear. That is, you can just go to whatever part you want for information about the topics in that part. You don't need to finish one chapter to go on to the next; each chapter is meant to stand alone.

Part 1: Becoming Familiar with Enterprise Linux

You have a system with Enterprise Linux, and you are wondering what to do with it. This first part covers everything you need to know about the different versions of Enterprise Linux. You'll discover how to log in and use the GNOME desktop, including customizing it to suit your style. This part includes an expla-nation of some of the most useful programs that are included with Enterprise

Linux, like *OpenOffice,* which is a complete office suite that lets you do anything that you can do with MS Office — but for zero cost. You explore a Web browser and an e-mail client and even play around with graphics and sound. The last topic in this part introduces you to the Linux file system and the command shell. This part contains information useful to users of all four versions of Enterprise Linux.

Part II: Configuring Your Enterprise Linux Local Area Network

This part begins with a tour through the X Window System, which provides the graphical interface to Enterprise Linux and what you see when you log in. You explore how to configure your system to use TCP/IP to communicate with other PCs on your network and how to get different types of printers to work on your local area network. You can share your files with other Linux or Unix users by following the topics covered in this part. You can even share your files with Windows users by using Samba, which is the last topic in this part. This part contains information useful to users of all four versions of Enterprise Linux.

Part III: Securing Your Enterprise Linux System

Who isn't concerned with security these days? Just read the paper or watch the news, and you will hear more about computer security problems than you care to. Your Linux system isn't affected by the most of the problems that plague users of MS Windows, but there are some vulnerabilities that you should know about.

This part is where you will explore some security basics for your local network as well as external networks. You can read about intrusion detection and some tools that you can use to help you find out whether someone has entered your system without your permission. This part contains information useful to users of all four versions of Enterprise Linux.

Part IV: Configuring Your Enterprise Linux Internet Services

All the chapters in this part deal with setting up servers that provide services to other users. Your users won't be able to find anything on the Internet

without a DNS server on your network; in this part, I show you how to configure one. I also show you how to configure an e-mail server so your users can
send and receive e-mail. The last two chapters in this part get you ready to
share your files with other users across the Internet by showing you how to
set up an FTP server. And, finally, the last chapter in this part gives you the
details about setting up and maintaining a Web server. This part contains
information useful to users of all the AS and ES versions of Enterprise Linux.

Part V: Maintaining Your Enterprise Linux System

Most likely, after you have your system set up exactly as you want it and running smoothly, you'd like to keep it that way. The topics in this part help you
do just that. You can explore keeping your system updated by using the *Red
Hat Network,* a subscription service that keeps an eye on your systems and
lets you know when they need to be updated. If you've found some really
cool software that you want to install, this part helps you install it and also
upgrade software already on your system. Toward the end of the part, you'll
discover how to add users to your system as well as how to change user
properties. And finally, you end the part by finding out about backing up and
restoring your data. This part contains information useful to users of all four
versions of Enterprise Linux.

Part VI: The Part of Tens

Every *For Dummies* book concludes with a Part of Tens, and this book is no
different. Here, you find a chapter that mostly deals with optimizing the different servers and services that your systems provide to other users. You
can also read about ten of the most common problems new users have when
running Enterprise Linux and what you can do to solve them. ***Hint:*** Maybe if
you read this part first, you can avoid some of these pesky problems before
they strike. This part contains information useful to users of all four versions
of Enterprise Linux.

Part VII: Appendixes

The appendixes offer installation instructions. You can also find out what's
on the book's companion CD material.

Icons Used in This Book

Within each chapter, I use icons to highlight particularly important or useful information. You find the following icons in this book:

The Tip icon flags useful information that makes living with your Red Hat Enterprise Linux system even less complicated than you feared that it might be.

I sometimes use this icon to point out information you just shouldn't pass by — don't overlook these gentle reminders.

Be cautious when you see this icon — it warns you of things you shouldn't do. The bomb is meant to emphasize that the consequences of ignoring these bits of wisdom can be severe.

This icon signals technical details that are informative and interesting, but not critical to understanding and using Red Hat Enterprise Linux. Skip these if you want (but please come back and read them later).

Typographical Roadsigns

I don't use too many of these, but they come in handy. When I want you to type something, whether at a prompt or in a field, **it appears in bold.** A command path looks like this: Choose File⇨New. Finally, code and things onscreen look like this. Told you it was simple.

Part I
Becoming Familiar with Enterprise Linux

The 5th Wave   By Rich Tennant

"When we started the company, we weren't going to call it 'Red Hat'. But eventually we decided it sounded better than 'Beard of Bees Linux'."

In this part . . .

This part tells you about the history of Enterprise Linux and the differences between the four versions. You explore what you can do with Enterprise Linux depending on the version that you install. Chapter 2 explains the GNOME desktop and how to log in and log out of your system. In Chapter 3, you discover some of the many programs that are included with Enterprise Linux and what you can do with them. In the last chapter in this part, you explore the Linux file system and read about the command shell.

Chapter 1

Getting Acquainted with Enterprise Linux

In This Chapter

▶ Exploring the history of Enterprise Linux

▶ Examining the versions of Enterprise Linux

▶ Putting Enterprise Linux to work

*E*nterprise Linux has four versions: Two of the versions are designed for workstation and desktop usage, and the other two versions are designed for server applications. Don't get too bogged down trying to sort out the differences of these versions because the four versions of Enterprise Linux are really quite similar. In this chapter, I examine the different versions of Red Hat Enterprise Linux and what you can do with them. Before I go into the version descriptions, take a look at the history of Enterprise Linux.

Exploring the History of Enterprise Linux

Red Hat Enterprise Linux is one of many available distributions of Linux. Several companies make their own commercial Linux distributions, but in this book, I discuss the Enterprise Linux distribution by Red Hat. A *Linux distribution* is a complete version of the Linux operating system that contains the Linux kernel as well as other applications and programs that can be used for doing some type of work. The Linux *kernel* is the core of the Linux operating system and controls how the operating system functions with the hardware that makes up your PC. (Linux was originally developed by Linus Torvalds in 1991 while he was a college student in Finland.)

I don't want to bore you with a lot of historical information about Enterprise Linux, but a little background information for a better understanding of the Linux kernel and version numbers is helpful. Exact dates aren't important, so I'll just give you the quick rundown of the history of Red Hat Linux and the introduction of Enterprise Linux.

The first publicly available version of Red Hat Linux appeared in the summer of 1994 and was based on kernel version 1.09. (The kernel is identified by a number that refers to the particular version of the kernel.) Since the release of the first version of the Red Hat Distribution, there have been many more releases, with each release improving upon the earlier versions. Red Hat made no distinction between its version's suitability for home use or commercial (business) use of its distributions until May, 2002. By then, Red Hat was at release 7.3 of the Red Hat Linux distribution. Coinciding with the release of version 7.3 was the introduction of Red Hat Linux Advanced Server 2.1, which was renamed Enterprise Linux 2.1.

Enterprise version 2.1 was based on the Red Hat 7.3 version but was intended for commercial/business use. The major difference between the commercial and home versions of Red Hat Linux was in the support offerings available for the versions. The home version, if purchased through a boxed set, gave the user a limited number of technical support calls for a short time period, and then the users were on their own. The commercial version provided a longer time period for technical support and offered additional technical support that could be purchased at additional cost. Also, Red Hat had issued a new version of its operating system about every six months — changing far too often for most commercial uses. With the release of Enterprise Linux 2.1, Red Hat slowed the pace of system changes to give users a more stable platform (thus requiring less frequent updates) and focused its commercial efforts on the Enterprise version.

From this point forward, Red Hat continued development of its home user versions through version 8 and finally version 9, which was the last Red Hat distribution that was available for home user purchase. In the summer of 2003, Red Hat decided that it would merge its open development process with the Fedora Linux project — and the Fedora Project was born.

In October, 2003, Red Hat introduced Enterprise 3 that, like its predecessor Enterprise 2.1, was specifically geared toward business/enterprise users. Enterprise 3 was initially available in three versions — AS, ES, and WS — each designed for specific types of service. In the summer of 2004, Red Hat added another version of Enterprise 3 specifically for the desktop. That brings us to the present — Enterprise version 4 — which is the focus of this book.

Examining the Versions of Red Hat Enterprise

All versions of Enterprise Linux share some similarities in their product features. The most significant of these features are

- A 12–18 month release cycle
- A common operating system, applications, and management tools

> ✔ One year of support and updates using the Red Hat Network included with the initial purchase, which is then renewable annually for 5 years for an additional yearly fee

Having a 12–18 month release cycle makes the update process more predictable because a user knows that he won't have to make any major changes to his system configuration for at least a year and perhaps longer. With all versions are based on the same operating system, a system administrator can more easily configure and maintain consistency because the same skill set is used for all versions.

Probably the most significant feature of Enterprise Linux is the level(s) of support available from Red Hat. One of the most frequently heard criticisms of Linux is the lack of user support typically available. With Enterprise 3, and Enterprise version 4 covered in this book, Red Hat has seriously addressed the support issue.

In the following sections, I examine the different versions of Enterprise Linux 4. (For installation details, see Appendix A.) Then I conclude the chapter the remainder of this chapter with what Enterprise Linux can do for you.

Red Hat Enterprise AS

Red Hat Enterprise AS is the top-of-the-line server operating system available from Red Hat. Enterprise AS is designed for large departments or company data centers. The AS version provides the same server functions as the ES version but is best suited for servers that have more than two CPUs with greater than 8GB of system RAM. In addition to support for more than two CPUs in the same system, there is support for many different types of CPUs as well, such as the IBM iSeries, pSeries, and zSeries.

The greatest difference between the AS and ES (see the following section) versions is the level of support available with the AS version. Users can purchase the premium level support option that provides 24/7 support with a guaranteed one-hour response time.

Red Hat Enterprise ES

Red Hat Enterprise ES is intended to provide for an entry-level or midrange server environment with support for up to two CPUs and 8GB of system RAM. The ES version is quite similar to the AS version (see the preceding section) but is meant for smaller-scale operations and does not provide the same level of support as the AS version. The ES version includes the following applications:

- ✔ Web server
- ✔ Network services (DNS [Domain Name System], DHCP [Dynamic Host Configuration Protocol], firewall security, and more)
- ✔ File/print/mail servers
- ✔ SQL (Structured Query Language) databases

Red Hat Enterprise WS

Red Hat Enterprise WS provides nearly the same functionality as the Desktop version. Included with WS are the same Web browser, office suite, and e-mail client (Firefox, OpenOffice.org 1.1, and Evolution, respectively). The major difference between the WS and Desktop (see the following section) versions is the number of CPUs supported. The WS version supports up to two CPUs, but the Desktop version supports only one.

Red Hat Desktop

According to Red Hat, Enterprise 4 Desktop is "a high-quality, full-featured client system for use in a wide range of desktop deployments where security and manageability are key." What does this mean to the typical user?

This version focuses on the desktop, containing applications that are used on the desktop. Red Hat Desktop includes a mail client program, similar to MS Outlook, called Evolution. Also included is the Firefox Web browser; a complete office suite, OpenOffice.org 1.1; and GAIM, which is an instant messaging client.

To find out more about some of the applications available in Enterprise Linux, take a look at Chapter 3.

Third-party productivity applications are also installed by default during the system installation. This is an improvement over earlier versions of Red Hat Linux. Adobe Acrobat Reader, a Macromedia Flash plug-in, RealPlayer, and Java are just a few of the applications that work in Red Hat Desktop right out of the box.

As part of the Enterprise family of programs, Red Hat Desktop shares many of the features and tools of the other Enterprise versions. A user or administrator who is familiar with one of the versions of Enterprise 4 will be able to easily use a different version. Red Hat Desktop supports a system with one CPU and up to 4GB of system RAM.

Putting Enterprise Linux to Work

Whether you're planning to use the AS or ES server versions of Enterprise Linux or you'll be using the WS or Desktop versions, the choices of productivity software and what you can do with them are nearly infinite. You can use Enterprise Linux to manage all your system hardware, do system administration, create networks for sharing data, browse the Internet, serve Web pages, and much more. Take a look at just some of the tasks that you can do with Enterprise Linux.

Configuring your local network

All versions of Enterprise Linux include the X Window System (find more on this in Chapter 5), based on XFree86, which provides the foundation for a graphical user interface (GUI). However, you aren't stuck with just one GUI because Enterprise Linux supplies two well-known GUIs: KDE and GNOME.

- **KDE:** The K Desktop Environment is an optional GUI that can be selected at installation time.
- **GNOME:** This is the default GUI that's installed when the operating system is installed.

If you have both GUIs installed, a tool on either desktop makes switching between the desktops very easy.

You don't have to spend additional money to buy typical productivity applications such as word processing or spreadsheet programs. All versions of Enterprise Linux ship with a complete office productivity suite — OpenOffice. org — as well as many other graphical applications that can be used for editing graphics, building Web sites, and much more.

With either desktop, you can use the included graphical-based tools to configure and maintain your systems. You can also configure the hardware in your system and add or remove devices.

Additionally, you can configure printers to work with your local network. Enterprise Linux includes support for many types of printers from different manufacturers. You can configure a printer connected directly to your system as well as many types of network-connected printers. (Read more about configuring system printers in Chapter 6.)

Enterprise Linux gives you everything you need to set up a local network so that your systems can share data with each other. For example, you can configure the AS and ES versions to provide local network services, such as Network File System (NFS), that shares files between the servers and WS and Desktop clients. (Read all about NFS in Chapter 8.) Or, you can configure the

Network Information System (NIS) to give your users the ability to log in to the network and use all the network resources.

You will also be able to share data with computers running other operating systems, such as MS Windows, Novell NetWare, or Mac OS X. (See Chapter 9 for more.) Enterprise Linux gives you all the tools that you need to configure your system to communicate with these other operating systems and exchange information.

Using Enterprise Linux to maintain your system

Keeping your systems running properly and updated with the latest patches can be a daunting proposition. Don't worry, though, because Enterprise Linux gives you all the tools that you need to perform these tasks. All versions of Enterprise Linux include a subscription to the Red Hat Network as well as the up2date application that constantly scans your system configuration and installed packages looking for packages that can be updated.

Tools are available in all versions that you can use to create and remove system users and groups. You use these same tools to change properties and permissions for your users and groups as well.

Several applications are available for creating file archives for backing up your data. You can compress your data to maximize your storage space and speed up your backup and restore process.

Installing application software in Enterprise Linux is a relatively easy process because most applications are available in the Red Hat Package Manager (RPM) format. You can use the graphical-based RPM tool to install your application, or you can use the rpm command from a command prompt. In many instances, you can either choose to use the graphical based tool or you can use the command line to enter your commands.

Read more about security basics in Chapter 10.

Securing your system

Anyone who uses a computer these days is well aware of the increasing problems caused by unsecured systems. Enterprise Linux includes many of the tools that you need to secure your system from malicious attacks.

You can configure a firewall on your system by making a few choices and answering a few questions from the graphical-based firewall tool. If you want to go into more detail with your firewall configuration, you can use the command line firewall tool to create more complex firewall rules. You can protect your systems from *internal* attacks (attacks that originate inside your organization) as well as *external* (outside) attacks.

Applications are also available that you can use to actively detect system intrusions. You can configure how your system should respond to intrusions and what actions should be taken to ensure that your systems are not vulnerable to future attacks.

Find out more on intrusion prevention and detection in Chapter 11.

Providing Internet services

You can use Enterprise Linux to serve information across the Internet to users on different networks than your own. The ES and AS versions of Enterprise Linux include the following Internet servers:

- ✔ **Apache** `httpd` **Web server:** The Apache Web server is the most widely used Web server in use today. (See Chapter 15.)

- ✔ **FTP server:** The `vsftpd` server is an implementation of the File Transfer Protocol (FTP) that is used for transferring files across the Internet. (See Chapter 14.)

- ✔ `sendmail`**:** This is the most widely used mail transport agent in use today. (See Chapter 13.)

You can remotely log in to another computer on your own network or even on the Internet. Using the `telnet` program, or another more secure program called `ssh`, makes remote logins easy. After logging in remotely, you can control the remote computer as though you were sitting in front of it.

In Enterprise Linux, all Internet servers are based on the Transmission Control Protocol/Internet Protocol (TCP/IP), which is the protocol on which the Internet is based. Any network applications that use TCP/IP are supported natively by Enterprise Linux. (Read more on TCP/IP networking in Chapter 12.)

As you can see from this quick examination of the features of Enterprise Linux, you can do a lot with it. In fact, anything you can do with the most widely used operating system (MS Windows), you can do as well or better with Enterprise Linux. You systems will certainly be more secure and less vulnerable to attack if you are running Enterprise Linux. The remaining chapters of this book explain in more detail the features briefly discussed in this chapter.

Comparing Enterprise Linux and Fedora Core

In Fall, 2003, Red Hat announced that it would no longer sell nor support its retail box version of Red Hat Linux. Version 9 would be the last of many versions that I've seen over the years. Instead of continuing this long line of versions, Red Hat announced that it would provide support to the Fedora Project for development of what Red Hat described as a place for testing cutting-edge technology. What this means is that all development efforts for all Red Hat software would go into the Fedora Project and the Fedora software, which is known as *Fedora Core.* New releases of Fedora Core will occur about every six months, which is far too often for production-based systems, but allows for testing of features that would appear at some later date in the Enterprise versions. At the same time as the Fedora Project announcement, Red Hat placed nearly all its efforts into promoting its Enterprise Linux product and its features and benefits.

Many people were very confused by this move by Red Hat, and many users had a strong feeling that Red Hat Linux would no longer be available. This is simply not true. What was known as Red Hat Linux is simply now called Fedora Project. In my opinion, except for the name change and not being able to purchase a retail box version of Fedora, nothing has really changed as far as the features and functionality of the operating system.

The major advantages of Enterprise Linux over Fedora Core are the number of support options that are available from Red Hat. For many years, one of the biggest reasons given by the corporate world for not using Linux has been a lack of user support. With the promotion of Enterprise Linux, Red Hat has effectively removed lack of support as a reason for a company not to consider using Linux.

Another key feature of Enterprise Linux is the extended development and release cycle for new versions. Red Hat has stated that it plans to release new versions of Enterprise Linux every 12–18 months rather than every 6 months, as had been the case with Red Hat Linux.

However, probably the most significant difference between Fedora Core and Enterprise Linux is the difference in price. Purchasing the AS version of Enterprise Linux with the standard support option cost about $1,500, with the premium support package costing about $2,500. Fedora Core, on the other hand, is free.

What does all this mean to the users of Enterprise Linux or Fedora? Can you use Fedora Core to provide the same services and functionality as Enterprise Linux? The answer is a resounding yes. Users can do everything in Fedora that they can do with Enterprise Linux. This is good news to users of Enterprise Linux as well. Any user who is familiar with Fedora Core can easily make the move to Enterprise Linux because they are nearly identical in features and functionality.

Chapter 2

Exploring the Desktop

● ●

In This Chapter

▶ Examining the graphical login screen

▶ Logging in and using the GNOME desktop

▶ Using the Nautilus File Manager

▶ Adding bookmarks

▶ Configuring GNOME

▶ Logging out

▶ Taking a look at KDE

● ●

The GNOME (GNU Network Object Model Environment) desktop is a graphical user interface (GUI) that is installed as the default user interface during the installation process. Another popular desktop, KDE (K Desktop Environment), can also be selected as an option to be installed during system installation. Each of these user interfaces is similar to that of MS Windows or Mac OS X but with some notable differences. One large difference is the ability of the user to select which desktop to use upon system login. In this chapter, I take you on a tour of both of these GUIs to discover some of the features that they offer and show you how to configure them to your liking.

Examining the Graphical Login Screen

Before you can do any exploring of the GNOME or KDE desktops, you must first log in. You log in from the graphical login window that is shown in Figure 2-1. Take a quick look at the options that you can choose from the login window.

Figure 2-1:
The
graphical
login
window
waits for
you to log in.

At the bottom of the window are four choices that you can click to make additional selections:

- ✔ **Language:** Clicking this opens a box displaying the languages available on your system. If you want to use the system default language, which was installed during system installation, you don't need to do anything with this choice. In most cases, only one language is listed unless additional languages were installed during the system installation. The default language would typically be the language used at your location. If other languages have been installed, just click the language that you want to use.

- ✔ **Session:** Clicking Session gives you the opportunity to select the desktop that you use after you log in. GNOME is the default desktop, so you need to use this choice only if you want to change to a different desktop, such as KDE.

- ✔ **Reboot:** Clicking Reboot will (you guessed it) ask you whether you want to reboot the system.

- ✔ **Shut Down:** Clicking Shut Down asks you whether you want to shut down your system.

Directly in the center of the window is the login field. This is where you enter your username and password to login. Here's the way-too-easy drill:

1. **Type your username.**

2. **Press Enter.**

3. **Type your password.**

4. **Press Enter again.**

Logging In and Using the GNOME Desktop

In this section, I walk you through logging in to the GNOME desktop and do some exploring to help you become familiar with its features. As I mention earlier, the GNOME desktop is installed as the default desktop, so to enter GNOME, you can just enter your username and password in the graphical login window without having to make any choices from the four options, as explained in the preceding section. After entering your username and password, you see the GNOME desktop, as shown in Figure 2-2.

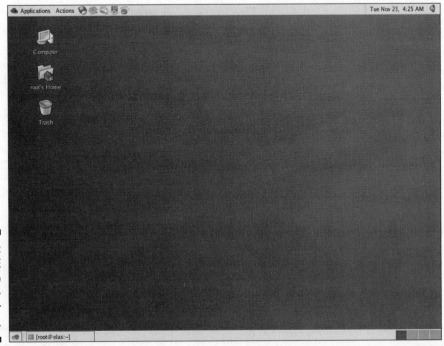

Figure 2-2:
The GNOME desktop immediately after logging in.

The GNOME desktop has a similar appearance to other well-known desktop environments like MS Windows or Mac OS X. If you can use either of these desktops, you can easily master GNOME in a short time. Notice that the GNOME desktop has a rather clean, almost Spartan, appearance.

The three icons in the upper-left corner of the desktop are links to your home directory, the system trash can that holds your deleted files until you empty the trash, and the Computer icon that opens the Nautilus graphical shell. The Nautilus File Manager gives you access to your files and directories so you can do typical file management tasks like copying and moving files. In addition to regular file management tasks, the Nautilus File Manager lets you perform desktop management as well. You look more closely at Nautilus in this chapter. Take a closer look at these icons.

- ✔ **Computer:** This icon also opens a Nautilus window. The Computer window contains four icons that are links to

   - *Floppy Drive:* The Floppy Drive icon is a link to the folder that contains the system mount point for the floppy drive. Double-clicking this icon displays the contents of the floppy disk that you inserted in the floppy drive.

   - *CD-R Drive:* The CD-R Drive icon is a link to the folder that contains the system mount point for the CD-R drive. Double-clicking this icon displays the contents of the CD-ROM disk that you inserted in the CD-R drive.

   - *Filesystem:* This icon is a link to the file system. Double-clicking this icon opens a new window displaying the root directory of the file system.

   - *Network:* Clicking the Network icon gives you access to the network file systems. Any files or directories that are available across your network are shown here.

- ✔ **Home directory:** This icon is a link to the user's home directory. The name of the user shown on the desktop corresponds to the user who is logged in. For example, Figure 2-2 shows the icon labeled as `root's Home` because I logged in with that user name. You can double-click this icon — or right-click and choose Open from the contextual menu — to open a Nautilus window that displays the user's home directory.

- ✔ **Trash:** This icon is a link to the system trash can. You can drag any icon, file, or directory and drop it here. When you're ready to empty the trash, just right-click and select Empty Trash from the contextual menu.

Playing with the panel

At the top and bottom of the desktop is a gray, horizontal bar. This area of the desktop is the *panel* and is similar to the taskbar in Windows. On the far left of the top panel is the Applications icon, indicated by the Red Hat icon. To the right of the Applications icon is an Actions menu that contains some actions you can do, such as locking the desktop or logging out. To the right of the Actions menu are icons representing programs that were installed during the system installation. You can start any of these programs by clicking them from the panel. Just move your mouse over any icon, and a pop-up appears with a description of the program represented by the icon.

At the far right of the bottom panel is a square gray area — the Workspace Switcher — that is divided into four sections. When you first log in to GNOME, the leftmost section of Workspace Switcher should be blue, indicating that you are in workspace one. You can switch between four workspaces in GNOME, so you actually get four distinct desktops that you can use. You can open different programs on the different desktops and switch between them by clicking the Workspace Switcher for the desktop that you want to see. Open some programs on the different desktops and then try clicking each of the four squares to see the effect of changing to a different workspace.

On the far left of the bottom panel is a Close Window icon that will hide, if visible, all open windows on the desktop. If the windows are already hidden, clicking this icon displays the windows. The open area on the bottom panel between the Workspace Switcher and the Close Window icon is used to show any programs that you're running on your desktop. You can switch between programs running on a single desktop by clicking the program name from the bottom panel. Also shown in this area are icons that you can add to the panel as well as applets. *Applets* are applications that provide some type of useful information or entertainment.

Managing applets on the panel

The icons on the top and bottom panels are links to applications — applets. Applets placed on the panel make it quick and convenient to start your chosen application with a single click. If you are familiar with MS Windows, applets in GNOME are like shortcuts. In addition to the applets that are already on the panel, you can add your own. You also can move applets that are already there or delete them to make more room.

To add applets to the panel, do the following:

1. **Right-click an empty area of the panel.**
2. **Choose Add to Panel from the contextual menu.**
3. **Choose the application that you want to add.**
4. **Click Add to add it to the panel.**

To move applets to another location on the panel

1. **Right-click the applet you want to move.**

2. **Click Move from the contextual menu.**

3. **Drag the applet to the desired location.**

4. **Click to release the applet to its new location.**

To remove an applet from the panel

1. **Right-click the applet you want to remove.**

2. **Choose Remove from Panel from the contextual menu.**

To modify the properties of an applet (or the panel)

1. **Right-click the applet (or an empty area of the panel).**

2. **Choose Properties from the contextual menu.**

3. **Change the parameters in the Properties dialog box.**

Right-clicking the panel or any applets on it presents a contextual menu, which gives you access to Help and some useful utilities for panel configuration. Contextual menus are different depending on the type of applet that you're selecting.

Choosing applications from the Applications menu

The Applications menu, represented by the Red Hat icon, is on the far-left corner of the top panel. The Applications menu button gives you access to a large number of applications. Click the Red Hat icon to open the Applications menu, and you see a menu, as shown in Figure 2-3, listing the many categories of applications from which you can choose.

Notice that many of the categories contain a right-pointing arrow. Moving your cursor over categories with a right-pointing arrow opens additional menus from which you can choose even more applications in that category. There are probably more than 100 applications from which you can choose, many more than I can describe in this book. However, I do provide a brief description of the main category of applications here so you can have some idea what they do. Begin by starting at the bottom of the menu and then work your way toward the top.

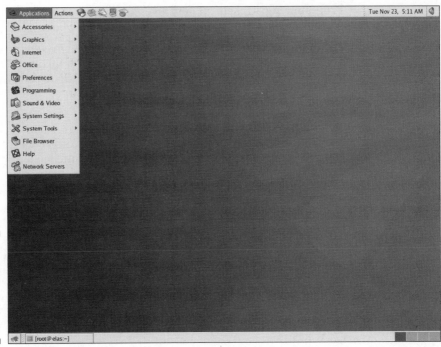

Your Applications menu might not be exactly as described in this section depending on the version of Enterprise Linux that you have installed.

- ✔ **Network Servers:** Choosing this menu item opens the Nautilus File Manager and displays any network servers that you might have.

- ✔ **Help:** This menu item opens the Help browser. You can get help on using GNOME by choosing this item.

- ✔ **File Browser:** This menu item is a link to the Nautilus File Manager and opens in the user's home directory.

- ✔ **System Tools:** This menu choice gives you access to many Enterprise Linux system administration utilities. You explore many of these tools in other chapters of this book.

- ✔ **System Settings:** This menu item contains Enterprise Linux system administration utilities and some GNOME configuration utilities as well.

- ✔ **Sound & Video:** Choosing this item gives you access to programs and utilities related to system sound and video. For example, if you want to adjust the system volume, use the utility here.

- ✔ **Programming:** This menu item gives you access to some programs that can be used for debugging programs.

- ✔ **Preferences:** This menu choice opens the System Preferences window. Most of the GNOME settings can be modified with this menu choice. Selecting this from the menu is the same as double-clicking the Computer icon on the desktop.

- ✔ **Office:** This menu choice gives you access to the OpenOffice.org office suite. The OpenOffice suite contains word processing, spreadsheet, presentation software, and much more. You can also start several of the OpenOffice applications by clicking the icons on the left side of the panel.

- ✔ **Internet:** Here you will find applications related to the Internet. For example, the Web browsers are located here as well as an FTP program.

- ✔ **Graphics:** This menu choice contains graphical programs. Here you find image viewing and editing applications.

- ✔ **Accessories:** Here you can find applications that don't fit well into the other categories, like the calculator, as well as some text editors.

You have several ways to start applications in Enterprise Linux. You can click the Applications menu icon in the left corner of the panel. You can also start any executable application by double-clicking its icon from the Nautilus File Manager.

Choosing actions from the Actions menu

To the right of the Applications menu is the Actions menu, as shown in Figure 2-4.

Items on this menu, listed from top to bottom, include the following:

- ✔ **Run Application:** This menu item opens a dialog box where you can enter the name of a program that you want to run.

- ✔ **Search for Files:** Choosing this menu item opens a file search dialog box.

- ✔ **Recent Documents:** Documents that you have recently opened appear in this list.

- ✔ **Take Screenshot:** You can use this menu choice to capture an image of your current display.

- ✔ **Lock Screen:** This menu option starts your system screensaver and locks your desktop. Move your mouse or press a key to open a dialog box that lets you enter your password to unlock the desktop.

- ✔ **Log Out:** Choosing Log Out opens a dialog box giving you the option to log out, shut down, or restart the computer. Select the radio button of your choice and then click OK.

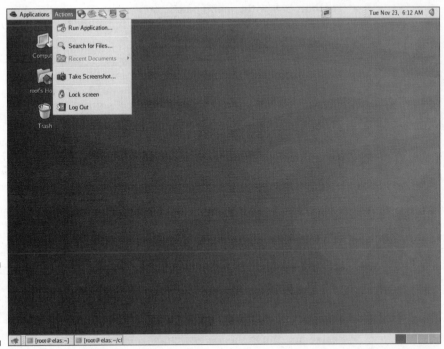

Figure 2-4:
The GNOME
Actions
menu.

Using the Nautilus File Manager

The Nautilus File Manager is a graphical shell for GNOME. You can use Nautilus not only to manage the files and directories on your system but also to perform many GNOME and system configurations. With Nautilus, you can even access your system applications.

To start the Nautilus File Manager, use any of the following methods:

✔ Select File Browser from the Applications menu.

✔ Right-click any folder and choose Browse Folder from the contextual menu.

Using any of the methods shown above will open the Nautilus File Manager, as shown in Figure 2-5.

A brief explanation of the items on the Nautilus File Manager window is in order:

✔ **Menu bar:** At the top of the window is the menu bar, similar to menu bars from other programs. From the menu bar, you can access to perform various actions.

✔ **Toolbar:** Below the menu bar is the toolbar. The toolbar holds buttons that you can use to perform the action indicated by the button, such as Back, Forward, and Reload.

✔ **Location bar:** The location bar contains a text field where you can enter a file, folder, or URL to go to. The location bar also has a zoom-in and a zoom-out button (magnifying glass icons) with which you can change the size of items. Finally, the View As Icons drop-down list lets you choose how you want to view the items.

✔ **Window panes:** Beneath the location bar, the Nautilus window is divided into two panes. The left, smaller pane (Information) shows a drop-down list that lets you choose what is displayed about items appearing in the larger, right pane. If you choose Tree from the list, you can see your entire file system tree in the left pane.

The larger, right pane displays the contents of the files or directories that you're viewing. *Note:* All directories appear as folders in Nautilus. You can view the contents of folders as either a list or as icons by choosing from the View As Icons drop-down list (in the location bar). You can also access FTP sites by entering the URL into the location text field.

✔ **Status bar:** At the bottom of the Nautilus window is the status bar, which displays status information about the files or folders that you are viewing.

✔ **Resize handle:** In the lower-right corner is a handle that you can use to resize the window. Move your mouse over the handle and then click and drag to resize the window. Release the mouse button at the desired size.

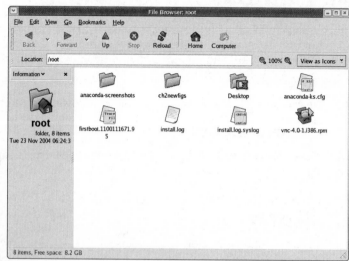

Figure 2-5:
The Nautilus
File
Manager
window.

When using the Nautilus File Manager, all directories are shown as folders. For the remainder of this section, I refer to directories as folders.

Displaying your home folder

If you start Nautilus by using one of the methods that I explain earlier, Nautilus opens to your home folder. However, if you changed folders while in Nautilus, you might want to return to your home folder. You can do this by

- ✔ Choosing Go➪Home from the Nautilus menu bar.
- ✔ Clicking the Home icon on the Nautilus toolbar.

If you want to refresh the display, click Reload on the toolbar.

Displaying the contents of a folder

You can easily move from one folder to another in Nautilus. Again, you have more than one way to navigate through your file system.

- ✔ **Double-click the folder.** If the folder that you want to view is visible in the large, right pane of the Nautilus window, you can open it by double-clicking it.
- ✔ **Enter the location.** You can enter the name of the folder that you wish to view by typing it into the location bar text field.
- ✔ **Use the tree view.** Choose Tree from the drop-down list in the small, left pane of the Nautilus window and select the folder that you wish to view.
- ✔ **Use the Search tool.** Click the Actions menu button and choose Search for Files from the menu.

To move forward and backward through your file system, you can use the Forward and Back buttons from the toolbar or you can choose Go➪ Forward/Back from the menu bar. To move up a level, you can use the Up button on the toolbar or you can choose Go➪Up from the menu bar.

Opening files

Whenever you double-click a file, Nautilus is configured by default to perform some type of action on the file depending on the type of file. Nautilus either opens the file by using a preconfigured viewer or runs the file if it is an executable file.

Nautilus has been configured to open the following types of files in the large, right pane:

- **Graphic image files:** Nautilus automatically displays a small icon of the graphic image in the folder view. Double-clicking the icon of the graphic opens the file in the left window. Click the Back button on the toolbar to return to the folder view. Nautilus can display GIF, JPEG, and PNG images.

- **Text files:** Nautilus opens any text files in the text viewer, which is displayed in the large, right pane of the Nautilus window. *Note:* You cannot edit text in the text viewer. Click the Back button on the toolbar to return to the folder view.

Accessing FTP sites

You can use the Nautilus File Manager to access an FTP site. All you need to do is enter the URL of the site in the location bar text field. If you need to log in to the site, you can use the following syntax.

```
ftp://username:password@hostname.domain
```

You can drag and drop files to move them from the FTP site to your desired folder.

Using bookmarks

With Nautilus, you can use bookmarks to keep track of your favorite locations. You can bookmark files, folders, and FTP sites as desired.

Adding a bookmark

To add a bookmark, do the following:

1. **Click the item that you wish to bookmark.**

2. **Choose Bookmarks⇨Add Bookmark from the menu bar.**

Editing bookmarks

To edit a bookmark, do the following:

1. **Choose Bookmarks⇨Edit Bookmarks to open the Edit Bookmarks dialog box, as shown in Figure 2-6.**

2. **Select the bookmark from the list on the left side of the dialog box.**

3. **Change the name and location as desired.**

4. **Click Close to finish editing the bookmark.**

Figure 2-6:
The Edit
Bookmarks
dialog box.

Deleting bookmarks

To delete a bookmark

1. **Choose Bookmarks⇨Edit Bookmarks from the menu bar.**

   The Edit Bookmarks dialog box opens.

2. **Select the bookmark that you want to remove.**

3. **Click the Remove button.**

4. **Click the Close button to close the dialog box.**

Managing your files and folders

You can take many actions when managing your file system with Nautilus.
Table 2-1 briefly explains the action that you want to perform and how you
should do it.

Table 2-1	Managing Files and Folders with Nautilus
Action	*Method*
Move an item.	Click item and drag it to desired location.
Copy an item.	Click item and hold Ctrl while dragging item.
Link to an item.	Click item and press Ctrl+Shift while dragging.
Select single item.	Click item.

(continued)

Table 2-1 *(continued)*

Action	Method
Select contiguous items.	In icon view, click and drag box around items. In list view, press Shift; click the first item, and then click the last.
Select multiple items.	Press Ctrl; click desired items.
Select all items.	Choose Edit⇨Select All File from menu bar.
Create folder.	Right-click and choose Create Folder from contextual menu.
Rename item.	Right-click and choose Rename from the contextual menu.
Move to trash.	Right-click and choose Move to Trash from the contextual menu.
Delete item.	Right-click and choose Move to Trash.
Change permissions.	Right-click, choose Properties, and click the Permissions tab.
Display trash.	Right-click the Trash icon and choose Open from the contextual menu.
Restore trashed item.	Open Trash folder and drag item to desired location.
Empty trash.	Right-click the Trash icon and choose Empty Trash.
Add emblem.	Right-click, choose Properties, click the Emblems tab, and choose desired emblem.
Change single icon.	Right-click, choose Properties, click Select Custom Icon, and choose desired icon.
Change item size.	Choose Zoom In or Zoom Out from toolbar.

Customizing the Nautilus File Manager

A very nice feature of Nautilus is its ability to be configured to make it work how you want it to. You can change many preferences; in this section, I tell you about them and how to change them.

Editing File Manager preferences

To open the Nautilus File Management Preferences dialog box, choose Edit⊅Preferences from the menu bar in a Nautilus window. The dialog box shown in Figure 2-7 appears.

On this dialog box are five tabbed pages:

- ✔ **Views:** Preferences on this tab give you options for setting the default view parameters for Nautilus, such as icon view, sort order, and showing hidden files.

- ✔ **Behavior:** Preferences on this tab are concerned with how Nautilus handles executable files and trash. You can also choose between single- and double-clicking here.

- ✔ **Display:** This tab lets you decide what information you want displayed with your icons, such as size, date created, date modified, and date format.

- ✔ **List Columns:** The settings on this tab let you choose what information is displayed as well as its order, when you choose list view.

- ✔ **Preview:** The settings on this tab determine how your files are displayed in their folders. For example, you can decide here whether you want thumbnail views of graphic files.

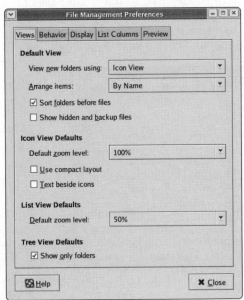

Figure 2-7:
Set
preferences
here.

You can change many preferences to alter the appearance and performance of Nautilus. I've touched upon only a few of them, so experiment with them to see for yourself what they do.

Changing the File Manager background and icon emblems

Another nice feature of Nautilus is the ability to display colors and patterns in the File Manager window. You can also assign emblems to icons. *Emblems* are small graphics that are used to make your icons more meaningful. For example, I like to change the background color for my home directory to light blue. That way, I can tell immediately when I'm in my home directory when I see the blue background. You can easily change the colors and patterns or add emblems by doing the following:

1. **Choose Edit⇨Backgrounds and Emblems from the Nautilus menu bar to open the Backgrounds and Emblems dialog box, as shown in Figure 2-8.**

2. **Click the Patterns, the Colors, or the Emblems button on the left side of the dialog box.**

3. **Click and drag the pattern, color, or emblem from the right side of the dialog box to where you want to place it.**

   You can drag a color or pattern to the large, right pane of the File Manager window to change the color or pattern. You can drag an emblem to an icon to attach it to the icon.

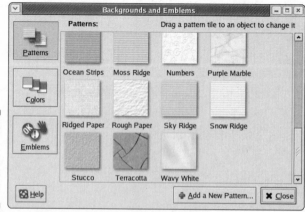

Figure 2-8: The Backgrounds and Emblems dialog box.

You can also drag the patterns or colors directly to the desktop and drop them there. Your desktop will change to reflect your new color or pattern.

Showing and hiding views

You can decide what you want to view and what you don't in your File Manager. You can view or hide the side pane, the status bar, the toolbar, and the location bar by choosing clicking the appropriate item from the View menu on the menu bar. These items are toggled items. If the item is checked, it is available for viewing; if not checked, it is not available. Clicking the item toggles it on or off.

Configuring GNOME

You can also customize your entire desktop as easily as you configure your Nautilus File Manager. Quite a few preferences can be modified in GNOME. I can't possibly explain all of them here in this chapter, but I can show you how to change one of them. You can play around with the rest and make changes as you desire. Take a look at setting up a screensaver. To set the preferences for the screensaver, do the following:

1. **Choose Applications⇨Preferences⇨Screensaver.**

   The Screensaver Preferences dialog box, as shown in Figure 2-9, opens.

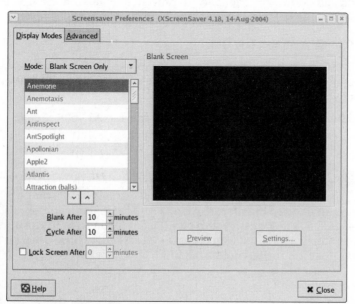

Figure 2-9: Configure the screensaver here.

2. **Choose the mode for the screensaver by making your choice from the drop-down list.**

3. **Select the image or images that you want for your screensaver by selecting the check box in front of your choice.**

4. **Pick the times that you want to use.**

Also be sure to look at the Advanced tab to see whether you want to change any items there. Items on the Advanced tab include image manipulation settings, display power managements settings, color map settings, and diagnostic settings.

5. **When you finish making choices, test your screensaver by clicking the Preview button.**

Don't forget to have a look at the settings for the screensavers that you chose. (Click the Settings button to see them.) In many cases, you can create some interesting effects by changing the settings. For example, you can change the speed of the screensaver or the number of colors displayed.

6. **Click the Close button when you're finished.**

Your new screensaver is enabled.

Logging Out

After you finish working in GNOME, you should log out before leaving the PC. Logging out is always a good idea to prevent anyone from using your system. You can log out of GNOME as follows:

1. **Choose Actions⇨Log Out.**

2. **From the Log Out dialog box, you can choose to log out, restart the system, or shut down the system by selecting the radio button in front of your choice.**

3. **After making your choice, click OK to execute your choice.**

Taking a Look at KDE

The default desktop in Enterprise Linux is GNOME, but another desktop — KDE — is available if you want to give it a try. If you want to use it, you'll have to make sure that it is installed on your system because the default installation of Enterprise Linux does not install KDE.

In this section, I give you a brief overview of KDE just to make you aware of it and perhaps tempt you to try it. I will briefly explain the KDE desktop, show you the Applications menu where you can find some applications to try, and tell you about the Konqueror File Manager. After that, you are on your own to explore if you like.

You can check whether KDE is installed from the graphical login screen. Click Session (refer to Figure 2-1) and select KDE from the choices. If KDE is not a choice, it isn't installed — but you can easily install it by using the Package Management tool.

After selecting KDE for your session, enter your username and password to login. You will see the KDE desktop, as shown in Figure 2-10.

The KDE desktop has a similar appearance to other well-known desktop environments like GNOME or MS Windows or Mac OS X. If you can use these desktops, you will easily master KDE in a short time. Notice that the KDE desktop has a rather clean appearance with little desktop clutter — just one icon at the top and a panel at the bottom. A description of the KDE desktop is in order here.

Figure 2-10:
The KDE desktop after logging in.

At the bottom of the desktop is a gray, horizontal bar. This area of the desktop is the *panel* and is similar to the taskbar in Windows. On the far left of the top panel is the Applications icon, indicated by the Red Hat icon. To the right of Applications are icons representing programs that were installed during the system installation. You can start any of these programs by clicking them from the panel. Just move your mouse over any icon, and a contextual menu appears with a description of the program represented by the icon.

To the right of the program icons on the panel is a square gray area — the Workspace Switcher — that is divided into four sections. When you first log in to KDE, the leftmost section of Workspace Switcher should be white, indicating that you are in workspace one. You can switch between four workspaces in KDE, so you actually get four distinct desktops that you can use. You can open different programs on the different desktops and switch between them by clicking the Workspace Switcher for the desktop that you want to see. Open some programs on the different desktops and then try clicking each of the four squares to see the effect of changing to a different workspace.

On the far right of the panel is a display of the current date and time. The open area on the panel between the Workspace Switcher and the date and time display is used to show any programs that you're running on your desktop. You can switch between programs running on a single desktop by clicking the program name from the bottom panel. Also shown in this area are icons that you can add to the panel as well as applets. *Applets* are applications that provide some type of useful information or entertainment.

Managing applets

The icons on the panel are links to applications — applets. Applets placed on the panel make it quick and convenient to start your chosen application with a single click. If you are familiar with MS Windows, applets in KDE are like shortcuts in Windows. In addition to the applets that are already on the panel, you can add your own. You also can move applets that are already there or delete them to make more room.

To add applets to the panel, do the following:

1. **Right-click an empty area of the panel.**

2. **Choose Add to Panel from the contextual menu.**

3. **Choose the application that you want to add.**

4. **Click Add to add it to the panel.**

To move applets to another location on the panel

1. **Right-click the applet that you want to move.**
2. **Click Move from the contextual menu.**
3. **Drag the applet to the desired location.**
4. **Click to release the applet to its new location.**

To remove an applet from the panel

1. **Right-click the applet that you want to remove.**
2. **Choose Remove from Panel from the contextual menu.**

To modify the properties of an applet (or the panel)

1. **Right-click the applet (or an empty area of the panel).**
2. **Choose Properties from the contextual menu.**
3. **Change the parameters in the Properties dialog box.**

Right-clicking the panel or any applets on it presents a contextual menu, which gives you access to Help and some useful utilities for panel configuration. Contextual menus are different depending on the type of applet that you're selecting.

Choosing applications from the Applications menu

The Applications menu, represented by the Red Hat icon, is on the far-left corner of the top panel. The Applications button gives you access to a large number of applications. Click the Red Hat icon to open the Applications menu, and you see a menu, as shown in Figure 2-11, listing the many categories of applications from which you can choose.

Notice that many of the categories contain a right-pointing arrow. Moving your cursor over categories with a right-pointing arrow opens additional menus from which you can choose even more applications in that category. There are probably more than 100 applications from which you can choose, many more than I can describe in this book. However, I do provide a brief description of the main category of applications here so you can have some idea what they do. Begin by starting at the bottom of the menu and work your way toward the top.

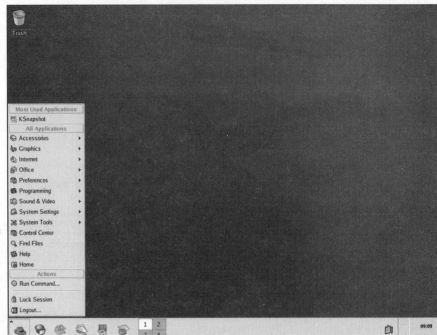

Figure 2-11:
The
Applications
menu on
the KDE
desktop.

Your Applications menu might not be exactly as described in this section, depending on the version of Enterprise Linux you have installed.

- ✔ **Logout:** Choosing Logout opens a dialog box giving you the option to log out or cancel. Select the radio button of your choice and then click OK.

- ✔ **Lock Session:** This menu option starts your system screensaver and locks your desktop. Move your mouse or press a key to open a dialog box that lets you enter your password to unlock the desktop.

- ✔ **Run Command:** This menu item opens a dialog box where you can enter the name of a program that you want to run.

- ✔ **Home:** This menu item is a link to the user's home directory.

- ✔ **Help:** This menu item opens the Help browser. You can get help on using KDE by choosing this item.

- ✔ **Control Center:** The Control Center is used for making configuration changes to the KDE desktop.

- ✔ **System Tools:** This menu choice gives you access to many Enterprise Linux system administration utilities. Tools for configuring your network and printers are located here.

✔ **System Settings:** This menu item contains Enterprise Linux system administration utilities and some KDE configuration utilities as well. Some of the tools here can be used to configure your Web server as well as other servers.

✔ **Sound & Video:** Choosing this item gives you access to programs and utilities related to system sound and video. For example, if you want to adjust the system volume, use the utility here.

✔ **Programming:** This menu item gives you access to some programs that can be used for debugging programs.

✔ **Preferences:** This menu choice opens the System Preferences window. Most of the GNOME settings can be modified with this menu choice. Selecting this from the menu is the same as double-clicking the Computer icon on the desktop.

✔ **Office:** This menu choice gives you access to the OpenOffice.org office suite. The OpenOffice suite contains word processing, spreadsheet, and presentation software, and much more. You can also start several of the OpenOffice applications by clicking the icons on the left side of the panel.

✔ **Internet:** Here you will find applications related to the Internet. For example, the Web browsers are located here as well as an FTP program.

✔ **Graphics:** This menu choice contains graphical programs. Here you find image viewing and editing applications.

✔ **Accessories:** Here you can find applications that don't fit well into the other categories, like the calculator, as well as some text editors.

Using the Konqueror File Manager

The Konqueror File Manager is a graphical shell for KDE. You can use Konqueror not only to manage the files and directories on your system but also as a Web browser to access the Internet.

To start the Konqueror File Manager, select Home from the Applications menu to open the Konqueror File Manager, as shown in Figure 2-12.

A brief explanation of the items on the Konqueror File Manager window is in order:

✔ **Menu bar:** At the top of the window is the menu bar, similar to menu bars from other programs. From the menu bar, you can access tools to perform various actions.

✔ **Toolbar:** Below the menu bar is the toolbar. The toolbar holds buttons that you can use to perform the action indicated by the button, such as back, forward, or reload. The toolbar also has a zoom-in and a zoom-out button (magnifying glass icons) with which you can change the size of items. Finally, the toolbar contains icons that let you choose how you want to view the items in the folder.

✔ **Location bar:** The location bar contains a text field where you can enter a file, folder, or URL to go to.

✔ **Window panes:** Beneath the location bar, the Konqueror window is divided into two panes. The left, smaller pane shows information about the icon selected from the far left side of the pane. Moving your mouse over an icon displays information about the icon. Clicking an item from the list in the left pane displays items in the larger, right pane. If you choose the Root Folder icon, you can see your entire file system tree in the left pane.

✔ The larger, right pane displays the contents of the files or directories that you're viewing. *Note:* All directories appear as folders in Konqueror. You can view the contents of folders as either a list or as icons by choosing from the View As icons (in the toolbar). You can also access Web or FTP sites by entering the URL into the location text field.

✔ **Status bar:** At the bottom of the Konqueror window is the status bar, which displays status information about the files or folders that you are viewing.

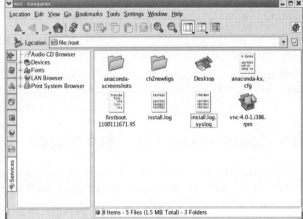

Figure 2-12: The Konqueror File Manager window.

Logging out

After you finish working in KDE, you should log out before leaving the PC. Logging out is always a good idea to prevent anyone from using your system. You can log out of KDE as follows:

1. **Choose Applications➪Log Out.**

2. **From the Log Out dialog box, you can choose to log out or cancel to return to the desktop.**

3. **After making your choice, click OK to execute your choice.**

Chapter 3

Putting Your System to Work

● ●

In This Chapter

▶ Browsing the Web

▶ Sending and receiving e-mail

▶ Working at the office

▶ Keeping yourself entertained

▶ Working with images

● ●

Many applications are installed by default during the Enterprise Linux installation. As soon as your system is installed, you can start doing productive work with the Firefox Web browser, the Evolution e-mail program, OpenOffice.org (the complete office software suite), and many others. You can even do some not-so-productive work with the audio, video, and graphics applications also included with Enterprise Linux. In this chapter, I show you how to use these applications.

Getting Started

After you log in to your desktop, you can select many of the most-used applications from the panel at the bottom of the desktop. As shown in Figure 3-1, on the left side of the panel are links to the Firefox Web browser, the Evolution e-mail client, OpenOffice.org Writer, OpenOffice.org Impress, and OpenOffice.org Calc.

Figure 3-1:
Panel icons
link to
frequently
used
programs.

The AS and ES versions of Enterprise Linux do not install OpenOffice.org, the Evolution mail client, or the Firefox Web browser during the default installation. If you are using one of these versions, you might have to install these applications if they weren't manually installed during system installation.

OpenOffice.org Writer is a word processing program similar to MS Word. OpenOffice.org Impress is a presentation program similar to MS PowerPoint, and Calc is a spreadsheet program similar to MS Excel.

Move you mouse over the icons to make a small help window appear with information about the icon.

Browsing the Web

Begin with the Web browser. The Firefox Web browser is an open source, full-featured, Web-standards-compliant browser that performs similarly to other Web browsers that you might have used. If you've used other graphical-based Web browsers, using Firefox will be easy for you. Starting Firefox is easy:

1. **Click the Firefox Web browser icon from the panel.**

   The icon looks like a globe with a mouse — a computer mouse, not the cheese-snatching critter — and its tail wrapped around it.

2. **Alternatively, you can choose Applications⇨Internet⇨Firefox Web Browser.**

   Regardless of your method, the Firefox program opens the main browser window to the Enterprise Linux default page, as shown in Figure 3-2.

As you can see from Figure 3-2, Firefox has a similar appearance to many other Web browsers, and its functionality is also similar. Take a quick look at the main browser window to familiarize yourself with what is there and how you can use it.

Beginning at the top of the browser window is the typical menu bar that contains the following choices:

- **File:** Items on this menu let you open a new browser window, e-mail pages or links to pages to others, open the page in Composer (Web page creation utility), print the current page, and quit the browser.

- **Edit:** Items on this menu let you copy and paste text, select items, find items, and edit your preferences.

- **View:** Items on this menu include selections related to how your pages appear and what you want to see on your pages.

- **Go:** Items on this menu let you go forward or backward or jump to other pages that you have visited.

✔ **Bookmarks:** These menu items let you add and manage *bookmarks* (favorite pages) so that you can quickly jump to them.

✔ **Tools:** From this menu, you can set many of your browsing preferences for handling cookies, images, passwords, forms, and pop-ups.

✔ **Help:** From this menu, you can choose from various online help options.

Under the menu bar is the navigation toolbar that contains the following options:

✔ **Back:** Clicking this button takes you to the previous page that you were viewing.

✔ **Forward:** Clicking this button takes you forward.

✔ **Reload:** Clicking this button reloads the current page.

✔ **Stop:** Clicking this button stops the current page from loading.

✔ **Home:** This link takes you to the home page that is listed in the browser preferences.

✔ **Location field:** In this field, you can type the address or Uniform Resource Locator (URL) that you want to go to.

✔ **Search:** Click Search to search one of the listed sites.

✔ **Firefox icon:** Click this button to go to the Firefox Web site.

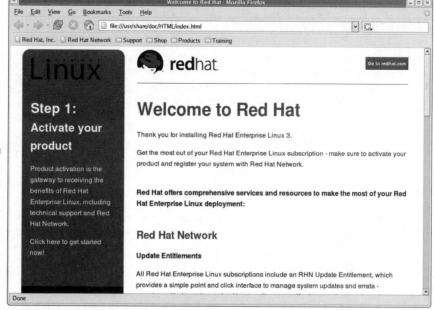

Figure 3-2:
The Firefox
Web
browser
opens to the
Enterprise
Linux
welcome
page.

Beneath the navigation bar is the personal toolbar that contains the following choices:

- **Red Hat, Inc.:** This link takes you to the Red Hat Web site.
- **Red Hat Network:** This link takes you to the Red Hat Network Web site.
- **Support:** Clicking this icon opens a menu that takes you to the support page of the Red Hat Web site:
  - Red Hat Linux Documentation
  - Red Hat Support
  - Red Hat Professional Services
  - Red Hat Search
- **Shop:** This link opens a menu with a selection that takes you to the Red Hat Store.
- **Products:** This link opens a menu that takes you to the Red Hat Web site pages with information about Red Hat Enterprise Linux and Red Hat software.
- **Training:** This link goes to the Red Hat Global Learning Services.

The area below the personal toolbar is the main display area. The current Web page is displayed in the main display area.

Changing Browser Preferences

You can customize many areas of the browser to your liking. Most of the areas that you can configure are reachable by choosing Edit⇨Preferences from the menu bar. The Preferences dialog box, as shown in Figure 3-3, appears.

When this dialog box opens, it opens to the General preferences page. On the left of the dialog box are five icons that open additional dialog boxes. The General dialog box is already shown, and you can click the other icons to open those dialogs boxes. From this dialog box, you are able to change the preferences for the following items:

- **General:** This includes items that you can change to affect the appearance of your browser, including fonts, colors, themes, languages/content packs, and browser home page.
- **Privacy:** These preferences are used to tell Firefox how to handle cookies, pop-ups, passwords, forms, and security certificates.
- **Web Features:** Preferences for this option are related to using Java and JavaScript at Web sites, loading images, and blocking pop-ups.

✔ **Downloads:** These preferences are used to control download options such as locations for saving files, using the Download Manager, and file type associations.

✔ **Advanced:** These preferences are used to control accessibility features, browsing options, and SSL security.

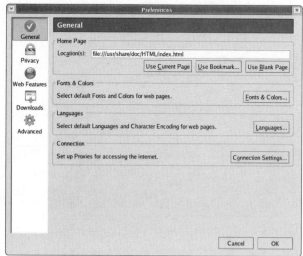

Figure 3-3:
Change the
browser
preferences
here.

Sending and Receiving E-mail

Enterprise Linux has several e-mail clients that you can use for sending and receiving e-mail. The Ximian Evolution e-mail client included with Enterprise Linux works well and is easy to configure and use. You use it to send and receive mail as well as manage your schedule. In this section, I take a look at the Evolution e-mail clients.

The Ximian Evolution e-mail client is a full-featured e-mail program and more. With Evolution, you can manage all your daily tasks with ease. Before you can use Evolution to send and receive mail, though, you must first configure it with your e-mail account settings.

1. **Start Evolution by clicking the Evolution icon from the desktop panel (the envelope and stamp icon) or by choosing Applications⇨Internet⇨ Evolution Email.**

   The Ximian Evolution Setup Assistant window, as shown in Figure 3-4, appears.

2. **Click Forward to go to the Identity page, as shown in Figure 3-5.**

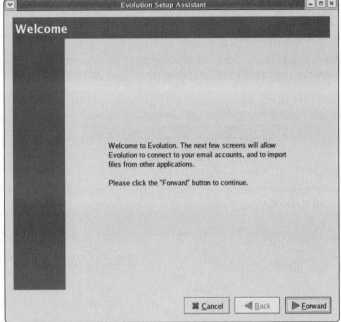

Figure 3-4:
The Ximian
Evolution
Setup
Assistant
e-mail client
window.

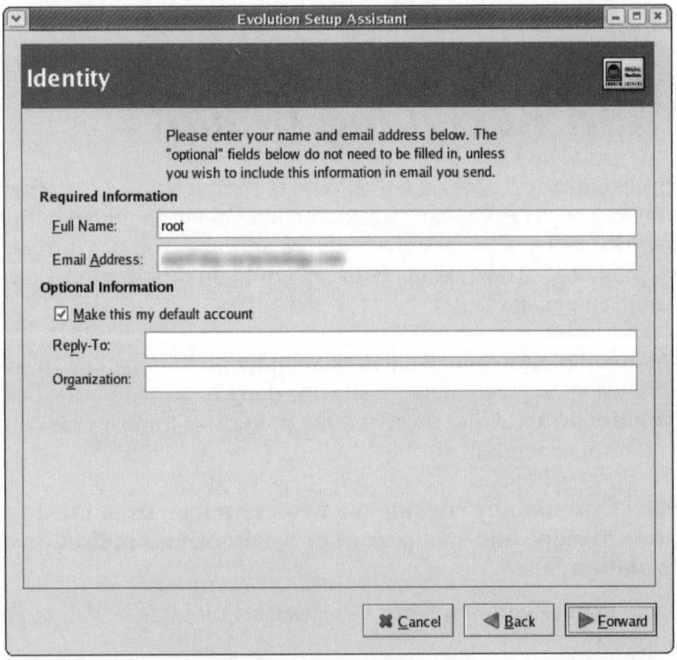

Figure 3-5:
Configure
your e-mail
client
identity
here.

3. **Enter your name and e-mail address in the required fields and then click Forward to continue.**

4. **In the Receiving Mail dialog box that opens, identify the type of mail server that you will be connecting to, as shown in Figure 3-6. Click the down arrow to the right of the Server Type field and choose the appropriate type of mail server for your location.**

   Depending on your choice, other fields will appear on the page in which you need to enter additional information. If you are running the WS or Desktop version of Enterprise Linux, check with your system administrator if you aren't sure what to choose here.

5. **Click Forward to continue to the Send Email dialog box where you choose the type of mail server for sending e-mail.**

6. **Click the down arrow next to the Server Type field and choose either SMTP or Sendmail.**

   If you are running the WS or Desktop version of Enterprise Linux, Check with your system administrator if you aren't sure what to choose here.

7. **Click Forward to continue to the Account Management dialog box, where you will enter a name for the account that you are creating.**

8. **After entering a name, click Forward to go to the Timezone dialog box and select your time zone.**

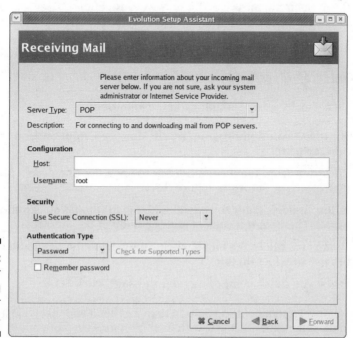

Figure 3-6:
Specify your
incoming
mail server
here.

9. **Click Forward and then click Apply.**

   Your account is created, and the newly created account appears on the right side of the Evolution Settings dialog box.

Receiving e-mail

To receive e-mail by using Evolution, do the following:

1. **Start the Evolution program by clicking the Evolution icon from the desktop panel.**

2. **Click the Send/Receive button on the navigation bar.**

   The program retrieves your messages from the server that you configured earlier (see the preceding section).

   If you have any new messages, a number appears behind the Inbox icon on the left side of the window indicating how many messages there are.

3. **Click the Inbox icon to open the Inbox.**

4. **Either click the message to view it in the bottom pane of the Evolution window or double-click the message to open it in a new window.**

5. **To reply to the message, click Reply on the navigation bar.**

6. **If you open the message in a new window, choose File⇨Close from the menu bar or click the X in the upper-right corner to close the window.**

Sending e-mail

To send e-mail by using Evolution, do the following:

1. **Start the Evolution program by clicking the Evolution icon from the desktop panel.**

2. **Click New from the navigation bar to open the Compose a Message dialog box, as shown in Figure 3-7.**

3. **In the To field, enter the e-mail address to whom you are sending the e-mail. Then enter a subject and the body of the message.**

4. **To attach a file to the email, click Attach from the navigation bar and browse to select the file.**

5. **When you finish composing your message, click Send.**

You can do a lot more with Evolution than just send and receive e-mail. You should do some experimenting with Evolution to learn more about its scheduling and time management features. You can begin your exploration of scheduling by clicking the Calendars button on the left side of the Evolution window. The calendar opens, showing today's date and hourly listings in a large calendar as well as a smaller calendar showing the entire month. You can double-click a time in the large calendar display to open a dialog box to schedule an event for that time. If you click a date on the small calendar, the date changes on the large calendar to show the date that you selected.

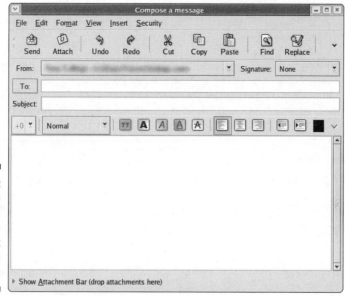

Figure 3-7:
Use the
Compose a
Message
dialog box
to send
e-mail.

Working at the Office

Enterprise Linux includes the complete office application suite OpenOffice.org. OpenOffice.org includes a word processing application, a presentation application, a spreadsheet application, a drawing application, a math equation editor, and an HTML page creation tool. In most cases, OpenOffice.org is compatible with documents created with other office suite applications such as MS Office. I have successfully created documents with OpenOffice.org and then exchanged those documents MS Office users and vice versa. The great thing about OpenOffice.org is its price — namely, free. And when you consider that it works with documents, presentations, and spreadsheets created with MS Office, it is an incredible value. In this section, I explain the basic steps for using OpenOffice.org Writer for creating documents, OpenOffice.org Impress for creating presentations, and OpenOffice.org Calc for creating spreadsheets.

For a detailed look at OpenOffice.org, check out *OpenOffice.org For Dummies* by Gurdy Leete, Ellen Finkelstein, and Mary Leete (Wiley).

Writing with OpenOffice.org Writer

As I mention in the preceding paragraph, OpenOffice.org Writer is a word processing program. If you've ever used a word processing program before, you should be able to easily begin using OpenOffice.org Writer. To start the program, click the OpenOffice.org Writer icon from the desktop panel (it looks like a pen and two sheets of paper) or choose Applications➪Office➪ OpenOffice.org Writer. The first time you open the program, you're prompted to register the program and then you are presented with a blank document, as shown in Figure 3-8.

I can't go into a detailed explanation about using OpenOffice.org Writer; that could be a complete book in itself. However, I will show you how to open documents and save them in other formats. So instead of using MS Office to do your work, you can use OpenOffice.org instead and share your work with others still using MS Office.

Opening documents

To open a document in OpenOffice.org Writer, do the following:

1. **Choose File➪Open from the menu bar at the top of the window.**

   A standard Open window appears (see Figure 3-9).

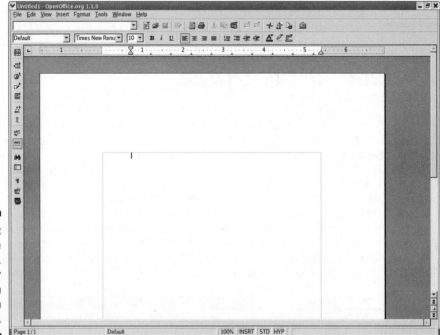

Figure 3-8:
The
OpenOffice.
org Writer
program
main
window.

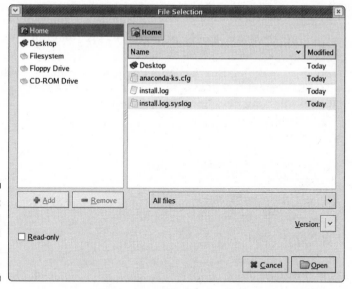

As you can see from Figure 3-9, OpenOffice.org Writer recognizes the file extension .doc as a MS Word file. With OpenOffice.org, you can open any MS Word-formatted file.

2. Select the file that you want to open and then click Open.

The document opens in the main window.

3. After you open the document, you can make any changes that you desire. When you are finished, be sure to save your document (as explained in the following section).

If you're interested in seeing all the file types that OpenOffice.org can handle, click the down arrow next to the File Type field in the file browser when you are looking for files to open.

Saving documents

Saving documents in OpenOffice.org Writer is a very simple procedure, and you probably already know what to do. The reason why I bring this up is to tell you how to save the document in formats that other word processing programs can understand. By default, OpenOffice.org writer uses the file extension .sxw for documents, but if you want to be able to use the document in another program, you will need to save the file with a different extension. To save your file, follow these steps:

1. Choose File⇨Save from the menu bar (or File⇨Save As if you want to change its name).

If you are saving a file that you previously opened, the program saves it in the same format that it was opened with. For example, if you're saving a file that was opened as a MS Word file, the program will save it as an MS Word file (look for a .doc extension).

2. **In the Save As dialog box that appears, you can change the file type to a different format by clicking the down arrow next to the File Type field and selecting the type of file you want.**

Figure 3-10 illustrates choosing a different file type.

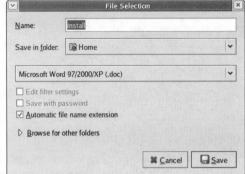

Figure 3-10:
Choose a
different file
type here.

When you save your files by using a different file type, the program warns you that using a different file type might affect your formatting. The program will prompt you to use the default OpenOffice.org file type. You can safely answer No and save the file with the type that you desire.

3. **Be sure to enter a name for your file as well as the file type. Then click Save to save the file.**

Calculating with OpenOffice.org Calc

Another member of the OpenOffice.org office suite is the Calc program. Calc is a full-featured spreadsheet program similar to MS Excel. In fact, anything that you can do with Excel, you can most likely do with Calc. To start the program, click the OpenOffice.org Calc icon from the desktop panel (it looks like a pie chart on top of a spreadsheet) or choose Applications⇨Office⇨ OpenOffice.org Calc. You are presented with a blank document, as shown in Figure 3-11.

OpenOffice.org Calc is a typical spreadsheet application. If you've used a spreadsheet program, you can soon master Calc. Many of the commands and formulas that you might have used in MS Excel also work in Calc. You can also save your spreadsheets in MS Excel format (.xls) so that you can share your files with Windows users or use them yourself on Windows PCs.

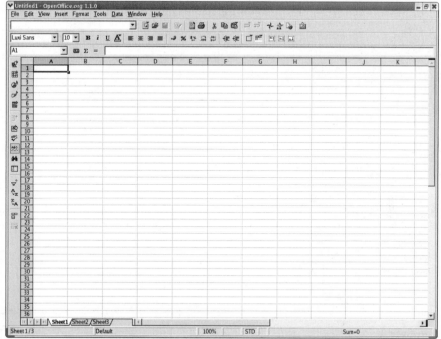

Figure 3-11:
The
OpenOffice.
org Calc
program
main
window.

Opening and saving spreadsheets in Calc works exactly the same as opening and saving documents using OpenOffice.org Writer. The best way to learn how easy it is to use OpenOffice.org Calc is to open the program and experiment with it. I strongly encourage you to do so.

Impressing with OpenOffice.org Impress

Impress is the presentation software included with the OpenOffice.org office suite. With Impress, you can make those fancy presentations that everyone seems to be using these days. If you've used MS PowerPoint to make your presentations, you should give Impress a try.

To start the program, click the OpenOffice.org Impress icon from the desktop panel (it looks like a slide on top of a bar graph) or choose Applications➪ Office➪OpenOffice.org Impress. When you open Impress, a presentation wizard opens to help you create your presentation. You can select to create a blank presentation or one from a template, or you can open an existing presentation. Figure 3-12 shows a presentation that I created with MS PowerPoint and then opened using OpenOffice.org Impress.

Figure 3-12:
Opening a
presentation
created in
PowerPoint
with
OpenOffice.
org Impress.

Not only can you open presentations created with MS PowerPoint, but you can also save presentations that you create with Impress as MS PowerPoint presentations. This means that you can use your presentations on just about any PC and share your files with nearly everyone.

Configuring OpenOffice.org

You can customize many areas of the OpenOffice.org office suite to your own liking. I can't cover the seemingly endless options in this book, but I can tell you where to go to begin your configuration. From there, you can explore and experiment on your own to get the settings that you want. To begin your customizing, do the following:

1. **Choose Tools⇨Options from the menu bar at the top of any open OpenOffice.org program.**

   The Options dialog box (see Figure 3-13) appears.

2. **On the left, click the area that you want to customize.**

A page related to that area opens (on the right of the Options dialog box).

3. **Enter the information or choose the options that you desire.**

   For example, I can fill in my user data by clicking this item and filling in the information requested. Or, I could click Print and specify printing options.

4. **After you finish your configuring, click OK to apply your changes.**

Click the Help button on the Options dialog box to get help on the specific page that you are viewing.

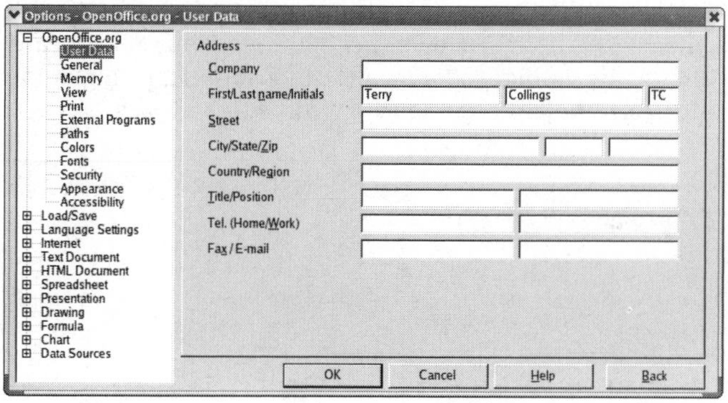

Figure 3-13:
Change
OpenOffice.
org options
here.

Options - OpenOffice.org - User Data	
OpenOffice.org	Address
User Data	Company
General	
Memory	First/Last name/Initials Terry Collings TC
View	
Print	Street
External Programs	
Paths	City/State/Zip
Colors	
Fonts	Country/Region
Security	
Appearance	Title/Position
Accessibility	
Load/Save	Tel. (Home/Work)
Language Settings	
Internet	Fax / E-mail
Text Document	
HTML Document	
Spreadsheet	
Presentation	
Drawing	
Formula	
Chart	
Data Sources	OK Cancel Help Back

Keeping Yourself Entertained

If you've followed this chapter to this point, you've done a lot of work and you're probably ready for a break. (Can't have Jack becoming a dull boy, now can we?) Not only can you do productive work with the applications included with Enterprise Linux, but you can also play. Audio and video applications are installed that you can use when you want to take a break from work. In this section, I show you some of them.

Configuring your sound card

Probably the first thing that you want to check before you start using any of the audio and video applications is your sound card. You want to be sure that it's working, or you won't be able to hear anything that might be coming from the applications. In most cases, if your system has a sound card installed, it will be detected and properly configured when Enterprise Linux itself is installed. However, there's always the possibility that the sound card isn't detected, or maybe you just got around to installing one. To check for a sound card and do the configuration, use the sound card detection utility:

1. **Choose Applications⇨System Settings⇨Soundcard Detection.**

   The utility runs and displays the sound card information, as shown in Figure 3-14.

2. **Click Play Test Sound to hear a sample sound play.**

   • *Tah-dah!:* If your sound card is detected and the sound plays, your sound card is configured and ready to go.

   • *Nah-dah:* If your sound card is not detected, you receive a message stating so. If you receive this message, your sound card is not automatically configured. Please read Chapter 21 on troubleshooting for more help on configuring your soundcard.

Figure 3-14:
The sound card detection utility shows the sound card installed in your system.

> **Audio Devices**
>
> The following audio device was detected.
>
> **Vendor:** VIA Technologies
> **Model:** VT8233/A/8235/8237 AC97 Audio Controller
> **Module:** via82cxxx_audio
>
> [Play test sound]
>
> [✔ OK]

Playing audio files

Enterprise Linux WS and Desktop include an audio player — Rhythmbox — that you can use to play many types of audio files. You open the player by choosing Applications⇨Sound & Video⇨Audio Player. The Rhythmbox player shown in Figure 3-15 appears.

Choose Music from the menu bar to open a menu that lets you choose files to play from your hard drive or other locations, including the Internet. You can set your player preferences, like the information you want displayed about the track you are listening to, by choosing Preferences from the Edit menu.

You won't be able to play MP3 files because Red Hat didn't include support for them because of patent and licensing issues. Check the Rhythmbox Web site at www.rhythmbox.org/faq.html for more information about MP3 files.

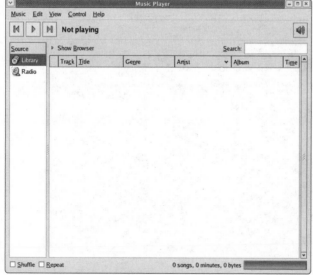

Figure 3-15:
The
Rhythmbox
Music
Player
application.

Playing video files

Earlier versions of Enterprise Linux included a movie player, called Xine,
which you could use to play many video file formats. Xine plays the majority
of file types such as MPG, AVI, MOV, ASF, and WMV. With version 4 of
Enterprise Linux, Xine is no longer included with Enterprise Linux.
Fortunately, you can get Xine from http://heidelberg.freshrpms.net. At
the Fresh RPMs Web site, look for and download the following packages:

- xine
- xine-lib
- aalib
- ilbdvdcss
- lib-fame

Install the packages by using the following command:

```
rpm -Uvh libdvd* aalib lib-fame xine-lib xine*
```

After installing Xine, you start it by typing **xine** at a terminal prompt. Right-
click an open area of the Xine window to open a menu that lets you select
files to play and configure Xine. Figure 3-16 shows the Xine main display.

Figure 3-16:
The Xine
movie
player.

Another movie player that I like a lot is MPlayer. You have to download and install it, but it can sometimes play movies that Xine refuses to play. You can find MPlayer at

```
www.mplayerhq.hu/homepage/design7/dload.html
```

Working with Images

Enterprise Linux has many applications that you can use to view and manipulate graphic images. In this section, I talk about one of my favorites, the GIMP (used for modifying images). I can't go into a long detailed explanation of the GIMP, but I can introduce it to you and perhaps make you curious to learn more.

The GIMP — an acronym for Gnu Image Manipulation Program — is a very powerful, image editing program quite similar to Adobe Photoshop. I used to use Photoshop frequently when I was still a Windows user and was quite pleased to find The GIMP when I switched to Linux. You can start The GIMP by choosing Applications⇨Graphics⇨The Gimp. The first time you select the application, it installs itself on your system; then the application window opens, as shown in Figure 3-17.

As you can see from Figure 3-17, the opening window doesn't look how one typically expects an open program to look. There is no large open white area, no menu bar, or navigation bar — just The GIMP toolbar — but everything you need to do can be done from that toolbar.

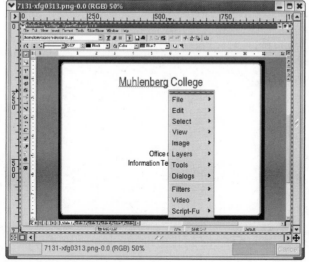

Figure 3-17:
The GIMP
toolbar is
the initial
interface
after
starting the
program.

Move your mouse over a tool icon to get a description of what the tool does. Click a tool icon to select that tool; double-click a tool icon to open the options for that tool.

To open a file, choose File➪Open and select the file that you want to open. You can also choose to acquire an image either from a screen capture or from a SANE-compliant scanner. Scanner Access Now Easy (SANE) refers to the program used by Linux systems to control scanners. After you open an image, you can right-click anywhere on the image to get a pop-up menu that gives you many more choices.

You can set preferences for the program by choosing File➪Preferences. You can set hundreds of preferences, so I recommend that you open the Preferences dialog box and go through it slowly to understand your options. Then make some changes and see what effect they have on your programs' functionality. Remember, often times the best way to learn about an application is to experiment.

Chapter 4

Exploring the File System and Command Shell

• •

In This Chapter

▶ Examining the file system structure

▶ Commanding the shell

▶ Commonly used shell commands

▶ Writing shell scripts

• •

*A*nyone who has used a computer, regardless of the operating system that the computer uses, knows that information stored on the computer is organized by files and directories into a hierarchical structure typically known as a *file system.* Red Hat Enterprise Linux is no different in this respect: Its file system is also organized similarly. However, you need to be aware of some significant differences when comparing an Enterprise Linux file system with the most widely used file system, MS Windows. In this chapter, I explain the Enterprise Linux file system organization and how it differs from Windows. I also show you how to use the command shell to navigate the file system and perform many routine file system tasks, such as creating and deleting files and directories as well as changing file permissions and ownership.

Examining the Enterprise Linux File System Structure

If you've used Windows before (and most of us have), the biggest difference that you'll notice when looking at the Enterprise Linux file system structure is that no drive letters are shown in a file system listing. For example, you won't find the typical C drive as the hard drive, A drive as the floppy drive, or D drive as the CD drive. All devices in Enterprise Linux, including disk drives, are just a part of the file system. Figure 4-1 shows a typical Enterprise Linux file system.

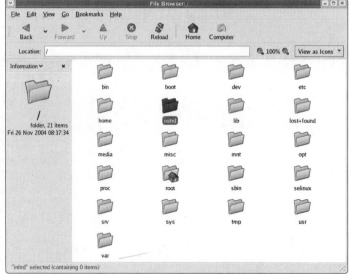

Figure 4-1:
The
structure
of the
Enterprise
Linux file
system
hierarchy.

The Enterprise Linux file system is based on the standards outlined in the Filesystem Hierarchy Standard (FHS). All Unix and Unix-based systems, like Enterprise Linux, follow this standard. The FHS provides specific require- ments for the placement of files in the directory structure. Placement is based on the type of information contained in the file. The two basic cat- egories of file information are

✔ **Shareable and unsharable**

  • *Shareable* files are files that can be accessed by other hosts.

  • *Unsharable* files can be accessed only by the local system.

✔ **Variable or static**

  • *Variable* files contain information that can change at any time on their own, without anyone actually changing the file. A log file is an example of a variable file.

  • A *static* file contains information that does not change unless a user changes it. Program documentation and binary files are exam- ples of static files.

Although you don't need to know the complete details of the FHS to work with the Enterprise Linux file system, if you want more information about the FHS, including the complete standard, go to www.pathname.com/fhs.

Understanding the organization or layout of the Enterprise Linux file system is one of the most important aspects of system use and administration. As you can see by looking at the tree structure on the left side of Figure 4-1, the Enterprise Linux file system contains a single top-level directory that is identified by a single / (forward slash character) and is known as the *root directory* or *root* of the file system. Take a look at the Location field of the file browser, and you will see the single forward slash that shows you are in the root directory of the file system. The system root contains a number of other directories, and each of these directories has a specific function as specified by the FHS. According to the FHS, the / directory must contain or have links to the following directories.

Not all the directories shown in Figure 4-1 are shown in the following list. The directories not shown are initially empty.

Unlike some other operating systems, Enterprise Linux is case-sensitive. I think it is a really good idea to always use lowercase for all my filenames. By doing this, I never have to remember whether I used uppercase or lowercase: I know that the name is always lowercase.

- ✔ `bin`: This directory contains command files for use by the system administrator or other users. *Note:* The `/bin` directory cannot contain subdirectories.

- ✔ `boot`: The `/boot` directory contains the *system kernel,* which is the core of the Enterprise Linux operating system. This directory also contains files related to booting the system.

- ✔ `dev`: This directory contains files with information about devices, either hardware or software, on the system.

- ✔ `etc`: The `/etc` directory and its subdirectories contain most of the system configuration files. If you have the X Window System installed on your system, the X11 subdirectory is located here. Networking-related configuration files are located in the `sysconfig` subdirectory.

- ✔ `home`: This directory contains the directories of users on the system. Subdirectories of `/home` are created and named automatically for each user who has an account on the system. For example, my home directory is identified as `/home/terry`.

- ✔ `lib`: The `/lib` directory and its subdirectories contain shared system files and kernel modules.

- ✔ `media`: This directory is the location of the mount point for temporary file systems, such as a floppy or CD drive.

  Before any file system can be used by Enterprise Linux, it must first be *mounted.* Mounting a file system requires that it be given a location on the / file system that can be referenced. Most administrators use the `/mnt` directory for this purpose. Mounting drives and other file systems will be explained later in the section, "Mounting and unmounting drives."

✔ opt: This directory is frequently used to hold applications that are installed on the system.

✔ proc: The /proc directory is a virtual file system that acts as an interface to the kernel's internal data structure. You can get detailed information about your system hardware and even change kernel parameters while the system is running.

✔ root: This is the home directory of the root user.

Don't confuse this directory with the / directory, which has the same name.

✔ sbin: This directory contains system binaries (programs) that are used by the system administrators or root user.

✔ tmp: The /tmp directory holds temporary files that are used by the running system.

✔ usr: This directory contains shareable, read-only data. Subdirectories can be used for holding applications, typically in /usr/local.

✔ var: Files and subdirectories under /var contain variable information such as system logs and print queues.

Commanding the Shell

Most of us who have been using PCs for a long time can remember a time when there were no GUIs with icons to click for whatever we wanted to do. Back in the old days of computing, in order to communicate with the PC, you had to enter commands by typing them into a text screen at a command prompt. This was more commonly known as working in a *shell.* In this section, I introduce you to the Enterprise Linux shell.

Perhaps you are wondering what I'm talking about when I mention working *in the shell.* Don't worry; after reading this section, you will know enough to make the shell work for you. Although using a GUI desktop environment has become commonplace, a lot can be said for using the shell. For example, sometimes a problem can occur with the GUI that prevents you from using it. Or, you might find using the shell to be faster and more efficient than constantly clicking icons.

Opening a terminal window

If you're logged into GNOME and wondering how you can type in commands at the desktop, well . . . you can't just yet. However, if you open a terminal window, you will be able to enter shell commands.

From either GNOME or KDE, you can open a terminal window by choosing Applications⇨System Tools⇨Terminal. A window similar to that shown in Figure 4-2 appears.

The terminal window is also known as the *console*.

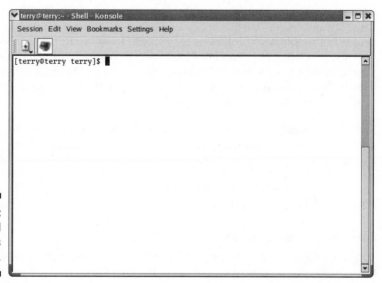

Figure 4-2:
Enter shell
commands
here.

Even if the GUI is locked up and won't respond to mouse clicks, you can still get to a console by going to a virtual console. You can get to six virtual consoles in Enterprise Linux by pressing Ctrl+Alt+F1 to enter the first virtual console, Ctrl+Alt+F2 to enter the second, Ctrl+Alt+F3 to enter the third, and so on. To return to the GUI, press Ctrl+Alt+F7.

The default shell in Enterprise Linux is called bash, which is an acronym for *Bourne again shell.* The bash shell is what gives you the command prompt and waits for you to enter commands. You can enter any valid shell command as well as enter any valid executable program name.

In Figure 4-2, you can see that the shell prompt is [terry@terry terry] $. This prompt gives you some valuable information. The first name shown is the user who is logged in, @terry is the name of the system to which the user is logged in, and the final name is the directory in which the user is currently located. The dollar sign at the end of the prompt shows that the user is logged in as a regular user. A pound sign (#) indicates that the user is logged in as the root user. Of course, you must follow a specific syntax when entering shell commands; the following section explains the command syntax.

Shell command syntax

All shell commands have the same basic syntax, as shown here.

```
command option(s) argument(s)
```

Be sure to pay close attention to this syntax because the most common cause for command line failures are mistakes in typing the commands. The syntax is the command, followed by a space, followed by one or more options, another space, and finally one or more arguments. The shell uses the spaces to keep the command and options separated. *Note:* Because you can have options that contain spaces, be sure to put any option containing spaces inside quotation marks.

Not all commands have options, so you might not need to enter them depending on the command that you're using. For example, if you just want a listing of the files in your current directory, you can enter **ls** with no options.

You can always get help by entering the command man followed by the command on which you want help.

Combining shell commands

You can pass more than one command at a time to the shell by separating the commands with a semicolon. For example, if you want to change to the /etc directory and then get a listing of that directory, you type **cd /etc;ls**.

You can also use another special character to pass the output from one command into the input of a following command. You do this by using a vertical bar — | — which is also known as the *pipe* symbol. For example, suppose you want to get a count of the files in a particular directory. You could use the command

```
ls /etc | wc -l
```

This command lists the contents of the /etc directory and then "pipes" the output of the ls (list) command into the wc (word count) command, which then shows the output as the number of lines (-l) in the /etc directory.

Redirecting input and output

Whenever you type in a shell command, the output of the command is displayed on your system monitor. This output is typically referred to as stdout. Information that you enter at the shell prompt is referred to as stdin. By using special characters, you can tell the shell to get its input from a different location, usually a file, other than stdin. You can also tell the shell to redirect the output to a different location, usually a file, other than stdout.

The character that is used for telling the shell to read the stdin from a file instead of the keyboard is the < (less-than) character. For example, suppose that you want to sort the contents of your group file. You could use the command

```
sort < /etc/group
```

In this case, the sort command reads the /etc/group file as stdin because it was redirected to do so by the less-than (<) character. The output of the command is displayed on the system monitor, or stdout.

If you wanted, you could redirect the output from stdout to a file by using another redirection character — this time, the > (greater-than) sign. By entering the command in the following example, you direct the output of the sort command to the file sortedgroup.

```
sort < /etc/group > sortedgroup
```

Using command completion

With command completion, you can save yourself some typing. Just type in the first few letters of the command that you want to use and then press Tab twice. The bash shell shows a list of all commands that begin with the letters that you typed. For example, if you want to use the grep command, just enter **gr** and then press Tab twice. On my system, I see the following output.

```
[terry@terry terry] $ gr
grefer      grepjar     groff       grops
grep        grip        groffer     grotty
(output shortened)
```

You can also use the command completion method to complete filenames that you might enter after the command. For example, if you have a file in your home directory named upstrack.txt that you want to view with the cat command, you could enter **cat /home/terry/ups** and then press Tab. The bash shell fills in the rest of the filename for you, saving you some typing and also reducing the chance of a typo.

If you don't enter enough characters to uniquely identify the command or filename, press Tab again. bash will show all the commands or filenames that begin with the letters that you typed.

Searching files with wildcards

If you've ever used MS-DOS or a command window in MS Windows, you know that you can use wildcard characters when searching your file system. In Enterprise Linux, you can also use two of the same wildcards, plus an additional one. You can use the following characters:

> ✔ **Asterisk:** The * (asterisk) character can be used to represent an unlimited number of characters. For example, a search for tennis* finds all words beginning with *tennis* and containing any number of other characters.

> ✔ **Question mark:** The ? (question mark) character is used to represent one character. For example, a search for `tennis?` finds all words beginning with *tennis* and containing one additional character after the *s*.
>
> ✔ **Characters inside brackets:** Using [. . .] (characters inside brackets) finds any of the characters inside the brackets. For example, a search for [Aa]* finds all files that begin with *A* or *a* and containing any other characters.

Repeating commands with history

The `bash` shell has an interesting feature that stores up to 1,000 commands that you might have used. To view the command history, you can use the `history` command. `bash` displays a numbered list of the commands that you've used, even commands from previous logins.

To use a command from the list, first type an exclamation point and then the number of the command. For example, to use command number 15 from the history list, type **!15**.

The easiest way to repeat a previous command is to press the up-arrow key. `bash` displays the commands that you've used, one at a time, in reverse order. Pressing the down-arrow key moves you one command at a time forward through the command history.

Frequently Used Shell Commands

I cannot possibly list all the hundreds of commands that you can use from the `bash` shell. You can find commands for working with files and directories, commands used to get help, commands used to manage system processes, and many, many other types of commands. In this section, I organize alphabetically some of the most frequently used commands into groups based on the commands' functions, and I also explain how to use them. Be sure to use the `man` command, which I explain in the following "Getting help" section, to get more details about the commands that I reference here.

To get a listing of the `bash` built-in commands, type **man command** at a terminal prompt.

Getting help

These commands are used to get more information about commands. To use these commands, type the command name (shown first) followed by the name of the command for which you want help.

✔ info: This command displays help for the command entered. For example, to search for help about ls, use

```
info ls
```

✔ man: This command displays help for the command entered. For example, to search for help about ls, use

```
man ls
```

✔ whatis: This command is used to get basic information about what a command is used for. This command does not provide detailed help on how to use the command. For example, entering **whatis ls** displays

```
ls (1) - list directory contents
```

Working with files and directories

This group contains the largest and most frequently used shell commands. Commands in this grouping are used to create and delete files and directories, list directory contents, change file and directory ownership, and much more.

Creating and removing directories

You can use directories to organize your files to make them easier to find when you need them. For example, I created a directory called rhelfd in my home directory to hold the files for this book. Inside that directory, I created a subdirectory for each of the chapters. To create my directory, I used the mkdir command, as shown here:

```
mkdir rhelfd
```

Then I created my chapter directories inside rhelfd by entering this command:

```
mkdir rhelfd/ch04
```

You don't have to be inside the directory in which you want to create another directory. In fact, you can create an entire directory tree by using the -p option with the mkdir command. The -p option tells the mkdir command to create the parent directories for the subdirectory that you are creating.

Changing directories

The cd command is used to change to another directory. For example, to change to the directory rhelfd from my home directory (/home/terry), I use the following:

```
cd rhelfd
```

To change to a subdirectory of the current directory, you don't need to specify the full (or absolute) path. Instead, you can just type the subdirectory (or relative) pathname. For example, to change to the `bin` subdirectory of `/usr/local`, you just need to type **cd bin**. To move up a level, or return to the parent directory, just enter **cd ..** (c, d, space, and then two periods).

To return to your home directory from any location, just type **cd** and then press Enter.

Determining the working directory

Whenever you're using the command prompt, the prompt shows the directory in which you are located. However, only the directory itself and not the entire path is shown. So, if the prompt shows `bin` as the directory, you can't tell from the prompt whether this is the `/bin` directory or the `/usr/local/bin` directory. Fortunately, using the `pwd` (print working directory) command will tell you where you are. To get the path name listing, use the following command:

```
pwd
```

which returns this output:

```
/usr/local/bin
```

Listing the directory contents

You probably already know this command from some of the earlier examples that I use in this chapter. But in case you don't, you can use the `ls` command to get a listing of a directory's contents. For example, to get a listing of the `/bin` directory, you type **ls /bin**. You will see the listing shown in Figure 4-3.

Notice that the shell uses different colors to differentiate the types of files and directories that are displayed. The colors used and what they typically represent are

- **Blue:** Directories
- **Green/red:** Executable files
- **Teal:** Links to other files or directories
- **Black:** Regular files

By default, the Enterprise Linux is set up to show different types of files in color to make them easy to distinguish. However, this setting might have been changed on your system. If you don't see colors, you can still determine the file type by using the `ls` command with the `-F` (yes, that's a capital F) option. To see the differences between files and directories in your listing, type the following:

```
ls -F
```

```
terry@terry:/bin - Shell - Konsole
Session  Edit  View  Bookmarks  Settings  Help

ash              dnsdomainname   kbd_mode        ping6      touch
ash.static       doexec          kill            ps         tracepath
aumix-minimal    domainname      link            pwd        tracepath6
awk              dumpkeys        ln              red        traceroute
basename         echo            loadkeys        rm         traceroute6
bash             ed              login           rmdir      true
bash2            egrep           ls              rpm        umount
bsh              env             mail            rvi        uname
cat              ex              mkdir           rview      unicode_start
chgrp            false           mknod           sed        unicode_stop
chmod            fgrep           mktemp          setfont    unlink
chown            gawk            more            setserial  usleep
cp               gettext         mount           sh         vi
cpio             grep            mt              sleep      view
csh              gtar            mv              sort       ypdomainname
cut              gunzip          netstat         stty       zcat
date             gzip            nice            su
dd               hostname        nisdomainname   sync
df               igawk           pgawk           tar
[terry@terry bin]$ ls ping
ping
[terry@terry bin]$ ls -l ping
-rwsr-xr-x   1 root     root         27924 Sep  3  2003 ping
[terry@terry bin]$ ▮
```

Figure 4-3:
Use the ls
command to
show the
contents of
a directory.

Now when you look at your directory listing, you see the following appended to the names.

- ✔ /: A slash indicates that the name is a directory.

- ✔ *: An asterisk indicates that the file is an executable file.

- ✔ @: An @ sign indicates that the file is a link to another file or directory.

Listing file permissions

The ls -l command is used to show the file permissions. When I enter this command by typing ls -l at the command prompt, I see the listing shown in Figure 4-4.

Each line in the directory listing provides permission and ownership information about the file or directory shown by the name at the end of the line. Take a more detailed look at the first line, beginning at the far left and moving toward the right, as shown in Figure 4-5.

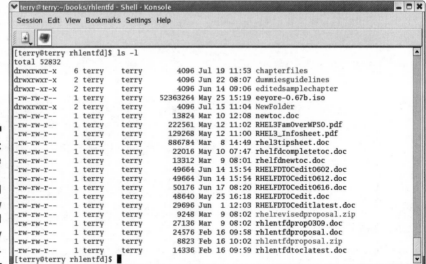

Figure 4-4:
Use the
ls -l
command
to show
file and
directory
permissions.

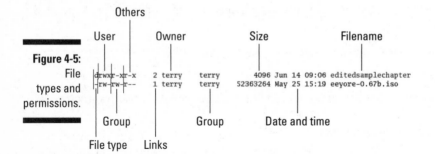

Figure 4-5:
File
types and
permissions.

The leftmost column shows the type of file and the file permissions and ownership of the file or directory. The first letter of this column indicates the type of file or directory and can be one of five characters, with the following meaning:

- b: The file is a block device — a disk drive, for example.

- c: The file is a character device, perhaps a terminal.

- d: The file is a directory.

- l: The file is a link to another file.

- - (hyphen): The file is a regular file.

Following the first character is a series of nine characters shown in the listing as `rwxrwxr-x`. Each group of three letters (`rwx`) represents the permissions granted to a particular user:

✔ r: Read permission

✔ w: Write permission

- *If the file is a program,* having the `x` permission means that the user can run the program.

- *If the file is a directory,* the `x` permission means that the user can open and read the contents of the directory.

✔ x: Execute permission

A hyphen in the series means that the permission for a particular item has not been given.

There are always three types of users for every file or directory in the Enterprise Linux file system, and the permissions correspond to the position of the three groups: user, group members, or others.

✔ **User:** The leading `rwx` shows the permissions that are granted to the owner of the file or directory. In this case, the owner can read, write, and execute the file. Because the first listing in Figure 4-5 shows a directory, the `x` means that the owner can open and view the contents of the directory.

✔ **Group members:** The middle group of `rwx` letters shows the read, write, and execute permissions of users who are members of the file's group.

✔ **Others:** The concluding group of `rwx` letters shows the read, write, and execute permissions of other users. These other users are usually referred to as *the world.* Look at some examples of permissions. A file with permission `rw-------` is readable and writable to the file's owner and no one else. A file with permission `rw-rw-r--` is readable and writable to the file's owner and group members but only readable by the world. Hopefully, you get the idea by now.

The column to the right of the permissions column shows the number of links to the file. Links in Linux are similar to shortcuts in Windows or aliases in Mac OS.

The third column (to the right of the links column) shows the owner of the file. The column to the right of the owner column shows the group the file belongs to.

Continuing to the right, the column after the group ownership shows the size of the file in bytes. Following the file size column is the date and time of the last modification to the file.

Finally, the last column on the right is the name of the file or directory.

After you master how reading permissions for files and directories, read on to see how to change them.

Changing file permissions

By changing file permissions, you can prevent unauthorized users from seeing or changing information in files and directories. Knowing how to change file permissions is one of the most basic requirements for running a secure system. The command for changing file permissions is chmod. The basic syntax for the command is

```
chmod options filename
```

The options that you use determine the file permissions for the specified file and are shown here. You can set permissions for three types of users:

- u: Owner of the file
- g: Group of the file
- o: Others who can use the file
- a: All

With these letters, you can add, remove, or assign permissions (respectively) by using a + (plus sign) to add, a - (minus sign) to remove, and an = (equal sign) to assign following the letters. Are you confused yet? Here are some examples to make it clearer.

Suppose you create a file in your home directory called testfile. You want to give yourself read (r), write (w), and execute (x) permissions and also remove permissions for the group and others. Enter the following command:

```
chmod u+rwx,go-rwx testfile
```

The preceding command adds rwx to the user (u+rwx) and removes rwx (go-rwx) from the group and others. A listing of the file using ls -l shows

```
-rwx------   1 terry    terry        0 Jul 20 13:04 testfile
```

Look at one more example. You now want testfile to be readable by everyone but readable and writable only by you, the owner of the file. Enter the following command:

```
chmod u-x,go+r testfile
```

Taking a look at the permissions (by using `ls -l`) shows the following permissions:

```
-rw-r--r--    1 terry     terry         0 Jul 20 13:04 testfile
```

One final example should do it. Now give everyone the ability to execute the file. Do this by entering the following command:

```
chmod a+x testfile
```

A listing of the file (by using `ls -l`) shows you exactly what you wanted to do — to add the execute (x) permission to everyone:

```
-rwxr-xr-x    1 terry     terry         0 Jul 20 13:04 testfile
```

You can also use the `a` character to remove permissions from everyone by using a minus sign instead of a plus sign for the permission that you want to remove.

Copying and moving files

Being able to copy and move files and directories is critical for keeping your file system organized. You can use two commands to copy or move files. Begin by looking at the copy command — `cp`. The following command shows the `cp` command being used to copy a file called `testfile` from my home directory to a temporary directory:

```
cp /home/terry/testfile /tmp
```

The preceding command keeps the original file in the original directory and also creates another file with the same name in the `/tmp` directory. You can give the file a new name during the copy operation, as shown here:

```
cp /home/terry/testfile /tmp/newtestfile
```

This command keeps the original file in the original directory — but in this case, a file with a new name is created in the `/tmp` directory. You can copy the entire contents of a directory, including any subdirectories and their contents, by using the `-r` option with the `cp` command. For example, to copy my home directory and all its subdirectories to the `/tmp` directory, I type the following command:

```
cp -r /home/terry /tmp
```

Using the copy command always keeps the original copy intact in its original location, even if you're copying the file to a new location. If you want to move the file to a new location but don't want to keep the original, use the `mv` command. For example, suppose you want to move the file `testfile` from your home directory to the `/tmp` directory without changing the name of the file. Use the following command:

```
mv /home/terry/testfile /tmp
```

You can also use the mv command to rename files, either in the same directory or when you move the file to another directory. For example, to change the name of the file testfile to newtestfile in the same directory, enter the following command:

```
mv /home/terry/testfile newtestfile
```

Searching for files

Sometimes you might look for a file in your file system but can't remember where it is. Fortunately, the shell provides a command that you can use to help you find the file. Easy to remember, the command is find. For example, if you want to find the file testfile but don't remember where it is, enter this command:

```
find / -name testfile -print
```

The basic syntax for the find command is

```
find path options filename options
```

The preceding command begins searching in the system root directory for a file named testfile and displays the results of the search to the system display.

The find command is very powerful and useful for finding files. It is also a complex command that lets you specify a large number of options for finding many types of files. Be sure to use the command man find to see the complete list of options for this command.

Deleting files

To remove files from your system, you can use the rm command. For example, if you want to delete the file testfile, enter the following command:

```
rm testfile
```

Be careful when using the rm command because you can easily delete files by accident. Deleted files cannot be recovered.

Viewing file contents

You have several ways to view the contents of any text file. Here are two methods. The first is using the more command, as follows:

```
more testfile
```

Using the `more` command displays the contents of the file one screen at a time. To go to the next screen, press the spacebar. Unfortunately, the `more` command will let you go in only one direction; after you pass a screen, you can't go back. However, you can use the `less` command to let you move down a screen as well as up a screen at a time:

```
less testfile
```

You see the first screen of text displayed. To move to the next screen, press the Page Down key. To go back to the previous screen, press the Page Up key.

Changing file group and owners

Sometimes you need to change the user or group that owns a file. Sometimes a program that you want to run requires that the program run as a particular user or group. For example, you might be running a Web server that requires that the file owner is the Apache user. In this example, look at the file `testfile` that is in my home directory. A listing of this file (by using `ls -l`) shows the following:

```
ls -l testfile
-rw-rw-r--   1 terry    terry        0 Jul 21 10:20 testfile
```

To change the owner of this file to `apache`, you use the `chown` command as follows:

```
chown apache testfile
```

A listing of this file now shows the owner as the Apache user.

```
rw-rw-r--   1 apache   terry        0 Jul 21 10:20 testfile
```

To change the group ownership of the file, enter the following command:

```
chgrp apache testfile
```

A listing of this file now shows the group as the `apache` group:

```
-rw-rw-r--   1 apache   apache       0 Jul 21 10:20 testfile
```

You can possibly change the file's owner and group at the same time with one command by entering the owner and group, separated by a period. For example, to change the owner and group of `testfile` to `apache`, enter the command

```
chown apache.apache testfile
```

Gaining superuser (root) privileges

Usually, when you want to use your system for doing your typical work, you should log in as a regular user. Sometimes you might need more privileges to be able to properly administer your system, so you need to become the root, or *superuser*. Fortunately, you can use the su command to gain superuser privileges to accomplish your administration task. When you are finished, you can give up the superuser privileges and return to being a regular user. Using the following command makes you the root user:

```
su -
```

Be sure to include the dash after the command so you will also have the path of the root user instead of the regular user. After entering the command, you will be prompted to enter the root password. When you are finished working as root, type exit to return to being your regular user.

Changing your system path

Your *system path* is a list of directories that are searched by the shell when it looks for files. You don't have to specify the location of any files that are in the system path because it will always be searched. Sometimes you might want to add additional directories to the search path. You can do this by using the export command. Before you add to your path, you might want to see the directories that are currently listed there. You can use the echo command to tell the system to display your path by entering the following command:

```
echo $PATH
```

The output of this command is the following:

```
/usr/kerberos/bin:/usr/local/bin:/usr/bin:/bin:/usr/X11R6/bin:/home/terry/bin
```

Now you know what your current path is. Usually, you would want to append additional directories to the current path. For example, if I want to add my home directory to the search path, I enter the following command (note the use of quotes):

```
Export PATH="$PATH:/home/terry"
```

By using this command, I added my home directory to my search path. Now my home directory will always be searched as part of my search path.

Mounting and unmounting drives

Before you can use any storage device in Enterprise Linux, the device must first be made a part of the file system. This process is *mounting;* to attach the drive, you use the mount command. The basic syntax of the mount command is

```
mount devicename mountpoint
```

The devicename identifies the device that you want to mount. All files that identify a device are located in the /dev directory. Thus, the system CD-ROM drive is typically identified as /dev/cdrom, and the system floppy drive is usually /dev/fd0.

You usually must be logged in as the root user to mount and unmount drives.

Mount point identifies the directory location on the file system where the device will be accessible. The top-level directory, /mnt, is the typical mount point for other devices, which are listed as subdirectories of /mnt. For example, if you want to access files from your CD-ROM drive, first mount the drive by entering the following command:

```
mount /dev/cdrom /mnt/cdrom
```

The preceding command mounts the cdrom device onto the file system at the directory /mnt/cdrom. To access files from the CD-ROM, all you need to do is to change into the /mnt/cdrom directory.

Although you can mount a device to any directory, I recommend using an empty directory as the mount point. Mounting a device on a directory that contains files will make those files inaccessible while the device is mounted.

To unmount a device from your file system, you use the umount command. For example, if you no longer need to access the CD-ROM drive, you can unmount the device by entering the following command:

```
umount /mnt/cdrom
```

This command tells the system to remove the mount point that was created at /mnt/cdrom.

Before you can remove a CD from the CD-ROM drive, you must unmount the device.

Viewing and stopping processes

Every program that runs on your system, including the shell itself and any commands that you might have issued, creates a process. You can get a list of all running process on your system by using the ps command. For example, entering the ps command on my system gives the following output:

```
ps -ax
    PID TTY     STAT   TIME COMMAND
      1 ?         S    0:04 init [5]
      2 ?        SW    0:01 [keventd]
      3 ?        SW    0:00 [kapmd]
      4 ?       SWN    0:00 [ksoftirqd/0]
      6 ?        SW    0:00 [bdflush]
<output shortened>
    23580 ?      S    1:38 /usr/lib/openoffice/
          program/soffice.bin private:factory/swriter
    23766 pts/1 R    0:00 ps ax
```

Sometimes processes don't behave nicely and can stop responding or working as you expected. You can use the output of the ps command to find the process that is misbehaving and stop it. Notice in the preceding listing the column labeled PID: In this column is the Process ID number of the process. For example, take a look at the next-to-last PID, number 23580. If you follow the line beginning with 23580 across to the command column, you can see that this is the process started by OpenOffice. The command column always shows the command that started the process. If OpenOffice were not responding, I could force it to stop running by using the kill command as follows:

```
kill -9 23580
```

The -9 in the command is referred to as a signal. In some cases, a running program can catch a signal and not act on the command. By using the -9, you are forcing the program to end because the -9 signal cannot be caught by a running program.

Checking disk space

You can use two commands to find out how much space you have used on your file system. First, using the df command shows how much space is used and still available on all devices that are mounted. On my system, this command shows the following output. In this example, I use the -h option to force the output to display the space in megabytes and gigabytes rather than the standard output of 1-kilobyte blocks.

```
df -h
Filesystem            Size  Used Avail Use% Mounted on
/dev/hdb5              27G   5.1G   21G  20% /
/dev/hdb1             198M   6.3M  182M   4% /boot
/dev/hdb2             9.7G   4.0G  5.3G  43% /home
none                 125M      0  125M   0% /dev/shm
/dev/hda2            5.9G   3.4G  2.2G  61% /mnt/drive2
```

Second, to find out how much disk space is used by a directory and its subdirectories, you can use the du command. In the following listing, I again use the -h option to have the output displayed in megabytes and gigabytes rather than 1-kilobyte blocks.

```
du -h /home/terry/website
80K      website/html/cgi-bin/fileman
8.0K     website/html/cgi-bin/log_files
8.0K     website/html/cgi-bin/my_db
44K      website/html/cgi-bin/my_html
28K      website/html/cgi-bin/system_db
60K      website/html/cgi-bin/system_db_html
344K     website/html/cgi-bin
512K     website/html/colonial
24K      website/html/.xvpics
904K     website/html
8.0K     website/.xvpics
1.1M     website
```

Creating an alias

Many times you will use the same commands frequently. For example, whenever you want to find permission information about a file or directory, you use the ls -l command. With the alias command, you can create new commands that already contain the options you might want to use, thus saving you time. The basic syntax for the alias command is

```
alias command='the command you want to run'
```

For example, to create an alias for the ls -l command so I can just type ls, enter the command

```
alias ls='ls -l'
```

Now whenever you run the ls command, you receive the output from ls -l.

If you want to know the already defined aliases, just enter the alias command without any options.

Writing Shell Scripts

A shell script is basically a sequence of commands that are contained in a single file. If you are familiar with MS-DOS and batch files, you're already familiar with the concept of shell scripts. A shell script can be very complex or very simple, depending on what you want to do. In this section, I introduce you to a simple shell script just to give you an idea of what you can do.

When I'm at work, I sometimes want to be able to use the files located on a Novell network on my Enterprise Linux PC. To do this, I need to configure my PC to connect to the Novell network by running several commands. Rather than having to enter these commands every time I start my system, I created a simple shell script that runs when my system boots up. The script that I created is called novell, and a listing of it follows.

```
more novell
#!/bin/bash
/sbin/modprobe ipx
/sbin/modprobe ncpfs
sleep 2
/sbin/ipx_configure --auto_interface=on -auto_primary=on
```

Take a closer look at this script and what it does. The first line of the script specifically tells the shell that it is using bash as the shell. The next two lines run the modprobe command, which is located in the /sbin directory. The line beginning with sleep 2 adds a two-second pause to the runtime of the script. The last line runs the ipx_configure program to set up the parameters for the IPX network protocol.

The purpose of the script is to load the modules required to connect to an IPX network and to configure the IPX connection. Although this is a short, fairly simple script, it isn't something you would want to have to type every time the system is started.

To create the script, I opened a simple text editor and entered each command as a separate line in the text file. After I finished entering the commands, I saved the file to my home directory. One more required step was to make the file executable by using the chmod command (chmod a+x novell) to change the file permissions. And that's all there is to making a simple shell script.

Of course, shell scripts can be much more complex than this and can perform nearly any operation you want. You can have a lot of fun learning how to write shell scripts. You can also become more productive and efficient while you customize your system with your scripts.

Part II
Configuring Your Enterprise Linux Local Area Network

The 5th Wave   By Rich Tennant

Despite its inclusion on the Hardware Compatability List, Martin shuddered at the thought of having to install Red Hat Enterprise Linux on the workstation from the early 1950s.

In this part . . .

*T*his part is all about your local area network (LAN) and getting network services working for you. The part begins with Chapter 5, which has an explanation of the X Window System that controls your desktop GUI. So you want to print something? Look in Chapter 6 for details about configuring different types of printers. Need to share some files with other Linux users, or maybe some Windows users? Have a look at Chapters 8 and 9. What about Chapter 7? In this chapter, you can find out what you need to know about configuring your system to communicate via TCP/IP. Don't know what TCP/IP is? Read Chapter 7.

Chapter 5

Configuring and Managing the X Window System

• •

In This Chapter

▶ Introducing the X Server

▶ Configuring the X Server with the X Configuration tool

▶ Fine-tune your X Server with the X Server Configuration file

▶ Restarting your X Server

▶ Disabling the X Server

• •

*T*he heart of Red Hat Enterprise Linux is the kernel, but for many users, the face of the operating system is the graphical environment provided by the X Window System, also called simply *X*. This chapter is an introduction to the behind-the-scenes world of *XFree86,* which is the open source implementation of X provided with Red Hat Enterprise Linux.

Introducing the X Server

Enterprise Linux began as a powerful, server-based operating system, excelling at efficiently processing complicated programs requiring high CPU utilization and handling requests from hundreds or thousands of clients through network connections. However, because of its open nature and stability, Enterprise Linux has quickly developed into a popular GUI-based operating system for workstations, both in the home and in the workplace.

In the Unix world, of which Enterprise Linux is a part, windowing environments have existed for decades, predating many of the current mainstream operating systems. The X Window System is now the dominant graphical user interface (GUI) for Unix-like operating systems. To create this GUI for the user, X uses a client-server architecture. An X Server process is started, and X client processes can connect to it via a network or local loopback interface. The server process handles the communication with the hardware, such as the video card, monitor, keyboard, and mouse. The X client exists in the user space, issuing requests to the X Server.

On Red Hat Enterprise Linux systems, the XFree86 server fills the role of the X Server. As a large-scope, open source software project, with hundreds of developers around the world, XFree86 features rapid development, a wide degree of support for various hardware devices and architectures, and the ability to run on different operating systems and platforms.

Most Red Hat Linux desktop users are unaware of the XFree86 server running on their system. They are much more concerned with the particular desktop environment in which they spend most of their time. The Red Hat Linux installation program does an excellent job of configuring your XFree86 server during the installation process, ensuring that X performs optimally when first started.

The X Server performs many difficult tasks using a wide array of hardware, requiring detailed configuration. If some aspect of your system changes, such as the monitor or video card, XFree86 needs to be reconfigured. In addition, if you are troubleshooting a problem with XFree86 that cannot be solved by using a configuration utility (such as the X Configuration tool), you might need to access its configuration file directly.

Configuring the X Server with the X Configuration Tool

You have basically two ways to configure the X Server on your Enterprise system. One, you can use the *X Configuration tool,* which is a graphical tool that gives you the ability to change some of the most significant settings, such as display, monitor, and video card settings. The X Configuration tool is a graphical front-end to the X configuration file, Xorg.conf, which is located in the /etc/X11 directory. Any changes that you make using the graphical utility are written to the /etc/X11/xorg.conf file. Two, you can edit the X Configuration file directly by using a text editing application. In this section, I show you how to make X Server configuration changes by using the X Configuration tool beginning with changing the display resolution.

Changing the display resolution

The X Configuration tool makes it easy for you to change your display resolution. To change your display resolution, do the following:

1. **Choose Applications⊏⊅System Settings⊏⊅Display to open the Display Settings dialog box, as shown in Figure 5-1.**

If you are not logged in as root, you will be prompted to enter the root password.

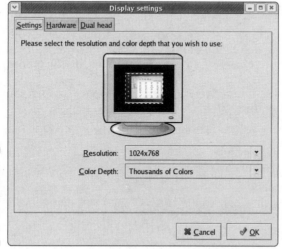

Figure 5-1:
Change
your screen
resolution
here.

2. **Select your desired resolution from the drop-down Resolution list.**

3. **Click OK to accept your choice and close the dialog box.**

Any time you make changes to the X Server configuration, you must restart the X Server. When using the X Configuration tool, you see a window reminding you to restart the X Server.

Changing the display color depth

The system display color depth setting determines the number of colors that are shown on the display. A higher color depth displays more colors on the monitor. To change the system color depth, do the following:

1. **Choose Applications⇨System Settings⇨Display to open the Display Settings dialog box. (Refer to Figure 5-1.)**

   If you are not logged in as root, you will be prompted to enter the root password.

2. **Select your desired color depth from the Color Depth drop-down list.**

3. **Click OK to accept your choice and close the dialog box.**

Changing monitor type settings

The Enterprise installer can usually detect the type of monitor that is connected to your system and set the configuration accordingly. Sometimes, however, the installer might not properly configure your monitor, requiring you to change the monitor settings. You also want to change your monitor settings if you get a different monitor with different parameters than your previous monitor. To change your monitor settings, do the following:

1. **Choose Applications⇨System Settings⇨Display to open the Display Settings dialog box. (Refer to Figure 5-1.)**

   If you are not logged in as root, you will be prompted to enter the root password.

2. **Click the Hardware tab (see Figure 5-2).**

Figure 5-2:
Access
monitor and
video card
settings
here.

3. **Click the top Configure button (to the right of the monitor type listing) to open the Monitor dialog box, as shown in Figure 5-3.**

4. **Find the manufacturer of your monitor in the list and then click the arrow to the left of the manufacturer name to see a list of models.**

5. **Click the model number that matches your monitor.**

6. **Click OK twice to accept your choice and exit the Display Settings dialog box.**

If you can't find your monitor manufacturer or model number on the monitor list, choose one of the generic monitors from the top of the monitor list.

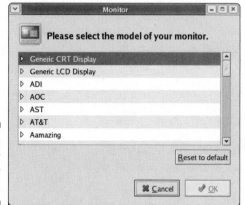

Figure 5-3:
Choose your
monitor
type.

Changing your video card type

The Enterprise installer can usually detect the type of video card that is connected to your system and set the configuration accordingly. However, if the installer doesn't properly detect your video card, you might need to change the video card type. You would also want to change your video card type if you install a different video card. To change your video card type, do the following:

1. **Choose Applications⇨System Settings⇨Display to open the Display Settings dialog box (refer to Figure 5-1).**

   If you are not logged in as root, you will be prompted to enter the root password.

2. **Click the Hardware tab (refer to Figure 5-2).**

3. **Click the bottom Configure button (to the right of the video card type listing) to display the Video Card dialog box, as shown in Figure 5-4.**

4. **Find the manufacturer of your video card in the list and click the appropriate model.**

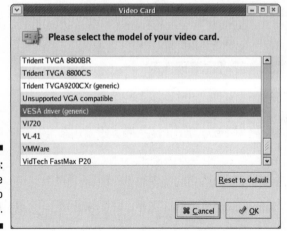

Figure 5-4:
Configure
your video
card.

Configuring dual monitors

In Enterprise Linux, you can use two video cards and monitors on your system if you desire. To configure a second video card and monitor, do the following:

1. **Choose Applications➪System Settings➪Display to open the Display Settings dialog box (refer to Figure 5-1).**

   If you are not logged in as root, you will be prompted to enter the root password.

2. **Click the Dual Head tab (see Figure 5-5) from the Display Settings dialog box.**

3. **Select the Use Dual Head check box.**

4. **Click the Configure button (next to the Second Monitor Type), choose your monitor from the list, and then click OK.**

5. **Enter the appropriate information for the video card type, display resolution, and color depth.**

6. **Select whether you want individual desktops on each display or a single desktop spanning both displays by selecting the appropriate choice.**

7. **Click OK twice to exit the configuration tool.**

Figure 5-5:
Use the
Dual Head
tab to
configure
dual
monitors.

Manually Configuring Your X Server from the X Configuration File

The XFree86 server configuration files are stored in the /etc/X11/ directory. The XFree86 version 4 server uses /etc/X11/xorg.conf. When Red Hat Enterprise Linux is installed, the configuration files for XFree86 are created by using information gathered during the installation process.

Although you rarely need to manually edit these files, you should know about the various sections and optional parameters found in them. Each section begins with a Section *section-name* line and ends with an EndSection line. Within each of the sections are several lines containing an option name and at least one option value, occasionally seen in quotes. The following list explores the most useful sections of an XFree86 version 4 file and the roles of various popular settings.

Device

The Device section specifies information about the video card used by the system. You must have at least one Device section in your configuration file. You might have multiple Device sections in the case of multiple video cards or multiple settings that can run a single card. The following options are required or widely used:

✔ Bus ID: Specifies the bus location of the video card. This option is necessary only for systems with multiple cards. However, it must be set so that the Device section uses the proper settings for the correct card.

✔ Driver: Tells XFree86 which driver to load in order to use the video card.

✔ Identifier: Provides a unique name for this video card. Usually, this name is set to the exact name of the video card used in the Device section.

✔ Screen: An optional setting used when a video card has more than one head (or connector) to go out to a separate monitor. If you have multiple monitors connected to one video card, separate Device sections must exist for each of them with a different Screen value for each Device section. The value accepted by this option is a number starting at 0, increasing by one for each head on the video card.

✔ Videoram: The amount of RAM available on the video card, in kilobytes. This setting is not normally necessary because the XFree86 server can usually probe the video card to autodetect the amount of video RAM. However, because there are some video cards that XFree86 cannot correctly autodetect, this option allows you to specify the amount of video RAM.

Direct Rendering Infrastructure

Direct Rendering Infrastructure (DRI) is an interface that primarily allows 3-D software applications to take advantage of the 3-D hardware acceleration capabilities on modern supported video hardware. In addition, DRI can improve 2-D hardware acceleration performance when using drivers that have been enhanced to use the DRI for 2-D operations. This section is ignored unless DRI is enabled in the Module section.

Because different video cards use DRI in different ways, read the /usr/ X11R6/lib/X11/doc/README.DRI file for specific information about your particular video card before changing any DRI values.

Files

This section sets paths for services vital to the XFree86 server, such as the font path. Common options include

✔ Fontpath: Sets the locations where the XFree86 server can find fonts. Different fixed paths to directories holding font files can be placed here, separated by commas. By default, Red Hat Linux uses xfs as the font server and points FontPath to unix/:7100. This tells the XFree86 server to obtain font information by using Unix-domain sockets for inter-process communication (IPC).

- ✔ Modulepath: Allows you to set up multiple directories to use for storing modules loaded by the XFree86 server.

- ✔ RGBpath: Tells the XFree86 server where the RGB (red/green/blue) color database is located on the system. This database file defines all valid color names in XFree86 and ties them to specific RGB values.

InputDevice

In this section, you can configure an input device, such as a mouse or keyboard, used to convey information to the system using the XFree86 server. Most systems have at least two InputDevice sections: keyboard and mouse. Each section includes these two lines:

- ✔ Driver: Tells XFree86 the name of the driver to load to use the device.

- ✔ Identifier: Sets the name of the device, usually the name of the device followed by a number, starting with 0 for the first device. For example, the first keyboard InputDevice has an Identifier of Keyboard0.

Most InputDevice sections contain lines assigning specific options to that device. Each of these lines starts with Option and contains the name of the option in quotes, followed by the value to assign to that option. Mice usually receive options such as Protocol, PS/2, and Device, which designates the mouse to use for this section. The InputDevice section is well commented, allowing you to configure additional options for your particular devices by uncommenting certain lines.

Module

This section tells the XFree86 server which modules from the /usr/X11R6/lib/modules/ directory to load. Modules provide the XFree86 server with additional functionality.

Be careful when editing these values. Changes made to the modules can prevent your X Server from starting. If necessary, you can enter rescue mode to get to a shell where you can edit the xorg.conf file to correct the problem.

Monitor

The Monitor section shows the type of monitor used by the system. Although one Monitor section is the minimum, there may be several Monitor sections — one for each monitor in use by the machine.

Be careful when manually editing values in the options of the `Monitor` section. Inappropriate values in this section could damage or destroy your monitor. Consult the documentation that came with your monitor for the safe operating parameters available.

The following options are usually configured during installation or when using the X Configuration tool:

- ✔ `HorizSync`: Tells XFree86 the range of horizontal sync frequencies compatible with the monitor in kHz. These values are used as a guide by the XFree86 server so that it will know whether to use a particular `Modeline` entry's values with this monitor.

- ✔ `Identifier`: Provides a unique name for this monitor, usually numbering each monitor starting at 0. The first monitor is named `Monitor0`, the second `Monitor1`, and so on.

- ✔ `Modeline`: This parameter is used to specify the video modes used by the monitor at particular resolutions, with certain horizontal sync and vertical refresh resolutions. `Modeline` entries are usually preceded by a comment that explains what the mode line specifies. If your configuration file does not include comments for the various mode lines, you can scan over the values (also called *mode descriptions*) to determine what the mode line is attempting to do. See the `xorg.conf man` page for detailed explanations of each mode description section by entering **man xorg.conf** at a terminal prompt.

- ✔ `ModelName`: An optional parameter that displays the model name of the monitor.

- ✔ `VendorName`: An optional parameter that displays the name of the vendor that manufactured the monitor.

- ✔ `VertRefresh`: Shows the vertical refresh range frequencies supported by the monitor, in kHz. These values are used as a guide by the XFree86 Server so that it will know whether to use a particular `Modeline` entry's values with this monitor.

Screen

The `Screen` section binds a particular `Device` and `Monitor` that can be used as a pair and contain certain settings. You must have at least one `Screen` section in your configuration file. The following options are common:

- ✔ `DefaultDepth`: Gives the `Screen` section the default color depth to try, in bits. The default is 8, specifying 16 provides thousands of colors, and using 32 displays millions of colors.

- ✔ `Device`: Specifies the name of the `Device` section to use with this `Screen` section.

- ✔ Identifier: Identifies the Screen section so that it can be referred to by a ServerLayout section and be utilized.

- ✔ Monitor: Tells the name of the Monitor section to be used with this Screen section.

You might also have a Display subsection within the Screen section that tells the XFree86 Server the color depth (Depth) and resolution (Mode) to try first when using this particular monitor and video card.

For more information, refer to the XF86Config man page. To review the current configuration of your XFree86 Server, enter the xset -q command. This provides you with information about the keyboard, pointer, screen saver, and font paths.

Restarting Your X Server

Sometimes you might be running a program that stops responding to mouse clicks or keyboard commands. Or, the entire GUI stops responding, and your system appears to be frozen. In these instances, you can stop and restart the X Server to reset your desktop. You can restart your X Server by doing the following:

1. **Press Ctrl+Alt+Backspace.**

2. **After the X Server restarts, log in to enter your desktop.**

Disabling the X Server

If you are using the server versions of Enterprise Linux and will be using the command line to do your server configurations, you might want to disable the X Server from starting automatically to conserve system resources. Although I don't recommend this action for inexperienced users, an experienced user doing configurations from the command line can usually work much faster and efficiently than a user doing the same configurations through the GUI tools. If you want to disable the X Server, do the following:

1. **Using a text editing program, open the /etc/inittab file.**

2. **Find the line in the file that looks like this:**

```
id:5:initdefault
```

3. **Change the numeral 5 to 3.**

4. **Save the changes to the file.**

5. **Restart your system.**

When your system restarts, instead of seeing the graphical login screen, you see a command line login.

If you have disabled the X Server from automatically starting, you can manually start it by typing **startx** at a command line prompt.

Chapter 6

Configuring and Managing Printers

In This Chapter

▶ Setting up printers with the Printer Configuration tool

▶ Changing printer configurations

*H*ave you ever sent a job to your printer, and it didn't print? Or maybe the job did print, but the output wasn't what you were expecting? Many times, these problems are caused by a printer that's not properly configured or uses an incorrect print driver. If you're thinking, "Hey, this is exactly what happened to me," then you're in luck reading this chapter.

In this chapter, I tell you all you need to know to successfully configure and manage your system printers. Included with Red Hat Enterprise Linux is the Printer Configuration tool to help you configure your printing system. The Printer Configuration tool is an easy-to-use, graphical tool that will help you to set up whatever type of printer you choose. And configuring your printers if you aren't using a graphical user interface (GUI) won't be a problem because you can also configure your printers from the command line in a terminal window.

After your printer is configured, you might want to gather information about jobs that you sent to the printer. You will also want to be able to change print job priority, see the contents of your print queue, and maybe even delete some of your scheduled print jobs. You will be able to do all these functions and more after going through this chapter.

Starting the Printer Configuration Tool

Because the Printing Configuration tool is a graphical-based utility, you can start it by choosing it from the Applications menu. To start the Printer Configuration tool, follow these steps:

1. **Choose Applications⇨System Settings, and then choose Printing.**

   If you aren't logged in as the root user, the system prompts you for the root password before you can continue.

2. **Type the root password, if necessary.**

   The Printer Configuration tool opens, as shown in Figure 6-1.

Figure 6-1:
The Printer Configuration tool.

3. **Click the New button in the main Printer Configuration tool window.**

   The window shown in Figure 6-2 appears.

   Notice that this window tells you that your changes are not saved until you click the Apply button on the last window.

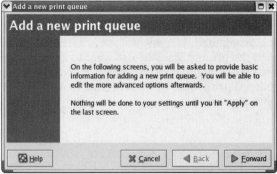

On the following screens, you will be asked to provide basic information for adding a new print queue. You will be able to edit the more advanced options afterwards.

Nothing will be done to your settings until you hit "Apply" on the last screen.

Figure 6-2:
The Add A New Print Queue window.

4. **Click the Forward button.**

   The Queue Name screen, as shown in Figure 6-3, appears.

5. **Enter a unique name for the printer in the Name text field.**

   Choose a descriptive name for your printer and follow these parameters:

   - The printer name must begin with a letter and can't contain spaces.

   - You can use any valid characters for the remainder of the printer name. The valid characters are lowercase and uppercase letters *a* through *z,* numeral *0* through *9,* – (dash), and _ (underscore).

   If you want, you can enter a description for the printer in the Short Description field.

6. **When you finish entering a name for your printer, click Forward.**

   The Queue Type window appears (as shown in Figure 6-4), and the Printer Configuration tool attempts to detect your printer.

   The following sections detail the various possibilities available for configuring your print queue and selecting your print driver.

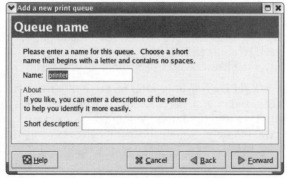

Figure 6-3:
The Queue
Name
window.

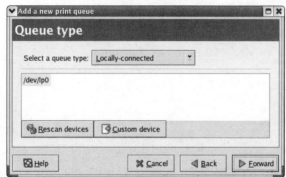

Figure 6-4:
The Queue
Type
window.

Configuring the print queue

You can configure six types of print queues. A *print queue* is a directory that holds the print jobs for the type of printer that you configure to work with the queue. The print queue is associated with the type of printer that you want to configure. At the top of the Queue Type window (see Step 6 of the preceding list) is a drop-down list containing the six types of print queues that you can configure. The queue type is set to Locally-Connected by default. If the printer is connected *locally* — that is, to either the parallel or the USB port on the PC, and is also recognized — it is shown in the list.

The following list shows the six types of queue that you can install; to choose one, select the type that you desire from the drop-down list.

✓ **Locally-Connected:** A printer attached directly to your computer through a parallel or USB port. If your printer isn't listed, click the Custom Device button, type the name of your printer, and then click OK to add it to the printer device list. A printer attached to the parallel port is usually referred to as /dev/lp0. A printer attached to the USB port is usually referred to as /dev/usblp0.

✓ **Networked CUPS (IPP):** A printer that can be accessed over a TCP/IP network. *CUPS,* the Common Unix Printing System, is based on the Internet Printing Protocol (IPP), which was created in an attempt to set some standards for printing over the Internet. If you choose this type of queue, you need to enter the server name and the path to the server. Figure 6-5 shows the Networked CUPS queue dialog box.

✓ **Networked UNIX (LPD):** A printer attached to a different Unix system that can be accessed over a TCP/IP network (for example, a printer attached to another Red Hat Linux system on your network). If you choose this type of queue, you need to enter the server name and path to the server, as shown in Figure 6-6.

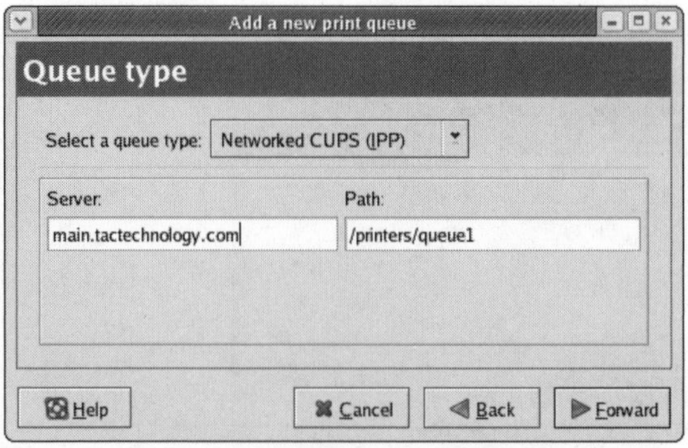

Figure 6-5:
The Networked CUPS (IPP) screen is where you enter the server name and path.

Add a new print queue

Queue type

Select a queue type: Networked CUPS (IPP)

Server:	Path:
main.tactechnology.com	/printers/queue1

Help   Cancel   Back   Forward

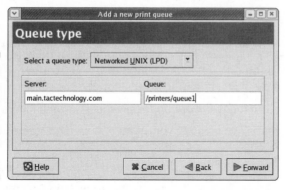

Figure 6-6:
Enter the
server and
queue for a
networked
Unix (LPD)
printer.

- ✓ **Server:** The hostname or IP address of the remote machine to which the printer is attached.

- ✓ **Queue:** The remote printer queue. The default printer queue is usually lp. By default, the Strict RFC1179 Compliance option is not chosen. If you are having problems printing to a non-Linux lpd queue, choose this option to disable enhanced LPR printing features. LPR is an older printing protocol used by many Unix systems.

   The remote machine must be configured to allow the local machine to print on the desired queue. As root, create the file /etc/hosts.lpd on the remote machine to which the printer is attached. On separate lines in the file, add the IP address or hostname of each machine that should have printing privileges.

- ✓ **Networked Windows (SMB):** A printer attached to a different system that shares a printer over an SMB network (for example, a printer attached to a Microsoft Windows machine). *SMB,* the Server Message Block protocol, is the native protocol that computers running Windows use to communicate with each other. See Figure 6-7.

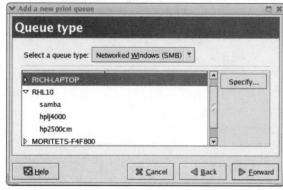

Figure 6-7:
Configuring
the
Networked
Windows
(SMB)
printer
screen.

On this screen, you see a list of shares from which you can select the networked Windows printer that you want to use. To the left of the share name is an arrow that you can click to expand the share listing and show any configured printers. Figure 6-7 shows the RHL10 share expanded and also lists three printers. Click the printer that you wish to use and then click Forward. An Authentication screen appears, as shown in Figure 6-8.

Text fields for the following options appear as shown in Figure 6-8:

- **Workgroup:** The name of your Windows workgroup needs to be entered here.

- **Server:** The name of the print server needs to be entered here.

- **Share:** This is the name of the shared printer on which you want to print. This name must be the same name defined as the Samba printer on the remote Windows print server.

- **User Name:** This is the name of the user of which you must log in to access the printer. This user must exist on the Windows system, and the user must have permission to access the printer. The default user name is typically *guest* for Windows servers or *nobody* for Samba servers.

- **Password:** The password (if required) for the user specified in the User Name field.

✔ **Networked Novell (NCP):** A printer attached to a different system that uses the Novell NetWare network technology. After choosing this type of queue, you need to enter additional information into the Queue Type window, as shown in Figure 6-9.

You need to enter information for the following fields in Figure 6-9:

- **Server:** The host name or IP address of the NCP system to which the printer is attached.

- **Queue:** The remote queue for the printer on the NCP system.

- **User:** The name of the user you must log in as to access the printer.

- **Password:** The password for the user specified in the User field.

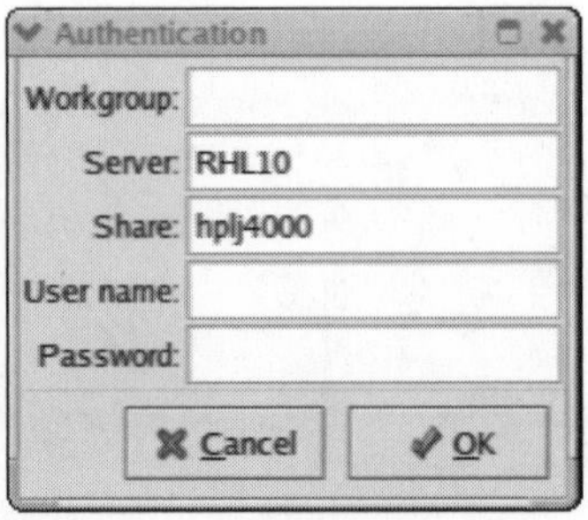

Figure 6-8:
The Authentication screen for connecting to a SMB printer.

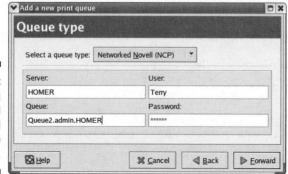

Figure 6-9:
Configuring
a networked
Novell
(NCP)
printer.

✔ **Networked JetDirect:** A printer connected directly to the network through HP JetDirect instead of to a computer. (See Figure 6-10.)

You need to enter the appropriate information for the following text fields:

• **Printer:** The hostname or IP address of the JetDirect printer.

• **Port:** The port on the JetDirect printer that is listening for print jobs. The default port is 9100.

Figure 6-10:
Configuring
a networked
JetDirect
printer.

Whenever you add a new print queue or change an existing one, you must restart the printer daemon for the changes to take effect. See the upcoming "Editing the Printer Configuration" section. In case you are wondering what a *daemon* is, it means *disk and execution monitor*. It is basically a program that runs in the background, waiting for some event to occur. In this case, the printer daemon is waiting for print jobs.

If you require a username and password for a Networked SMB or NCP (NetWare) print queue, they are stored. Thus, another person can learn the username and password. To avoid this, the username and password to use the printer should be different from the username and password used for the user's account on the local Red Hat Linux system. If they are different, the only possible security compromise would be unauthorized use of the printer.

Selecting the print driver

The next step in configuring a printer is to select the print driver. The *print driver* processes the data that you want to print into a format that the printer can understand.

1. **After you select the queue type of the printer and enter the required information, click Forward to go on to the Printer Model window, as shown in Figure 6-11.**

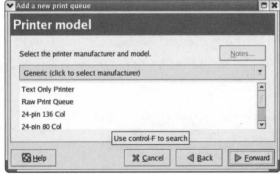

Figure 6-11:
Select the
printer
manufac-
turer and
model.

2. **Select the driver from the list.**

   a. Click the arrow beside the manufacturer for your printer.

   b. Find your printer from the expanded list and then click the arrow beside the printer name.

   A list of drivers for your printer appears. The printers are listed by manufacturer.

   c. Select one.

   Sometimes you might need to try several of the listed drivers to find one that works properly.

To read more about the print drivers, go to www.linuxprinting.org/printer_list.cgi. You can select a different print driver after adding a printer by starting the Printer Configuration tool, selecting the printer from the list, clicking Edit, clicking the Printer Driver tab, selecting a different print driver, and applying the changes.

3. **Click Forward to go to the printer information confirmation page where you can check your printer configuration choices.**

   • Click *Apply* to add the print queue if the settings are correct.

   • Click *Back* to modify the printer configuration if necessary.

4. **Click the Apply button in the main window to save your changes to the printer configuration file and restart the printer daemon (lpd).**

   Click Back to modify the printer configuration if necessary.

Editing the Printer Configuration

After adding your printer(s), you can edit settings by selecting the printer from the printer list of the Printer Configuration tool and then clicking the Edit button. The tabbed window shown in Figure 6-12 appears. The window contains the current values for the printer that you selected to edit. Make any changes and click OK. Then click Apply in the main Printer Configuration tool window to save the changes and restart the printer daemon.

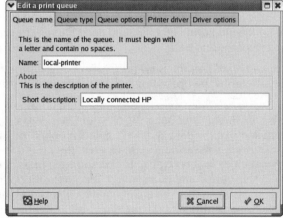

Figure 6-12:
The Edit a
Print Queue
screen.

The tabs and what they hold are as follows:

✔ **Queue Name:** To rename a printer, change the value of Name on the Queue Name tab. Click OK to return to the main window. The name of the printer changes in the printer list. Click Apply to save the change and restart the printer daemon.

✔ **Queue Type:** The Queue Type tab shows the queue type that you selected when adding the printer and its settings. You can change the queue type of the printer or just change the settings. After making modifications, click OK to return to the main window. Click Apply to save the changes and restart the printer daemon. Depending on which queue type you choose, you will see different options. Refer to the section of this chapter that describes your particular printer; options unique to your printer are listed there.

✔ **Queue Options:** From the Queue Options tab, you can select banner pages before and after your print job. You can also set the printable area of the page. To modify filter options, highlight the option and click Edit to modify or click Delete to remove it. Click OK to accept your changes and return to the main window. Click Apply to save the change and restart the printer daemon.

✔ **Printer Driver:** The Printer Driver tab shows which print driver is currently being used. This is the same list that you use when you add the printer. If you change the print driver, click OK to accept your changes and return to the main window. Then click Apply to restart the printer daemon.

✔ **Driver Options:** The Driver Options tab displays advanced printer options. Options vary for each print driver. Common options include

- Select *Send Form-Feed (FF)* if the last page of your print job is not ejected from the printer (for example, the form feed light flashes). If selecting this option does not force the last page out of the printer, try selecting Send End-of-Transmission (EOT) instead. Some printers require both Send Form-Feed (FF) and Send End-of-Transmission (EOT) to eject the last page.

- Select *Send End-of-Transmission* (EOT) if sending a form feed does not work. Refer to the preceding bullet on the Send Form-Feed (FF) option.

- Select *Assume Unknown Data Is Text* if your print driver does not recognize some of the data sent to it. Select it only if you are having problems printing. If this option is selected, the print driver assumes that any data it cannot recognize is text and tries to print it as text. If you select this option and the Convert Text to PostScript option, the print driver assumes that the unknown data is text and then converts it to PostScript.

- Select *Prerender PostScript* if you are trying to print characters outside of the basic ASCII character set (such as foreign language characters) that won't print correctly. If your printer doesn't support the fonts you are trying to print, try selecting this option. You should also select this option if your printer cannot handle PostScript level 3. This option converts it to PostScript level 1.

- *Convert Text to PostScript* is selected by default. If your printer can print plain text, try deselecting this when printing plain text documents to decrease the time it takes to print.

- *Page Size* allows you to select the paper size for your printer, such as US Letter, US Legal, A3, and A4.

- *Effective Filter Locale* defaults to C. If you are printing Japanese characters, select ja_JP. Otherwise, accept the default of C.

- *Media Source* defaults to Printer default. Change this option to use paper from a different tray.

If you modify the driver options, click OK to return to the main window. Then click Apply to save the changes and restart the printer daemon.

Deleting a printer

To delete an existing printer, select the printer and click the Delete button on the toolbar. The printer will be removed from the printer list. Click Apply to save the changes and restart the printer daemon.

Setting the default printer

To set the default printer, select the printer from the printer list and click the Default button on the toolbar. The default printer icon appears in the first column of the printer list beside the default printer.

Chapter 7

Configuring the Network

In This Chapter

▶ Discovering the Enterprise Linux Network Configuration tool

▶ Adding an Ethernet network interface card

▶ Adding a wireless network interface card

▶ Adding a modem

▶ Editing your network configuration

*P*robably one of the first things that you want to do with your Enterprise Linux system is to connect to some type of network. Who could imagine in today's world having a PC that was not connected to the Internet or to a local area network (LAN)? To be able to connect to a LAN or the Internet, every PC needs to have a network interface card (NIC) installed and properly configured.

The Enterprise Linux Network Configuration Tool

Red Hat Enterprise Linux provides a graphical network configuration tool that you can use to configure network interface devices installed in your system. With this tool, you can configure Crypto IP Encapsulation (CIPE), Ethernet, Integrated Services Digital Network (ISDN), modem, token ring, wireless, and xDSL (*x* refers to different variations of DSL) devices. In this chapter, I cover the most common types of devices: Ethernet, modem, and wireless.

You can access the Network Configuration tool by using the Applications menu from the GNOME desktop. To start the Network Configuration tool, choose Applications➪System Settings➪Network. The Network Configuration window, as shown in Figure 7-1, appears.

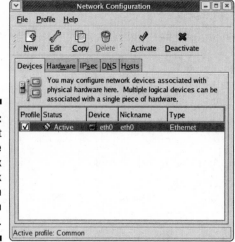

Figure 7-1:
The Red Hat
Enterprise
Linux
Network
Configuration
tool main
window.

The main Network Configuration tool window (shown in Figure 7-1) has five tabbed pages and opens to the Devices tab by default. Read on for a more detailed look at the five tabbed pages.

✔ **Devices:** This tab shows the network devices that are installed and configured on your PC. Network devices are associated with the actual physical hardware in the PC.

If you have a supported NIC installed on your system during installation of Red Hat Enterprise Linux, your NIC should already be listed in the Network Configuration tool. Click the Hardware tab to see information about the device.

✔ **Hardware:** This tab shows the actual physical hardware installed in your PC.

✔ **IPSec:** This tab is where you can configure IPSec tunnels used for secure communications.

✔ **DNS:** This tab shows the system hostname, domain, and nameservers used for DNS lookups. You can configure this information here.

✔ **Hosts:** This tab shows the PC hostname to static IP address mapping.

Adding an Ethernet device

With the Network Configuration tool, you can easily add and configure your Ethernet device. To add an Ethernet device, do the following:

1. **Click the New button from the toolbar of the Network Configuration tool main window. (Refer to Figure 7-1.)**

   The Select Device Type window appears, as shown in Figure 7-2.

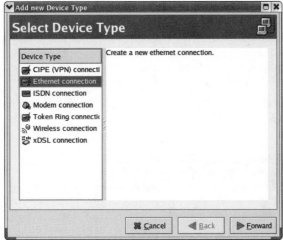

Figure 7-2:
Select your
network
device here.

2. **Choose Ethernet Connection from the Device Type list and then click Forward to go to the Select Ethernet Device list.**

3. **If your NIC is shown in the Select Ethernet Device list, select it and then click Forward to go to the Configure Network Settings window (see the upcoming Figure 7-4).**

4. **If your NIC is not listed, choose Other Ethernet Card and then click Forward to open the Select Ethernet Adapter window, as shown in Figure 7-3.**

5. **Select your card from the Adapter drop-down list.**

6. **Choose the device name from the Device drop-down list.**

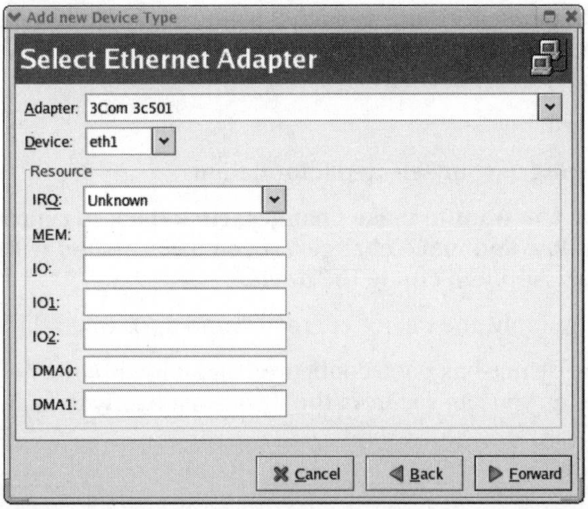

Figure 7-3:
The Select
Ethernet
Adapter
window.

You should choose eth0 for the first device, eth1 for the second, eth2 for the third, and so on. You can also enter the system resources that the adapter will use, if desired. Usually this is not necessary because the OS automatically assigns resources to devices. But in the event that you need to manually control the resource assignments because of other hardware that you are using, you are able to do so.

7. **Click Forward to continue to the Configure Network Settings window, as shown in Figure 7-4.**

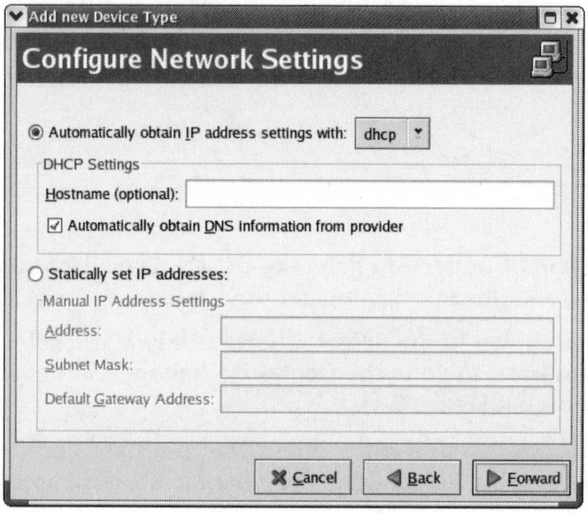

Figure 7-4:
The
Configure
Network
Settings
window.

Configure Network Settings

Add new Device Type

◉ Automatically obtain IP address settings with: dhcp ▾

DHCP Settings
Hostname (optional):
☑ Automatically obtain DNS information from provider

○ Statically set IP addresses:
Manual IP Address Settings
Address:
Subnet Mask:
Default Gateway Address:

✖ Cancel   ◀ Back   ▶ Forward

8. **Choose whether you want to use DHCP to automatically obtain your IP address or whether you want to enter a static IP address.**

Make your choice by selecting the appropriate radio button. If you choose to set your address statically, you must enter the IP address, the network mask, and the address of the default gateway. You can also enter a hostname for your PC, if you desire.

9. **Click Forward.**

You see a listing of your selected information.

10. **(Optional) If you want to make changes, click Back to return to the desired window and make changes. If you are satisfied with your choices, click Apply to create the device.**

After clicking Apply, the device is created and appears in the device list.

Although the device has been configured and added to the list of devices, it is inactive, as you can see from the device listing. By default, the device will start at boot time, but you can activate it immediately by highlighting it and then clicking the Activate button from the menu bar at the top of the window.

11. **Choose File⇨Save from the menu to save your changes.**

Adding a wireless NIC

With the Network Configuration tool, you can easily add and configure your wireless NIC. To add a wireless NIC, do the following:

1. **Click the New button from the toolbar of the Network Configuration tool main window. (Refer to Figure 7-1.)**

   The Select Device Type window (refer to Figure 7-2) appears.

2. **Choose Wireless Connection from the Device Type list and then click Forward to go to the Select Wireless Device list.**

3. **If your NIC is shown in the Select Wireless Device list, select it and click Forward to go to the Configure Wireless Connection dialog box, as shown in Figure 7-5. If your NIC is not listed, go to Step 6.**

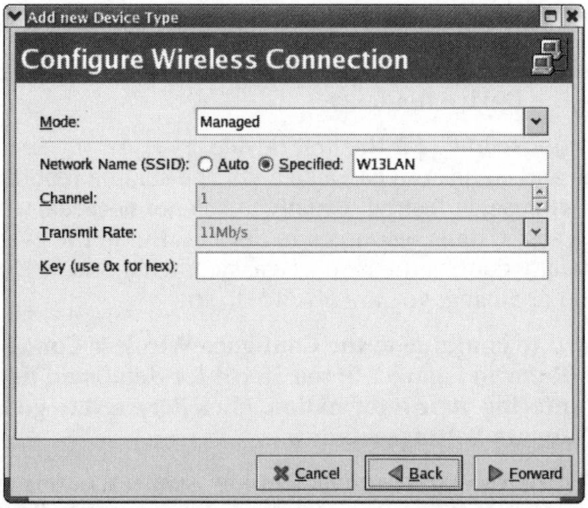

Figure 7-5: The Configure Wireless Connection dialog box.

4. **In the Configure Wireless Connection dialog box, enter the appropriate information for your wireless connection as follows.**

✔ **Mode:** From the drop-down list, choose from

- *Auto* to have the system automatically determine the connection type

- *Managed* to set your configuration to connect to a wireless access point

- *Ad-hoc* if you will be connecting directly to other wireless NICs

✔ **Network Name (SSID):** Either select the Specified radio button and enter the name of your network here, or select the Auto radio button to have the system determine the name.

✔ **Channel:** Enter the channel that your wireless network uses.

✔ **Transmit Rate:** Choose Auto or a specific transmission rate for your network.

✔ **Key:** If your network uses Wired Equivalent Privacy (WEP), enter the appropriate encryption key here.

5. **After you enter your network information, click Forward to go to the Configure Network Settings dialog box (refer to Figure 7-4).**

6. **If your NIC is not listed, choose Other Wireless Card and then click Forward to open the Select Ethernet Adapter window (refer to Figure 7-3).**

7. **Select your card from the drop-down list in the Adapter field.**

8. **After choosing your card, choose the device name from the drop-down list in the Device field.**

    You should choose eth0 for the first device, eth1 for the second, eth2 for the third, and so on. You can also enter the system resources that the adapter will use, if desired. Usually this is not necessary because the OS automatically assigns resources to devices. But in the event that you need to manually control the resource assignments because of other hardware you are using, you are able to do so.

9. **Click Forward to continue to the Configure Wireless Connection dialog box. (Refer to Figure 7-5; see Step 4 for details on this dialog box.) After entering your information, click Forward to go to the Configure Network Settings window.**

10. **In the Configure Network Settings window, you can choose whether you want to use DHCP to automatically obtain your IP address or whether you want to enter a static IP address.**

    Make your choice by selecting the appropriate radio button. If you choose to set your address statically, you must enter the IP address, the network mask, and the address of the default gateway. You can also enter a hostname for your PC, if you desire.

11. **After you make the appropriate entries, click Forward.**

    You see a listing of your selected information.

12. **If you want to make changes, click Back to return to the desired window and make changes. If you are satisfied with your choices, click Apply to create the device.**

    After clicking Apply, the device is created and appears in the device list.

    Although the device has been configured and added to the list of devices, it is inactive, as you can see from the device listing. By default, the device starts at boot time, but you can activate it immediately by highlighting it and then clicking the Activate button from the menu bar at the top of the window.

13. **Choose File⇨Save from the menu to save your changes.**

Adding a modem connection

With the Network Configuration tool, you can easily add and configure your modem. To add a modem, do the following:

1. **Click the New button on the toolbar.**

2. **Choose Modem Connection from the Device Type list and then click Forward.**

    The configuration tool searches your system to try to detect a modem.

    If you have a modem installed in your system during installation of Red Hat Enterprise Linux, your modem should already be listed in the Network Configuration Tool. Click the Hardware tab to see information about the device.

    If you have a modem in your hardware list, the configuration tool uses that modem and opens the Select Modem window, as shown in Figure 7-6, with values appropriate for the modem. If no modem is found, a message appears, stating that no modem was found and prompting you to click OK. After clicking OK, the Select Modem dialog box appears, but the values might not be correct for the modem that you have installed.

3. **If your modem was successfully found, you can accept the default values for modem device, baud rate, flow control, and modem volume; otherwise, enter the values appropriate for your modem.**

    If you don't have touch-tone dialing, remove the check mark from the Use Touch Tone Dialing check box.

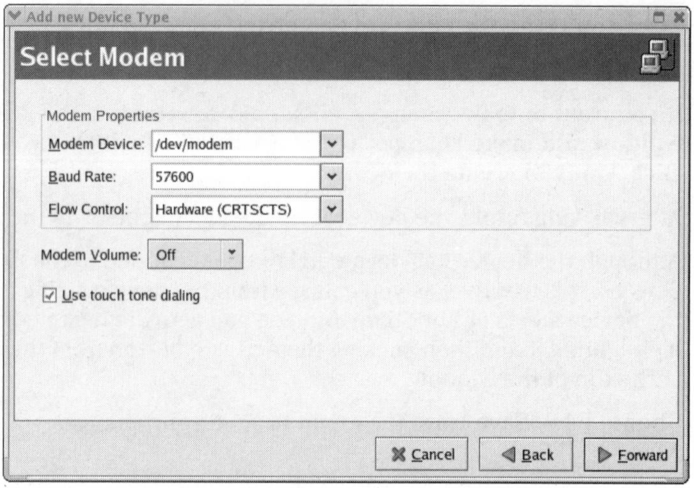

Figure 7-6:
The Select
Modem
dialog box.

4. **When you are satisfied with the settings, click Forward to go to the Select Provider window, as shown in Figure 7-7.**

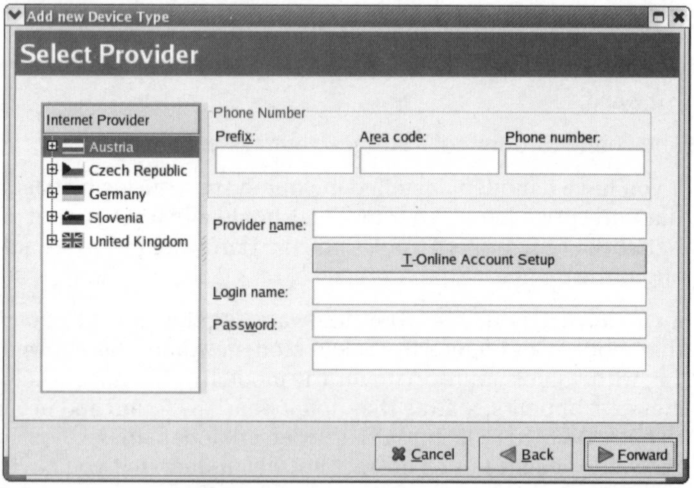

Figure 7-7:
The Select
Provider
dialog box.

5. **Here you need to enter the name of your ISP and the telephone number that you dial to connect. Enter your login name and password that were given to you by your ISP.**

6. **Click Forward to go to the IP Settings window, as shown in Figure 7-8.**

You can probably accept the default setting here to obtain IP addressing information automatically.

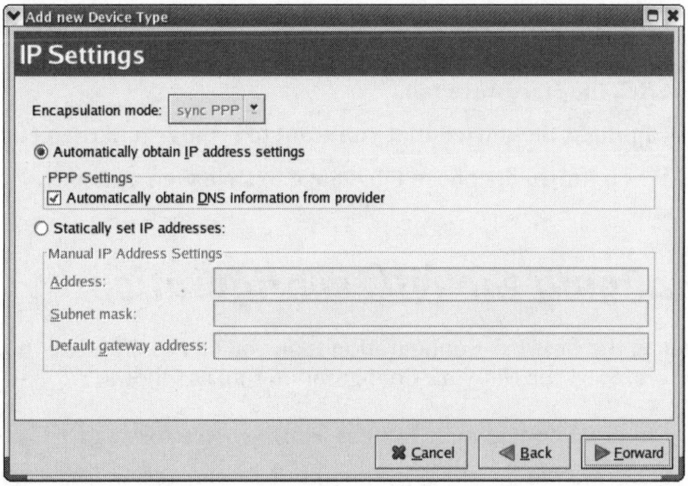

Figure 7-8:
The IP
Settings
dialog box.

7. **Click Forward to continue.**

   You see a listing of your selected information. If you want to make changes, click Back to return to the desired window and make changes. If you are satisfied with your choices, click Apply to create the device.

   The device is created and appears in the device list. Although the device has been configured and added to the list of devices, it is inactive, as you can see from the device listing. By default, the device starts at boot time, but you can activate it immediately by highlighting it and then clicking the Activate button from the menu bar at the top of the window.

8. **Choose File⇨Save from the menu to save your changes.**

Editing Your Network Configuration

After you add and configure your network connection device, whether it is a wired NIC, wireless NIC, or modem, you usually don't need to change the configuration. You might need to modify the configuration, though, if you change to a different NIC.

Removing a NIC

By using the Network Configuration tool, you can easily make the necessary changes. Start the Network Configuration tool as follows:

1. **Choose Applications⇨System Settings⇨Network.**

If you are not logged in as the root user, you will be prompted to enter the root password.

2. **Click the Hardware tab.**

3. **Highlight the device that you want to remove and then click Delete.**

4. **When finished, choose File⇨Save to save your changes.**

Changing the NIC configuration

By using the Network Configuration tool, you can easily make the necessary changes. Start the Network Configuration tool as follows:

1. **Choose Applications⇨System Settings⇨Network.**

   If you are not logged in as the root user, you will be prompted to enter the root password.

2. **Highlight the device that you want to modify and then click Edit (on the toolbar).**

   The Ethernet Device properties dialog box for the device you selected, as shown in Figure 7-9, appears.

3. **The three tabs available from this dialog box are used for the following:**

   ✔ **General:** Here you can enter a nickname for the device and choose whether the device is activated when the system starts. You can also choose to allow other users to be able to enable and disable the device. You can choose to obtain IP information automatically by using DHCP, or you can manually enter the IP information for the device.

Figure 7-9: The Ethernet Device properties dialog box.

In most cases, you can accept the default setting and let the system obtain IP information using DHCP. If you need to use a static IP address, you can usually get the IP information from your system administrator. If you are the system administrator, you should know what IP information to use.

✔ **Route:** Here you can enter static routes to other network. You need to enter the network IP number as well as the gateway IP number. In most cases, you don't need to enter any information here if you are using DHCP.

✔ **Hardware Device:** This tab contains information about the hardware associated with the Ethernet device. You can assign device aliases here if you desire.

Device aliases are virtual devices associated with the same physical hardware, but they can be activated at the same time to have different IP addresses. They are commonly represented as the device name followed by a colon and a number (for example, eth0:1). They are useful if you want to have more than one IP address for a system but the system has only one network card.

If you have configured a device, such as eth0,

    a. Click the Add button in the Network Administration tool to create an alias for the device.

    b. Select the network device and configure the network settings.

The alias will appear in the device list with a device name, followed by a colon and the alias number.

4. After you make the changes you desire, click OK to return to the Network Configuration dialog box.

5. Choose File⇨Save to write your configuration changes to a file.

Managing DNS settings

The DNS tab of the Network Configuration tool is where you configure the system's hostname, domain, nameservers, and search domain. *Nameservers* are used to look up other hosts on the network. To enter or change these settings, do the following:

1. Choose Applications⇨System Settings⇨Network.

If you are not logged in as the root user, you will be prompted to enter the root password.

2. Click the DNS tab from the Network Configuration dialog box.

3. On the DNS tab, enter the appropriate information for your system.

4. After you finish, choose File⇨Save to save your changes.

The Nameservers section does not configure the system to be a nameserver. If the DNS server names are retrieved from DHCP (or retrieved from the ISP of a modem connection), do not add primary, secondary, or tertiary DNS servers.

Managing hosts

On the Hosts tab of the Network Configuration tool, you can add, edit, or remove hosts to or from the /etc/hosts file. This file contains IP addresses and their corresponding hostnames. When your system tries to resolve a hostname to an IP address or determine the hostname for an IP address, it refers to the /etc/hosts file before using the nameservers (if you are using the default Red Hat Enterprise Linux configuration). If the IP address is listed in the /etc/hosts file, the nameservers are not used. If your network contains computers whose IP addresses are not listed in DNS, it is recommended that you add them to the /etc/hosts file.

1. **Choose Applications⇨System Settings⇨Network.**

   If you are not logged in as the root user, you will be prompted to enter the root password.

2. **Click the Hosts tab from the Network Configuration dialog box.**

   The Hosts tab that appears shows the hostname to static IP address mappings, if any.

3. **Click New from the toolbar to open the Add/Edit Hosts Entry dialog box.**

4. **Enter the hostname and its IP address. If there is an alias for the hostname, enter it as well.**

5. **Click OK to add the entry to the list.**

6. **Choose File⇨Save to save your changes.**

Do not remove the Localhost entry from the Hosts section, or your network will not work properly.

Working with profiles

Multiple logical network devices can be created for each physical hardware device. For example, if you have one Ethernet card in your system (eth0), you can create logical network devices with different nicknames and different configuration options, all associated with eth0. These logical network devices are different from device aliases. Logical network devices associated with the same physical device must exist in different profiles and cannot be activated simultaneously. Device aliases are also associated with the same physical hardware device, but device aliases associated with the same physical hardware can be activated at the same time.

Profiles can be used to create multiple configuration sets for different networks. A configuration set can include logical devices as well as hosts and DNS settings. After configuring the profiles, you can use the Network Administration tool to switch back and forth between them.

By default, there is one profile called Common. To create a new profile, do the following:

1. **Choose Applications⇨System Settings⇨Network.**

   If you are not logged in as the root user, you will be prompted to enter the root password.

2. **Choose Profile⇨New from the menu.**

3. **Enter a unique name for the profile.**

4. **After creating a new profile, if all the devices are not listed for all the profiles, add them by clicking the Add button.**

   If a device already exists for the physical device, use the Copy button to copy the existing device.

In the list of devices is a column of check boxes labeled Profile. For each profile, you can check (mark) or uncheck (clear) devices. Only the checked devices are included for the currently selected profile.

A profile cannot be activated at boot time. Only the devices in the Common profile, which are set to activate at boot time, are activated at boot time. After the system has booted, execute the following command to enable a profile (replacing *profilename* with the name of the profile):

```
redhat-config-network-cmd --profile profilename
```

Chapter 8

The Network File System

In This Chapter

▶ Explaining Network File System (NFS)

▶ Configuring and managing an NFS server

▶ Configuring an NFS client

As you can see from the title of this chapter, NFS is an acronym for *Network File System*. So now you know what the abbreviation means, but just what exactly is NFS?

NFS is a protocol that was developed by Sun Microsystems to allow computers to access shared directories across a network yet appear as if those directories were on the computers' local file system. NFS is widely used by systems running Unix and Unix variants, like Enterprise Linux, but it can also be used by computers running different operating systems, such as MS Windows or Mac OS.

In this chapter, I show you how to configure an NFS server to share some directories to other computers on the network. You can also read how to configure an NFS client to access the directories that you share from the NFS server.

Configuring and Managing an NFS Server

In order for the NFS server to be able to share files and directories with other computers on the network, you must tell it which directories and files to share. The term used to express the sharing of files and directories from an NFS server is *exporting*. The directory or directories that is/are exported are *shares*. Red Hat Enterprise Linux has a graphical tool — the NFS Server

Configuration tool — that you can use to configure the server and choose the directories that you want to export. You can use the graphical tool if you have an X Server installed and are running X. If you don't have an X Server installed, see the section, "Command Line Configuration."

Adding Shares to Export

To start the NFS Server Configuration tool and choose the directories to export, do the following:

1. **Choose Applications⇨System Settings⇨Server Settings⇨NFS.**

   If you are not logged in as the root user, you will be prompted for the root password.

   The NFS Server Configuration dialog box, as shown in Figure 8-1, appears.

2. **Choose File⇨Add Share from the menu, or click Add from the toolbar.**

   The Add NFS Share dialog box, as shown in Figure 8-2, appears. Of the three tabs of this dialog box, the Basic tab is displayed by default.

3. **In the Directory field, enter the directory that you want to export.**

   Alternatively, you can click the Browse button to locate the directory by browsing your file system.

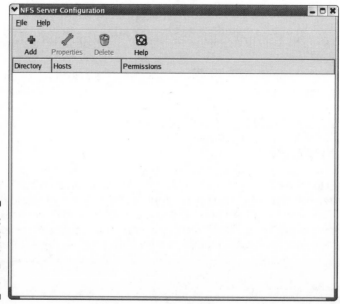

Figure 8-1:
The NFS
Server Con-
figuration
dialog box.

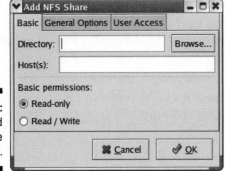

Figure 8-2:
The Add
NFS Share
dialog box.

4. **In the Host(s) field, enter the host or hosts to which you want to export the directory.**

   Hostnames can be entered with the following formats:

   ✔ **For a single computer:** A fully qualified domain name, hostname, or an IP address.

   ✔ **For groups of computers:** You can list groups of computers in the same domain by using wildcards. For example, `*.muhlenberg.edu` would share the selected directory with any hostname at the domain `muhlenberg.edu`.

   ✔ **By IP network addresses:** You can also list hosts by using their IP network address and netmask: for example, 192.168.2.0/24 or 192.168.2.0/255.255.255.0. In the first example, the netmask is expressed as the number of bits in the netmask. In the second example, the actual netmask is specified. Either of these formats is acceptable.

5. **Select the type of access (permissions) that you want to allow, either read-only or read/write.**

6. **Click the General Options tab (see Figure 8-3) and make the appropriate selections there.**

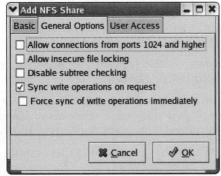

Figure 8-3:
The General
Options tab.

Five options can be configured from this tab. These options are

✔ **Allow Connections from Port 1024s and Higher:** Services started on port numbers less than 1024 must be started as root. Select this option to allow the NFS service to be started by a user other than root.

✔ **Allow Insecure File Locking:** Do not require a lock request.

✔ **Disable Subtree Checking:** If a subdirectory of a file system is exported but the entire file system is not exported, the server checks whether the requested file is in the subdirectory exported. This check is *subtree checking.* Select this option to disable subtree checking. If the entire file system is exported, selecting to disable subtree checking can increase the transfer rate.

✔ **Sync Write Operations on Request:** Enabled by default, this option does not allow the server to reply to requests before the changes made by the request are written to the disk.

✔ **Force Sync of Write Operations Immediately:** Do not delay writing to disk.

7. **Click the User Access tab (see Figure 8-4) and make the appropriate selections there.**

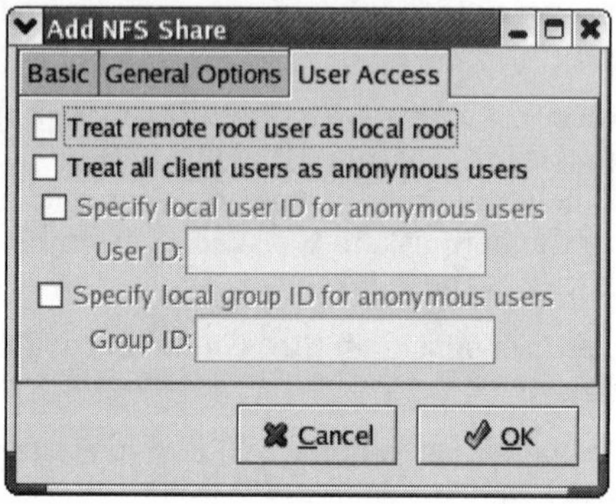

Figure 8-4:
The User
Access tab.

> **Add NFS Share**
> Basic | General Options | User Access
> ☐ Treat remote root user as local root
> ☐ Treat all client users as anonymous users
> ☐ Specify local user ID for anonymous users
>   User ID:
> ☐ Specify local group ID for anonymous users
>   Group ID:
>   ✖ Cancel   ✔ OK

These options can be configured from this tab:

✔ **Treat Remote Root User as Local Root:** If this option is selected, the root on a client has root privileges to exported directories.

Selecting this option negatively affects system security. You should not select it unless it is absolutely necessary.

✔ **Treat All Client Users as Anonymous Users:** If this option is selected, all user and group IDs are mapped to the anonymous user. The following two options are available only if this parent option is enabled:

    • *Specify Local User ID for Anonymous Users:* This option lets you specify a user ID for the anonymous user.

- *Specify Local Group ID for Anonymous Users:* This option lets you specify a group ID for the anonymous user.

8. **Click OK to close the Add NFS Share dialog box and return to the NFS Server Configuration dialog box.**

   You see the share that you just added in the list of directory exports.

9. **(Optional) If you wish to add more shares, repeat the procedure.**

10. **Choose File⇨Quit to close the NFS Server Configuration dialog box.**

Editing and Deleting NFS Exported Shares

With the NFS Server Configuration tool, you can easily change share properties or delete shares. To modify share properties or delete shares, do the following:

1. **Choose Applications⇨System Settings⇨Server Settings⇨NFS.**

   If you are not logged in as the root user, you will be prompted for the root password.

   The NFS Server Configuration dialog box appears (refer to Figure 8-1).

2. **Click to highlight the share that you want to edit and then click Properties from the toolbar.**

   The Edit NFS Share dialog box, as shown in Figure 8-5, appears.

3. **Edit the share as needed.**

   Refer to the preceding section for a description of the NFS properties and make the changes you desire. After you finish editing the share, click OK to apply the changes.

4. **To delete a share, click the share to highlight it and then click Delete from the toolbar.**

Figure 8-5:
The Edit
NFS Share
dialog box.

Command Line Configuration

You don't have to use the graphical NFS Configuration tool to configure the NFS server. Perhaps you don't have an X Server installed, or maybe you just want to use the command line because it's usually faster to do so. In either case, the only file that needs to be changed to configure the NFS server is the /etc/exports file. This is the file that's modified if you do use the graphical tool. To enter the directories that you want to export via the command line, do the following:

1. **From a command prompt, open the** /etc/exports **file by using any text editor.**

   I usually use the vi editor for making changes to configuration files. Although it takes a little while to get used to vi, it's very quick and easy to use after you become familiar with it. An added advantage is that vi is installed by default on just about every Unix and Linux system. If you aren't comfortable using vi, you can try using gedit, which is the GNOME text editor. To open gedit, choose Applications➪Accessories➪ Text Editor.

2. **Enter the information about the directory that you want to export and to which hostnames by using the following syntax:**

   ```
   /export_directory hostname(options)
   ```

   The only option that you must specify is either sync or async, which tells the server whether to respond to requests before the changes requested are written to disk. The recommended option is sync.

   For example, if I want to export the /musicfiles directory to terry.muhlenberg.edu with read and write permissions, I enter

   ```
   /musicfiles terry.muhlenberg.edu(rw,sync)
   ```

3. **Save the changes that you make to the** /etc/export **file.**

4. **Restart the NFS server by issuing the following command:**

   ```
   /sbin/service nfs restart
   ```

After you have the /etc/exports file open, you can make changes to existing exported shares and even delete shares by using the text editor to make the changes.

Any time that you manually change the /etc/exports file, you need to reload the file to let the NFS server know about the changes. Restarting the NFS service reloads the /etc/exports file.

Configuring an NFS Client

Before you can access directory shares that have been exported by an NFS server, you need to do some configuration of the NFS client. The client configuration is quite simple and easy. All you need to do is to *mount* (access) the exported directories onto your file system. There are several ways that you can mount the exported directories, and I show them to you here.

Mounting an NFS directory

You can always use the `mount` command to mount the exported directory on your file system. The basic syntax for mounting an exported share is

```
mount NFS_Server_Name:/exported_directory /mount_point
```

For example, suppose that my NFS server is named `terry.muhlenberg.edu`, the directory that I exported is `/musicfiles`, and I want to mount the exported directory on my file system at `/mnt/temp`. I use the following command:

```
mount terry.muhlenberg.edu:/musicfiles /mnt/temp
```

After executing the `mount` command, the `/musicfiles` directory exported by the NFS server is accessible on my file system at the mount point that I specified — in this case, at `/mnt/temp`. Now the files are available to me locally, but I wouldn't want to manually mount the exported directory every time I start my system. I want the directory to be mounted automatically when my system starts. I show you how in the next section.

The mount point on your file system for the exported directory must already exist. Be sure that you create the directory before you issue the `mount` command.

Mounting NFS directories automatically at system start

By placing the mount information for my NFS server into one of your system startup files, you can have the exported directories available automatically every time your system starts. The file that you need to modify is the `/etc/fstab` file. An example of the `/etc/fstab` file is shown in Figure 8-6.

```
root@terry:/misc - Shell - Konsole

Session  Edit  View  Bookmarks  Settings  Help

[root@terry misc]# cat /etc/fstab
LABEL=/1                /                       ext3    defaults          1 1
LABEL=/boot             /boot                   ext3    defaults          1 2
none                    /dev/pts                devpts  gid=5,mode=620    0 0
LABEL=/home             /home                   ext3    defaults          1 2
none                    /proc                   proc    defaults          0 0
none                    /dev/shm                tmpfs   defaults          0 0
/dev/hdb3               swap                    swap    defaults          0 0
/dev/cdrom              /mnt/cdrom              iso9660 noauto,owner,kudzu,ro 0
0
/dev/fd0                /mnt/floppy             auto    noauto,owner,kudzu 0 0
/dev/hda2               /mnt/drive2             ext3    defaults          0 0
/dev/sda1               /mnt/thumb              auto    noauto,owner,user  0 0
/dev/sda4               /mnt/zip                auto    noauto,owner,user  0 0
[root@terry misc]#
```

Figure 8-6:
The /etc/
fstab file.

This file contains information about the file systems that my system knows
about and will automatically mount for me. I just need to add one line of the
exported directory that tells my system where to go to find the directory and
where to mount it on my system:

```
NFS_server_name:/export_directory /mnt_point filetype options
```

For example, suppose that my NFS server is named terry.muhlenberg.edu,
the directory that I exported is /musicfiles, and I want to mount the
exported directory on my file system at /mnt/temp. I add the following line
after the last line of my /etc/fstab file by using any text editor:

```
terry.muhlenberg.edu:/musicfiles  /mnt/temp  nfs  rsize=8192,wsize=8192
```

The options shown in the preceding example specify the read and write size
in bytes. The default size is 1024 bytes, but increasing the size to 8192 greatly
increases system performance. Of the many options that can be specified for
mounting the NFS shares, these two are the most common. You can see a
complete list of available options by reading the nfs manual page, which you
can access by entering the following command at a teminal prompt:

```
man nfs
```

Chapter 9

Connecting to Windows PCs Using Samba

• •

In This Chapter

▶ Installing Samba

▶ Configuring Samba

▶ Creating Samba users

▶ Starting the Samba server

▶ Connecting to a Samba server

▶ Connecting to a Samba client

• •

*B*y using the Samba program, you can emulate the Windows file sharing protocol and connect your Red Hat Network to a Windows network to share files and printers. In this chapter, I show you how to install and configure Samba to connect a Red Hat Linux network to a Microsoft network.

In this chapter, I refer to the Red Hat Enterprise Linux PC as the *Samba server* and the Windows PC as the *Samba client*.

Installing Samba

Before you can use Samba to connect to the Windows computers, it must first be installed on the Linux PC. All current versions of Red Hat Enterprise Linux include Samba, but it might not have been installed during the system installation. Even if it has been installed, you should always check for the latest version to find out whether any problems have been fixed by the latest release and to install it if necessary. To see whether Samba is installed on your system, type the following at a terminal window:

```
rpm -q samba
```

If Samba is not installed, the command returns the output stating that Samba is not installed. If Samba is installed, the `rpm` query returns the version number of the Samba program installed on your system.

The latest version of Samba (3.0.9 as of this writing) can be obtained at the Samba Web site, located at `www.samba.org`. To install Samba, proceed as follows:

1. **Download the file** `samba-3.0.9.tar.gz`.

2. **Extract the file by using the following command:**

   ```
   tar -xfvz samba-3.0.9.tar.gz
   ```

3. **Change to the directory containing the extracted files (usually** `/usr/src`**) and then type**

   ```
   ./configure
   ```

4. **Press Enter and wait for the command prompt to return. From the command prompt, type**

   ```
   make
   ```

5. **Press Enter and wait for the command prompt to return.**

6. **Type** make install **from the command prompt and then press Enter.**

Samba is installed when the command prompt returns. Now you need to configure it. In order for Samba to provide its services, the Red Hat Enterprise Linux PC needs to be configured.

Configuring the Samba Server

Before you can use Samba to connect with your Windows PCs, it must be configured. The several graphical-based programs available for configuring Samba are just front-ends that make changes to the Samba configuration file behind the scenes. Editing the Samba configuration file directly is much quicker and easier. The Samba configuration file is `smb.conf` and is typically located in the `/etc/samba` directory by the installation program. A sample `smb.conf` file was created during the installation that can be used for reference and modification.

The `smb.conf` file is divided into several sections, called *shares,* the names of which I show as bracketed subsection titles in Listing 9-1. Shown in Listing 9-1 is the `smb.conf` file from one of the computers that I use at school. Following the listing is a description of the sections in the Samba configuration file. Refer to this listing to see what a section looks like as it is described.

Listing 9-1:   The Samba Configuration File

```
# This is the main Samba configuration file. You should read the
# smb.conf(5) manual page in order to understand the options listed
# here. Samba has a huge number of configurable options (perhaps too
# many!) most of which are not shown in this example
# Any line which starts with a ; (semi-colon) or a # (hash)
# is a comment and is ignored. In this example we will use a #
# for commentry and a ; for parts of the config file that you
# may wish to enable
# NOTE: Whenever you modify this file you should run the command "testparm"
# to check that you have not made any basic syntactic errors.
#======================= Global Settings =======================================
[global]
          log file = /var/log/samba/%m.log
          smb passwd file = /etc/samba/smbpasswd
          load printers = yes
          passwd chat = *New*password* %n\n *Retype*new*password* %n\n
                  *passwd:*all*authentication*tokens*updated*successfully*
          socket options = TCP_NODELAY SO_RCVBUF=8192 SO_SNDBUF=8192
          obey pam restrictions = yes
          encrypt passwords = yes
          passwd program = /usr/bin/passwd %u
          dns proxy = no
          netbios name = rhl
          writeable = yes
          server string = Samba Server
          printing = lprng
          path = /home
          default = homes
          unix password sync = Yes
          workgroup = Tardis
          printcap name = /etc/printcap
          security = user
          max log size = 50
          pam password change = yes

[homes]
          comment = Home Directories
          browseable = yes
          writeable = yes
          create mode = 0664
          directory mode = 0775
          max connections = 1

[printers]
          browseable = yes
          printable = yes
          path = /var/spool/samba
          comment = All Printers
```

Global

The first section of the `smb.conf` file is the `global` section. The `global` section contains settings that apply to the entire server as well as default settings that can apply to the other shares. The `global` section contains a list of options and values in this format:

```
option = value
```

Of the hundreds of options and values at your disposal, the most common ones are shown here. For a complete listing of options, refer to the `smb.conf` `man` page. Some of the more significant options are

- ✔ `workgroup = Tardis`: This is the name of the workgroup shown in the identification tab of the network properties box on the Windows computer.

- ✔ `smb passwd file = /etc/samba/smbpasswd`: This shows the path to the location of the Samba password file. Be sure that you include this option/value pair in your `smb.conf` file.

- ✔ `encrypted = yes`: Beginning with Windows NT Service Pack 3 and later, passwords are encrypted. If you are connecting to any systems running these versions of Windows, you should choose encrypted passwords.

- ✔ `netbios name = RHEL`: This is the name by which the Samba server is known to the Windows computer.

- ✔ `server string = Samba Server`: This is shown as a comment on the Windows PC in the network browser.

- ✔ `security = user`: This is the level of security applied to server access. Other possible options are

  - • `share`: Using `share` makes it easier to create anonymous shares that do not require authentication, and it is useful when the NETBIOS names of the Windows computers are different from other names on the Linux computer.

  - • `server`: This is used if the password file is on another server in the network.

  - • `domain`: This is used if the clients are added to a Windows NT domain by using `smbpasswd`, and login requests are by a Windows NT primary or backup domain controller.

- ✔ `log file = /var/log/samba/log`: This is the location of the log file.

- ✔ `max log size = 50`: This is the maximum size in kilobytes that the file can grow to.

✔ socket options = TCP_NODELAY SO_RCVBUF=8192 SO_SNDBUF=8192: This enables the server to be tuned for better performance. TCP_NODE-LAY is a default value, and the BUF values set send and receive buffers.

✔ dns proxy = No: This indicates that the NETBIOS name will not be treated like a DNS name and that there is no DNS lookup.

Homes

The next section of the smb.conf file, homes, is used to enable the server to give users quick access to their home directories. Refer to the smb.conf man page for a more complete description of how the homes section works.

✔ comment = Home Directories is a comment line.

✔ browseable = yes means that the directory will appear in the Windows file browser.

✔ writeable = yes means that users can write to their directories.

✔ create mode = 0664 sets the default file permissions for files created in the directory.

✔ directory mode = 0775 sets the default permissions for directories that are created.

✔ max connections = 1 is the maximum number of connections allowed.

Printers

This section sets the options for printing.

✔ path = /var/spool/samba is the location of the printer spool directory.

✔ printable = yes enables clients to send print jobs to the specified directory. This option must be set, or printing does not work.

✔ browseable = yes means that the printer appears in the browse list.

TIP

Be sure to have your printer properly configured for your Linux network before you attempt to set it up for use with Windows clients. You might need to enter the location of the path to the print spool for the printer that you want to use in the smb.conf file.

The `smb.conf` file shown in the examples allow users that already have Red Hat Enterprise Linux system accounts to access their home directories and to use printers. After modifying your configuration file to fit your specific needs and saving the `/etc/samba/smb.conf` file, you should check the syntax of the file. To do this, you can use the `testparm` command, as shown here:

```
[root@terry terry]# testparm
Load smb config files from /etc/samba/smb.conf
Processing section "[printers]"
Processing section "[homes]"
Loaded services file OK.
Press enter to see a dump of your service definitions
```

If you see the line `Loaded services file OK`, your file does not contain any syntax errors, and the `smb.conf` file is now ready to use. If you receive any error messages, go back to the file and carefully check the syntax of the configuration.

Creating Samba Users

Next you need to create a Samba users' password file. You can convert all your system users to Samba users by running the following command:

```
cat /etc/passwd | mksmbpasswd.sh > /etc/samba/smbpasswd
```

This utility creates only the users' accounts — not their passwords. You need to create passwords for your users by using the `smbpasswd` command and the user's name as shown in the following example:

```
[root@terry terry]# smbpasswd terry
New SMB password:
Retype new SMB password:
Password changed for user terry.
            Password changed for user terry.
            [root@terry terry]#
```

Starting the Samba Server

The next step is to start the Samba server. The command to start Samba is

```
[root@terry terry]# service smb start
```

At this point, you should have a functioning Samba server running on your system. It is configured to allow all those who have an account on your Red Hat Enterprise Linux system to access their home directories from a Windows PC. Logged in users will also be able to use the printers configured with the Red Hat Enterprise Linux system.

Connecting to the Samba Server

Now you are ready to test your connection to the Samba server from the Windows PC. There is no configuration required on the Windows PC to be able to connect to the Samba server. To connect to the Samba server, do the following:

1. **On the Windows computer, open the My Network Places window by clicking its icon from the desktop.**

2. **In the My Network Places window, you should now see a listing for the Red Hat Enterprise Linux computer, which is called *sabrina* on RHL10.**

   Figure 9-1 shows the Samba server as it appears in the My Network Places window on my Windows 2000 PC.

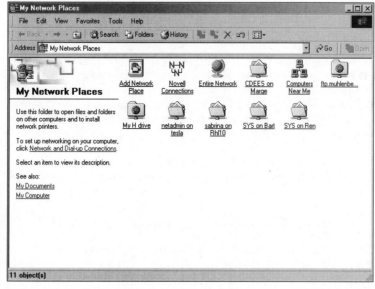

Figure 9-1:
The My Network Places window showing the Samba server.

3. Double-click the rhl10 PC icon (or whatever you called the Samba server) to see the shares that you made available.

If you double-click the directory share from the rhl10 PC, you are prompted for a username and password to enter the directories. That's all there is to it. Now you can share files between your Linux and Windows computers.

Connecting to a Samba Client

You can connect your Red Hat Enterprise Linux system to any computer that is running the smb protocol, whether it is a Windows PC or another Linux system running Samba. The connection can be made from the command line by using two methods. The first uses a utility called smbclient, and the command syntax is smbclient //computer name/directory, as shown in Listing 9-2. Be sure to replace computer name in the example with the name of your computer.

Listing 9-2: Logging into a Samba Client

```
[root@terry terry]# smbclient //terrycollings/c
added interface ip=192.168.9.93 bcast=192.168.9.255 nmask=255.255.255.0
Got a positive name query response from 192.168.9.102 (192.168.9.102)
Password:
Domain=[Tardis] OS=[Windows 5.0] Server=[Windows 2000 LAN Manager]
smb: \>
```

Listing 9-2 shows me logging into my Windows PC from my Red Hat system. I was prompted for a password to login and then was given some information about the Windows system and a command prompt. You can type **help** at the command prompt to get a list of possible commands. The commands at the smb prompt are very similar to command line ftp commands. To exit the connection, type **exit**.

Another way to make the files on the Samba client accessible on your Red Hat Linux system is to mount the client file system on your file system. You can do this by using the smbmount command. The syntax for this command is

```
smbmount //computer name/directory /system_mount_point
```

An example of the command and its output follows:

```
[root@terry terry]# smbmount //terrycollings/c /mnt/windows
Password:
[root@terry terry]# cd /mnt/windows
```

```
[root@terry windows]# ls
arcldr.exe              MSDOS.SYS               quicktime
arcsetup.exe            Muhlnet Setup           QuickTimeInstaller.zip
AUTOEXEC.BAT            My Download Files       Recycled
boot.ini                My Music                rhsa
camtasia                NALCache                W2K.CD
CONFIG.SYS              netplus                 Windows Update Setup Files
Documents and Settings  Novell                  WINNT
Drivers                 NTDETECT.COM            WSREMOTE.ID
fgc                     ntldr                   WT61CE.UWL
hiberfil.sys            p2.pdf                  WT61OZ.UWL
IO.SYS                  pagefile.sys            WT61UK.UWL
lconfig.aot             Program Files           WT61US.UWL
Local Muhlnet           PUTTY.RND
```

In this example, I am connecting to the same Windows PC that I connected to in the earlier example. However, by using the smbmount command, I am mounting the Windows file system on to my Red Hat Linux file system. After entering the password for the Windows PC and returning to the command prompt, I change to the directory that I just mounted and run the ls command to obtain a directory listing of the Windows PC share that I mounted. I can now easily move files between the two systems via regular file system utilities. I could put the mount information into my /etc/fstab file so that the directories would be mounted at system boot if I desired.

To unmount the client file system, enter the smbumount command and the path to the directory to unmount, as shown here:

```
# smbumount /mnt/windows
```

After pressing Enter, the file system will be unmounted.

Part III

Securing Your Enterprise Linux System

The 5th Wave   By Rich Tennant

Now, maybe that's an enterprise file server and maybe it ain't. Let's just you turn that thing on and show me some data rates for streaming reads and writes.

Airport SECURITY

In this part . . .

There are only two chapters in this part, but the topic they cover — security — is big, really big. In Chapter 10, you explore some basic security concepts that can be used for local and Internet security. You'll also see how to set up a basic firewall. Chapter 11 tells you about intruder detection and shows you some tools that you can use to test your vulnerability and detect intruders.

Chapter 10

Security Basics

In This Chapter

▶ Understanding basic security

▶ Developing a security policy

▶ Implementing host security

▶ Implementing network security

▶ Building a firewall

*I*n this chapter, you discover basic security concepts as they apply to a local area network (LAN) as well as security concepts that apply to outside networks, such as the Internet. For the purposes of this chapter, I refer to LAN security as *host security* because the goal of securing your LAN starts with the security of the individual hosts on your network. I refer to network security as *securing your network from outside threats* because the goal here is to secure your entire network from any outside threat.

Developing a Security Policy

Before you can implement any security on your systems, whether host or network security, you need to develop a security policy. A *security policy* is a written set of rules that describes how your organization will implement the security procedures. The security policy should include a good definition of the following items as well as the procedures to follow to implement good security practices:

▶ Physical security

▶ Document security

▶ Network security

▶ Consequences for not following the security policy

▶ Responsibility

Each of these items is equally important, and one item's position on the list does not indicate any kind of increased importance over other items. The following sections contain a more detailed look at each of these items.

Physical security

Physical security can refer to several methods that you can use to keep your systems safe from unauthorized access. When used in reference to individual hosts, physical security usually means choosing a strong password that cannot be easily guessed.

When used in reference to your network servers, physical security typically means making sure that the servers are locked in a secure location. A malicious user doesn't need to be able to log in to your servers to do them harm if your servers can be physically accessed. If a user can physically access your servers, he can do all sorts of damage to them — from simply turning off the power to picking them up and carrying them away. Keeping your servers locked away as well as limiting access to the locked location keeps unauthorized users from doing any harm to your servers. Other aspects of physical security include

- **Identification badges:** Requiring all employees to wear identification badges makes it easy to identify someone who does not belong inside your organization.

- **Door locks:** All doors to data centers or server rooms should be locked, with limited access to only those who need it.

- **Security cameras:** Cameras should cover all building entrances and exits and should be monitored continuously.

Document security

Document security refers to the ability of a company or organization to prevent loss of important information by maintaining strong control over company documents. One of the easiest and most effective ways to maintain good document security for an organization is to have a *clean desk policy* in place. This doesn't refer to not eating at your desk or wiping the surfaces of the desk clean (although both are probably good ideas). Rather, a clean desk policy means that all important documents, such as schematics, engineering drawings, company policy statements, confidential correspondence, and other similar items are locked away when employees leave their work areas. Someone can easily pick up items from a desk in an empty office with no one even knowing that it happened.

Another way to help ensure document security is to use encryption. *Encryption* uses a special key to change the document to make it unreadable to anyone who doesn't have the key that is used to decrypt the document. Using encryption won't prevent someone from obtaining your documents, but it can keep them from reading them.

Network security

Many items can be listed under the category of network security. The primary goal of network security is to keep your network safe from inside and outside vulnerabilities. As you can read in the preceding section, physical security and document security are major parts of network security. Other items of significance are shown in the following list:

- **Network access:** You should disable any unused network ports to prevent unauthorized users with laptops from connecting to your network.

- **Network wiring:** If possible, you should not run your network wiring where it's easily accessible. Network devices such as routers and firewalls should be in locked closets or other secure areas.

- **Modems:** Company employees should not be allowed to use desktop modems for any reason.

Many more items could be included on this list, but these are enough to provide a good starting point for network security as well as overall company security. Besides, I wouldn't want you to think that I'm some kind of security nut, after all.

Consequences for breaking security policy

Your security policy should include a section on the consequences of not following the policy. You must specifically state the actions that your organization will take against users who fail to comply with the policy. Typically, infractions can be categorized as either major or minor infractions.

Usually, a user who commits a major infraction could be subject to immediate termination. Many infractions could be considered major, such as using the Internet to browse to inappropriate sites as determined by the policy. Any user who commits a major infraction and is to be terminated should be immediately escorted out of the building after the employee is given the chance to gather any personal belongings from his or her work area.

A minor infraction is typically caused when a user breaks a security policy rule that usually results in the user having network access or privileges revoked for a certain period of time. For example, an employee might be spending too much time on the Internet instead of doing his or her work. She isn't browsing inappropriate sites, which would be a major infraction, but is just spending too much time browsing. In this case, her Internet usage could be suspended for a specified time period.

Responsibility

You need to determine who is responsible for your security policy. Who will implement the policy, make sure that it is maintained, and report any violations of the policy? You also need to determine who is responsible for fixing any problems that might arise from infractions of the policy or from events occurring that were not expected or planned for in the existing policy.

Performing a security audit

Before you can develop your security policy, you need to determine the specific areas that you need to secure. You can do this by performing a security audit of your hosts as well as your outside network connections. The items that you would examine can all be classified under the heading of *risk assessment*. Your risk assessment should look at the following areas:

- ✔ **Threats:** From what do you need to protect your hosts and network? Typical threats to your systems can be from both external sources as well as from internal users. Some typical threats to your systems from external sources can be Denial of Service attacks (DoS) and IP spoofing.

  - • **DoS attack:** Your servers become so overloaded with bogus requests for service that authorized users cannot use the services that they need.

  - • **IP spoofing attack:** Someone uses your system IP addresses to launch attacks against other systems. Internal threats can come from users who attempt to access systems that they shouldn't be accessing.

- ✔ **System weaknesses:** You need to determine the areas where your system is vulnerable to attack based on the threats that you identified.

- ✔ **Affects of attack:** You must examine the possible implications that an attack could have on your systems.

- ✔ **Vulnerability reduction:** If your system is attacked or otherwise compromised, determine what you can do to lessen the effect of the attack and also prevent future occurrences.

After you conduct your security audit, you are ready to create your security policy based on the information that you obtained from the risk assessment phase of the security audit. Additional areas that you need to cover in your security policy relate to those users who are authorized to use your systems as well as how those users will authenticate, or log in, to your system.

The services that you decide to offer to your users will greatly affect your security policy. For example, if you plan to offer Internet services to your users — such as FTP, e-mail, Internet chat, and Web access — you must consider the access level for your users. You might also need to consider virus scanning for incoming e-mail and downloaded files.

You must also consider protecting company data as well as other sensitive data from unauthorized users. You might need to consider legal requirements for securing your data and legal ramifications for the unauthorized release of data.

The final step in crafting a security policy is actually putting it in place. Whomever you assigned the responsibility for your system security will implement the policy and perform periodic checks to be sure that the policy is working and is being followed.

Implementing Host Security

After you have a basic understanding of system security (as explained in the first part of this chapter), look at specific examples of securing your hosts to make them less vulnerable to threats. In this section, I look at some system administration security functions, such as employing good usernames and strong passwords and also assigning proper access rights to files and directories to keep out unauthorized users.

System administrator security functions

As the system administrator, you have a lot of control over securing the hosts on your network. You can do many administrator functions to make your systems less vulnerable. One of the most important functions of the system administrator is creating user accounts. In fact, the primary method that you have for securing your systems is to assign good usernames and strong passwords to your user accounts. However, creating user accounts by assigning good usernames and strong passwords is not the only user security function that you can apply to your systems. The following list shows the common tasks that an administrator performs on user accounts.

- ✔ Creating accounts
- ✔ Assigning passwords

✔ Assigning rights

✔ Setting concurrent logins

✔ Setting account properties

✔ Setting password and account expiration

These are discussed in the next few sections.

Creating accounts

As a system administrator, one of your responsibilities is creating user accounts. User accounts usually comprise the user's first or last name — or some combination of both — but they can be anything that the administrator wants. You should try to make the username easy for the user to remember for the user.

In many cases, you might create special accounts for users who have additional system level privileges. A good example of a special user account is the root account. Everyone knows that the root user is the most powerful user on the system, and anyone who wants to break into your system already has the username of this most powerful user. So, a good idea from a security perspective is to use a name that does not describe the functions of the user. Instead of giving a system administrator the name *sysadmin,* use a different name. You can still give system administrator rights to the user, but the username won't give it away.

Administering users, which includes assigning passwords and their properties, is covered in Chapter 17.

Assigning passwords

Assigning passwords to accounts that you create is another job of the system administrator. You should always keep the following rules in mind when you are assigning passwords to your users:

✔ **Use strong passwords.** Passwords should be a combination of alphanumeric characters and special characters. Good education is the key to your users using strong passwords.

✔ **Make passwords easy for users to remember.** If passwords are too hard for your users to remember, they will change them to something too easy to break.

✔ **Make passwords difficult for others to guess.** User passwords should be difficult for other to guess. Don't use birthdays, proper names, license plate numbers, or Social Security numbers.

✔ **Never write down a password.** Be sure that you or your users never write down passwords on paper.

✔ **Passwords should have a minimum length.** Your passwords should be at least eight characters long.

✔ **Passwords should have a maximum length.** Your passwords should be no longer than 15 characters, or your users will have trouble remembering them.

✔ **Don't use common words found in a dictionary.** Any word that can be found in a dictionary — in any language — is a poor choice for a password. There are programs specifically designed to search through dictionaries looking for a password match.

✔ **Don't use the same password on different systems.** Never use the same password on more than one system because if someone does break your password, he might also gain access to the other system.

✔ **Educate your users.** Because your users will most likely be able to change their passwords, you need to be sure that they are properly educated in proper password selection.

Password management

As the system administrator, you can set properties affecting your user's password and account usage. You can set the following properties:

✔ **Password expiration:** You can force users to change their passwords by setting a password expiration date in the User Manager. See Chapter 17 to read about the User Manager tool.

✔ **Password lockout:** You can prevent a user from logging in by locking the password in the User Manager, thus essentially disabling the account. If a user is on extended leave or if you've set up a temporary or maintenance account for outside contractors, you can use this feature to lock the account and prevent access.

✔ **Account expiration:** You can set an expiration date for the entire account in the User Manager.

Assigning file and directory permissions

All users need to have permissions, or rights, to the files and directories that they use to do their work. Be sure that you do not assign more permissions than the user needs. You should periodically review, perhaps every 90 days, the permissions assigned to users to be sure that they aren't allowed to access any more than they need to. You can assign rights to files and directories by using the chmod command from the command line.

See Chapter 4 for instructions on using the chmod command to assign rights to files and directories.

You can also assign permissions to files and directories by browsing for the file in the File Manager and following the procedure here.

1. **Find the file whose permissions you want to change, right-click the file, and choose Properties from the contextual menu, as shown in Figure 10-1.**

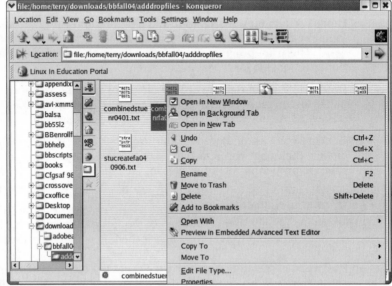

Figure 10-1:
Select a
file to
change its
properties.

After choosing Properties, the Properties dialog box for the selected file opens, as shown in Figure 10-2.

2. **Click the Permissions tab to open the Permissions dialog box for the selected file, as shown in Figure 10-3.**

Figure 10-2:
The
Properties
dialog box.

Figure 10-3:
Set file
permissions
here.

3. **Set the appropriate permissions for the file by selecting the check box(es) for the permissions that you want to apply for the user, group, or others.**

4. **After setting the file permissions, click OK to save your choices.**

If you're setting permissions for an executable file, you can also choose to have the program run with the user ID (UID) or group ID (GID) of the file owner by selecting the Set UID or the Set GID check boxes, respectively.

Having executable files running with Set UID enabled can be dangerous to your system. If this permission is set, the program runs with the permissions of the file's owner. If the file owner is root, the program has the same permissions as the root user; thus, the program can create new files, read all system files, and delete any file. If the program has security vulnerabilities, someone can gain root access to your system by exploiting the vulnerability.

You can find all the files on your system that have the UID set by entering the following command at a command line prompt:

```
find / -type f -perm 4000
```

You might be surprised at the long list of files that you will see. Don't be alarmed, however, because these programs need to run with the UID set. You should check the list, looking for files that have the permission set and are located in a user's home directory. Files with the UID set are not typically found in a user's home directory, and finding such files can be an indication that someone has compromised your system.

You can safely ignore the Sticky option because the Linux kernel will ignore this option if it is set.

Keeping your system updated

Another area that can cause security problems for your system is failing to keep it updated. Many users will spend considerable time installing and configuring their system until it is just the way they want it to be, but then they never download and install important system updates that might be specifically designed to fix security problems. Fortunately, Enterprise Linux users have access to the Red Hat Network and can use the tools provided to keep their system updated.

Chapter 16 explains the Red Hat Network and how to keep your system updated.

Implementing Network Security

Whether your systems are part of a LAN that is not accessible from the outside or whether they are open to the world, many of the security principles are the same. Having strong passwords and proper file and directory permissions are just as important for host security as they are for network security. In this section, I look at securing services that are typically known as *Internet services*. I also take a look at some system services that you can disable to prevent access and make your system less vulnerable to intruders.

Defining Internet services

Many of the services that are described as Internet services are typically programs that run on a system that provide requested services. For example, when you send an e-mail, you're actually requesting that an e-mail server responds to your request to send an e-mail. Or when you browse to a Web site, you're asking a Web server for a response to your request.

The programs that provide these services can be on your own network or located at some distant location. The common thread for these systems is that they all use the TCP/IP protocol. So, in short, you can say that an Internet service is any service that can be accessed over a TCP/IP-based network through a secure or an unsecured connection. Common secure Internet services are

✔ **SSH:** Secure Shell is a replacement for Telnet that encrypts all traffic, including passwords, via a public/private encryption key exchange protocol. ssh provides terminal access to remote computers across TCP/IP networks.

✔ **SCP:** Secure Copy is part of the `ssh` package and can be used to securely copy files from one system to another across a TCP/IP network.

✔ **SFTP:** Secure File Transfer Protocol is similar to regular FTP, but all file transfers are done by using `ssh` over a TCP/IP network.

Commonly used non-secure Internet services are

✔ **Telnet:** Telnet provides terminal access to remote computers across a TCP/IP network. Telnet is a non-secure service that passes all information in clear text.

✔ **FTP:** File Transfer Protocol is widely used for transferring software packages across the Internet. For most uses, this is perfectly acceptable, but for sensitive data transfer, SCP or SFTP should be used.

✔ **HTTP:** HyperText Transfer Protocol is the protocol used to transfer information from Web servers to Web clients.

✔ **SMTP:** Simple Mail Transfer Protocol is the protocol used by the mail server to send information across TCP/IP networks.

Disabling standalone servers

For a server to provide a requested service, it needs to run the appropriate program that listens to the proper TCP/IP port to establish a connection. Some of the programs start when the system starts and then run continuously, and other server programs are started as needed.

Servers that run continuously are *standalone services.* Because these servers are constantly listening on many TCP/IP ports, they present an opportunity for someone to find a vulnerability and exploit it. By disabling the services that you don't need to run, you can make your system less vulnerable to attack. In this section, I look at standalone services. You use a utility found in Enterprise Linux to disable the services that you don't need to run.

1. **To see a list of the services currently running on your system, choose Applications⇨System Settings⇨Server Settings⇨Services.**

   If you are not logged in as root, you will be prompted for the root password.

   The Service Configuration dialog box, as shown in Figure 10-4, appears.

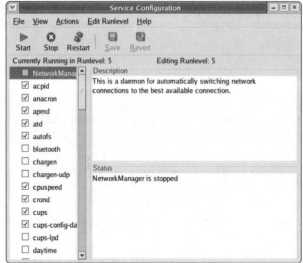

Figure 10-4:
The Service
Configura-
tion dialog
box.

In the left column is a list of all the services running on your system. Services marked with a check in front of the service name are started when the system boots.

In the right column are two areas:

✔ *Description:* The top area is a description of the service. Click the service name, and a description of the service appears in the top of the right column.

✔ *Status:* In the bottom of the right column is a status area. Click the service name and look here to see the status of the selected service.

Just above the list of services, you notice that you are currently in run-level 5. Runlevels 3 and 5 are the most significant because both are indicators of a fully functional Linux system. Runlevel 3 is a non-graphical system, and runlevel 5 is a graphical system.

2. Make any changes to both runlevels 3 and 5.

✔ You are in runlevel 3 if you are not running an X server and log in at a terminal prompt.

✔ You are in runlevel 5 if you are running an X server and use a graphical login.

Stopping services

To stop a running service and prevent it from starting at boot time, do the following:

1. **Choose Applications⇨System Settings⇨Server Settings⇨Services to open the Services Configuration dialog box (refer to Figure 10-4). Then determine which services you want to stop on your system.**

   If you are providing Internet services such as e-mail or Web services, your choices will be different than if you are running a personal workstation or desktop. To help you decide which services to run or disable, click the service and read the description of the service. Then decide whether you need it, depending on your system.

2. **Click the service that you want to stop and then click Stop from the toolbar.**

3. **Clear (remove) the check from the check box.**

   This will prevent the service from starting when the system boots.

4. **After you stop and disable the services that you desire, click Save to save your changes.**

Disabling xinetd server services

The `xinetd` server is sometimes called the *Internet superserver*. `xinetd` is started at boot time, and it listens for connections on network ports. When the `xinetd` server starts, it reads the configuration file `/etc/xinetd.conf` that points the server to the configuration files located in the `/etc/xinetd.d` directory. You can see the services that are started by the `xinetd` server by viewing the contents of the `/etc/xinetd.d` directory. The files on my system are shown in Listing 10-1.

Listing 10-1:   Contents of My /etc/xinetd.d Directory

```
[root@main root]# ls /etc/xinetd.d
chargen       daytime-udp  gssftp        ktalk    services  time
chargen-udp   echo         klogin        mtftp    sgi_fam   time-udp
cups-lpd      echo-udp     krb5-telnet   mtftp~   tftp
daytime       eklogin      kshell        rsync    tftp~
```

You can check whether a service is enabled or disabled by viewing the contents of the configuration file for that service. For example, to see whether TFTP is enabled, you can use the `cat` command to view the contents of the `tftp` configuration file, as shown in Listing 10-2.

Listing 10-2:   Contents of the /etc/xinetd.d/tftp File

```
[root@main root]# cat /etc/xinetd.d/tftp
# default: off
# description: The tftp server serves files using the trivial file transfer \
#       protocol.  The tftp protocol is often used to boot diskless \
#       workstations, download configuration files to network-aware printers, \
#       and to start the installation process for some operating systems.
service tftp
{
        disable                 = no
        socket_type             = dgram
        protocol                = udp
        wait                    = yes
        user                    = root
        server                  = /usr/sbin/in.ftpd -p -c -U 002 -u nobody -s
                /tftpboot
        server_args             = /tftpboot
        per_source              = 11
        cps                     = 100 2
        flags                   = IPv4
}
```

The most significant line in this listing shows

```
        disable                 = no
```

which indicates that `tftp` is enabled. To disable `tftp`, just change the `no` to a `yes`.

Conversely, if a service is disabled, just change the `yes` to a `no` to enable the service. You can use this same procedure to enable or disable any service controlled by `xinetd`.

If you make any changes to your `xinetd` configuration files, you must restart the `xinetd` server for the changes to take effect by issuing the command `service xinetd restart`.

Building a Firewall

A *firewall* is typically used to isolate an internal network from an external network. Most likely, this means that you want to protect your internal network from the Internet. A firewall can be a dedicated piece of hardware whose sole function is to protect your network, or it could be a server that provides other functions in addition to the firewall. Several types of firewalls can be used to protect your internal network from outside attack, and they work in different ways. Common types of firewalls can be configured to restrict access by using the following methods:

- ✔ **Access control lists:** This type of firewall contains lists of IP addresses that are allowed to use Internet services.

- ✔ **Demilitarized zone (DMZ):** This type of firewall passes network traffic to a separate network segment isolated from the internal network that contains servers running the desired services.

- ✔ **Protocol switching:** In this scheme, a protocol other than TCP/IP is used, either on the internal network or in a dead zone between the internal and external network.

- ✔ **Packet filtering:** In this firewall setup, only packets that meet specified requirements are allowed to pass through.

In this section, I look at setting up a packet-filtering firewall on a system that also provides other services.

Configuring a simple firewall with the Security Level Configuration tool

Red Hat Enterprise Linux provides a graphical tool that you can use to configure a basic firewall for your system. You can start the Security Level Configuration tool and configure your firewall by following these steps.

1. **Choose Applications⇨System Settings⇨Security Level to start the Security Level Configuration tool, as shown in Figure 10-5.**

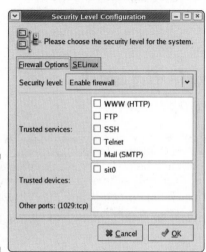

Figure 10-5:
The Security Level Configuration tool.

2. **Choose the security level that you desire by choosing either Enable Firewall or Disable Firewall from the Security Level drop-down list.**

   If you are inside a protected LAN, you can safely choose to disable the firewall.

3. **In the Trusted Services area, select the types of inbound traffic that you want to allow as a trusted service; select the type of traffic based on the services that you are running.**

   It is generally not a good idea to make an external network connection a trusted service because you don't know who will try to connect and whether that person can be trusted.

4. **Select the check box for your Ethernet connection to make it a trusted device.**

   Be aware that setting this device as trusted will allow all traffic to pass through. If you are directly connected to an external network, you should not do this.

5. **After making your choices, click OK to save your configuration.**

   The choices that you make are written to the `iptables` file, and the firewall is immediately started.

If you are not running any of the services listed, you should choose to enable the firewall but not select any devices as trusted. This will install a firewall that allows only inbound requests that are in response to outbound requests from your system.

For your firewall to be active when you boot your system, you must change your services configuration by using the Services Configuration tool or the `chkconfig` command from a command prompt. The fastest way to change the services configuration is to issue the following command:

```
/sbin/chkconfig -level 345 iptables on
```

Configuring a simple firewall with the iptables command

If you need a more complex and robust firewall than you can configure by using the graphical Security Level Configuration tool, you can use the `iptables` command from the command line. The `iptables` command is more difficult to use than the graphical tool, but you can definitely make a much more sophisticated firewall.

The iptables tool uses a series of rules that are collectively known as a *chain*. The iptables program begins with the first rule in the chain and executes each one in sequence applying the rules as appropriate. Three separate chains are examined:

- ✔ INPUT **chain:** Incoming packets are first subjected to the rules in this chain. Packets are sent to the next chain unless the packet fits the conditions of a rule that specifies DROP or REJECT, in which case they are either dropped or rejected.
- ✔ FORWARD **chain:** This chain holds rules that apply to packets that use your system to pass through to another system.
- ✔ OUTPUT **chain:** This chain tells your system what to do with packets that are outbound from your system.

To view the current iptables that was configured by using the graphical tool, you can use the /sbin/iptables -L command. The command produces the output shown in Listing 10-3.

Listing 10-3:   Output from the iptables -L Command

```
Chain INPUT (policy ACCEPT)
target     prot opt source               destination
RH-Firewall-1-INPUT  all  --  anywhere            anywhere

Chain FORWARD (policy ACCEPT)
target     prot opt source               destination
RH-Firewall-1-INPUT  all  --  anywhere            anywhere

Chain OUTPUT (policy ACCEPT)
target     prot opt source               destination

Chain RH-Firewall-1-INPUT (2 references)
target     prot opt source               destination
ACCEPT     all  --  anywhere             anywhere
ACCEPT     all  --  anywhere             anywhere
ACCEPT     icmp --  anywhere             anywhere          icmp any
ACCEPT     ipv6-crypt--  anywhere            anywhere
ACCEPT     ipv6-auth--  anywhere            anywhere
ACCEPT     all  --  anywhere             anywhere          state
               RELATED,ESTABLISHED
REJECT     all  --  anywhere             anywhere          reject-with icmp-
               host-prohibited
```

With the iptables command, you can add to the existing chains or create new ones. Here is an example of adding a rule to accept all traffic from my local network. An explanation of the syntax of the command follows the command:

```
iptables -A INPUT -s 192.168.2.0/24 -j ACCEPT
```

In the preceding command, -A INPUT tells the command to append the information that follows to the existing INPUT chain. -s 192.168.2.0/24 means from source 192.168.2.0/24, and -j ACCEPT tells the command to immediately accept all traffic.

The basic syntax for most iptables commands is similar to the following line. *Note:* This line is shown split here because of space constrictions but should be entered on a single line.

```
iptables [-t <table-name>] <command> <chain-name> <parameter> <option>
              <parameter> <option>
```

Your commands might contain more or less options and parameters than shown here, depending on the complexity of your rules. For a complete list of all options and parameters available with the iptables command, use the command iptables -h.

Although the iptables command might seem difficult to use at first, you will soon discover that it's not that difficult. For a complete list of options and some samples, refer to the man file by issuing man iptables at a terminal prompt.

Chapter 11

Intrusion Detection and Prevention

* *

In This Chapter

▶ Types of intrusion detection

▶ Using software detection tools to test your system security

* *

*I*n this chapter, I discuss *intrusion detection,* which comprises determining whether someone has entered your system without authorization. Intrusion detection is a complex subject, to say the least, and I can't possibly go into great detail in the confines of this chapter.

However, I do show you the different types of intrusion detection as well as a tool that you can use to test how vulnerable your systems are to attack. By discovering your vulnerabilities, you will be able to implement a plan to prevent future intrusions of the type that you detected. Finally, I look at a tool, called Tripwire, which you can use to keep an eye on your systems and find unauthorized users who might have entered your systems.

Discovering the Types of Intrusion Detection

Having unauthorized users entering your systems is definitely something that you don't want to happen. Of course you want to stop them before they get in. But before you can do something about keeping out unwanted visitors, you first need to know whether someone has entered your systems. This is what intrusion detection is all about: finding out whether someone is in your system who doesn't belong there. In this section, I examine two types of intrusion detection: active and passive.

Active detection

Most of us check to be sure that our doors are locked before we go to bed at night or leave the house. We do this to keep someone from getting into our house while we are sleeping or while we are away. In much the same way, you can actively check the locks on your system "doors" to be sure that no unauthorized users can get in. You can check the security of your systems by actively checking your systems for known attack methods by using special software designed for this purpose.

One such program that is commonly used to check systems for open ports and other types of connectivity information is nmap. With nmap, which is a network exploration tool and security scanner that is included with the default installation of Enterprise Linux, you can scan your systems to determine which ones are up and what services they are offering. You can then use the information that you obtain from the scan to determine how secure your systems are and what you can do to make them more secure if required. I look at nmap more closely in the upcoming section, "Using Software Detection Tools to Test Your System Security."

Passive detection

As its name implies, with passive detection, no direct action is taken to test the system for open ports or other vulnerabilities. This method of intrusion detection uses system log files to track all connections to the system. The log files are continuously reviewed by the system administrator for details that would indicate that the system has been compromised.

You can use the Tripwire program (see the upcoming section, "Using Tripwire to detect system changes") to take a snapshot of the system when it is fully configured and operating as it would be when connected to the network. The snapshot contains information about system configuration files and operating parameters and is stored on the system. Periodically, the snapshot is compared with the same parameters on the running system, looking for any changes. If changes are discovered, Tripwire informs you of the changes, and thus you know that your system might have been compromised.

Although passive detection can tell you that your system has been compromised, it tells you only after the break-in has occurred. Any damage that the intruder might have caused will be yours to deal with. Active detection, on the other hand, gives you the opportunity to test your systems for open vulnerabilities and to close the open holes.

Using Software Detection Tools to Test Your System Security

There are many tools that you can use to check your system security. In this section, I look at two of these tools — nmap, which you use to actively check our system ports for vulnerability; and Tripwire, which you use to passively log all system activity for you to look at and compare.

Scanning your network with nmap

nmap is a tool that you use to scan your network looking for hosts that are up as well as for open ports on those hosts. You can check to see whether nmap is installed on your system by issuing the following command:

```
rpm -q nmap
```

If nmap is installed, you see the following output, which shows the most recent release of nmap:

```
nmap-3.75.1
```

If you do not have nmap installed, you can find the rpm (Red Hat Package Manager) file on the installation CD-ROMs. Install it by using the Package Manager tool. See Chapter 18 for more information about using the Package Manager tool.

You can also install a graphical front-end to nmap to enable an easy-to-use interface. If you choose to not install the graphical front-end, you have to enter all your nmap commands from a terminal command line. You can install the graphical front-end by using the Package Manager tool.

After you are sure that nmap is installed, gather some information about your system. To start the nmap front-end, you issue the following command from a terminal command line:

```
nmapfe
```

After issuing the command, the nmap front-end opens, as shown in Figure 11-1.

You should run nmap as the root user so you can use all the scanning options. If you run nmap as a non-root user, some scanning options will be unavailable.

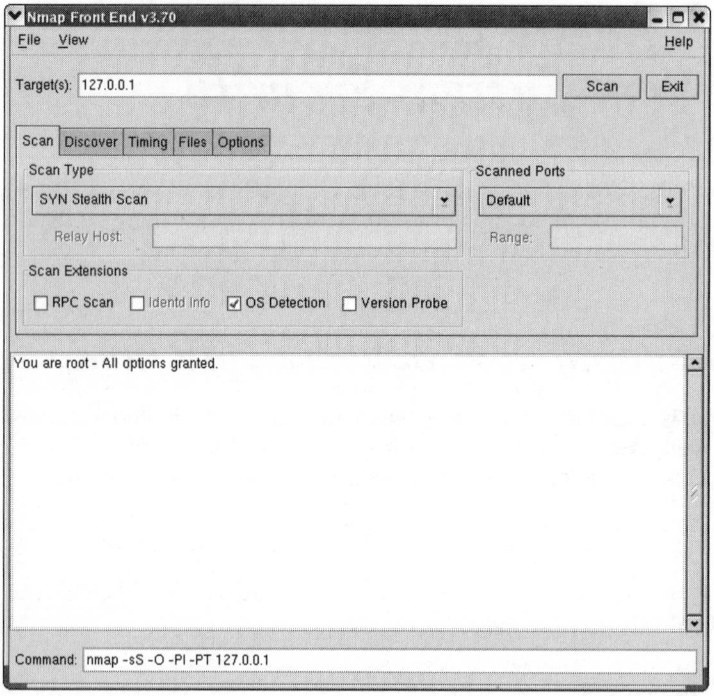

Figure 11-1:
The nmap
front-end
is an easy-
to-use
graphical
interface.

You should not run indiscriminate port scans on systems that do not belong to you. Port scanning is considered by many administrators to be an actual attack, and they will not react favorably to your scans.

Scanning your system ports with nmap

The most common use of nmap is to scan systems for open ports. An open port is like an open door into your system although having open ports is not necessarily a bad thing. For example, if you are running a Web server, you want to have at least port 80 open because this is the default port used by HTTP. You just want to make sure that you have only those ports open that you need and no more. Some commonly used port numbers and their services are

- ✔ **Port 21:** Used by FTP
- ✔ **Port 22:** Used by SSH
- ✔ **Port 25:** Used by SMTP
- ✔ **Port 53:** Used by DNS
- ✔ **Port 80:** Used by HTTP
- ✔ **Port 110:** Used by POP3

To get a list of ports and their uses, go to

```
www.iana.org/assignments/port-numbers
```

To begin scanning your system, follow these steps:

1. **In the Target(s) field (refer to Figure 11-1), enter the IP address or host and domain name of the system that you want to scan.**

   Hint: Accept the default or enter **localhost**.

2. **Click the down arrow in the Scan Type field and choose from one of the following options:**

   ✔ **Connect Scan:** This is the most basic form of TCP scanning. The connect() system call provided by your operating system is used to open a connection to every commonly used port on the machine. If the port is listening, connect() will succeed; otherwise, the port isn't reachable.

   ✔ **SYN Stealth Scan:** In this scan, you send a SYN packet — like you are opening a real connection — and you wait for a response. A SYN|ACK response means the port is listening, and an RST response means the port is not listening. If a SYN|ACK is received, an RST is immediately sent to tear down (close) the connection. Most sites will not log this type of scan. This is the default scan type for the root user.

   Whenever one system (call it system A) attempts to connect with another system (call it system B) by using the TCP protocol, it sends a packet — known as a SYN (synchronize) packet, requesting a connection. System B responds to system A with a SYN|ACK (acknowledgement) packet. System A then replies to system B with an ACK packet, and the connection is established. When system A sends an RST (reset) packet, it tells system B to close the connection.

   ✔ **ACK Stealth Scan:** This scan type sends an ACK packet to the ports specified. If an RST comes back, the port is listed as *unfiltered,* meaning there is no firewall performing packet filtering. If nothing is returned or if an ICMP (Internet Control Message Protocol) unreachable response is returned, the port is shown as filtered. ICMP is the protocol used to transmit messages about events occurring on TCP/IP networks. This type of scan can be used to determine firewall rules in place on the scanned system.

   ✔ **FIN|ACK Stealth Scan:** This scan sends a FIN (finished signal used to terminate a session) and an ACK packet to the specified system. A closed port is required to reply to your probe packet with an RST, and an open port must ignore the packets. These scans are designed to be even more nondetectable by the target systems.

✓ **FIN Stealth Scan:** This scan sends a FIN to the specified system. A closed port is required to reply to your probe packet with an RST, and an open port must ignore the packets. These scans are designed to be even more nondetectable by the target systems.

✓ **NULL Stealth Scan:** This scan type turns off all flags and doesn't send any packet information. A closed port is required to reply to your probe packet with an RST, and an open port must ignore the packets. These scans are designed to be even more nondetectable by the target systems.

✓ **Xmas Tree Stealth Scan:** This scan type sends a FIN, an URG (urgent pointer flag set, indicating priority of packet), and a PUSH flag. The *PUSH flag* means that the sender called the push operation, telling the receiver that it should notify the receiving process. A closed port is required to reply to your probe packet with an RST, and an open port must ignore the packets. These scans are designed to be even more nondetectable by the target systems.

✓ **TCP Window Scan:** This scan is like the ACK scan in that it finds filtered and unfiltered ports. The difference between the Window scan and an ACK scan is that sometimes the Window scan can detect open ports.

✓ **UDP Port Scan:** This scan type is used to determine which User Datagram Protocol (UDP) ports are open on the target host.

✓ **IP Protocol Scan:** This scan type is used to determine which IP protocols are supported by the scanned system.

✓ **Ping Sweep:** Choosing this scan option sends an ICMP ping request to the targeted hosts but will not do any other type of scan.

✓ **Host List:** This scan type is used to get a list of IP addresses or hostnames. No scanning is done on any of the listed systems.

✓ **FTP Bounce Attack:** This scan type looks for an error in the FTP protocol that allows a user to send data from an FTP server to anywhere.

✓ **Idle Scan:** This scan type lets you scan a target but send the IP address of another system as the source of the scan to the target.

3. **For this example, select the SYN Stealth Scan default scan type.**

This scan does not implement a full connection to the scanned system and is not detectable by most systems.

4. **For Scanned Ports, accept the default choice.**

This scans the most commonly used ports.

5. **Click the Scan button next to the Target(s) field.**

The scan begins. After a few seconds, your results appear. Figure 11-2 shows the results of running the SYN Stealth Scan on my system.

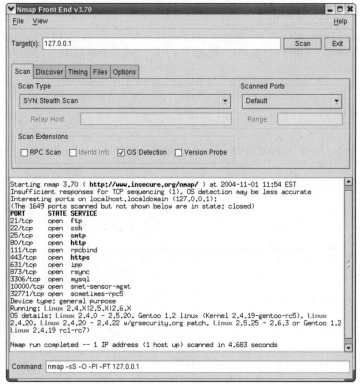

Figure 11-2:
The results
of running
nmap on my
system.

 The Command field at the bottom of the nmap graphical front-end shows the actual command that is being executed. These are the same commands that can be entered at the command line if desired.

Take a closer look at the output of the nmap command. The output shows the port number and protocol, the state of the port (open or closed), and the service that is running on that port. Looking at Figure 11-2, you can see that nearly all the ports are closed and that only a few services are running.

Closing ports for unused services

In Figure 11-2, you can see that one of the services running is ftp. This is fine if you're running an FTP server, but suppose that you are not. You would want to close port 21 to prevent someone from attempting to access your system through that port. Similarly, if you are running a Web server, you need to have port 80 open. Conversely, if you're not running a Web server, you don't need to have port 80 open. (For more on running a Web server, see Chapter 15.)

How you close an open port depends on how the service is controlled. In Enterprise Linux, some of the services are run as standalone servers, and some are controlled by the `xinetd` server. You can find out which services are standalone and which are controlled by `xinetd` by running the `chkconfig` command. Issuing this command lists all services, both those controlled by `xinetd` and those that are standalone. Issue the `chkconfig -list` command at a terminal command line to obtain the output similar to that shown in Listing 11-1:

Listing 11-1:   chkconfig -list Command Output

```
[root@terry xinetd.d]# chkconfig --list
ntpd            0:off   1:off   2:off   3:off   4:off   5:off   6:off
syslog          0:off   1:off   2:on    3:on    4:on    5:on    6:off
vmware          0:off   1:off   2:off   3:off   4:off   5:off   6:off
wine            0:off   1:off   2:on    3:on    4:on    5:on    6:off
netfs           0:off   1:off   2:off   3:on    4:on    5:on    6:off
network         0:off   1:off   2:on    3:on    4:on    5:on    6:off
random          0:off   1:off   2:on    3:on    4:on    5:on    6:off
rawdevices      0:off   1:off   2:off   3:on    4:on    5:on    6:off
saslauthd       0:off   1:off   2:off   3:on    4:on    5:on    6:off
xinetd          0:off   1:off   2:off   3:on    4:on    5:on    6:off
portmap         0:off   1:off   2:off   3:on    4:on    5:on    6:off
apmd            0:off   1:off   2:on    3:off   4:on    5:off   6:off
atd             0:off   1:off   2:off   3:on    4:on    5:on    6:off
gpm             0:off   1:off   2:off   3:off   4:off   5:off   6:off
autofs          0:off   1:off   2:off   3:on    4:on    5:on    6:off
irda            0:off   1:off   2:off   3:off   4:off   5:off   6:off
isdn            0:off   1:off   2:off   3:off   4:off   5:off   6:off
smartd          0:off   1:off   2:on    3:on    4:on    5:on    6:off
kudzu           0:off   1:off   2:off   3:on    4:on    5:on    6:off
nscd            0:off   1:off   2:off   3:off   4:off   5:off   6:off
sshd            0:off   1:off   2:on    3:on    4:on    5:on    6:off
snmpd           0:off   1:off   2:off   3:off   4:off   5:off   6:off
snmptrapd       0:off   1:off   2:off   3:off   4:off   5:off   6:off
sendmail        0:off   1:off   2:on    3:on    4:on    5:on    6:off
iptables        0:off   1:off   2:on    3:on    4:on    5:on    6:off
nfs             0:off   1:off   2:off   3:off   4:off   5:off   6:off
nfslock         0:off   1:off   2:off   3:on    4:on    5:on    6:off
rhnsd           0:off   1:off   2:off   3:on    4:on    5:on    6:off
pcmcia          0:off   1:off   2:off   3:off   4:on    5:off   6:off
crond           0:off   1:off   2:on    3:on    4:on    5:on    6:off
anacron         0:off   1:off   2:on    3:on    4:on    5:on    6:off
xfs             0:off   1:off   2:on    3:on    4:on    5:on    6:off
ypbind          0:off   1:off   2:off   3:off   4:off   5:off   6:off
named           0:off   1:off   2:off   3:off   4:off   5:off   6:off
lisa            0:off   1:off   2:off   3:off   4:off   5:off   6:off
firstboot       0:off   1:off   2:off   3:off   4:off   5:off   6:off
```

```
httpd           0:off   1:off   2:off   3:on    4:on    5:on    6:off
aep1000         0:off   1:off   2:off   3:off   4:off   5:off   6:off
bcm5820         0:off   1:off   2:off   3:off   4:off   5:off   6:off
winbind         0:off   1:off   2:off   3:off   4:off   5:off   6:off
smb             0:off   1:off   2:off   3:off   4:off   5:off   6:off
squid           0:off   1:off   2:off   3:off   4:off   5:off   6:off
tux             0:off   1:off   2:off   3:off   4:off   5:off   6:off
webmin          0:off   1:off   2:on    3:on    4:off   5:on    6:off
microcode_ctl   0:off   1:off   2:on    3:on    4:on    5:on    6:off
irqbalance      0:off   1:off   2:off   3:off   4:off   5:off   6:off
eloq6           0:off   1:off   2:on    3:on    4:on    5:on    6:off
messagebus      0:off   1:off   2:off   3:on    4:on    5:on    6:off
cups            0:off   1:off   2:on    3:on    4:on    5:on    6:off
vsftpd          0:off   1:off   2:off   3:off   4:off   5:off   6:off
mysqld          0:off   1:off   2:off   3:on    4:on    5:on    6:off
lircd           0:off   1:off   2:off   3:off   4:off   5:off   6:off
nagios          0:off   1:off   2:off   3:on    4:on    5:on    6:off
innd            0:off   1:off   2:off   3:off   4:off   5:off   6:off
yum             0:off   1:off   2:off   3:off   4:off   5:off   6:off
snortd          0:off   1:off   2:on    3:on    4:on    5:on    6:off
xinetd based services:
        chargen-udp:    off
        rsync:          on
        chargen         off
        daytime-udp:    off
        daytime:        off
        echo-udp:       off
        echo:           off
        services:       on
        servers:        off
        time-udp:       off
        time:           off
        swat:           on
        rsh:            on
        cups-lpd:       off
        sgi_fam:        on
        ktalk:          off
        rexec:          on
        vsftpd:         on
```

The output is divided into two sections. The services listed at the top are standalone services, and those listed under the xinetd-based services heading are controlled by xinetd. (For more information on xinetd, see Chapter 10.)

To turn off a standalone service — the httpd Web server for example — issue the following command:

```
/sbin/service httpd stop
```

To prevent the service from starting when the server is rebooted, enter the following command:

```
/sbin/chkconfig -level 345 httpd off
```

To turn off a service that is controlled by xinetd, you need to change the configuration file for the service in the /etc/xinetd.d directory. For example, suppose that you want to disable the FTP server to close its port. Use a text editor to open the vsftpd configuration file and then change the line disable = no to disable = yes. Then issue the following command to restart the xinetd server:

```
/sbin/service xinetd restart
```

Now you can run the nmap scan on your system again; this time, the ftp service does not appear in the list of services, and its respective port is also no longer open. Figure 11-3 shows the results of turning the ftp service off for my system.

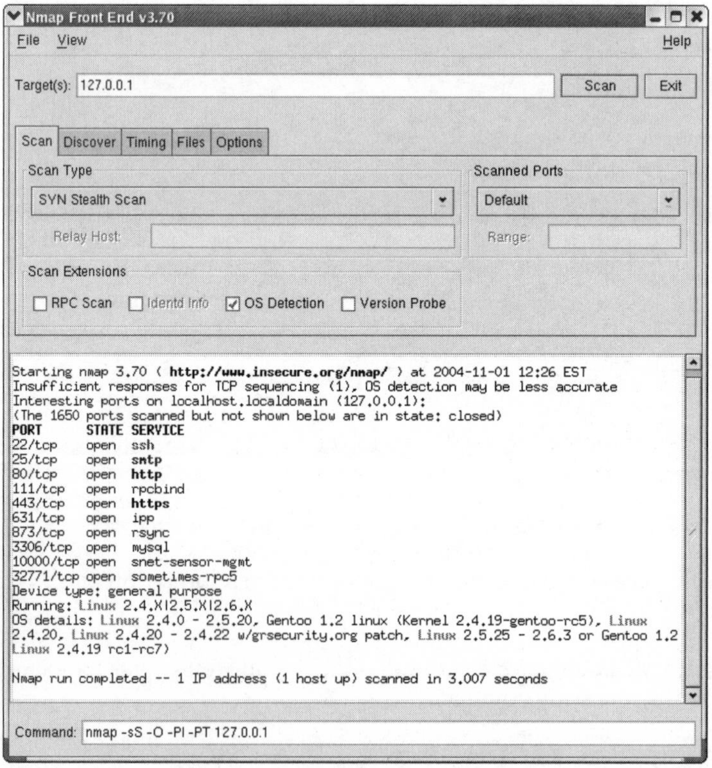

Figure 11-3: The results of the nmap scan after turning off the ftp service.

Many options can be chosen when running nmap scans of your systems. I suggest that you run the program and try different options to see their effect on your scan output. You can also try enabling and disabling different services to see their effect on the nmap scans.

Using Tripwire to detect system changes

Tripwire is often referred to as *file integrity software*. Tripwire works by creating a database of important files and file systems on your system. The program compares the saved database information with the same information on the operating system at some time in the future. A report that lists changes to the files or file systems is generated by Tripwire. The changes might or might not be an indicator of an intrusion or that the system has been compromised.

Depending on the use of the system, it might not be necessary or even advisable to install Tripwire. If you use your system for testing or if you frequently change system files, you probably don't want to use software that is meant to detect changes to system files because you will receive many notices about the changes.

Before you can put Tripwire to work for you, you must first install and configure it.

Installing Tripwire

Tripwire was included in previous versions of Red Hat Linux, but since the move to Enterprise Linux by Red Hat, Tripwire is no longer included with the standard distribution. However, I believe that Tripwire is useful enough to warrant installing it on an Enterprise system. You can find Tripwire, at no cost, at

```
http://rpm.chaz6.com/?p=fedora/tripwire/tripwire-2.3.1-18.fdr.3.1.fc2.i686.rpm
```

I recommend installing Tripwire immediately after installing the operating system. You should not connect your system to any network until you have installed and configured Tripwire. After you download the rpm file, install it by entering the following command:

```
rpm -Uvh tripwire-2.3.1-18.fdr.3.1.fc2.i686.rpm
```

Installing the Tripwire rpm file places several files and directories on your system. The directories and the files that they contain are

- /usr/sbin: This directory contains the Tripwire executable files. These files are tripwire, twadmin, and twprint.

- ✔ /etc/tripwire: This directory contains the installation script, the configuration and policy files, and the local and site keys. *Policy files* contain details about the files on your system.

- ✔ /var/lib/tripwire: This directory contains the Tripwire database file, which is typically named *your.host.name*.twd.

- ✔ /var/lib/tripwire/report: This directory contains the reports generated by Tripwire. By default, Tripwire is scheduled to run once each day. Tripwire report files are typically named *your.host.name-date and time*.twr.

The documentation for Tripwire is installed in /usr/share/doc/trip wire-2.3.1. Be sure to read the release notes and readme files for important information about Tripwire.

Configuring Tripwire

After installing the Tripwire rpm, you must run the Tripwire install script that will ask you for passphrases and generate the encryption keys to protect the Tripwire configuration and policy files. To run the installation script, do the following:

1. **Open a terminal and enter** su – **to become the root user.**

2. **Change to the** /etc/tripwire **directory with the command** cd /etc/tripwire.

3. **Enter** ./twinstall.sh **at the command line and then press Enter.**

4. **After the script starts to run, you are prompted to enter site and local keyfile passphrases.**

   Figure 11-4 shows the beginning of the install process. Be sure to pay attention to the suggestions about choosing passphrases.

   After the keys have been generated and the files signed, you see a message about the file being written.

5. **Set up the initial database for Tripwire to use. Enter the command** tripwire -m i **at a command prompt.**

6. **Enter your local passphrase when prompted.**

   The command to create the database runs for a few minutes. While the command runs, you might see error messages about missing files, as shown in Figure 11-5. You can safely ignore these messages for now; however, in the future when you run Tripwire reports, you need to pay attention to the messages because they could be an indication of an intruder in your system.

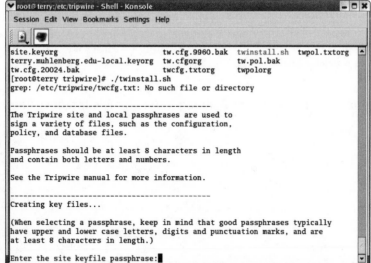

Figure 11-4:
Running the
`twinstall`
script to set
up Tripwire
on your
system.

After the database is created, you see a message to that effect, as shown
in Figure 11-5.

7. **Run the first Tripwire integrity check to compare your newly created
   database with your system files. Enter the command** tripwire -m c **at a
   terminal prompt to start the integrity check.**

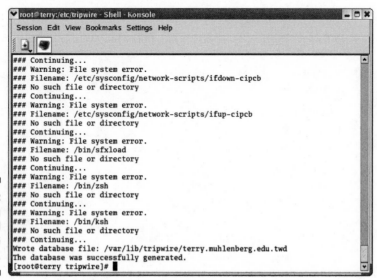

Figure 11-5:
Creating
the initial
Tripwire
database.

Running the integrity check can take some time to complete while Tripwire compares the system files with those listed in its database. After the integrity check completes, a report is written to the screen and also to the `/var/lib/tripwire/report` directory. A typical Tripwire report is shown in Listing 11-2.

Listing 11-2:   Results of Running a Tripwire File Integrity Check

```
Tripwire(R) 2.3.0 Integrity Check Report

Report generated by:        root
Report created on:          Tue 02 Nov 2004 10:50:08 AM EST
Database last updated on:   Never


===============================================================================
Report Summary:
===============================================================================


Host name:                  terry.muhlenberg.edu
Host IP address:            127.0.0.1
Host ID:                    None
Policy file used:           /etc/tripwire/tw.pol
Configuration file used:    /etc/tripwire/tw.cfg
Database file used:         /var/lib/tripwire/terry.muhlenberg.edu.twd
Command line used:          tripwire -m c


===============================================================================
Rule Summary:
===============================================================================


-------------------------------------------------------------------------------
  Section: Unix File System
-------------------------------------------------------------------------------


  Rule Name                          Severity Level   Added   Removed  Modified
  ---------                          --------------   -----   -------  --------
  Invariant Directories              66               0       0        0
  Temporary directories              33               0       0        0
* Tripwire Data Files                100              1       0        0
  Critical devices                   100              0       0        0
  User binaries                      66               0       0        0
  Tripwire Binaries                  100              0       0        0
  Critical configuration files       100              0       0        0
  Libraries                          66               0       0        0
  Operating System Utilities         100              0       0        0
  Critical system boot files         100              0       0        0
  File System and Disk Administraton Programs
                                     100              0       0        0
  Kernel Administration Programs     100              0       0        0
  Networking Programs                100              0       0        0
```

```
         System Administration Programs  100              0          0          0
         Hardware and Device Control Programs
                                         100              0          0          0
         System Information Programs      100              0          0          0
         Application Information Programs
                                         100              0          0          0
         Shell Related Programs           100              0          0          0
         Critical Utility Sym-Links       100              0          0          0
         Shell Binaries                   100              0          0          0
         System boot changes              100              0          0          0
         OS executables and libraries     100              0          0          0
         Security Control                 100              0          0          0
         Login Scripts                    100              0          0          0
    *    Root config files                100              2          2          2

    Total objects scanned:  52230
    Total violations found:  7


    ================================================================================
    Object Summary:
    ================================================================================


    --------------------------------------------------------------------------------
    # Section: Unix File System
    --------------------------------------------------------------------------------


    --------------------------------------------------------------------------------
    Rule Name: Tripwire Data Files (/var/lib/tripwire)
    Severity Level: 100
    --------------------------------------------------------------------------------


    Added:
    "/var/lib/tripwire/terry.muhlenberg.edu.twd"


    --------------------------------------------------------------------------------
    Rule Name: Root config files (/root)
    Severity Level: 100
    --------------------------------------------------------------------------------


    Added:
    "/root/.xauth8xykPy"
    "/root/mbox"

    Removed:
    "/root/.xauthG449Xj"
    "/root/.xauthv7qdP3"

    Modified:
    "/root"
    "/root/.viminfo"
```

(continued)

Listing 11-2: *(continued)*

```
===================================================================
Error Report:
===================================================================


-------------------------------------------------------------------
  Section: Unix File System
-------------------------------------------------------------------


1.   File system error.
     Filename: /usr/sbin/fixrmtab
     No such file or directory
2.   File system error.
     Filename: /bin/sfxload
     No such file or directory


-------------------------------------------------------------------
*** End of report ***

Tripwire 2.3 Portions copyright 2000 Tripwire, Inc. Tripwire is a registered
trademark of Tripwire, Inc. This software comes with ABSOLUTELY NO WARRANTY;
for details use --version. This is free software which may be redistributed
or modified only under certain conditions; see COPYING for details.
All rights reserved.
Integrity check complete.
```

Next, you modify the Tripwire policy file. You might notice that the report has generated some errors, indicating missing files or directories. You can edit the twpol.txt file to comment out the entries for these files to prevent future error messages from occurring.

Editing the Tripwire policy file

You can edit the /etc/twpol.txt policy file to comment out files that are not on your system. Then when Tripwire does its next integrity check, you won't see error messages about files that you know aren't on your system. To comment out a filename, do the following:

1. **Open the /etc/tripwire/twpol.txt file via your favorite text editor.**

2. **Find the line that matches the filename of the file that you want to comment out.**

    For example, in Listing 11-2, one of the files shown is /bin/sfxload.

3. **Scroll down the twpol.txt file until you find the line containing /bin/sfxload and then place a pound sign (#) in front of the filename that you want commented out, as shown in Figure 11-6.**

4. **Comment out all the filenames for which you received errors in the report.**

```
/etc/tripwire/twpol.txt - Text Editor

File  Edit  Go  Tools  Settings  Help


# Hardware and Device Control Programs.

(
  rulename = "Hardware and Device Control Programs",
  severity = $(SIG_HI)
)
{
  /bin/setserial                    -> $(SEC_CRIT) ;
  #/bin/sfxload                       -> $(SEC_CRIT) ;
  /sbin/blockdev            |        -> $(SEC_CRIT) ;
  /sbin/cardctl                     -> $(SEC_CRIT) ;
  /sbin/cardmgr                     -> $(SEC_CRIT) ;
  #/sbin/cbq                          -> $(SEC_CRIT) ;
  /sbin/dump_cis                    -> $(SEC_CRIT) ;
  /sbin/elvtune                     -> $(SEC_CRIT) ;
  /sbin/hotplug                     -> $(SEC_CRIT) ;

                                        INS   Line: 449 Col: 29
```

Figure 11-6: Commenting out a file name in the /etc/ tripwire /twpol. txt file.

5. **After you make changes to the policy file, you need to create a new signed policy file and create a new database file based on the new policy information. To create a new policy file, enter the following command:**

   ```
   twadmin -m P -S /etc/tripwire/site.key /etc/tripwire/twpol.txt
   ```

6. **Update the Tripwire database file by first removing the old database file and then creating a new database file. To delete the database file, enter the following command:**

   ```
   rm /var/lib/tripwire/your.host.name.twd
   ```

7. **Create the new database by running the following command:**

   ```
   tripwire -m i
   ```

   You successfully installed and configured Tripwire.

Viewing Tripwire reports

After you install and configure Tripwire to detect changes to your file system integrity, you want to see the results of Tripwire's scans. Tripwire saves all its reports in the /var/lib/tripwire/report directory. If you want to see a list of the reports, you can use the ls command to get a listing of the directory. For example, a listing of my /var/lib/tripwire/report directory shows the following:

```
[root@terry tripwire]# ls /var/lib/tripwire/report
terry.muhlenberg.edu-20040929-104529.twr
terry.muhlenberg.edu-20040930-045900.twr
terry.muhlenberg.edu-20041001-051950.twr
terry.muhlenberg.edu-20041002-041007.twr
terry.muhlenberg.edu-20041003-040932.twr
```

```
terry.muhlenberg.edu-20041004-040936.twr
terry.muhlenberg.edu-20041005-041014.twr
terry.muhlenberg.edu-20041006-041003.twr
terry.muhlenberg.edu-20041007-041553.twr
terry.muhlenberg.edu-20041008-040700.twr
terry.muhlenberg.edu-20041009-040634.twr
```

To view the contents of any of the Tripwire reports, you can use the `twprint` command. The basic syntax for `twprint` is

```
twprint -m r -r reportname
```

If you want to see the report from October 9, 2004, you enter the following command (amended for your database, of course):

```
twprint -m r -r /var/lib/tripwire/report/terry.muhlenberg.
        edu-20041009-040634.twr
```

The report is far too long to display here, but the most significant area of the report is the error section. This is where you see the instances of file system integrity violations.

If you recently installed or upgraded software on your system, these changes will be shown as errors by Tripwire. You can correct these errors so they won't appear in future reports by editing the `/etc/twpol.txt` file as discussed earlier in this section.

If you didn't make any changes to your system, the errors shown could be an indication that your system was broken into. In this case, you should replace the changed files by restoring them from the originals or reinstalling the application in question.

Part IV

Configuring Your Enterprise Linux Internet Services

The 5th Wave   By Rich Tennant

"...so if you have a message for someone, you write it on a piece of paper and put it on their refrigerator with these magnets. It's just until we get our e-mail system fixed."

In this part . . .

This part is all about sharing with others. You remember when you were a kid, and your parents taught you to share? Well, this part has nothing to do with that kind of sharing: Its' all about sharing *services*. Chapter 12 explains DNS and how to set up your DNS servers. In Chapter 13, you get to be a mailman. Not really, but you do read about configuring an e-mail server. If you have ever wanted to get on the Web and be able to upload and download files, Chapters 14 and 15 are for you. In Chapter 14, you discover how easy it is to set up an FTP server; in Chapter 15, you configure your very own Web server.

Chapter 12

Configuring and Managing DNS Servers

In This Chapter

▶ Translating Web names to IP addresses

▶ Discovering the types of DNS servers

▶ Examining the DNS server configuration files

▶ Configuring a caching DNS server

▶ Configuring a secondary master DNS server

▶ Configuring a primary master DNS server

▶ Checking your configuration

*I*n this chapter, you discover the *Domain Name System* (DNS), which is used for name address resolution. The DNS is controlled by a program called bind, which is used for finding hosts on TCP/IP networks. I also talk about the different types of DNS servers and how to configure them for your own network. After configuring your servers, you can read about some diagnostic tools that can be used to check the configuration and performance of your DNS servers.

Translating Web Names to IP Addresses

Translating Web names to IP addresses is properly known as *name address resolution*. Name address resolution is, simply stated, the conversion of people-friendly names into computer-friendly numbers. Each interface on the network has an IP address that is expressed as a dotted quad group: for example, 192.168.2.1. These groups of numbers present no problem to the computers in the network, but it's not so easy for people to remember many groups of numbers. Thus, you need to be able to enter names and then have these names converted into numbers. Each time you type a Web site's address into your browser, the DNS goes to work. You enter names that are easy for you to remember, like www.redhat.com, and the names are resolved into numbers that computers find easy to understand. Enabling efficient human/machine interaction is the function of name address resolution.

For example, take a look at domain names and their organization, using the domain name muhlenberg.edu. The first part of this domain name, muhlenberg, is the name of the company, institution, or organization. The next part, after the period (*dot* in today's vernacular) is the top-level domain. In addition to the edu top-level domain, you will find a few others. Table 12-1 shows other top-level domains in the United States.

Table 12-1	United States Top-Level Domains	
Top-Level Domain	*Meaning*	*Example*
com	Typically a business	www.tactechnology.com
edu	An educational institution	www.muhlenberg.edu
gov	A U.S. government agency	www.whitehouse.gov
mil	A branch of the U.S. military	www.army.mil
net	A network-affiliated organization	www.tellurium.net
org	A noncommercial organization	www.lvcg.org
int	An international organization	www.wipo.int
us	The U.S. domain, with each listing as a lower level	www.state.pa.us

Top-level domains in other countries include a two-letter suffix, such as fr for France or su for Switzerland. Not all top-level domains are the same as the top-level U.S. domains, but a company in France could be http://www.frenchcompany.com.fr.

Large domains can be further broken down into subdomains. For example, the (state of) Pennsylvania Web site is www.state.pa.us. The Pennsylvania state government includes many agencies, such as the Road Weather Information Service (RWIS). To find the RWIS, the state.pa.us domain contains the subdomain www.rwis.state.pa.us. An individual computer in the RWIS also has a host name: for example, lehigh. The complete name for this computer is then lehigh.rwis.state.pa.us, and you can find its IP address by using the DNS to look it up. When you type in a hostname, your system uses its resources to resolve names into IP addresses.

Types of DNS Servers

A top-level domain server, one that provides information about the domains shown in Table 12-1, is typically referred to as a *root nameserver*. When you try to find a Web site, `www.muhlenberg.edu` for example, your system sends a query to the root nameserver for `.edu` for information. The root nameserver then directs the search to a lower-level domain nameserver until the information is found.

After you find the domain that you're looking for, information about that domain is provided by its local domain nameservers. The three types of local domain nameservers are the *master server,* the *slave* (or *secondary*) *server* and the *caching server.*

✔ **Master server:** This contains all the information about the domain and supplies this information when requested. A master server is listed as an authoritative server when it contains the information that you are seeking and it can provide that information.

✔ **Slave server:** This is intended as a backup in case the master server goes down or is not available. This server contains the same information as the master and provides it when requested if the master server cannot be contacted.

✔ **Caching server:** A caching server does not provide information to outside sources; it is used to provide domain information to other servers and workstations on the local network. The caching server remembers the domains that have been accessed. Use of a caching server speeds up searches because the domain information is already stored in memory, and the server knows exactly where to go rather than having to send out a request for domain information.

Where does the information that the master and slave servers provide come from? The server(s) have to be configured, either by you or someone else, to provide it when asked. DNS configuration information is contained in files that are referred to as *zone files.* In the next sections, you see how to configure the servers to provide domain name information.

Examining the DNS Server Configuration Files

Before you begin to configure your servers, you need to take a closer look at the files you need to configure. You need five files to set up the named server. Three files are required regardless of the configuration as a master, slave, or caching-only server, and two additional files are used on the master server.

The three required files are

- named.conf: Found in the /etc directory, this file contains global properties and sources of configuration files.
- named.ca: Found in /var/named, this file contains the names and addresses of root servers.
- named.local: Found in /var/named, this file provides information for resolving the loopback address for the localhost.

The two additional files required for the master domain server are

- zone: This file contains the names and addresses of servers and workstations in the local domain and maps names to IP addresses.
- reverse zone: This file provides information to map IP addresses to names.

You begin with the /etc/named.conf file, which is shown in Listing 12-1.

Listing 12-1:   The /etc/named.conf file

```
//
// named.conf for Red Hat caching-nameserver
//

options {
             directory "/var/named";
             dump-file "/var/named/data/cache_dump.db";
             statistics-file "/var/named/data/named_stats.txt";
             /*
             * If there is a firewall between you and nameservers you want
             * to talk to, you might need to uncomment the query-source
             * directive below.  Previous versions of BIND always asked
             * questions using port 53, but BIND 8.1 uses an unprivileged
             * port by default.
             */
             // query-source address * port 53;
};


//
// a caching only nameserver config
//
controls {
             inet 127.0.0.1 allow { localhost; } keys { rndckey; };
};

zone "." IN {
             type hint;
             file "named.ca";
};
```

```
zone "localdomain" IN {
          type master;
          file "localdomain.zone";
          allow-update { none; };
};

zone "localhost" IN {
          type master;
          file "localhost.zone";
          allow-update { none; };
};

zone "0.0.127.in-addr.arpa" IN {
          type master;
          file "named.local";
          allow-update { none; };
};
include "/etc/rndc.key";
```

The named.conf file

Look at this file in more detail beginning with the lines starting with //. These are comment lines and anything following them is ignored. Commands are passed to the file in the form of statements. Several of these statements are shown in the sample file, but you actually can use seven configuration statements. The following list briefly explains their functions:

- ✔ options: Lists global configurations and defaults.
- ✔ include: Gets information from another file and includes it.
- ✔ acl: Specifies IP addresses used in an access control list.
- ✔ logging: Specifies log file locations and contents.
- ✔ server: Specifies properties of remote servers.
- ✔ zone: Specifies information about zones.
- ✔ key: Specifies security keys used for authentication.

Information about the statement is contained within curly braces and terminated by a semicolon: {information about server};.

Options

The options statement is typically the first section of named.conf, and it contains information about the location of the files used by named. You can use only one options statement, but you can have more than one value for that statement. In the sample file shown in Listing 12-1, the options statement shows the path to where additional configuration files used by named are located. By specifying the directory where other files are located, it is not necessary to list the entire path to the file, just the name of the file for any files shown in the remainder of named.conf. Options statements use the following syntax:

```
options {
     value "property";
}
```

The list of values that can be used in the options statement is quite long. These values are shown, listed alphabetically, in Table 12-2.

Table 12-2	Options Values and Their Meanings	
Value	*Meaning*	*Usage*
allow-query	Accepts queries only from hosts in the address list (by default, queries are accepted from any host).	allow-query {"address-list"};
allow-transfer	Zone transfers are accepted only by hosts in the address list (by default, transfers are allowed to all hosts).	allow-transfer {"address list"};
auth-nxdomain	The server responds as an authoritative server (defaults to yes).	auth-nxdomain "yes or no"; (choose one)
check-names	Host names are checked for compliance with the RFC.	check-names "master or slave or response warn or fail or ignore"; (choose one from each group)
cleaning-interval	Specifies the time period before the server removes expired resource records (defaults to 60 minutes).	cleaning-interval "number"; (specify number in minutes)
coresize	Specifies largest size for core dump files.	coresize "size"; (specify size in bytes)
datasize	Limits server memory usage.	datasize "size"; (specify size in bytes)
deallocate-on-exit	Detects memory leaks (default is no).	deallocate-on-exit "yes or no"; (choose one)

Value	Meaning	Usage
directory	Path of the directory where server configuration files are located.	directory "path to directory"; (specify path)
dump-file	If named receives a SIGINT signal, it dumps the database to the file specified here (defaults to named_dump.db).	
fake-iquery	If set to yes, the server sends a fake reply to inverse queries rather than an error (default is no).	fake-iquery " yes or no"; (choose one)
fetch-glue	If set to yes, the server obtains the glue records for a response (default is yes).	fetch-glue "yes or no"; (choose one)
files	Limits number of concurrently open files (default is unlimited).	files "number"; (specify number)
forward	If set to first, the servers listed in the forwarders option are queried first, and then the server tries to find the answer itself. If set to only, just the servers in the forwarders list are queried.	forward "first or only"; (choose one)
forwarders	Shows IP addresses of servers to forward queries (default is none).	forwarders "IP addresses of servers"; (specify IP addresses)
host-statistics	If set to yes, the server keeps statistics on hosts (default is no).	host-statistics "yes or no"; (choose one)
interface-interval	Specifies interval for searching the network for new or removed interfaces (default is 60 minutes).	interface-interval "time"; (specify time in minutes)
listen-on	Specifies port and interfaces on which server listens for queries (default is port 53).	listen-on "port {address list}"; (specify port number and address list)

(continued)

Table 12-2 *(continued)*

Value	Meaning	Usage
max-transfer-time-in	Specifies the time the server waits for completion of inbound transfer (default is 120 minutes).	max-transfer-time-in "time"; (specify time in minutes)
memstatistics-file	When deallocate-on-exit is set, specifies the file where memory statistics are written (defaults to named.memstats).	memstatistics-file "path to file"; (specify path and file name)
multiple-cnames	When set to yes, enables multiple CNAME usage (default is no).	multiple-cnames "yes or no"; (choose one)
named-xfer	Specifies path to the named-xfer program.	named-xfer "path to file"; (specify path)
notify	When zone files are updated, this option, when set to yes, sends DNS NOTIFY messages (default is yes).	notify "yes or no"; (choose one)
pid-file	Name of file holding process ID.	pid-file "path to file"; (specify path and file name)
query-source	Specifies port and IP address used to query other servers.	query-source "address port"; (specify IP address and port)
recursion	The server recursively searches for query answers (default is yes).	recursion " yes or no"; (choose one)
stacksize	The amount of stack memory the server can use.	stacksize "number"; (specify the amount of memory)
statistics-interval	The time interval for logging statistics (default is 60 minutes).	statistics-interval "time"; (specify the time in minutes)
topology	Sets server preference for remote servers.	topology {"address list"};

Value	Meaning	Usage
transfer-format	When set to one-answer, only one resource record per message is sent. When set to many-answers, as many records as possible are transmitted in each message. (default is one-answer).	transfer-format "one-answer many-answers"; (choose one)
transfers-in	Maximum concurrent inbound zone transfers (default is 10).	transfers-in "number"; (specify the number)
transfers-out	Maximum concurrent outbound transfers.	transfers-out "number"; (specify the number)
transfers-per-ns	Limits inbound transfers from a single server (default is two).	transfers-per-ns "number"; (specify the number)

Include

The include statement lists the path and name of any files that you want to be included with the named.conf file. Use the same syntax as used in the options statement to specify the path.

Acl

This option lets you specify a list of IP addresses in an access control list. Only hosts on this list have access to the server.

Logging

The logging statement is where you specify your server's logging options. The logging statement contains two additional items, the channel and the category.

The channel is where you specify the location of the logged information. Logged information can be written to a file, sent to the syslog, or thrown away by specifying the appropriate command. Choosing to send the information to a file gives you several additional choices on how to handle the information. You can set the number of versions to keep, the size of the files, and whether the severity of the information and the time and category are included with the other information in the file.

The syntax for the `logging` statement is similar to the syntax for the `option` statement. The following commands send the information to a file (items in italics indicate information you need to enter):

```
logging {
       channel channel_name {
       (file    path to file
       versions specify number or unlimited
       size specify size in bytes }If you want to send the information to the
              syslog, the syntax is
logging {
       channel channel_name {
       syslog (choose where to send from following choices)
(kern,user,mail,daemon,auth,syslog,lpr,news,uucp,cron,\
       authpriv,ftp,local0 thru local7)
To discard the information, choose null as the destination.
logging {
       channel channel_name {
       null;)
```

Next, you can set the severity level for the information written to the file or syslog. This section follows the sections shown previously for file or syslog. You also indicate here if you want the time, category, and severity included. If you are discarding the information, you don't need to set these parameters.

```
severity choose from critical,error,warning,notice,info,debug\ level,dynamic
print-time choose yes or no
print-severity choose yes or no
print-category choose yes or no
};
```

The `category` is where you specify the type of information to log. This value follows the severity and print parameters and takes the following syntax:

```
category  category name {
channel name; channel name;
};
```

You can choose from over 20 categories. These are shown, alphabetically, in Table 12-3.

Table 12-3	Logging Categories
Category	*Type of Information Logged*
cname	Information about CNAME references
config	Information about configuration files
db	Information about databases

Category	Type of Information Logged
default	The default if nothing is selected
eventlib	Information about event system debugging
insist	Details about failures from internal consistency checking
lame-servers	Information about lame servers
load	Information about zone loading
maintenance	Information about maintenance
ncache	Information about negative caching
notify	Information about tracing the NOTIFY protocol
os	Information about operating system problems
packet	Dumps of all sent and received packets
panic	Information about faults that shut down the server
parser	Information about processing configuration commands
queries	Information about all received DNS queries
response-checks	Information about response-checking results
security	Information about security status of server
statistics	Information about server statistics
update	Information about dynamic updates
xfer-in	Information about inbound zone transfers
xfer-out	Information about outbound zone transfers

Using the categories from the logging statement, you can obtain a large quantity of information about your server. This information can be useful if you are having problems with your DNS. You can enable logging for the area that you think is causing your problem and then read the appropriate log to find any messages that might indicate an error with your configuration.

Server

In the server statement, you can set the properties of a remote server. You can specify whether to send queries to the remote server from the local server, and you can set the method used for transferring information. The syntax for this statement is the same as for other statements. The valid values are

- ✔ `bogus`: Specify `yes` or `no` (`no` is the default and indicates that queries are sent to the remote server). `yes` means that the remote server is not queried.
- ✔ `transfer`: Specify the number of transfers you want to allow.
- ✔ `transfer-format`: Specify whether you want `one-answer` or `many-answers`.
- ✔ `keys`: Specify key ID (currently not implemented).

Zones

The remainder of the listings in `/etc/named.conf` shown in Listing 12-1 are `zone` statements. These `zone` statements refer to files that are called zone files. Additional options for `zone` statements exist, of course. Each `zone` statement begins with the word `zone` followed by the domain name and the data class. The four data classes are `in`, `hs`, `hesiod`, and `chaos`. If no type is specified, the default is `in`, for Internet.

Next follows the type option, which specifies whether the server is a master, a slave/stub, or is the hints file. A stub server loads only NS records, not the entire domain. The hints file is used to initialize the root cache and contains a list of root servers.

Next is the name of the zone file for the specified zone. This is a pointer to the file containing the data about the zone. You look at a zone file in detail a little later in this chapter.

The following list shows the other options for the `zone` statements and explains their functions:

- ✔ `allow-query`: Accepts queries only from hosts in the address list (by default, queries are accepted from any host).
- ✔ `allow-transfer`: Zone transfers are accepted only by hosts in the address list (by default, transfers are allowed to all hosts).
- ✔ `allow-update`: Hosts in the address list are allowed to update the database.
- ✔ `also-notify`: Servers in the address list are sent a notify message when the zone is updated.
- ✔ `check-names`: Host names are checked for compliance with the RFC.
- ✔ `max-transfer-time-in`: Specifies the time the slave waits for a zone transfer.
- ✔ `notify`: When zone files are updated, this option, when set to `yes`, sends DNS NOTIFY messages (default is `yes`).

These options are the same as those shown in the `options` statement section and have the same function here. When listed in the options section, they apply to all zones, but if listed with a specific zone, they apply only to that zone. Settings listed in a specific zone section override those globally set in the `options` statement.

Zone files

Zone files contain resource records (RR) about IP addresses. A typical zone file is shown in Listing 12-2.

Listing 12-2:   A Zone File Is Used to Provide Information about a DNS Server

```
@                        IN SOA      localhost root (
                                     42                  ; serial
                                     3H                  ; refresh
                                     15M                 ; retry
                                     1W                  ; expiry
                                     1D )                ; minimum
                     IN NS   localhost
localhost            IN A            127.0.0.1
```

A zone file can contain many types of RRs, which are listed in the order in which they generally appear in the zone files, and explained next.

SOA — Start of Authority

The Start of Authority (SOA) is the first line in the zone file. The SOA identifies the name server as the authoritative source for information about this domain. Each zone file has only one SOA, and it contains the following data:

```
@  IN  SOA  main.tactechnology.com.    mail.tactechnology.com. (/
                2000052101 ; Serial
                8h          ;Refresh
                2h          ;Retry
                1w          ;Expire
                1d)         ;Minimum TTL
```

The first character in the SOA line is a special symbol that means "to look at this domain." IN means Internet. SOA means Start of Authority.

In this example, the authoritative server for this domain is `main.tac technology.com.`, and `mail.tactechnology.com.` is the e-mail address of the administrator. Note the trailing period after the domain names: If the period is not included, the domain name is appended to the entry.

The opening parenthesis enables the first line to be extended so that anything between the opening and closing parenthesis is considered one line.

The information within the parenthesis is passed to other name servers, secondary masters, which use this information to update their records. The line containing 2000052101 ; Serial is the serial number of the file. Secondary servers compare this number with their stored information. If the numbers are the same, the information has not changed and it is not necessary to download this file. If the serial numbers are different, the file is downloaded to update the information in the secondary server. The serial number can be any number desired, as long as it can be incremented to indicate a revision to the file. The semicolon indicates that what follows to the end of the line is a comment.

- Refresh: This is the amount of time the server should wait before refreshing its data.

- Retry: This is the amount of time the server should wait before attempting to contact the primary server if the previous attempt failed.

- Expire: This means that if the secondary master is unable to contact a primary master during the specified period, the data expires and should be purged.

- TTL: This specifies the Time to Live for the data. This parameter is intended for caching name servers and tells them how long to hold the data in their caches.

All of the information contained by the SOA may be placed on one line, but it is usually written as shown previously. The order of the items is significant in the SOA header. Following the SOA header information are lines containing additional server information. Two of these lines, which contain the abbreviations NS and A, are shown in Listing12-2. The following list explains the meanings of these abbreviations:

- NS: Name servers in this domain.

- A: The IP address for the name server.

- PTR: Pointer for address name mapping.

- CNAME: Canonical name, the real name of the host.

- MX: The Mail exchange record. The MX record specifies the mail servers for the domain. If more than one MX server is present,the address with the lowest number receives the highest priority.

- TXT: Text information. You can enter descriptive information here.

- WKS: Well-known service. You can enter descriptive information here.

- HINFO: Host Information usually shows type of hardware and software.

The reverse zone file

The previous example shows a sample zone file that uses the domain name. This method is called *forward address resolution* because it uses a name to find an IP number and is the most common use of name resolution.

You can also find a name from an IP number, and this is called *reverse address resolution.* All you need to do is enter the IP address, and the server returns the domain name. Reverse address resolution requires the use of a reverse zone file. Listing 12-3 shows a sample reverse zone file.

Listing 12-3:   A Typical Reverse Lookup Zone File

```
@       IN      SOA     localhost. root.localhost.  (
                        1997022700 ; Serial
                        28800      ; Refresh
                        14400      ; Retry
                        3600000    ; Expire
                        86400 )    ; Minimum
        IN      NS      localhost.
1       IN      PTR     localhost.
```

Configuring a Caching DNS Server

The previous sections show which files need to be configured and what information needs to be placed in them, which prepares you to set up your own domain name servers. In this section, you set up a caching server. As stated earlier, you use three files in all three types of server configurations. In a caching-only server, these three files make up the entire configuration. Fortunately, the default installation of BIND used on Red Hat Enterprise Linux creates the configuration files needed for a caching name server, but it is always a good idea to look at the files to be sure that they are correct.

Begin by verifying the zone information in /etc/named.conf. When you installed the BIND package, the /etc/named.conf file was created and it contained zone information for your localhost, but you need to check it to be sure. You are looking for two zone lines: one indicated by a period, referencing the file named.ca, and one shown as 0.0.127.in.addr.arpa, referencing named.local.

Next, you need to check the configuration of the /var/named/named.local file. This file contains the domain information for the localhost and is typically created when BIND is installed. You usually don't have to make any changes to /var/named/named.local. This domain is a reverse domain in that it is used to map the loopback address 127.0.0.1 to the localhost name.

You need to check the /etc/nsswitch file to be sure it contains the following line:

```
hosts:        files dns
```

You need to check the /etc/resolv.conf file to make sure that the IP address (127.0.0.1) of your localhost is listed as a name server.

Finally, you need to check that your /etc/host.conf contains the word *bind*.

After you have completed all of the previous steps, it is time to start the named daemon and check your work.

Type service named start at a command prompt, press Enter, wait for the prompt to return, and then type rndc status and press Enter. You will see output similar to this:

```
number of zones: 8
debug level: 0
xfers running: 0
xfers deferred: 0
SOA queries in progress: 0
query logging is off
server is up and running
```

You have successfully configured and started your caching name server.

Configuring a Secondary Master DNS Server

Next, you set up a secondary master or slave server for your domain. The procedure is similar to, and not much more difficult than, the procedures described previously in this chapter. You already have three of the files in place and only need to slightly modify the /etc/named.conf file and add two more files to complete the slave configuration.

On the server you want to be the slave, go to the /etc/named.conf file and add two more zones, one for the forward lookup of your server, and one for the reverse lookup. For the forward lookup, you need to add the following. (For this example, the master server is called main.tactechnology.com, and the slave is p200.tactechnology.com. Be sure to use your own domain name and IP address instead of the examples shown.)

```
zone "tactechnology.com" {
    notify no;
    type slave;
    file "tactech.com";
    masters { 192.168.1.1; };
};
```

For the reverse lookup, you add this section:

```
zone "1.168.192.in-addr.arpa" {
    notify no;
    type slave;
    file "tac.rev";
    masters { 192.168.1.1; };
};
```

After modifying the /etc/named.conf file, configuration of the slave server is now complete, and you can move on to configuring the master server.

Configuring a Primary Master Server

The /etc/named.conf file on the master server also needs to be modified. Assuming that you already set up this server as a caching-only server, you just need to add the following lines to /etc/named.conf. (This example uses the names defined as described earlier in this chapter; be sure to use your own names and IP addresses.)

```
zone "tactechnology.com" {
    notify no;
    type master;
    file "tactech.com";
};
```

For the reverse lookup, you add this section:

```
zone "1.168.192.in-addr.arpa" {
    notify no;
    type master;
    file "tac.rev";
};
```

Notice that you used the same names for the files on the master server as the slave server. This is because these files are downloaded by the slave in a zone file transfer and stored on the slave in the files shown by the file option. You did not create the files on the slave but created them on the master server.

The file names, host names, and IP addresses I use here are just examples for the purpose of this explanation. Be sure to use file names, host names, and IP addresses appropriate to your organization.

You now need to create the zone files that are referenced by the /etc/named.conf file. First, you create the file /var/named/tactech.com by beginning with the Start of Authority section (SOA). For an explanation of the information contained in zone files, refer to the "Zone files" section, earlier in this chapter.

```
@   IN  SOA   main.tactechnology.com.mail.tactechnology.com. ( /
              200005203    ; Serial/
                 8h; Refresh/
                 2h; Retry/
                 1w; Expire/
                 1d); Minimum TTL/
```

Next, you add name server and mail exchange information.

```
    NS         main.tactechnology.com./
    NS         terry.tactechnology.com./
    MX         10 main;Primary Mail Exchanger/
    MX         20 p200;Secondary Mail Exchanger/
```

Finally, you add information about your localhost, mail, FTP, and Web server. You can also add information about every workstation on your network.

Next, you set up the reverse lookup zone file called tac.rev. Again, you need to start with the SOA header as shown:

```
@  IN  SOA  main.tactechnology.com.  mail.tactechnology.com.(
          200005203;Serial
          8h       ; Refresh
          2h       ; Retry
          1w       ; Expire
          1d)      ; Minimum TTL
```

Next, you add the information about your name servers and their IP addresses:

```
        NS     main.tactechnology.com.
  1     PTR    main.tactechnology.com.
  2     PTR    p200.tactechnology.com.
```

If you have done everything as explained here, your name server should be working. You made some changes to the /etc/named.conf file, so before you can check what you did, you need to restart the named daemon.

The `named` daemon must be restarted whenever you make changes to
`/etc/named.conf`. To restart `named`, you just need to enter the following
command:

```
service named restart
```

Checking Your Configuration

After you finish configuring your master DNS server, you can check your configuration to be sure that it's working. You can use several tools to do your
check. I talk about two of them here. Just be sure to substitute your domain
and IP information when you run the commands. If your system is set up correctly, you should obtain similar results.

The host program

`host` enables you to find an IP address for the specified domain name. All
that is required is the domain name of the remote host, as shown here with
the command on the first line and the output from the command on the
second line.

```
[root@laptop root]# host tactechnology.com
tactechnology.com has address 12.129.206.112
```

You can also search for resource record types by using the `-t` option and the
type of resource record that you want to search. For example, if you want to
find information about the mail server for a domain, enter the following command and receive the following output:

```
[root@terry named]# host -t mx tactechnology.com
tactechnology.com mail is handled by 10 mail.tactechnology.com.
```

The dig program

`dig` can be used for debugging and obtaining other useful information. The
basic syntax is

```
dig (@server) domain name (type)
```

Items shown in parentheses are optional. Listing 12-4 shows an example of
using `dig` to request information about the DNS servers at my school.

Listing 12-4:   Using dig to Search for IP Addresses

```
[root@terry named]# dig muhlenberg.edu

; <<>> DiG 9.2.2-P3 <<>> muhlenberg.edu
;; global options:  printcmd
;; Got answer:
;; ->>HEADER<<- opcode: QUERY, status: NOERROR, id: 50760
;; flags: qr aa rd ra; QUERY: 1, ANSWER: 1, AUTHORITY: 1, ADDITIONAL: 1

;; QUESTION SECTION:
;muhlenberg.edu.                      IN      A

;; ANSWER SECTION:
muhlenberg.edu.         86400   IN      A       192.104.181.5

;; AUTHORITY SECTION:
muhlenberg.edu.         86400   IN      NS      hal.muhlenberg.edu.

;; ADDITIONAL SECTION:
hal.muhlenberg.edu.     86400   IN      A       192.104.181.5

;; Query time: 5 msec
;; SERVER: 192.104.181.5#53(192.104.181.5)
;; WHEN: Thu Sep  9 14:37:54 2004
;; MSG SIZE  rcvd: 82
```

dig can also be used to do reverse lookups by using the -x switch and specifying the IP address, as seen in Listing 12-5. The first line in the listing is the command entered at the command prompt, and the remaining lines are the output from the command.

Listing 12-5:   Using dig to Search for Domain Names

```
[root@terry named]# dig  -x 192.104.181.5

; <<>> DiG 9.2.2-P3 <<>> -x 192.104.181.5
;; global options:  printcmd
;; Got answer:
;; ->>HEADER<<- opcode: QUERY, status: NOERROR, id: 26961
;; flags: qr aa rd ra; QUERY: 1, ANSWER: 1, AUTHORITY: 2, ADDITIONAL: 2

;; QUESTION SECTION:
;5.181.104.192.in-addr.arpa.     IN      PTR

;; ANSWER SECTION:
5.181.104.192.in-addr.arpa. 86400 IN    PTR     hal.muhlberg.edu.

;; AUTHORITY SECTION:
181.104.192.in-addr.arpa. 86400 IN      NS      hal.muhlberg.edu.
181.104.192.in-addr.arpa. 86400 IN      NS      stimpy.nwip.muhlberg.edu.
```

```
;; ADDITIONAL SECTION:
hal.muhlberg.edu.          86400   IN       A       192.104.181.5
stimpy.nwip.muhlberg.edu. 86400 IN         A       192.104.181.207

;; Query time: 6 msec
;; SERVER: 192.104.181.5#53(192.104.181.5)
;; WHEN: Thu Sep  9 14:39:46 2004
;; MSG SIZE  rcvd: 170
```

Both of the listings provide information about the exact same servers. In Listing 12-4, I used a domain name for the search, and I received the IP addresses associated with the domain name. In Listing 12-5, I searched using an IP address, and I received the host and domain name of the servers.

Chapter 13

Configuring and Managing an E-Mail Server

***

In This Chapter

▶ How e-mail works

▶ Configuring your mail server

▶ Maintaining e-mail security

***

*W*ith your computer, you can send messages to and receive them from other computer users anywhere in the world. E-mail, as it's more commonly known, is a very powerful and useful tool. In this chapter, I show you how e-mail works and then how to configure your systems to put e-mail to work for you.

How E-Mail Works

An e-mail message, just like a letter sent through regular mail, begins with a sender and ends with a receiver. In between these two people are many postal workers who ensure that the letter is properly handled. Even though the sender and receiver might never see these workers, their functions are essential in moving the mail. E-mail works in a similar fashion, and although there are not many people between the sender and receiver, programs perform the same function. These programs use network protocols to do the job of ensuring that the message goes from sender to receiver. In this chapter, I show you how to configure e-mail to run across TCP/IP protocols.

Before configuring an e-mail client or server, you need to understand how e-mail works as well as the programs to use or make available to your users. Several key components are essential for e-mail to work properly. As a system administrator, your responsibility is to configure the following items, which are explained in more detail later in this chapter:

- ✔ A **Mail User Agent** (MUA) for users to be able to read and write e-mail
- ✔ A **Mail Transfer Agent** (MTA) to deliver the e-mail messages between computers across a network
- ✔ A **Local Delivery Agent** (LDA) to deliver messages to users' mailbox files
- ✔ The **TCP/IP protocols** for storing e-mail messages and transferring e-mail between MTAs

To see how all the various components work to accomplish their jobs, read on to discover how to track an e-mail message through the process from sending to delivery. After seeing how the components work, you then configure these components to build a fully functioning e-mail system for your server and clients.

Mail User Agent (MUA)

To be able to send mail, you (or your users) need a Mail User Agent (MUA) program. The MUA, also called a *mail client,* enables users to write and read mail messages. Two types of MUAs are available:

- ✔ A **graphical user interface (GUI):** example, Evolution
- ✔ A **command line interface:** example, `mail`

Whether your MUA is a GUI or command line interface, after the message is composed, the MUA sends it to the Mail Transfer Agent (MTA). The MTA is the program that sends the message across the network and does its work without any intervention by the user. In fact, most users are unaware of the MTA: They just see their mail client. The next section explains how to configure Evolution to send and receive e-mail.

The Ximian Evolution e-mail client

The Ximian Evolution e-mail client is a full-featured e-mail program and more. With Evolution, you can manage all your daily tasks with ease. Before you can use Evolution to send and receive mail, though, you must first configure it with your e-mail account settings.

Configuring the Evolution e-mail client

Before you can send or receive e-mail, you must configure your e-mail client as follows:

1. **Start Evolution by clicking the Evolution icon from the desktop panel (the envelope and stamp icon) or by choosing Applications⇨Internet⇨ Evolution Email.**

   The Ximian Evolution Setup Assistant window, as shown in Figure 13-1, appears.

2. **Choose Forward to go to the Identity page as shown in Figure 13-2. Then choose Tools⇨Settings from the menu bar at the top of the Evolution window.**

3. **Enter your name and e-mail address in the required fields and then click Forward to continue.**

4. **In the Receiving Email dialog box that opens, as shown in Figure 13-3, identify the type of mail server that you will connect to.**

5. **Click the down arrow to the right of the Server Type field and choose the appropriate type of mail server for your location.**

   Depending on your choice, other fields will appear on the page that require you to enter additional information. If you're not the system administrator and aren't sure what to choose here, check with your system administrator.

6. **Click Forward to continue to the Send Email dialog box in which you choose the type of mail server for sending e-mail. Click the down arrow next to the Server Type field and choose either SMTP or Sendmail.**

Figure 13-1:
Evolution
Setup
Assistant is
where you
configure
your e-mail
client.

Evolution Setup Assistant

Welcome

Welcome to Evolution. The next few screens will allow Evolution to connect to your email accounts, and to import files from other applications.

Please click the "Forward" button to continue.

✖ Cancel   ◀ Back   ▶ Forward

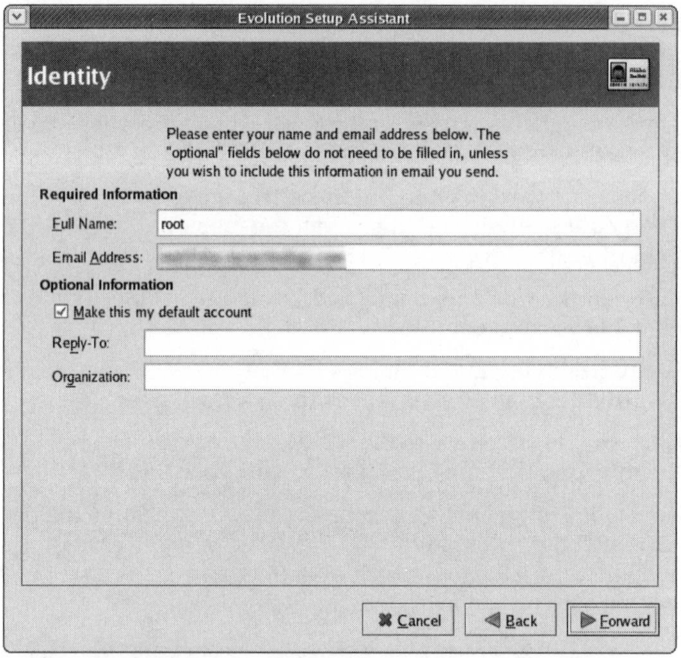

Figure 13-2:
Enter your
e-mail
identity
information
here.

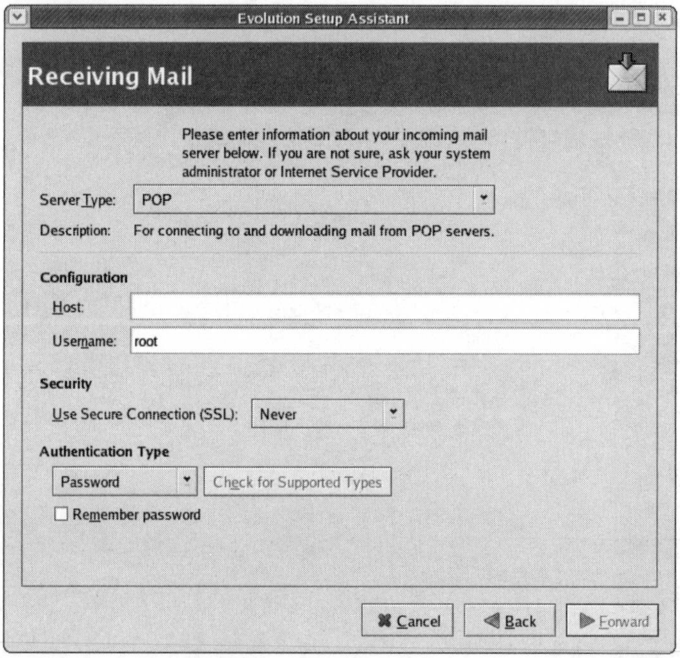

Figure 13-3:
Specify your
incoming
mail server
here.

Check with your system administrator if you aren't sure what to choose here. Read more about SMTP in the upcoming section, "Introducing SMTP," and find out about Sendmail in "Using Sendmail."

7. **Click Forward to continue to the Account Management dialog box. Here you enter a name for the account that you are creating. After you enter a name, click Forward to go to the Done dialog box.**

8. **Click Apply.**

   Your account is created, and the newly created account appears on the right side of the Evolution Settings dialog box.

Receiving e-mail

To receive e-mail via Evolution, do the following:

1. **Start the Evolution program by clicking the Evolution icon (looks like an envelope and stamp) from the desktop panel.**

2. **Click the Send/Receive icon from the navigation bar.**

   The program retrieves your messages from the server that you configured earlier. (See the preceding section.)

   If you have any new messages, a number appears behind the Inbox icon on the left side of the window, indicating how many messages you have.

3. **Click the Inbox icon to open the Inbox.**

4. **Click the message to view it in the bottom pane of the Evolution window, or double-click the message to open it in a new window.**

   If you opened the message in a new window, choose File➪Close from the menu bar or click the X in the upper-right corner to close the window.

5. **To reply to a message, click Reply from the navigation bar.**

Sending e-mail

To send e-mail via Evolution, do the following:

1. **Start the Evolution program by clicking the Evolution icon from the desktop panel.**

2. **Click New from the navigation bar to open the Compose a Message dialog box, as seen in Figure 13-4.**

3. **In the To field, enter the e-mail address for your recipient. Then enter a subject (in the same-named field) and the body of the message (in the open text field, below).**

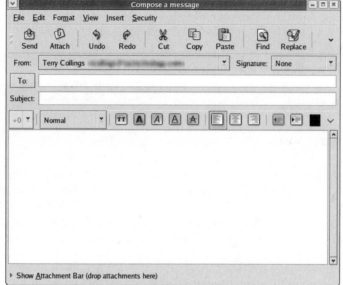

Figure 13-4:
Compose
new
messages
here.

> Show Attachment Bar (drop attachments here)

4. **To attach a file to your e-mail, click the Attach icon from the navigation bar and then browse to select the file.**

5. **When you finish composing your message, click Send.**

You can do a lot more with Evolution than just send and receive e-mail. Experimenting with Evolution to discover more about its address book as well as scheduling and time management features.

The address book in Evolution is actually called Contacts. You can open the contacts by clicking the Contacts icon on the left side of the Evolution main window. This opens a page where you see your existing contacts and from where you can add additional contacts by clicking New and entering the contact information in the Contact dialog box.

You can begin your exploration of scheduling by clicking the Calendars button on the left side of the Evolution window. The calendar opens showing today's date and hourly listings in a large calendar as well as a smaller calendar showing the entire month. You can double-click a time in the large calendar display to open a dialog box to schedule an event for that time. If you click a date on the small calendar, the date changes on the large calendar to show the date that you selected.

Mail Transfer Agent (MTA)

After the MTA receives the message from the MUA, it can do its job. The MTA installed by default on your Red Hat Enterprise system is Sendmail. The MTA reads the information in the To section of the e-mail message and determines the IP address of the recipient's mail server. Then the MTA tries to open a connection to the recipient's server through a communication port, typically port 25. If the MTA on the sending machine can establish a connection, it sends the message to the MTA on the recipient's server by using the Simple Message Transfer Protocol (SMTP).

The MTA on the receiving server adds header information to the message. The header contains information that is used for tracking the message and ensuring that it is delivered. Next, the receiving MTA passes the message to another program to inform the receiver that new mail has arrived.

Local Delivery Agent (LDA)

After the LDA receives the message from the MTA, it places the message in the receiver's mailbox file that is identified by the username. On your Red Hat system, this is a program called `procmail`. The location of the user's mailbox file is `/usr/spool/mail/<user's name>`.

The final step in the process happens when the user who is the intended receiver of the message reads the message. The user does this by using the MUA on his or her PC.

An optional program is a mail notifier that periodically checks your mailbox file for new mail. If you have such a program installed, it notifies you of the new mail.

The Red Hat Enterprise Linux shell has a built-in mail notifier that looks at your mailbox file once a minute. If new mail has arrived, the shell displays a message just before it displays the next system prompt. It won't interrupt a program that you're running. You can adjust how frequently the mail notifier checks and even which mailbox files to watch.

If you are using a GUI, like Evolution, a mail notifier is available as part of the application itself that plays sounds to let you know that new mail has arrived. You can turn on sound notification for new e-mail in Evolution by choosing Tools⇨Settings from the main menu. Then choose Mail Preferences and select either Beep When New Mail Arrives or Play Sound File When New Mail Arrives. Enter the name of the file to play and then click OK. See Figure 13-5.

Figure 13-5:
Enable
sound
notifications
for new
e-mail here.

Introducing SMTP

In the earlier section describing the MTA, you can read that messages are sent between MTAs via SMTP. This section explains SMTP and two other protocols used to deliver mail: Post Office Protocol (POP3) and Internet Message Access Protocol (IMAP4). SMTP is the TCP/IP protocol for transferring e-mail messages between computers on a network. SMTP specifies message movement between MTAs. Messages can go directly from the sending to the receiving MTA or through other MTAs on other network computers. These other computers briefly store the message before they forward it to another MTA (if it is local to the MTA) or to a gateway that sends it to an MTA on another network.

The SMTP protocol can transfer only ASCII text. It can't handle fonts, colors, graphics, or attachments. If you want to be able to send these items, you need to add another protocol to SMTP, such as Multipurpose Internet Mail Extensions, or MIME. MIME enables you to add colors, sounds, and graphics to your messages while still enabling them to be delivered by SMTP. In order for MIME to work, you must have a MIME-compliant MUA.

The Post Office Protocol (POP3)

POP3 is the Post Office Protocol version 3. This protocol runs on a server that is connected to a network and continuously sends and receives mail. The POP3 server stores any messages that it receives. POP3 was developed to solve the problem of what happens to messages when the recipient is not connected to the network.

Without POP3, the message could not be sent to the recipient if the recipient were offline. But with POP3, when you want to check your e-mail, you connect to the POP3 server to retrieve your messages that were stored by the server. After you retrieve your messages, you can use the MUA on your PC to read them. Of course, your MUA has to understand the POP3 to be able to communicate with the POP3 server.

The messages that you retrieve to your PC are then typically removed from the server. This means that they are no longer available to you if you want to retrieve them to another PC.

The Internet Mail Access Protocol (IMAP4)

The Internet Message Access Protocol version 4 (IMAP4) provides sophisticated client/server functionality for handling e-mail. IMAP4 has more features than POP3. IMAP4 enables you to store your e-mail on a networked mail server, just as POP3 does. The difference is that POP3 requires you to download your e-mail before your MUA reads it, whereas IMAP4 enables your e-mail to reside permanently on a remote server, from which you can access your mail. And you can do so from your office, your home, or anywhere else. Your MUA must understand IMAP4 to retrieve messages from an IMAP4 server.

Using Sendmail

A number of mail transport agents are available for Red Hat Enterprise Linux, including Qmail, Postfix, and Sendmail. The most widely used MTA is Sendmail, which is the default MTA for Red Hat Enterprise Linux.

Checking that Sendmail is installed and running

Before you start to configure Sendmail, be sure that it's installed on your computer. It probably is because the Red Hat Enterprise Linux installation program installs Sendmail. But just to be sure, check it out. The following example shows how to check, using the `rpm -q` command.

```
root@main# rpm -q sendmail
```

The following output shows not only that Sendmail is installed but also which version of Sendmail is installed.

```
Sendmail-8.13.1-2
```

Next, make sure that Sendmail starts when your computers boot. You have several ways to check whether Sendmail is running. Pick your favorite. The next example uses ps to look for Sendmail.

```
root@main# ps -auwx | grep sendmail
```

Here is sample output from the command:

```
root  8977  0.0  0.3  1488  472  ?  S  12:16  0:00 sendmail: accepting
                   connections on port 25
```

If Sendmail is not running, you can start it by entering the following command at a command line prompt:

```
root@main# service sendmail start
```

Configuring Sendmail

Many system administrators think that Sendmail is difficult to configure. If you look at its configuration file, /etc/sendmail.cf, this might seem to be the case. However, Red Hat Enterprise Linux provides you with a default Sendmail configuration file that works for most sites. Your default Sendmail configuration file accepts mail deliveries to your computer, sends mail deliveries from your computer, and enables your computer to be used as a relay host.

If you need to edit the configuration file at all, you might need to make only a couple of minor changes. Here are the key lines that a Red Hat Enterprise Linux system administrator might want to edit in /etc/sendmail.cf. These are *not* in the order that you find them in the file. In Listing 13-1, the tactechnology.com domain is set up to be a relay host.

Listing 13-1:   Sample Relay Host Configuration

```
# Copyright (c) 1998-2000 Sendmail, Inc. and its suppliers.
#       All rights reserved.
# Copyright (c) 1983, 1995 Eric P. Allman. All rights reserved.
# Copyright (c) 1988, 1993
#The Regents of the University of California. All rights #reserved.
#
# By using this file, you agree to the terms and conditions
# set forth in the LICENSE file which can be found at the top
# level of the sendmail distribution.
```

```
##################################################################
#####              SENDMAIL CONFIGURATION FILE
#####
##################################################################
                   | File edited here |
==========
# "Smart" relay host (may be null)
DS

CHANGE THE LINE TO DEFINE THE NAME OF THE MAIL RELAY HOST (GATEWAY COMPUTER THAT
                HAS THE RESPONSIBILITY FOR SENDING/RECEIVING INTERNET MAIL).  NOTE
                -- NO SPACES!


DSmailrelay.tactechnology.com
==========
# my official domain name
# ... define this only if sendmail cannot automatically          #
                determine your domain
#Dj$w.Foo.COM
```

Fortunately, you do not have to be a Sendmail expert in order to perform most
configuration chores. In most cases, all you need is one of the predefined configuration files in `/usr/lib/sendmail.cf`. The basic process is to modify one
of the predefined configuration files for you own needs, regenerate `/etc/`
`sendmail.cf` by using the m4 macro processor (as explained in the following
section), and then test your configuration. This method enables you to make
incremental changes, thus minimizing the risk of major problems. Red Hat
Enterprise Linux comes with a generic Sendmail configuration file
(`/etc/sendmail.cf`).

The m4 macro processor

A *macro* is a symbolic name for a long string of characters, much like a keyboard macro is a shorthand way to type a long series of keystrokes. Sendmail
gets its rules from the entries in a Sendmail macro file. The location of the
generic Sendmail macro file for Red Hat is

```
/usr/lib/sendmail-cf/cf/generic-linux.mc
```

The rules in the Sendmail macro file generate the default Sendmail configuration file, `sendmail.cf`. The m4 is a macro processor that reads the macro file
and generates the configuration file. Unless you want Sendmail to use your
own customized rules in a complex configuration, you can leave the macro
file and macro processor alone. For more information on changing Sendmail's
rules in the macro file, see the `MailadminHOWTO` on the CD-ROM accompany-
ing this book.

An example of a macro in / is the OSTYPE macro that names the operating system. Remember that Sendmail runs on many different operating systems, not just Unix and Linux. On a Linux system, if you look at Sendmail's macro file, you see the following line, which tells Sendmail which operating system it's running on so that Sendmail runs properly:

```
OSTYPE('linux')
```

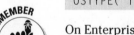

On Enterprise Linux, the OSTYPE macro comes predefined, so you don't need to worry about it.

If you really want complete, technical information about the macro file and how it works, read the /usr/lib/sendmail-cf/README file.

Managing the mail queue

Sometimes e-mail messages can't go out immediately, and the reasons are varied. Perhaps your network is down. Maybe your connection to the Internet is sporadic. Maybe the recipient's computer is unavailable. Whatever the reason, users can continue to compose e-mail with their MUAs. When they send the mail, Sendmail puts the message into the mail queue and keeps trying to send the message at intervals defined for the Sendmail daemon. You can find out what these intervals are by checking the initialization script that starts Sendmail.

The following brief excerpt is from the file /etc/rc.d/rc2.d/S80sendmail. The first line defines the interval to retry as one hour (1h). You can specify the interval in h (hours), m (minutes), or s (seconds). This Red Hat version defines the variable QUEUE and sets it to 1h. Some distributions hard-code the interval right into the Sendmail command (sendmail -q1h). The last two lines of Listing 13-2 show the Sendmail startup command. The -q$QUEUE in the last line sets the retry time to one hour. The -bd option in the next-to-last line of the excerpt starts Sendmail as a daemon.

Listing 13-2:   Excerpt from /etc/rc.d/rc2.d/S80sendmail

```
QUEUE=1h
fi

# Check that networking is up.
[ ${NETWORKING} = "no" ] && exit 0

[ -f /usr/sbin/sendmail ] || exit 0

RETVAL=0

start() {
```

```
      # Start daemons.

  echo -n "Starting sendmail: "
  /usr/bin/newaliases > /dev/null 2>&1
  for i in virtusertable access domaintable mailertable ; do
        if [ -f /etc/mail/$i ] ; then
              makemap hash /etc/mail/$i < /etc/mail/$i
        fi
  done
daemon /usr/sbin/sendmail $([ "$DAEMON" = yes ] && echo -bd) \
                          $([ -n "$QUEUE" ] && echo -q$QUEUE)
```

Configuring POP3

The steps involved in setting up POP3 include

1. Installing the package that contains the POP3 daemon.

2. Editing the file `/etc/xinetd.d/ipop3` to make POP3 services available.

   To edit this file, use your favorite text editor to change the line

   ```
   disable = yes
   ```

   to

   ```
   disable = no
   ```

3. Restarting the `xinetd` daemon to make the changes in Step 2 take effect by entering the following command at a command line prompt.

   ```
   Service xinetd restart
   ```

4. Checking that the POP3 daemon is accepting connections. You can telnet to your own computer on port 110, as shown here, to see whether POP3 is accepting connections:

   ```
   terry@main# telnet localhost 110
   Trying 127.0.0.1...
   telnet:Connected to localhost.
   Esc character is '^'.
   * OK POP3 localhost  v7.64 server ready
   ```

Your Enterprise Linux operating system installation procedure might have already set up POP3 for you. Before you start setting up POP3, therefore, you should use your favorite package manager to query whether POP3 is already installed.

Red Hat bundles IMAP4 and POP3 software together. When you query the RPM database for POP3, you need to look for it under the IMAP name:

```
root@main# rpm -q imap
```

Configuring IMAP4

To configure IMAP4, you follow the same basic steps as with POP3:

1. Installing the package that contains the IMAP4 daemon.

2. Editing the file `/etc/xinetd.d/imapconf` to make IMAP4 services available.

   To edit this file, use your favorite text editor to change the line

   ```
   disable = yes
   ```

   to

   ```
   disable = no
   ```

3. Restarting the `xinetd` daemon to make the changes in Step 2 take effect by entering the following command at a command line prompt.

   ```
   Service xinetd restart
   ```

4. Checking that the IMAP4 daemon is accepting connections. You can telnet to your own computer on port 143, as shown here, to see whether IMAP4 is accepting connections:

   ```
   terry@main# telnet localhost 143
   Trying 127.0.0.1...
   telnet:Connected to localhost.
   Esc character is '^'.
   * OK localhost IMAP4rev1 v12.264 server ready
   ```

Your Red Hat Enterprise Linux operating system installation procedure might have already set up IMAP4 for you. Before you start setting up IMAP4, therefore, you should use RPM to query whether it is already installed.

Setting up aliases to make life easier

Mail aliases are useful for creating distribution lists and for making access to users more convenient. For example, if people have trouble spelling someone's name, you can create an alias with alternate spellings — thus, if someone misspells the name, the mail still reaches the intended recipient. You can also alias a nonexistent user to a real user. For example, you could set up an alias — bozo, for example — that redirects all mail intended for bozo to user Wilson. The aliases file is usually `/etc/aliases`. Listing 13-3 contains entries for

- **System aliases for** `mailer-daemon` **and** `postmaster`, **which are required.**

- **Redirections for pseudo accounts such as** `lp`, `shutdown`, **and** `daemon`. Most of these are all aliased to `root` by default, but you can change them.

✔ **User aliases, such as** bozo.

✔ **Distribution lists, such as** TCPAuthors.

Listing 13-3: Mail Alias Creation

```
# Basic system aliases -- these MUST be present.
mailer-daemon:  postmaster
postmaster:     root
# General redirections for pseudo accounts.
daemon:         root
lp:             root
sync:           root
shutdown:       root
usenet:         news
ftpadm:         ftp
ftpadmin:       ftp
ftp-adm:        ftp
ftp-admin:      ftp

# trap decode to catch security attacks
decode:         root

# Person who should get root's mail
root:           terry

#Users
wilson:         bozo


#Distribution lists
terry,wilson:                       clowns
```

To create an entry in the aliases file, use your favorite editor. Each entry consists of the username, a colon, space(s) or tab(s), and the alias. After you save the file, you must run the newaliases command to make the changes take effect. This step is necessary because Sendmail looks at the binary file /etc/mail/aliases.db to read alias information. The newaliases command reads your aliases text file and updates the binary file. To run the newalias command, enter it at a command line prompt. The following example shows running the newalias command on the first line and the output of the command on the second line.

```
[root@terry etc]# newaliases
/etc/aliases: 63 aliases, longest 10 bytes, 625 bytes total
```

Maintaining E-Mail Security

Do you think you have nothing to hide? Maybe you don't, but e-mail security is always a privacy issue even if you aren't mailing credit card numbers or corporate secrets. Using Secure Multi-Purpose Internet Mail Extensions (S/MIME) for security is only a first step in protecting your users and yourself. *S/MIME* is a mail protocol used to add digital signatures and encryption to standard MIME messages. To find out more about S/MIME, go to `www.rsasecurity.com/rsalabs/node.asp?id=2292`.

Protecting against eavesdropping

Your mail message goes through more computers than just yours and your recipient's because of store and forward techniques. All a cracker has to do to snoop through your mail is use a packet sniffer program to intercept passing mail messages. A *packet sniffer* is intended to be a tool that a network administrator uses to record and analyze network traffic, but the bad guys use them, too. Dozens of free packet sniffing programs are available on the Internet. One such program that I have used and like is called Snort. You can find it at `www.snort.org`.

Using encryption

Cryptography isn't just for secret agents. Many e-mail products enable your messages to be *encrypted* (coded in a secret pattern) so that only you and your recipient can read them. Lotus Notes provides e-mail encryption, for example.

Using a firewall

If you receive mail from people outside your network, you should set up a firewall to protect your network. The *firewall* is a computer that prevents unauthorized data from reaching your network. For example, if you don't want anything from `ispy.com` to penetrate your net, put your net behind a firewall. The firewall blocks out all `ispy.com` messages. If you work on one computer dialed in to an ISP, you can still install a firewall. Several vendors provide personal firewalls, and some of them are free if you don't want a lot of bells and whistles.

Don't get bombed, spammed, or spoofed

Bombing happens when someone continually sends the same message to an e-mail address either accidentally or maliciously. If you reside in the U.S. and you receive 200 or more copies of the same message from the same person, you can report the bomber to the FBI. The U.S. Federal Bureau of Investigation has a National Computer Crimes Squad in Washington, DC, telephone +1-202-325-9164.

Spamming is a variation of bombing. A spammer sends junk mail to many users (hundreds and even thousands). You easily can be an accidental spammer: For example, if you choose your e-mail's Reply All function and then send a reply to a worldwide distribution list, you are a spammer.

Spoofing happens when someone sends you e-mail from a fake address. If spoofing doesn't seem like it could be major problem for you, consider this scenario. You get e-mail from a system administrator telling you to use a specific password for security reasons. Of course, many people comply because the system administrator knows best. Imagine the consequences if a spoofer sends this e-mail faking the system administrator's e-mail address to all the users on a computer. All of a sudden, the spoofer knows everyone's passwords and has access to private and possibly sensitive or secret data.

Spoofing is possible because plain SMTP does not have authentication capabilities. Without authentication features, SMTP can't be sure that incoming mail is really from the address it says it is. If your mail server enables connections to the SMTP port, anyone with a little knowledge of the internal workings of SMTP can connect to that port and send your e-mail from a spoofed address. Besides connecting to the SMTP port of a site, a user can send spoofed e-mail by modifying their Web browser interfaces.

If someone invades your mail system, you should report the intrusion to the Computer Emergency Response Team (CERT). You can find the CERT at `www.cert.org`.

Some SMTP cautions

Use dedicated mail servers. First of all, keep the number of computers vulnerable to SMTP-based attacks to a minimum. Have only one or a few centralized e-mail servers, depending on the size of your organization.

Allow only SMTP connections that come from outside your firewall to go to those few central e-mail servers. This policy protects the other computers on your network. If your site gets spammed, you have to clean up the central e-mail servers, but the rest of your networked computers are okay.

If you use packet filtering, you need configure only your e-mail servers. Packet filtering analyzes packets based on the source and destination addresses. The analysis decides whether to accept the packets and pass them through to your networks or to reject them as being unsafe. Firewalls often use packet filtering techniques, and Enterprise Linux provides the `iptables` tool for configuring your packet filtering firewall.

Chapter 14

Configuring and Managing an FTP Server

....

In This Chapter

▶ Installing an FTP server

▶ Configuring an FTP server

▶ Starting and testing an FTP server

▶ Logging in to FTP servers

....

*F**ile Transfer Protocol* (FTP) is an Internet protocol that can be used for transferring files not only across the Internet but on local networks as well. If you've ever downloaded a file from a Web site, you most likely used FTP to download the file. FTP is easy to install and configure on your system. In this chapter, I show you how to install and configure an FTP server as well as use the ftp client to access an FTP server.

Installing an FTP Server

Red Hat Enterprise Linux ES and AS include the vsftpd FTP server. Known as the Very Secure FTP daemon, vsftpd is by design a fast, stable, and secure FTP server that is capable of handling large numbers of connections simultaneously. In case you are wondering, a *daemon* (pronounced *dee*-mon) is a process that listens for requests and then provides its intended service. Depending on the options selected when your system was installed, the vsftpd server might not be installed. The first thing that you should do is to check for the installation as follows:

1. **Open a terminal window by choosing Applications⇨System Tools⇨ Terminal.**

2. **Type rpm -q vsftpd at the command prompt.**

   If the vsftpd server is installed, you see vsftpd-⟨version number⟩ as the result of running this command. If the server is not installed, you see a message stating that vsftpd is not installed.

If your `vsftpd` server software is already installed, skip to the section, "Configuring an FTP Server." If your server is not installed, continue with Step 3.

3. **Choose Applications⇨System Settings⇨Add/Remove Applications.**

If you are not logged in as root, you will be prompted for the root password. The Add or Remove Packages dialog box appears, as shown in Figure 14-1.

4. **Scroll down the list of packages until you find the FTP server in the list. Check the box in front of the name and then click the Update button.**

You are prompted to insert one of the Enterprise Linux installation CDs into the CD drive. After the installation completes, the Update Completed dialog box appears.

5. **Click OK on the Update Completed dialog box and then click Quit to exit the Add or Remove Packages dialog box.**

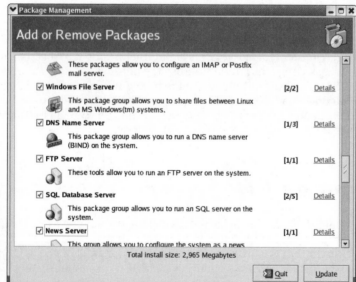

Figure 14-1: The Add or Remove Packages dialog box.

Configuring an FTP Server

After the `vsftpd` server is installed, you are ready to configure the server. Because no graphical tool is available for configuring the FTP server, you need to manually edit the configuration files. The installation process places the server startup and configuration files in several places on your system, which are

- ✔ `/usr/sbin/vsftpd`: The FTP daemon, which is the actual program that runs to provide FTP services.

- ✔ `/etc/rc.d/init.d/vsftpd`: The initialization script that is run to start the server.

- ✔ `/etc/vsftpd/vsftpd.conf`: The main configuration file for the `vsftp` server.

- ✔ `/etc/vsftpd.ftpusers`: Contains a list of users who are not allowed to use the FTP service.

- ✔ `/etc/vsftpd.user_list`: Contains a list of users who are, or are not, allowed to access the FTP server depending on the configuration directive in the `/etc/vsftpd/vsftpd.conf` file. If the directive `userlist_deny=YES` is set in the `/etc/vsftpd/vsftpd.conf` file, users in this list are denied access. If `userlist_deny=NO`, users on this list are allowed to access the FTP server.

If you set the `userlist_deny` directive to `NO`, be sure that you do not have the same users listed in the `/etc/vsftpd/ftpusers` file or the users won't be able to access the FTP server.

- ✔ `/var/ftp`: The `ftp` directory is created under `/var` to hold the publicly accessible files. If you are allowing anonymous users, another directory — `/var/ftp/pub` — is created for their use. You should place publicly available files in this directory.

The first two files in the preceding list do not require configuration because the first file is the `ftp` program and the second file is the script that starts the program. The configuration of the last three files is discussed in the following sections.

Configuring the /etc/vsftpd/vsftpd.conf file

The main configuration file for the `vsftp` server is `/etc/vsftpd/vsftpd.conf`. In most cases, you can usually accept the default settings and just start the FTP server. However, I recommend that you become familiar with the configuration file in case you need to change settings. An example of this file is shown in Listing 14-1, with an explanation of the file following the listing. The first line in the listing is the command entered at the command prompt, and the remainder of the listing is the output for the command.

Listing 14-1: The /etc/vsftpd/vsftpd.conf File

```
[root@terry root]# cat /etc/vsftpd/vsftpd.conf
# Example config file /etc/vsftpd/vsftpd.conf
#
# The default compiled in settings are fairly paranoid. This sample file
# loosens things up a bit, to make the ftp daemon more usable.
# Please see vsftpd.conf.5 for all compiled in defaults.
#
# READ THIS: This example file is NOT an exhaustive list of vsftpd options.
# Please read the vsftpd.conf.5 manual page to get a full idea of vsftpd's
# capabilities.
#
# Allow anonymous FTP? (Beware - allowed by default if you comment this out).
anonymous_enable=YES
#
# Uncomment this to allow local users to log in.
local_enable=YES
#
# Uncomment this to enable any form of FTP write command.
write_enable=YES
#
# Default umask for local users is 077. You may wish to change this to 022,
# if your users expect that (022 is used by most other ftpd's)
local_umask=022
#
# Uncomment this to allow the anonymous FTP user to upload files. This only
# has an effect if the above global write enable is activated. Also, you will
# obviously need to create a directory writable by the FTP user.
#anon_upload_enable=YES
#
# Uncomment this if you want the anonymous FTP user to be able to create
# new directories.
#anon_mkdir_write_enable=YES
#
# Activate directory messages - messages given to remote users when they
# go into a certain directory.
dirmessage_enable=YES
#
# Activate logging of uploads/downloads.
xferlog_enable=YES
#
# Make sure PORT transfer connections originate from port 20 (ftp-data).
connect_from_port_20=YES
#
# If you want, you can arrange for uploaded anonymous files to be owned by
# a different user. Note! Using "root" for uploaded files is not
# recommended!
#chown_uploads=YES
#chown_username=whoever
#
# You may override where the log file goes if you like. The default is shown
# below.
#xferlog_file=/var/log/vsftpd.log
```

```
#
# If you want, you can have your log file in standard ftpd xferlog format
xferlog_std_format=YES
#
# You may change the default value for timing out an idle session.
#idle_session_timeout=600
#
# You may change the default value for timing out a data connection.
#data_connection_timeout=120
#
# It is recommended that you define on your system a unique user which the
# ftp server can use as a totally isolated and unprivileged user.
#nopriv_user=ftpsecure
#
# Enable this and the server will recognise asynchronous ABOR requests. Not
# recommended for security (the code is non-trivial). Not enabling it,
# however, may confuse older FTP clients.
#async_abor_enable=YES
#
# By default the server will pretend to allow ASCII mode but in fact ignore
# the request. Turn on the below options to have the server actually do ASCII
# mangling on files when in ASCII mode.
# Beware that turning on ascii_download_enable enables malicious remote parties
# to consume your I/O resources, by issuing the command "SIZE /big/file" in
# ASCII mode.
# These ASCII options are split into upload and download because you may wish
# to enable ASCII uploads (to prevent uploaded scripts etc. from breaking),
# without the DoS risk of SIZE and ASCII downloads. ASCII mangling should be
# on the client anyway..
#ascii_upload_enable=YES
#ascii_download_enable=YES
#
# You may fully customise the login banner string:
ftpd_banner=Welcome to the TAC Technology FTP service.
#
# You may specify a file of disallowed anonymous e-mail addresses. Apparently
# useful for combatting certain DoS attacks.
#deny_email_enable=YES
# (default follows)
#banned_email_file=/etc/vsftpd.banned_emails
#
# You may specify an explicit list of local users to chroot() to their home
# directory. If chroot_local_user is YES, then this list becomes a list of
# users to NOT chroot().
#chroot_list_enable=YES
# (default follows)
#chroot_list_file=/etc/vsftpd.chroot_list
#
# You may activate the "-R" option to the builtin ls. This is disabled by
# default to avoid remote users being able to cause excessive I/O on large
# sites. However, some broken FTP clients such as "ncftp" and "mirror" assume
# the presence of the "-R" option, so there is a strong case for enabling it.
```

(continued)

Listing 14-1: (continued)

```
#ls_recurse_enable=YES

pam_service_name=vsftpd
userlist_enable=YES
#enable for standalone mode
listen=YES
tcp_wrappers=YES
```

As you can see from Listing 14-1, the basic format of the file is either a comment line, indicated by the pound sign (#) at the beginning of a line or a directive, which is in the form of

```
option=value
```

Comment lines are ignored by the program and are used either to provide information about the directive that follows the comment or to prevent a directive from being read. Many directives are shown commented out in the configuration file. To enable these directives, you just need to remove the comment (pound sign) from the beginning of the directive. Directives must not contain any spaces between the option equal sign and value. Values can be expressed as a Boolean value of YES or NO, numeric values, or string values.

There are probably over 100 options for which you can set a value. If you want to see the complete list, take a look at the vsftpd.conf man file. I briefly explain the most common options in the order that they are shown in the default /etc/vsftpd/vsftpd.conf file created during the server installation.

- ✔ anonymous_enable=YES: This directive enables anonymous FTP. Users of anonymous FTP can use the username *anonymous* and whatever password that they want. To disable anonymous FTP, change the value to NO or just comment out the entire directive.

- ✔ local_enable=YES: This directive controls whether local users can log in to the FTP server. If enabled, any user who has an account can log in.

- ✔ write_enable=YES: This directive enables or disables any of the FTP write commands.

- ✔ local_umask=022: The default file permissions are controlled by the umask setting.

- ✔ anon_upload_enable=YES: To allow anonymous users to upload files to your server, set this directive to YES. To disallow anonymous uploads, set the directive to NO or comment out the line.

- ✔ anon_mkdir_write_enable=YES: If you want to allow anonymous users to create new directories, uncomment this directive; otherwise, leave it commented out or set the value to NO.

- ✔ dirmessage_enable=YES: If you want to pass a message to users when they enter a directory, set this directive to YES. You also need to create a file with the name .message and place it in the directory from which you want the message to appear.

✔ xferlog_enable=YES: To enable logging of uploads and downloads, set this directive to YES.

✔ connect_from_port_20=YES: This directive controls whether port 20 is used on the server for data transfers. This directive is typically set to YES for security reasons.

✔ pam_service_name=vsftpd: This string value displays the pluggable authentication module service name used by the FTP server. The file is located at /etc/pam.d/vsftpd.

✔ userlist_enable=YES: If this directive is enabled, the FTP server reads the names from the file shown by the userlist_file directive and denies access to those users.

✔ listen=YES: If enabled, this directive instructs the FTP server to run in standalone mode.

✔ tcp_wrappers=YES: If this directive is enabled, access control for the FTP server is handled by tcp wrappers.

Configuring the /etc/vsftpd.ftpusers file

The /etc/vsftpd.ftpusers file lists users who are not allowed to log in to the FTP server. These users are typically users who have increased privileges on the server; allowing these users to log in could present a security vulnerability to your system. Listing 14-2 shows the contents of this file. You can add additional names to this list by editing the file in any text editing program. The first line in the listing is the command entered at the command prompt, and the remainder of the listing is the output for the command.

Listing 14-2: The /etc/vsftpd.ftpusers File

```
[root@main root]# cat /etc/vsftpd.ftpusers
# Users that are not allowed to login via ftp
bin
daemon
adm
lp
sync
shutdown
halt
mail
news
uucp
operator
games
nobody
```

Configuring the /etc/vsftpd.user_list file

Depending on the directive that you set in the /etc/vsftpd/vsftpd.conf file, the list in the /etc/vsftpd.user_list file can be used to block or allow access to users whose name appears on the list. Listing 14-3 shows the contents of the file. Notice the directions in the commented out lines at the beginning of the file. The first line in the listing is the command entered at the command prompt, and the remainder of the listing is the output for the command.

Listing 14-3:   The /etc/vsftpd.user_list File

```
[root@main root]# cat /etc/vsftpd.user_list
# vsftpd userlist
# If userlist_deny=NO, only allow users in this file
# If userlist_deny=YES (default), never allow users in this file, and
# do not even prompt for a password.
# Note that the default vsftpd pam config also checks /etc/vsftpd.ftpusers
# for users that are denied.
root
bin
daemon
adm
lp
sync
shutdown
halt
mail
news
uucp
operator
games
nobody
```

Starting the FTP Server

After you configure the FTP server to your liking, you need to start it. You start the server by entering the following command:

```
[root@main root]# service vsftpd start
Starting vsftpd for vsftpd:                          [ OK ]
```

This command starts the FTP server for this session but does not set up the server to start whenever the system does. To ensure that the FTP server starts at system start, enter the following command:

```
chkconfig -level 35 vsftpd on
```

This command tells the system to always start the vsftpd server whenever the system is in runlevel 3 or 5.

Testing the FTP Server

Always test your work to make sure that you properly configured your server. You can test your server locally by attempting to log in. Listing 14-4 shows the entire login process. The first line in the listing is the command entered at the command prompt, and the remainder of the listing is the output for the command.

Listing 14-4: The Login Process

```
[root@main root]# ftp localhost
Connected to localhost.localdomain.
220-    Welcome to the TAC Technology ftp server!
220-    Anonymous logins are allowed by using
220-    ftp or anonymous as the username and
220-    a valid e-mail address as the password.
220-    Please be advised that all activity on this site is logged.
220-    We hope you enjoy your visit with us!
220
530 Please login with USER and PASS.
530 Please login with USER and PASS.
KERBEROS_V4 rejected as an authentication type
Name (localhost:root): terry
331 Please specify the password.
Password:
230 Login successful.
Remote system type is UNIX.
Using binary mode to transfer files.
ftp>
```

If you can successfully log in to your server locally, your configuration is correct. To complete your testing, you should log in remotely as a regular user — and if you configured anonymous access, as an anonymous user.

Logging In to FTP Servers

You can log in to an FTP server by using a graphical ftp client or by using the command line ftp client. In this section, I show you how to use both a graphical ftp client and the command line ftp client.

Using gFTP for FTP access

Enterprise Linux includes a graphical FTP program — gFTP — that can be accessed from either the GNOME or KDE desktops. You can start gFTP by choosing Applications➪Internet➪More Internet Applications➪gFTP. The gFTP window, as shown in Figure 14-2, appears.

To log in to the FTP server via gFTP, proceed as follows:

1. **In the Host field, fill in the hostname or IP address of the server to which you want to connect.**

2. **In the Port field, enter the port number of the remote server.**

    Port 21 is the port typically used by ftp.

3. **In the User field, enter the username of the user.**

4. **In the Pass field, enter the appropriate password for the user.**

    If you are connecting to a host that you have previously connected to, you can click the down arrow next to the Host, User, and Pass fields and choose from the respective drop-down lists.

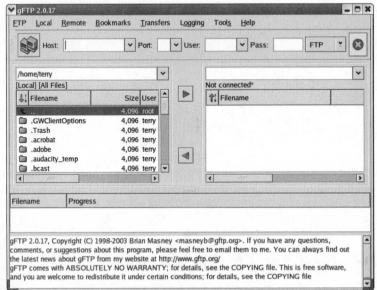

Figure 14-2:
The gFTP program is a graphical FTP client.

5. **Click the Host button to the left of the Host field. (The button has two computers on it.)**

   gFTP connects to the remote server and logs in the user that you entered.

6. **After you log in, you see a window similar to that shown in Figure 14-3.**

   On the left side of the window is a directory listing of the local system. On the right side of the window is the directory listing of the remote system. Between the two directory listings are arrows that can be used to transfer files between the two systems.

   - **To transfer a file from the local to the remote system,** select the files that you want to transfer from the local directory listing and then click the right-pointing arrow.

   - **To transfer a file from the remote to the local system,** select the files that you want to transfer from the remote directory listing and then click the left-pointing arrow.

   To quit your gFTP session, choose FTP⇨Quit from the menu at the top of the program window to close the program. If you want to disconnect from the remote server but keep gFTP open, click the Host button to disconnect but keep gFTP open.

Figure 14-3:
The gFTP program window after logging into the FTP server.

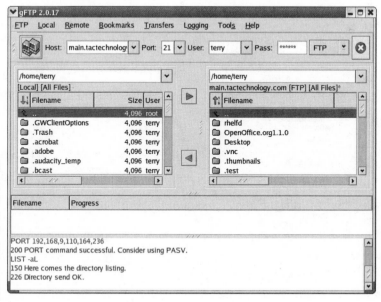

Accessing an FTP server with the command line FTP client

Perhaps you aren't running a graphical system, or you just prefer to use the command line for its speed advantage over the GUI. In either case, you can use the command line `ftp` client. To use it, do the following:

1. **Open a terminal window and type the following at the command prompt:**

   ```
   ftp <server name>
   ```

2. **Enter the username and password when prompted.**

   If you log in to an FTP server using your username and password, you will have access to your home directory structure.

   After you log in to the FTP server, you see a `login successful` message, and the prompt changes to `ftp>`. You can enter the command `help` to get a list of the `ftp` commands. Listing 14-5 shows the login process and using the `help` command to obtain a list of `ftp` commands that you have available.

Listing 14-5: Obtaining a Listing of Available ftp Commands

```
230 Login successful.
Remote system type is UNIX.
Using binary mode to transfer files.
ftp> help
Commands may be abbreviated. Commands are:

!            debug        mdir         sendport     site
$            dir          mget         put          size
account      disconnect   mkdir        pwd          status
append       exit         mls          quit         struct
ascii        form         mode         quote        system
bell         get          modtime      recv         sunique
binary       glob         mput         reget        tenex
bye          hash         newer        rstatus      tick
case         help         nmap         rhelp        trace
cd           idle         nlist        rename       type
cdup         image        ntrans       reset        user
chmod        lcd          open         restart      umask
cr           macdef       passive      runique      ?
delete       mdelete      proxy        send
```

Quite a few of the ftp commands are the same as the commands that you use in Linux for working with the file system. I cover some of the most common ftp commands here.

- ✔ bye: Using the bye command ends the session with the remote server and exits the ftp program.

- ✔ cd: The cd command is used to change to a different directory on the remote server.

- ✔ chmod: The chmod command is used to change file and directory permissions on the remote server.

- ✔ close: The close command is used to end the session with the remote server.

- ✔ get: The get command is used to transfer a single file from the remote server to the local computer.

- ✔ help: Using the help command displays a list of available ftp commands. When used with a command name, it displays help about the command.

- ✔ lcd: The lcd command is used to change the working directory on the local computer.

- ✔ ls: The ls command is used to obtain a directory listing of the remote server.

- ✔ mdelete: The mdelete command is used to delete files from the remote server.

- ✔ mget: The mget command is used to transfer multiple files from the remote server to the local computer.

- ✔ mkdir: The mkdir command is used to create a directory on the remote server.

- ✔ mput: The mput command is used to transfer multiple files from the local computer to the remote server.

- ✔ put: The put command is used to transfer a single file from the local computer to the remote server.

- ✔ pwd: The pwd command is used to show the current working directory on the remote server.

- ✔ quit: Using the quit command ends the session with the remote server and exits the ftp program.

To log in as an anonymous user, use the username *anonymous* and your email address as the password. After you log in, you can access the /var/ftp directory. Files that are available for download are in the /var/ftp/pub directory.

Chapter 15

Serving Web Pages

· ·

In This Chapter

▶ Installing and starting the Web server

▶ Configuring and managing your Web server

· ·

Whenever you go to a Web site on the Internet, you see the content provided by that site. What you don't see is the behind-the-scenes activity that makes viewing the Web site possible. This behind-the-scenes activity is all controlled by a Web server, and the Apache Web server is by far the most widely used Web server in use today. It is relatively easy to set up and maintain, as you can see by reading this chapter. If you're running the AS or ES versions of Enterprise Linux, you can find out what you need to know about your Apache server in this chapter. If you are running the WS or Desktop versions of Enterprise Linux, you won't be running a Web server — so you can skip this chapter.

 Setting up and running a Web server can be a very complex task; indeed, many books are devoted entirely to this topic. The information in this chapter, however, will enable you to set up a basic Web server. You should refer to the Apache Web site at www.apache.org for more detailed documentation.

Installing and Starting the Web Server

The Apache Web server software is usually installed automatically during the system installation, so you shouldn't have to install it manually. I recommend, though, checking to be sure that it is there before you try to start it. You can check for the Web server by entering the following command:

```
rpm -q httpd
```

If the Apache software is installed, the system responds with the name and version number of the installed software. If the Web server is not installed, your query results in the system responding that the server is not installed. You can install the Web server as follows:

1. **Choose Applications➪System Settings➪Add/Remove Applications.**

   If you're not logged in as the root user, you are prompted to enter the root password.

   The Package Management dialog box, as shown in Figure 15-1, appears.

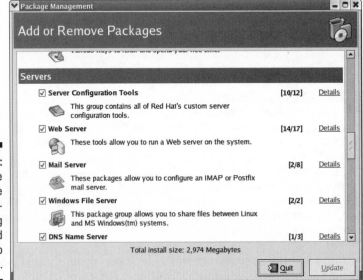

Figure 15-1:
Use the
Package
Manage-
ment dialog
box to add
packages to
your system.

2. **Scroll down to the Servers section and mark the Web Server check box.**

   Be sure to click the Details link for the Web server to see whether you need to install any additional Web server tools. For example, if you plan to use a database with your Web server, you want to install the tools for using databases with the Web server.

3. **Click the Update button, click Continue when the summary dialog box appears, enter the appropriate Enterprise Linux installation disk when prompted, and then click OK.**

4. **When the Update Complete dialog box appears, click OK and then click Quit to close the Package Management dialog box.**

After the Web server software is installed, you can start the Web server to check that it's working. After you're sure that the Web server is working, you can make any configuration changes for the Web server. You also need to put the files for your Web site into the proper directory on your system so that the Web server can find them. First things first. Start the Web server and then open a browser to see whether you can use the Web server. You start the Web server as follows:

1. **Choose Applications⇨System Settings⇨Server Settings⇨Services.**

   If you're not logged in as the root user, you are prompted to enter the root password.

   The Service Configuration dialog box, as shown in Figure 15-2, appears.

Figure 15-2:
Use the
Service
Configu-
ration dialog
box to start
and stop
services.

2. **Scroll down the list of services on the left side of the dialog box until you find httpd.**

3. **Mark the httpd check box.**

   This ensures that the Web server starts whenever the system boots up.

4. **Click the Start button on the tool bar to start the Apache server.**

   You see a small dialog box indicating that the server started successfully.

5. **Click OK to close the dialog box.**

6. **Click the Save icon from the toolbar and then choose File⇨Quit to close the Service Configuration dialog box.**

You can now check whether your Web server is functioning. You can get to it by following these steps:

1. **Open your Web browser by clicking the Web browser icon from the panel.**

2. **In the browser location box, enter the URL** http://localhost.

   You see a Test Page screen, as shown in Figure 15-3, indicating that your Web server is properly installed and working.

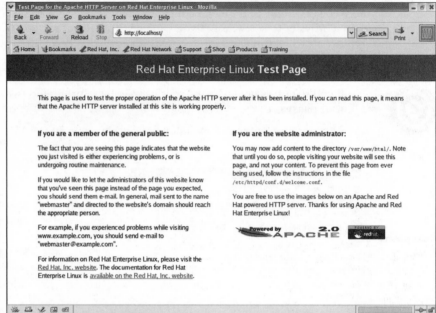

Figure 15-3:
The
Enterprise
Linux Web
server test
page.

Notice the text on the right of the screen meant for system administrators. This text tells you that you can now put your Web pages into the directory on your server. I show you how to do this in the next section.

Configuring and Managing Your Web Server

Before you place your Web files into the directory, I recommend finding out where all the Apache files are located on your system. Table 15-1 lists the files and directories related to the Apache Web server:

Table 15-1	Apache Web Server File and Directory Locations
Location	**Contains**
/etc/httpd	Directory containing httpd configuration files.
/etc/logrotate.d/httpd	The logrotate file for the httpd server.
/etc/rc.d/init.d/httpd	The startup script for the httpd server.
/usr/sbin/httpd	The httpd server daemon.

Location	Contains
/usr/lib/httpd	Directory containing the modules used by the httpd server.
/var/log/httpd	Directory containing the httpd log files.
/var/lock/subsys/httpd	The server lock file. The *lock file* contains the process ID of the running process and is used to prevent users from accessing the already running application.

The configuration file for the Apache Web server is /etc/httpd/conf/httpd.conf. You can manually edit this file to configure the Web server for the performance that you desire. Red Hat Enterprise Linux provides a graphical based tool that can be used to edit the Apache configuration file instead of manually editing it. I find it much faster to directly edit the configuration file, but many people prefer to use their mouse to click icons and then type information into text boxes. In the next section, you use the graphical based tool to edit the /etc/httpd/conf/httpd.conf file.

Editing the Apache Configuration File Using the HTTP Configuration Tool

With the HTTP configuration tool, you can set the parameters that control the operation of your Web server. You start the HTTP configuration tool by choosing Applications⇨System Settings⇨Server Settings⇨HTTP. The HTTP dialog box, as shown in Figure 15-4 appears.

Figure 15-4:
Use the HTTP configuration dialog box to set Web server parameters.

The HTTP configuration dialog box contains four tabs (Main, Virtual Hosts, Server, and Performance Tuning) that control different aspects of the server and its performance. There are also additional dialog boxes that are reachable from the four tabs of the HTTP configuration main dialog box. These are explained in the following sections.

Main tab

When the HTTP configuration tool is started, the Main tab is selected by default. On this page, you enter the following information:

- **Server Name:** Here you enter the name that people use to find your Web site, such as www.whatever.com.

- **Webmaster Email Address:** Enter the e-mail address of the person responsible for the Web server.

- **Available Addresses:** By default, the Web server listens to all addresses on port 80. If you want the Web server to listen to other ports or addresses, click the Edit button here to change the default settings or click Add to use additional addresses in addition to the default address. When you click either Edit or Add, another dialog box, as shown in Figure 15-5, opens.

If you click Add, the dialog box is labeled Add Address; if you click Edit, the dialog box is labeled Edit Address. Regardless of which one you choose, the options are the same on both. Figure 15-5 shows the Edit an Address dialog box.

Figure 15-5:
The Edit an Address dialog box lets you change addresses to which the Web server listens.

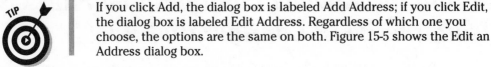

Virtual Hosts tab

The Virtual Hosts tab is where you enter information about other hosts that are available from your Web server. The term *virtual hosts* is typically used to refer to having more than one domain on a single server, but you can also use

them to set up separate Web sites on the same network for different departments in the same organization. You can have any number of virtual hosts on
your Web server. You can see the Virtual Hosts tab in Figure 15-6.

Figure 15-6:
Enter
information
about other
hosts on
your Web
server here.

On this tab, you can configure global parameters for the default virtual server
as well as add other virtual servers. You start by setting the global defaults
by clicking the Edit Default Settings button near the bottom of the tab. The
default Virtual Host Properties dialog box, as shown in Figure 15-7, opens.

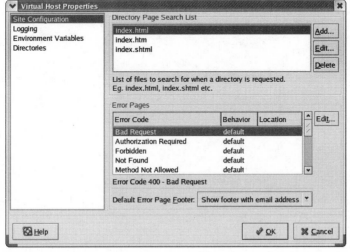

Figure 15-7:
Set default
virtual host
properties
here.

The Virtual Host Properties dialog box opens to the Site Configuration page;
three additional pages (Logging, Environment Variables, and Directories) are
available. The four pages available are seen in the column on the left of the
dialog box.

Site Configuration

On the Site Configuration page of the Virtual Host Properties dialog box, you can set the following:

- **Directory Page Search List:** This list contains the names of the files to look for in the document root directory in the order that they are listed here.

- **Error Pages:** This section shows the error codes and messages that are displayed for an error. You can change the default behavior by selecting the code and clicking the Edit button to the right of this section. An additional dialog box opens where you can then change the server behavior to either File or URL, which redirects the server to the specified location. If you select File, you need to specify the local location of the file. If you select URL, you need to enter the URL of the redirect.

- **Default Error Page Footer:** Here, you can select whether you want to display an error page footer with your e-mail address, without your e-mail address, or no footer at all.

Logging

The Logging page of the Virtual Host Properties dialog box, as shown in Figure 15-8, is where you can specify alternate log files and file locations.

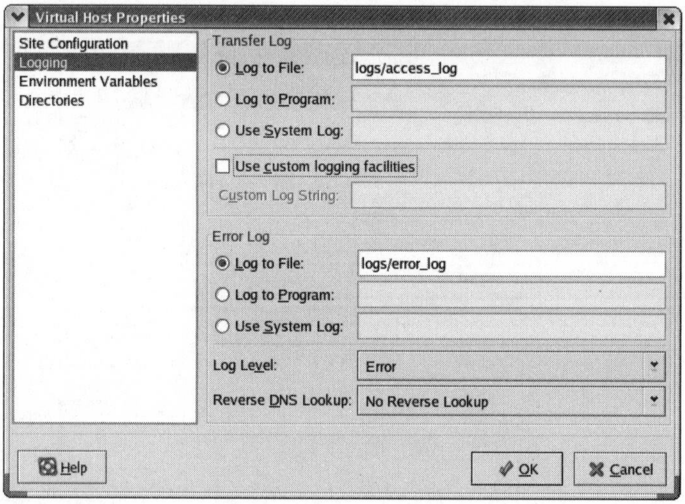

Figure 15-8:
Change
Web server
logging
settings
here.

Items on this page include

- **Transfer Log:** Any attempt to access your server is logged by default to `/var/log/httpd/access_log`. If you want to change the name or location, enter the appropriate information relative to the server root directory. If you want to use a different directory not relative to the server root, begin your path with a backslash.

✔ **Use custom logging facilities:** If you are using your own logging system rather than the system logs, enter the appropriate information for your logging system in the Custom Log String field. The information that you enter here is dependent on the logging system that you are using — and because I have no way of knowing that, I can't tell you what to enter here.

✔ **Error Log:** Any errors encountered by your server are logged by default to `/var/log/httpd/error_log`. If you want to change the name or location, enter the appropriate information relative to the server root directory. If you want to use a different directory not relative to the server root, begin your path with a backslash.

✔ **Log Level:** The options here let you set the amount of information that you want to receive about errors in your logs. Selecting the first choice in the drop-down list provides the least information. Each choice moving down the list provides more information; selecting the last choice provides the most information. Error messages contain information about server access and data transfers between clients and the server.

✔ **Reverse DNS Lookup:** This setting tells the server whether it should do reverse DNS lookups or do a double-reverse lookup. The default setting here is No Reverse Lookup; for most sites, this is fine. For more on reverse DNS lookups, read Chapter 12.

Environment Variables

The Environment Variables page of the Virtual Host Properties dialog box, as shown in Figure 15-9, is where you can specify variables passed, or not passed, to CGI (common gateway interface) scripts. Some commonly used CGI environment variables include `server_protocol`, `server_name`, `request_method`, `path_info`, and `script_name`.

You can set the following:

✔ **Set for CGI Scripts:** Here you can enter variables that are set for a CGI script. Click this section's Add button and enter the environment variable into the appropriate field and also the value of the variable in its field; then click OK. To edit or delete an item, select it and click the appropriate button.

✔ **Pass to CGI Scripts:** Here you can enter the environment variable to pass to a CGI script when the server starts. Click this section's Add button, enter the name of the environment variable into the field, and then click OK. To edit or delete an item, select it and click the appropriate button.

✔ **Unset for CGI Scripts:** Here you can enter environment variables whose values you do not want passed to CGI scripts. Click this section's Add button, enter the name of the environment variable into the field, and then click OK. To edit or delete an item, select it and click the appropriate button.

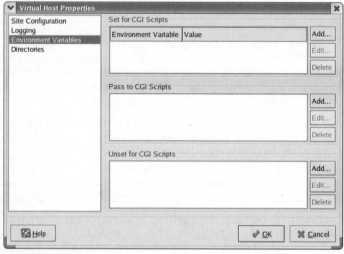

Figure 15-9:
Change
Web server
environment
variable
settings
here.

Directories

The Directories page of the Virtual Host Properties dialog box, as shown in Figure 15-10, is where you can set options for directories used by your Web server.

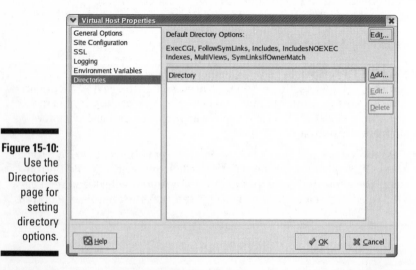

Figure 15-10:
Use the
Directories
page for
setting
directory
options.

On this page, you can set the following options:

✔ **Default Directory Options:** The default directory options are listed here. To change the options, click the Edit button in the upper-right corner to open the Default Directory Options dialog box from which you can select or deselect directory options. The directory options are

- **ExecCGI:** Select this option to allow execution of CGI scripts.

- **FollowSymLinks:** Select this option to allow symbolic links to be followed.

A *symbolic link* is a pointer to another file. For those of you who are familiar with MS Windows, you can think of a symbolic link as a shortcut.

- **Includes:** This option allows the server to use server side includes.

- **IncludesNOEXEC:** This option allows server side includes and disables the `exec` and `include` commands from CGI scripts.

- **Indexes:** If you don't have a directory index file, such as `index.html`, a request to the server displays a list of files in the directory.

- **MultiViews:** This option enables multiviews and is not enabled by default. When enabled, the Web server tries to find pages similar to the requested page if the requested page is not found. For example, if a user requests a page *whatever*.html and it is not found, the Web server will look for pages *whatever*.*.

- **SymLinksIfOwnerMatch:** This option allows symbolic links to be followed if the file or directory has the same owner as the symbolic link.

✔ **Directory:** In this area are listed directories that you specify. To add a directory, click the Add button and the Directory Options dialog box, appears, as shown in Figure 15-11.

From the Directory dialog box, you can select options for directories that you choose by entering the directory path into the Directory field and selecting your desired options from the right side of the dialog box. The options are the same as those listed for the default directory options. You can also specify the following:

- **Order:** This option specifies whether all users are allowed or in which order to process the allow or deny lists.

- **Deny List:** You can choose to deny all hosts or to deny hosts based on domain name, IP address, subnet, or Classless Interdomain Routing (CIDR) listing by entering this information in the Deny Hosts From field. CIDR lets routers group routes to minimize the amount of information transmitted by core routers. Multiple IP addresses are shown as a single address to routers outside your network.

• **Allow List:** You can choose to allow all hosts or to allow hosts based on domain name, IP address, subnet, or CIDR listing by entering this information in the Allow Hosts From field.

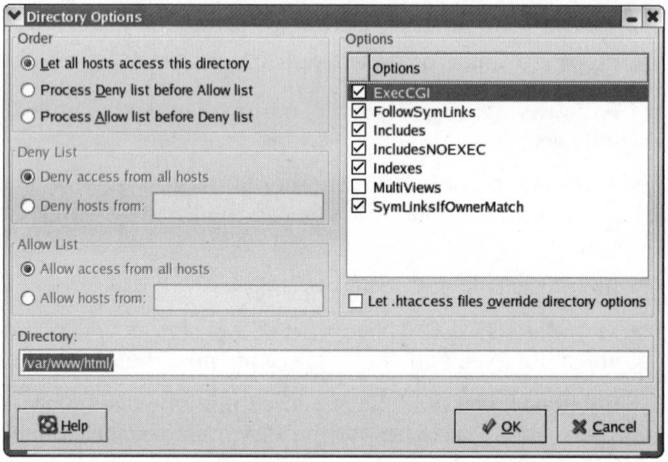

Figure 15-11:
Use the
Directory
Options
dialog box
for setting
directory
options.

To add a virtual host to your system, click the Add button from the Virtual Host dialog box, as shown in Figure 15-6, to open the Virtual Host Properties dialog box, as shown in Figure 15-12.

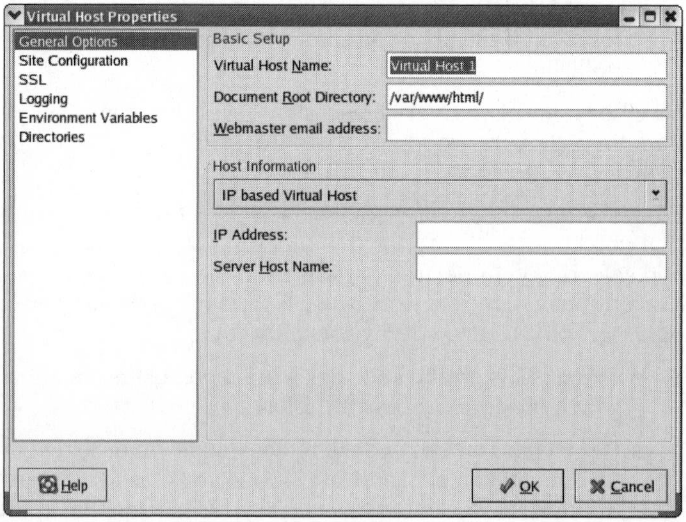

Figure 15-12:
Use the
Virtual Host
Properties
dialog box
to configure
a new
virtual host.

Four of the pages of this dialog box are the same as the default Virtual Host Properties dialog box shown in Figure 15-7. Refer to the description of Site

Configuration, Logging, Environment Variables, and Directories following Figure 15-7. The two pages not shown in the default Virtual Host Properties dialog box (General Options and SSL) are explained here.

General Options

On this page, you enter options for the virtual hosts that you are adding. You can set the following options:

- ✔ **Virtual Host Name:** Enter the name that you want to call the virtual host.

- ✔ **Document Root Directory:** Enter the directory that contains the root index file.

- ✔ **Webmaster Email Address:** Enter the e-mail address that will be displayed in the footer on error pages.

- ✔ **Host Information:** In this section, you specify Default Virtual Host, IP Based Virtual Host, or Name Based Virtual Host by clicking the down arrow and choosing from the list. Depending on your choice, text boxes appear beneath your selection for additional configuration information.

    - **Default Virtual Host:** Settings here are used if the requested IP address is not defined by another virtual host configuration.

      Be sure to not configure more than one default virtual host. If you do, the server will not know which default host to use, and you will get an error.

      If you do not configure a default virtual host, the main Web server settings are used.

    - **IP Based Virtual Host:** Selecting this option requires you to enter an IP address for the virtual Web server. You can enter multiple IP addresses by separating them with spaces. You can also specify ports by separating them from the IP address with a colon: for example, 192.168.2.1:80. You also need to enter the server host name.

    - **Name Based Virtual Host:** Electing this option requires you to enter the server host name for the virtual Web server. You can enter multiple IP addresses by separating them with spaces. Specify ports by separating them from the IP address with a colon: for example, 192.168.2.1:80. You also need to enter an IP address for the server. You can also enter an alias for the server by clicking the Add button next to the Aliases filed from the configuration options that appear when you selected the Name Based Virtual Host option and entering the alias.

SSL

Using Secure Socket Layers (SSL) allows you to provide a secure environment for your Web page users to send and receive personal or confidential information. If you are not serving such information, you probably don't need to enable SSL.

If you are planning to use SSL on your server, you want to enable it via the SSL page of the Virtual Host Properties Options dialog box, as shown in Figure 15-13.

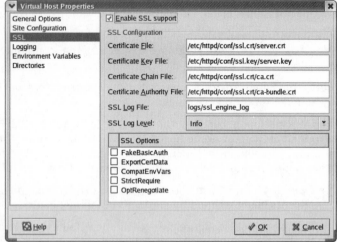

Figure 15-13: Set the SSL options for the virtual host here.

To enable SSL, mark the check box in front of the Enable SSL Support option. After selecting the Enable SSL Support option, the SSL Configuration text boxes are available for you to enter your SSL configuration information.

You need to obtain a valid digital certificate to use with your server. The configuration information supplied with the server is for testing purposes only, is not valid, and should not be used.

You cannot use SSL with name-based virtual hosts. You need to use IP-based virtual hosts if you want to use SSL. You can adjust these settings from the General Options page; see the preceding section.

Server tab

The third tab of the HTTP configuration dialog box (refer to Figure 15-4), the Server tab, is where you enter configuration information about your Web server. See Figure 15-14.

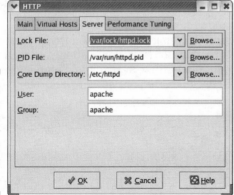

Figure 15-14:
Use the
Server tab
for
configuring
basic server
settings.

In most cases, you won't need to change these settings; just accept the default settings. The information that you can configure comprises

- ✔ **Lock File:** This setting shows the path to the location where the server lock file is located.

- ✔ **PID File:** This setting shows the path to the location where the server process ID file is located.

- ✔ **Core Dump Directory:** This setting shows the path to the location where the server core dump file is located.

- ✔ **User:** This setting specifies the user under which the Web server runs.

- ✔ **Group:** This setting specifies the group under which the Web server runs.

Setting the user or group to the root user can cause security problems with your Web server.

Performance Tuning tab

You can use the Performance Tuning tab, as shown in Figure 15-15, to set connection options for your server.

You can configure the following options:

- ✔ **Servers:** The Max Number of Connections setting determines how many simultaneous requests your server will accept. The maximum number that you can set here is 256.

- ✔ **Connections:** The Connection Timeout is how long the server waits, in seconds, for transmission and receipt of information in a communication session. You can select to either allow unlimited requests or change the number of requests accepted by entering another number in the appropriate field.

✔ **Requests per Connection:** Marking the Allow Persistent Connections check box enables the Timeout for Next Connection value to take effect: The server waits that amount of time, in seconds, before closing the session. A large number here can cause your server performance to slow down.

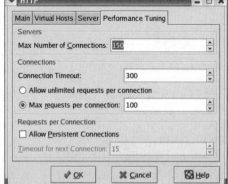

Figure 15-15: Set connection settings for your server here.

Saving Your Settings and Restarting the Web Server

After you finish configuring your Web server, you need to save your changes to the /etc/httpd/conf/httpd.conf file and restart the Web server for the changes to take effect. To do this, proceed as follows:

1. **Click OK and then Yes when asked whether you want to save and exit.**

2. **At a terminal prompt, and as the root user, enter the command**

```
service httpd restart
```

The server restarts, and your changes take effect.

Part V
Maintaining Your Enterprise Linux System

The 5th Wave   By Rich Tennant

"You the guy having trouble staying connected to the network?"

In this part . . .

This part is for all the neat freaks out there. You know who you are. You always want everything to be just right and in its place and working perfectly. In this part, you explore the tasks involved with keeping your system up-to-date using the Red Hat Network. Adding new users and configuring options for them is easy after you read Chapter 17. You install and upgrade software packages in Chapter 18. And, finally, in Chapter 19, you make some backups of your important data and figure out how to restore it to your system.

Chapter 16

Maintaining Your System with the Red Hat Network

· ·

In This Chapter

▶ Registering your system

▶ Configuring the up2date agent

▶ Using the up2date agent to keep your system current

▶ Accessing the Red Hat Network with a Web browser

· ·

*T*he Red Hat Network is a program that is installed by default when you install Red Hat Enterprise Linux. The Red Hat Network software is used to register a profile with Red Hat that contains information about your system hardware and the software packages installed on your system. Whenever a package update is available, for whatever reason, you can receive an e-mail notification from Red Hat as well as a visual notification of the update right on your desktop.

This might not sound like much at first, but think about the many steps involved in keeping your system up-to-date with the latest versions of the hundreds of packages that are installed on your system. The Red Hat Network practically eliminates the need for you to search for these packages because you can receive this information by e-mail. As a registered Red Hat Network user, you can also search for updates by using the up2date agent. With the Red Hat Network, you can now easily keep your system running reliably and securely. A few steps are involved in setting up the Red Hat Network, but they are well worth the effort. In this chapter, you can read how to register your system with Red Hat, configure the up2date agent, and then connect to look for updated files. The first step is registering, and this procedure is covered in the next section.

Registering Your System

Before you can begin using the Red Hat Network, you must first register your system with Red Hat by using the Red Hat Network registration client.

You can also register for the Red Hat Network at the Red Hat Web site by using your Web browser to go to http://rhn.redhat.com/network, creating a login, and filling in the online registration form.

You must be logged in as root to perform the registration, and you must also have a connection to the Internet to be able to log on to the Red Hat Web site. If you aren't connected to the Internet, you receive an error message, and the program closes when you click OK.

Start the registration client by following these steps:

1. **From the GNOME desktop, choose Applications⟶System Tools⟶ Red Hat Network.**

   You see the Red Hat Network Configuration screen where you can set a proxy server and authentication information if you need to. Click OK to go on and click Yes to install the GPG key. The Red Hat Update Agent screen appears that provides a description and lists the benefits of the Red Hat Network. If you choose not to use the Red Hat Network, you can click Cancel to end the process.

2. **Click Forward to continue to the Up2date Login Page dialog box, as shown in Figure 16-1.**

   You use this dialog box to create a new account or use an existing one if you've already created an account.

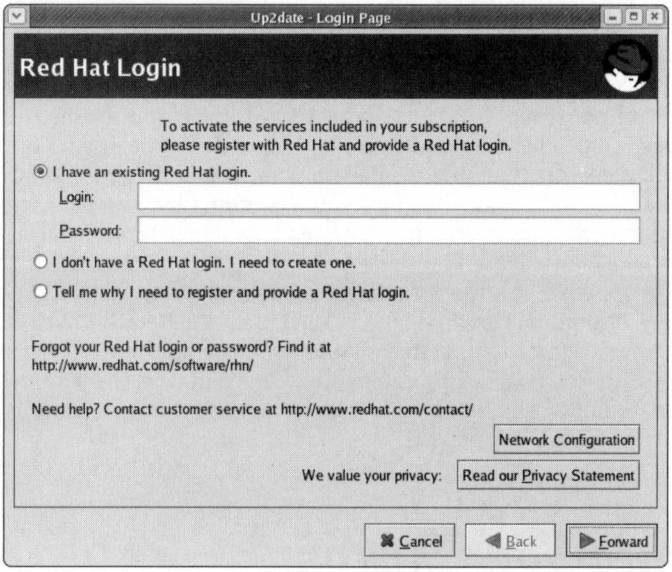

Up2date - Login Page

Red Hat Login

To activate the services included in your subscription,
please register with Red Hat and provide a Red Hat login.

● I have an existing Red Hat login.

    Login: [   ]

    Password: [   ]

○ I don't have a Red Hat login. I need to create one.

○ Tell me why I need to register and provide a Red Hat login.

Forgot your Red Hat login or password? Find it at
http://www.redhat.com/software/rhn/

Need help? Contact customer service at http://www.redhat.com/contact/

    [Network Configuration]

We value your privacy: [Read our Privacy Statement]

[✖ Cancel] [◀ Back] [▶ Forward]

Figure 16-1:
The
Up2date
Login Page
dialog box.

3. **If you already have an account, check the radio button for "I have an existing Red Hat login" and enter the username and password in the appropriate text boxes.**

   If you don't have a Red Hat Network login, you need to create one. Check the radio button for "I don't have ..." and click Forward. A new page opens where you can enter your information. All fields with an asterisk are required fields.

   The username must be at least five characters and cannot contain any spaces, tabs, line feeds, or reserved characters such as ', &, +, or %. You also enter your e-mail address here.

4. **After you enter the appropriate information, click Forward to continue to the Up2date Activation Page dialog box, as shown in Figure 16-2.**

   On this page, you can enter your subscription number, if you have one, and set your system name. By default, your system hardware information and installed packages are sent to the Red Hat Network but you can choose not to send them by deselecting the appropriate check box.

Figure 16-2:
The
Up2date
Product
Information
Page dialog
box.

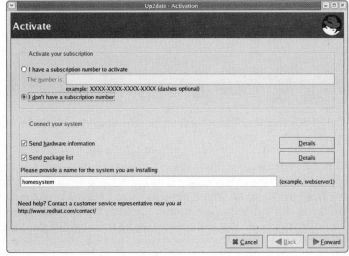

5. **Click Forward to continue.**

   Your system profile is sent to the Red Hat Network. After the registration process is finished, you receive a confirmation message stating that you have successfully registered your system profile on the Red Hat Network. Now you are ready to configure the up2date agent.

Configuring the Up2date Agent

Before you can use the Red Hat up2date agent, you need to configure it. To start and configure the Up2date Agent Configuration tool, do the following:

Open a terminal window and from the command line, type **up2date-config**. The Red Hat Network Configuration dialog box, as shown in Figure 16-3, now opens.

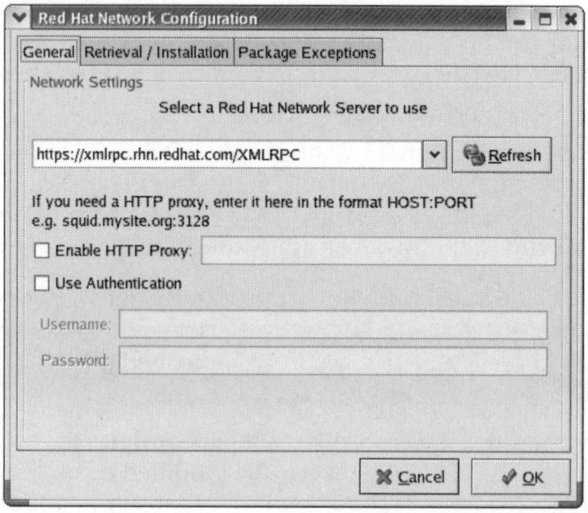

Figure 16-3: The Red Hat Network Configuration dialog box.

This dialog box has three tabs — General, Retrieval/Installation, and Package Exceptions:

✔ **General:** The General tab is the tab shown by default when the dialog box opens. A server is already selected for you to use, and you should not need to change it. If you need to use a proxy server to connect to the Web, you can enter this information here by first selecting the Enable HTTP Proxy check box and then entering the name of your server in the field next to the check box. If you need to use authentication, you can enable it by selecting the Use Authentication check box and filling in the Username and the Password fields.

✔ **Retrieval/Installation:** From this tab (see Figure 16-4), you can choose options that affect how the packages are retrieved and subsequently installed.

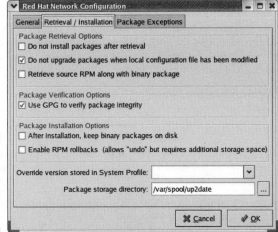

The Package Retrieval Options are

- **Do Not Install Packages After Retrieval.** By default, packages are automatically installed after they are retrieved. If you enable this option, packages are retrieved to the specified directory but not installed.

- **Do Not Upgrade Packages When Local Configuration File Has Been Modified.** If you have manually modified configuration files for packages on your system, these packages are not displayed by default. If you disable this option, the packages are displayed.

- **Retrieve Source RPM Along with Binary Package.** By default, the source Red Hat Package Manager (RPM) is not downloaded with the binary version of the package. By enabling this option, you also retrieve the source of the RPM.

The Package Verification Options has but one choice:

- **Use GPG to Verify Package Integrity.** By default, for security purposes, the packages are verified to ensure they contain the Red Hat GPG signature. If you disable this option, the security check is not performed.

GPG stands for GNU Privacy Guard, which is the open source replacement for PGP. PGP (Pretty Good Privacy) was developed in the mid 1990s by Phil Zimmerman to provide data encryption. GPG was developed to replace PGP because PGP contained a patented algorithm and its use was restricted. GPG can be freely used without concern for patented information.

The Package Installation Options are

- **After Installation, Keep Binary Packages on Disk.** By default, the packages are removed from the local disk after they are installed. Enabling this option leaves a copy of the package in the specified directory.

- **Enable RPM rollbacks.** Choosing this option lets you restore your system to its condition before the RPM was installed.

The last two items on this tab are

- **Override Version Stored in System Profile.** By filling in this field, you can override the version stored in your System Profile with the version in the field.

- **Package Storage Directory.** Here you can specify the storage location of the packages on your system.

✔ **Package Exceptions:** From this tab (see Figure 16-5), you can choose to exclude packages by either the name of the package or the name of the file.

- *To exclude a package by package name:* Type the name of the package in the Add New field in the Package Names to Skip section, and then click the top Add button.

- *To exclude a package by file name:* Type the name of the file in the Add New field in the File Names to Skip section, and then click the bottom Add button.

After you make any changes to the three tabs, click OK. Your configuration changes are saved, and you can now use the up2date agent.

Figure 16-5:
The Package Exceptions tab.

Using the Red Hat Enterprise Linux Up2date Agent

The up2date agent is a valuable tool for you because it helps you to keep your system running the most current versions of the packages installed on your system. During the system installation, an Alert icon is placed on the right side of the top desktop panel that provides visual notification when your system needs to be updated. Figure 16-6 shows the location of the Alert icon on the panel.

Red Hat Network Alert icon

Figure 16-6:
The Red Hat
Network
Alert icon.

The Alert icon is colored-coded, representing a different state of the update. The icons and their meaning are

- ✔ **Blue check mark:** The system is up-to-date.

- ✔ **Green double arrows:** The system is checking for updates.

- ✔ **Red exclamation point:** The system needs to be updated.

- ✔ **Gray question mark:** An error has occurred.

You can roll the mouse over the Alert icon to view a small pop-up window that gives additional information. To start the up2date agent to update your system, do the following:

1. **Right click the Alert icon and select Launch Up2date from the contextual menu.**

   If you are not logged in as root, you will be prompted for the root password.

   The first time you run the utility, a configuration dialog box appears that explains the terms of service and provides a dialog box from which you can configure a proxy server if necessary.

2. **You are prompted to install the Red Hat GPG key that is used to verify the Red Hat security signature on the downloaded packages. Click Yes to install the key.**

   You see the Red Hat Update Agent Welcome screen.

You can run the configuration utility at any time by choosing Config-uration from the Alert icon's contextual menu (right-click the icon).

3. **Click Forward to continue to the Channels dialog box, as shown in Figure 16-7.**

4. **Select the appropriate channel and click Forward to continue.**

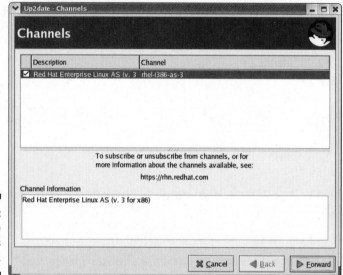

Figure 16-7:
The
Channels
dialog box.

The program connects to the Red Hat Network to search for package updates. If you chose to skip packages when you configured up2date earlier in this chapter, you see the Skipped Packages dialog box, as shown in Figure 16-8. Click Forward to continue.

If you did not choose to skip packages, you see the Package List dialog box, as shown in Figure 16-9, showing the available packages. If your system is updated, you won't see any packages listed.

5. **You can select packages individually by selecting the check box in front of the package name, or you can mark the Select All Packages check box to select all packages. After you finish selecting packages, click Forward.**

The up2date program gets the packages and prompts you to continue after the packages have been retrieved.

6. **Click Forward to install the packages.**

You see a progress dialog box during the package installation.

After all the packages that you selected for installation are installed, you see a dialog box indicating the package installation has finished.

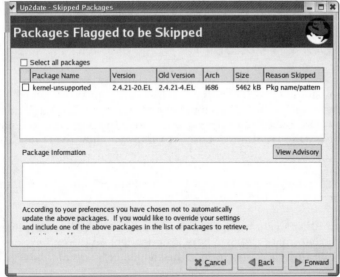

Figure 16-8:
The Skipped
Packages
dialog box.

Figure 16-9:
The
Package
List dialog
box.

7. Click Finish to complete the update process.

Click the Alert icon to open a dialog box listing all available packages. You can also launch up2date from here.

Accessing the Red Hat Network with a Web Browser

You can access the Red Hat Network by using any Web browser. In fact, if you have multiple machines, you can manage them at the same time through the browser interface. All you need to do is go to the Red Hat Web site at `http://rhn.redhat.com` and log in by using the username and password that you assigned to the account that I show you how to create earlier in this chapter.

After logging in, you see the Your RHN tabbed page for your system, as shown in Figure 16-10.

The Your RHN tab shown in Figure 16-10 might not look exactly like your page. The information shown here is dependent on the preferences that you might have chosen. Take a look at the significant areas of this page.

At the top of the page are seven tabs that can be used to take you to other pages where you can get more information about you systems and make configuration changes. The seven tabs are

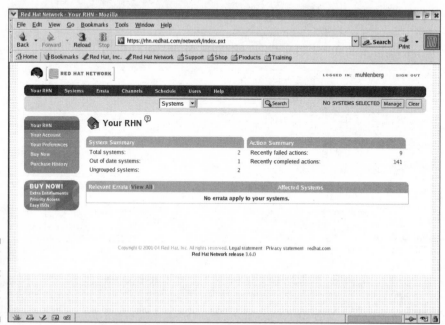

Figure 16-10: The Red Hat Network main page.

✔ **Your RHN:** This tab opens by default after you login to the Red Hat Network. In the center of the page is a summary of your system (or systems, depending on how many you have configured). Along the left side of the page are links to information about your account and settings that you can change.

✔ **Systems:** The Systems tab opens a page that provides a general overview of your systems, as shown in Figure 16-11.

You can click the link for your system that is shown in the body of the page to get information specific to that system. Along the left side of the page are links to pages that provide additional information about your systems.

✔ **Errata:** Clicking the Errata tab opens a page, as shown in Figure 16-12, listing any errata that applies to your system. As with the other tabs, there are additional links along the left side of the page that give additional information.

✔ **Channels:** The Channels tab, as shown in Figure 16-13, shows the software channels to which you have subscribed. You can download software for your systems from channels to which you have subscribed. Like the other tabbed pages, there are additional links on the left side of the page for obtaining more information or services.

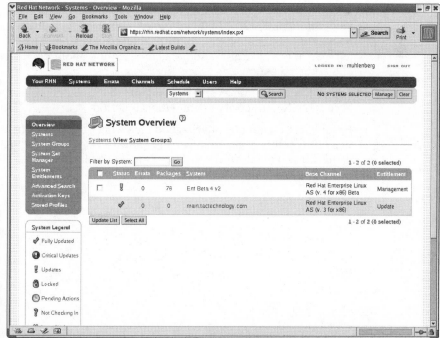

Figure 16-11:
The Systems tab shows general system information.

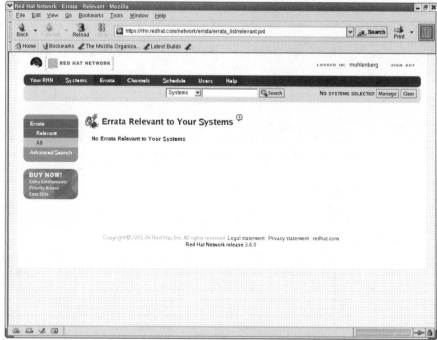

Figure 16-12:
The Errata
tab shows
system
errata
information.

✔ **Schedule:** The Schedule tab, as shown in Figure 16-14, gives you information about pending actions for the selected system. The links on the left side of the page give additional information about completed, failed, and archived actions.

✔ **Users:** The Users tab, as shown in Figure 16-15, shows the users who can access the Red Hat Network and their functions.

✔ **Help:** I bet you already have a good idea what you'll find when you click this link. On this page, as shown in Figure 16-16, you'll find links to many good sources of information about Enterprise Linux.

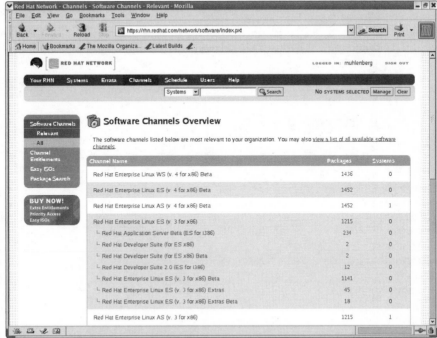

Figure 16-13:
The
Channels
tab shows
your
subscription
entitlements.

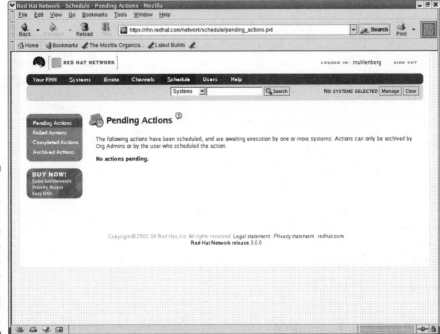

Figure 16-14:
The
Schedule
tab shows
pending,
failed,
completed,
and
archived
actions.

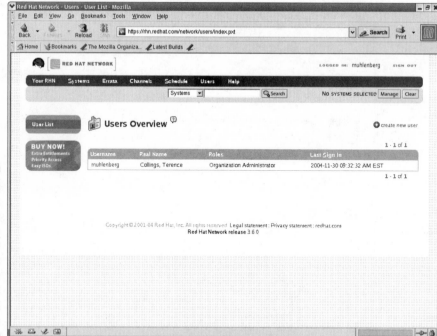

Figure 16-15:
The Users tab shows the administrators allowed to access the Red Hat Network account.

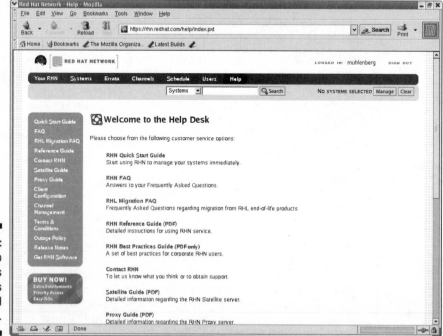

Figure 16-16:
The Help tab takes you to links to helpful information.

Chapter 17

Administering Users and Groups

- -

In This Chapter

▶ Working with users and groups

▶ Restricting disk space with quotas

- -

*O*ne of your primary tasks as a system administrator is creating and managing user accounts. You should always create user accounts for anyone who will be using your systems. Making the user log in by using a username and password is your first line of defense in keeping your system secure and giving you a trail to follow if security problems arise. You won't have to be so worried if only those to whom you have given permission can log in and use your system and its resources.

Working with Users and Groups

Enterprise Linux provides you with a graphical utility, the *Red Hat User Manager,* which you can use to create and modify user and group accounts. You open the User Manager by choosing Applications⇨System Settings⇨ Users & Groups. The Red Hat User Manager dialog box, as shown in Figure 17-1, appears.

Take a brief look at what is contained in the User Manager dialog box. At the top of the dialog box is a menu bar containing three submenus:

✔ **File:** The File menu offers the same choices as those appearing on the toolbar immediately beneath the menu bar.

✔ **Preferences:** Choosing Preferences offers one choice: namely, to filter system users and groups. This choice is a toggle. The first time that you run the User Manager, the filter is applied, and you see only those users listed that you created during the system installation. Toggle the option again, and you see a list of all system accounts, many of which are not actual log in accounts but are required for proper system and application operation. The purpose of the filter is to hide the list of the system accounts and show you only the real login accounts. You cannot make any changes to the filter; you can just choose to use it or not.

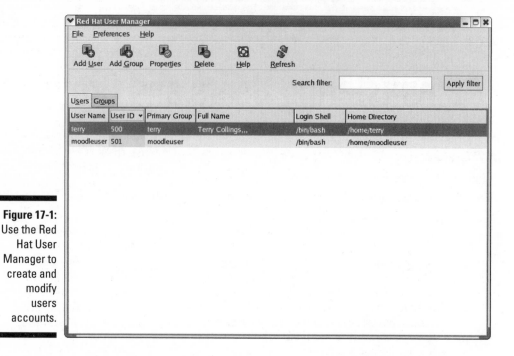

Figure 17-1:
Use the Red
Hat User
Manager to
create and
modify
users
accounts.

✔ **Help:** Clicking Help opens a browser window displaying help for the
User Manager program.

The toolbar contains the following icons:

✔ **Add User:** Click this icon to add a new user. (See the upcoming section,
"Adding a new user.")

✔ **Add Group:** Click this icon to add a new group. (See the upcoming section, "Adding a new group.")

✔ **Properties:** Select a user or group and then click this icon to view or
modify the user or group properties.

✔ **Delete:** Select a user or group and then click this icon to delete the user
or group.

✔ **Help:** Click this icon to open the help for User Manager.

✔ **Refresh:** Click this icon to refresh the display.

Below the toolbar, on the right side of the dialog box, is the Search Filter text
area. Here you can enter the first few letters of a user or group name and
either press Enter or click the Apply Filter button to search for and display
only the name that you're searching for.

Under the Search Filter field is the tabbed display of the users and groups on your system. The Users tab opens by default when you start the application. You can click the Groups tab to change to the groups view. To return to the users view, click the Users tab.

Adding a new user

Adding a new user to your system is easy when you use the Red Hat User Manager. To create a new user account, do the following:

1. **Start the User Manager by choosing Applications⇨ System Settings⇨Users & Groups.**

   If you are not logged in as the root user, you are prompted to enter the root password.

2. **Click the Add User icon from the toolbar to open the Create New User dialog box, as shown in Figure 17-2.**

Figure 17-2: Add new users to your system here.

3. **Enter the username that your user will use, the full name of the user, and the user's login password.**

4. **You can accept the default settings for the login shell, creating a home directory and creating a private group. To add the user to another group, modify the user's properties. (See the upcoming section, "Changing user properties." Click OK to create the user.**

5. **To create more users, repeat Steps 2–4. When you are finished creating users, choose File⇨Quit from the menu bar.**

When you create a new user on your system, a home directory is created by default for the user at `/home/username` unless you decide not to create the directory or to place it somewhere else. A *private group* — that is, belonging to just the user — is also created for the user unless you decide not to create the group when you create the user account. You can find out more about groups in the section "Adding a new group" later in this chapter. Finally, all users on the system have a user ID number (UID) assigned by the system. Enterprise Linux reserves UIDs less than 500 for system purposes, so all users that you create have UIDs beginning with 500 and greater. See the section, "Changing user properties" for more information about user rights assignments.

Adding a new group

Adding a new group to your system is easy when you use the Red Hat User Manager. To create a new group account, follow the procedure here.

After you create a group, you can assign rights to that group. Then, whenever you create new users and add them as members of that group — or add existing users to that group — they have the rights assigned to that group. This is a quick and easy way to assign rights to many users at the same time. For example, suppose that you have a drafting department in your company whose users need access to the same files and directories. You could create a group called *Drafting* and assign the rights to the files and directories to that group. Then you make the new or existing users in the drafting department members of the Drafting group, and they have all the rights that they need.

1. **Start the User Manager by choosing Applications⇨ System Settings⇨Users & Groups.**

   If you are not logged in as the root user, you are prompted to enter the root password.

2. **Click Add Group from the toolbar to open the Create New Group dialog box, as shown in Figure 17-3.**

Create New Group

Group Name: |

☐ Specify group ID manually

GID: 500

✖ Cancel   ✔ OK

3. **Enter the group name in the Group Name field. If you want to manually assign a group ID number (GID), select the check box in front of the option and click the up or down arrow to choose the number that you want.**

By default, all groups on the system have the group ID number (GID) assigned by the system. Enterprise Linux reserves GIDs less than 500 for system purposes, so all groups that you create have GIDs beginning with 500 and greater.

4. **Click OK to create the group.**

5. **To create additional groups, repeat Steps 2–4. When you are finished creating groups, choose File⇨Quit from the menu bar.**

Changing user properties

After you create your users, you might want to change the properties for their accounts. For example, you might want to force them to change their password at some specified interval, make their account expire at a specified time, or make them members of one or more groups. You can change user properties by following this procedure:

1. **Start the User Manager by choosing Applications⇨ System Settings⇨Users & Groups.**

If you are not logged in as the root user, you are prompted to enter the root password.

2. **Click the username from the list under User Name (refer to Figure 17-1) and then click Properties from the toolbar to open the User Properties dialog box, as shown in Figure 17-4.**

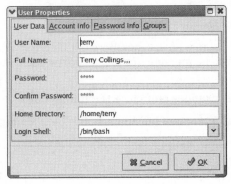

Figure 17-4: Modify user account properties here.

The User Properties dialog box contains four tabs.

- **User Data:** Here you can change the user's full name, password, home directory, and login shell.

- **Account Info:** On this tab, you can set an account expiration time and lock the local password.

- **Password Info:** On this tab, you can enable password expiration and set time limits related to password expiration.

- **Groups:** On this tab, you can view the groups to which the user belongs. You can select additional groups to which you want the user to be a member, or you can remove the user from groups.

3. **After you make your changes on all the tabs, click OK to apply them and close the dialog box.**

4. **Choose File⇨Quit from the menu bar to close the User Manager.**

Changing group properties

You can change your group's properties with the User Manager by following the procedure here:

1. **Start the User Manager by choosing Applications⇨ System Settings⇨Users & Groups.**

   If you are not logged in as the root user, you are prompted to enter the root password.

2. **Click the Groups tab and then the group name from the list of Group Names.**

3. **Click Properties from the toolbar to open the Group Properties dialog box, as shown in Figure 17-5.**

4. **Click the Group Users tab.**

   Here you can view the users who are members of this group. You can select additional users to be members of the group, or you can remove the user from this group.

5. **Click OK to apply your changes and close the dialog box.**

6. **Choose File⇨Quit from the menu bar to close the User Manager.**

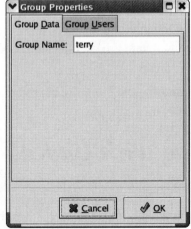

Figure 17-5:
Add users to
a group
here.

Removing a user

To remove a user from your system, do the following:

1. **Start the User Manager by choosing Applications⇨System Settings⇨ Users & Groups.**

   If you are not logged in as the root user, you are prompted to enter the root password.

2. **Click the username from the User Name list and then click Delete from the toolbar.**

   You will be asked whether you are sure that you want to delete the user. You are also offered the choice to delete the user's home directory. There are instances when you might want to keep a user's files even though you have deleted the user's account. For example, if an employee is terminated, you can prevent him from accessing your systems by removing his login account. Keeping the user's home directory gives you, or someone in his department perhaps, the ability to check through the files to see whether they are worth keeping. See Figure 17-6.

Figure 17-6:
User
Manager
prompts you
before
deleting
a user
account.

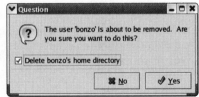

Before you delete a user's home directory, be sure that the files and directories there are no longer needed.

3. If you are sure that you want to delete the user account, click Yes.

The user account is deleted.

4. Choose File➪Quit from the menu bar to close the User Manager.

Restricting Disk Usage with Quotas

One of the problems that you might encounter as a system administrator is running out of disk space. Many times, this problem is caused by users who do not properly manage their home directories. Your users might be saving too many files and not periodically removing their unused files.

You can force users to be more efficient in their use of storage space by imposing disk quotas on their home directories. A *disk quota* is simply a restriction on the amount of disk space that a user can use. There is no graphical tool available in Enterprise Linux for managing disk quotas, but setting them up from the command line is a fairly simple process.

You need to do only a few steps to begin using disk quotas on your system. These steps are

1. Modify the /etc/fstab file.

2. Run the quotacheck program.

3. Unmount and mount the file system.

4. Run edquota to set up the user quotas.

Configuring disk quotas

When Enterprise Linux is going through its startup procedures, the /etc/fstab file is read by the system to obtain mounting information about the file systems. When you want to use quotas on your system, you need to put the options usrquota and grpquota into the options area of the file system to be mounted.

Disk quotas can be based on users, groups, or both. If you are using solely user-based quotas, you need to add only the usrquota option. If you are using solely group-based quotas, you need to add only the grpquota option. In this section, I discuss only user-based quotas, but the same rules apply to group-based quotas as well.

You must be the root user to change the /etc/fstab file. To modify your /etc/fstab file, do the following:

1. **From** vi **or a text editor of your choice, open the** /etc/fstab **file.**

   Figure 17-7 shows the /etc/fstab file from my system.

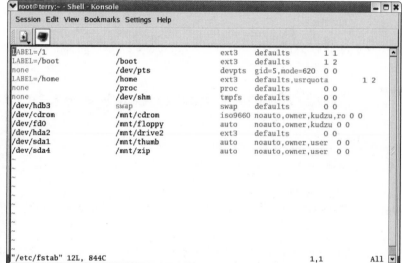

Figure 17-7:
The /etc/
fstab file
is where
you enable
disk quotas.

2. **Type in the option** usrquota **in the options section of the file system for which you want to enable quotas.**

   In Figure 17-7, you can see the usrquota option on the fourth line of the file. Your file will be different from mine, but try to find a similar line in your file to place the option.

3. **Save and close the file.**

4. **Run the** quotacheck **command to set up the quota files needed by the system. At a terminal prompt, enter**

   ```
   quotacheck /mounted file system
   ```

   where *mounted file system* is your file system.

   The quotacheck command also gets usage information about the mounted file system.

5. **Unmount and remount the file system.**

   a. Enter the following at a command prompt:

   ```
   umount /mounted file system
   ```

   where *mounted file system* is your file system.

b. Then enter

```
mount /file system
```

where *file system* is your file system.

6. **Set up the quotas for your users with this command:**

```
edquota user name
```

where *user name* is the name of the user for whom you want to set the quota.

Figure 17-8 shows the result of running the `edquota` command.

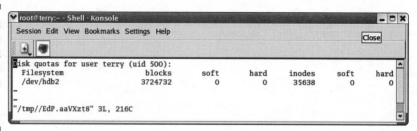

The `edquota` command starts a text editor that enables you to make changes to the quota limits. Statistics are displayed for the user that you specified when you ran the command. In Figure 17-8, you can see that user terry is using 3724732 1K blocks, or 35638 inodes, on file system `/dev/hdb2`. The number of inodes corresponds to the number of files used. The values for `soft` and `hard` are currently 0 (zero), indicating that no quotas have been set yet. (Read more about inodes in the section, "Obtaining disk quota statistics.")

✔ **Soft:** The *soft limit* is the maximum amount of blocks or inodes that a user can use permanently.

✔ **Hard:** The *hard limit* is the maximum amount of blocks or inodes that a user can use temporarily.

The soft limit is always set below the hard limit so that the user can temporarily go above the soft limit if necessary. The amount of time that the user can temporarily go over the soft limit is determined by the grace period set for the system. The default grace period is 7 days, but it can be changed by using the `edquota` program. (See how in the following steps.)

The `edquota` program opens the `vi` text editor for editing the quota file. If you are not familiar with `vi`, you can get help by typing **man vi** at a command prompt. Now you can finish the configuration process:

1. **Enter the soft and hard values for the disk quota in the appropriate places.**

   You enter 1K block values. For example, if you want to set a soft limit of 4.9GB, enter **4900000** as the block value.

2. **After you finish editing the file, be sure to save and exit.**

3. **To change the grace period, type** edquota -t **at a command prompt.**

   After the `vi` editor opens, you can change the time period as you desire.

You should run the `quotacheck` command about once a week to be sure that your quota files are current. If your system crashes for any reason, you definitely need to run `quotacheck` as soon as the system restarts.

Obtaining disk quota statistics

To get information about the disk quotas in place on your system, you can use the `repquota` command. Enter the command as follows:

```
repquota /file system
```

where *file system* is your mounted file system.

For the example command

```
[root@terry root]# repquota /home
```

you should obtain results similar to this:

```
*** Report for user quotas on device /dev/hdb2
Block grace time: 10days; Inode grace time: 10days
                        Block limits              File limits
User            used    soft    hard  grace  used  soft  hard  grace
----------------------------------------------------------------------
root       --  532656      0       0          2783    0    0
apache     --      84      0       0            16    0    0
terry      -- 3724732      0       0         35638    0    0
moodleuser --      80      0       0            20    0    0
bonzo      --      40 4900000 5000000          10    0    0
#10490     --   52740      0       0            11    0    0
#1000      --   18108      0       0          1092    0    0
#1004      --   15036      0       0            19    0    0
#1110      --    9180      0       0           944    0    0
#620       --    2804      0       0           189    0    0
```

In this example, you can see the disk quota set in 1K blocks for the user bonzo on the mounted file system /dev/hdb2. The information that appears in the File Limits columns shows the number of inodes used. An *inode* (information node) is a data structure containing information about a file. Each file on the system has an inode that contains information about the file such as ownership, permissions, and type of file. Inodes are created when the file system is created on the disk drive. The total number of inodes is dependent on the size of the disk drive and limits the number of files that you can have on your system.

Chapter 18

Installing and Upgrading Software Packages

In This Chapter

▶ Managing packages with the Red Hat Enterprise Package Manager

▶ Managing applications from binary rpm files

▶ Installing applications from compressed zip files

*O*ne of your primary tasks as a system administrator is managing the application packages that are installed on your system. At some point in your system administration duties, you'll need to install new packages or modify and remove already installed packages. In this chapter, you can read about the Package Manager application that you can use to install and remove packages that are part of the Enterprise Linux installation. You will also discover how to find other packages that you can install, either from binary files or from source files that you can compile and install on your system.

Managing Packages with the Red Hat Package Manager

Enterprise Linux provides you with a graphical utility — the Red Hat Package Manager — that you can use to install new applications or remove existing system applications. The Package Manager supplied with Enterprise Linux is used only to add or remove applications that were included with the original Enterprise Linux installation disks. For installing other packages, see the section, "Installing Applications from Compressed Zip Files," later in this chapter. You open the Red Hat Package Manager by choosing Applications⇨ System Settings⇨Add/Remove Applications. The Package Management dialog box, as shown in Figure 18-1, appears.

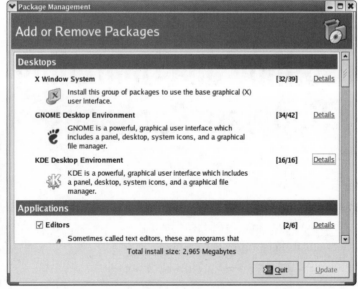

Figure 18-1:
Use the
Red Hat
Package
Manager
install and
remove
applications.

Take a brief look at what is contained in the Package Management dialog box. It contains a list of all the packages that can be or are already installed on your system. Each package listed has numbers that follow the package name and a Details link that you can click to get more information. The numbers after the package name indicate the number of installed applications related to the package. For example, the numbers 6/12 following the package name indicates that 6 of 12 applications related to the package are installed. You can click Details to open another dialog box that lists each application included in the package. Figure 18-2 shows the results of clicking the Details link for the GNOME Desktop Environment.

As you can see from Figure 18-2, many applications are installed with the GNOME Desktop Environment. If a check mark is in the box in front of an application's name, the application is installed. Conversely, if there is no check in the box, the application is not installed.

Installing system packages

From the Red Hat Package Manager, you can easily install additional system applications. To install additional applications, do the following:

1. **Choose Applications⇨System Settings⇨Add/Remove Applications.**

2. **Find the package that you want to install from the list of packages and click the box in front of the package name to place a check there.**

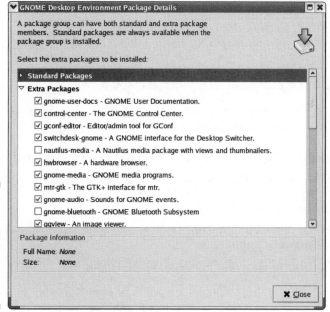

Figure 18-2:
Details
about the
applications
installed in
the GNOME
Desktop.

3. **Click the Details link for the package and then select other related packages to install.**

4. **Click Close to close the Package Details dialog box.**

5. **Click Update.**

   The system displays a dialog box with information about the packages that you selected.

6. **Click Continue to begin the package installation. If prompted to insert one of the installation CDs into the CD drive, insert the requested disc and click OK to continue.**

   After the packages that you selected are installed, you see a dialog box, as shown in Figure 18-3, indicating that the update is complete.

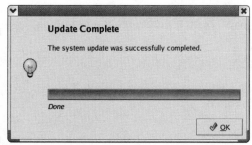

Figure 18-3:
You
successfully
updated
your
packages.

7. Click OK to close the Update Complete dialog box.

8. Click Quit to close the Package Manager.

Removing system packages

From the Red Hat Package Manager, you can also easily remove system applications. To remove system applications, do the following:

1. **Choose Applications➪System Settings➪Add/Remove Applications.**

2. **Find the package that you want to remove from the list of packages and click the box in front of the package name to remove the check in the box.**

3. **Click the Details link for the package and then select other related applications to remove.**

4. **Click Close to close the Package Details dialog box.**

5. **Click Update.**

   The system displays a dialog box with information about the packages that you selected to remove.

6. **Click Continue to begin the package removal.**

   After the packages that you selected are removed, you see a dialog box indicating that the update is complete.

7. **Click OK to close the Update Complete dialog box.**

8. **Click Quit to close the Package Manager.**

Managing Applications from Binary rpm Files

Although you can use the Package Manager that is included with Enterprise Linux to add or remove system packages and applications, you can't use it to install third-party packages. If you want to install other applications, you have two choices:

✔ Find binary files to install.

✔ Get the compressed zip file, extract and compile the package for your system, and then install it.

Either method is relatively simple.

Installing binary rpm files

There are thousands of applications that you can install on your system that can be obtained from many sources. If you can find a binary package already compiled for your system, the installation will be a little quicker and easier than compiling the application yourself. Binary files end with the extension .rpm, which stands for Red Hat Package Manager. In this section, I show you how to find an application by searching the Web and then how to install that application.

Be sure that the file you download does not end in .src.rpm because this is a source .rpm and can't be installed directly by using the procedure in this section.

One of my favorite applications for viewing pictures of my daughter is gqview. This package is not installed as part of an Enterprise Linux installation and must be installed separately. First, you need to find it. I did a search on the Web looking for *gqview*. The results showed the rpm file that I needed to download and then install to be able to use gqview to look at all the pictures of my daughter that I took with my digital camera. I installed the rpm file by following this procedure:

1. **Find the file that you want to download and then save it to a directory on your system.**

   Be sure that you download the appropriate file for your system and that it ends with the extension .rpm.

2. **Change to the directory containing the file that you downloaded.**

3. **Enter this command at a terminal prompt:**

   ```
   rpm -Uvh <name of rpm>
   ```

   where *<name of rpm>* is the file that you downloaded.

   Be sure that you are logged in as root.

   You see a progress dialog box while the rpm file is installed.

   When the command prompt returns, the rpm file is installed.

You can browse to the directory where you saved the downloaded file with a graphical file manager and then click the filename to install it.

Look a little deeper into the rpm command. The rpm command can be used to build, install, update, query, and remove packages from your system. The syntax for the command is

```
rpm <basic options> <general options> <specific options> name of application
```

The basic options are required, and your rpm command must contain one of the basic options. Basic options consist of the following:

- ✔ -q: Use this option to query the rpm database for information about the selected package.
- ✔ -e: Use this option to remove an already installed package.
- ✔ -F: Use this option to upgrade an existing package.
- ✔ -i: Use this option to install a package.
- ✔ -U: (note capitalization) Use this option to install a new package or upgrade an existing one and remove earlier versions after the upgrade.
- ✔ -V: (note capitalization) Use this option to verify information about the package compared with the rpm database.

General options can be used with any of the basic options. Some of the commonly used general options are

- ✔ -v: This option instructs the rpm command to display details about the command.
- ✔ --quiet: (note use of double hyphens) Using this option prints only error messages about the command.

In addition to the basic and general options, specific options are used, depending on the basic option chosen — for example, install-specific options that are used only with the install option, erase-specific options only used with the erase option, and so on.

Finding installed package files

By using the rpm command, you can find what packages you already have installed on your system. You can either search for a specific package or get a list of all packages installed. To search for a specific package, enter the following command from a terminal command prompt:

```
rpm -q <name of package>
```

For example, if I want to know whether the Samba package is installed, I enter

```
rpm -q samba
```

and receive this output indicating the package is installed and showing the version number of the installed package.

```
samba-3.0.7-1.3e
```

Removing installed packages

You can also use the rpm command to remove installed packages by using the -e option. For example, if you want to remove the Samba packages from your system, you enter the following command at a terminal command prompt:

```
rpm -e samba-3.0.7-1.3e
```

After the command executes, the package is removed from your system.

For a complete list of all options and more details about the rpm command, see the man page for the command.

Installing Applications from Compressed Zip Files

Although you can usually find a binary rpm file that contains the package you want to install, sometimes you can find the application only as a compressed zip file. Files of this type end with the extension .tar.gz and are commonly referred to as *tarballs,* from the tar command that is used to create the archive.

Before you can compile applications and install them on your system, you must be sure that you have the development tools installed on your system. Open the Package Manager and scroll down the list of installed packages until you find one called Development Tools. If it is installed, you'll see a check mark next to its name. If it isn't installed, follow the steps in the section, "Installing system packages."

Files with the extension .tar.gz are files that have been placed into an archive with the tar command and then compressed via the gzip command. In this section, I show you how to extract the files from the compressed archive and then compile and install them on your system. Be sure that you are logged in as the root user before beginning the following procedure. To extract, compile, and install a compressed zip file, do the following:

1. **Change to the directory containing the file that you downloaded.**

   In this example, I downloaded the file kstocks-2.02.tar.gz.

2. **Enter the following command at a terminal prompt:**

   ```
   tar -xzvf kstocks-2.02.tar.gz <name of your program>
   ```

The tar command has many options; the ones used in this example have the following meaning:

- x: Tells the tar command to extract the files from the archive

- z: Tells the tar command that the file has been gzipped, so it needs to be ungzipped

- v: Tells the tar command to be *verbose,* or to display what it is doing on the display

- f: Tells tar to use the archive file that you specify

After you run the tar command, the compressed archive is uncompressed, and the archive is extracted to a directory named for the program without the .tar.gz extension.

3. Change to the directory containing the extracted files and open the file named INSTALL.

The INSTALL file contains installation instructions. You will find a file like this in every directory created when you extract compressed archive files.

4. Run the configure **command after you extract the file.**

```
./configure
```

Running the configure command can take a while, depending on the speed of your system. While it's running, it displays messages on the screen so you can see what it is doing. After the command has finished, the system returns to a command prompt.

5. Type make **at the command prompt to compile the package.**

6. When make **has finished running, type** make install **to install the package.**

7. Type make clean **to remove the program binaries and object files from the source code directory.**

Although this chapter contains the basic procedure for extracting, configuring, compiling, and installing a compressed archive, sometimes the procedure is different. You should always look for the INSTALL file and also the README file in the directory containing the extracted files. Be sure to follow the instructions in these files to do the installation.

Chapter 19

Backing Up and Restoring Your Files

In This Chapter

▶ Planning your backup strategy

▶ Selecting your backup media

▶ Determining your backup method

▶ Using backup tools

Making backups of the file system is important to avoid the loss of important information in the case of catastrophic hardware or software failure. An efficient backup and restoration process can minimize downtime and avoid the need to re-create lost work. Red Hat Enterprise Linux provides several packages for backup and restoration of the file system. In this chapter, I show you how to create a backup strategy for your systems as well as choose your backup media and use the tools provided with Enterprise Linux to do your backups.

Planning Your Backup Strategy

Before you can back up your important files, you need to determine what you need to back up. Your choice of what to back up depends largely on what data the system contains and how you use the system. However, here are some basic guidelines that can help you determine what to back up.

Don't: Back up temp and cache files

Usually, temporary and cached files do not need to be backed up. The contents of the /tmp directory, for instance, are usually deleted when the system is rebooted. Therefore, not backing up these files is okay. You might find it worthwhile to check whether any other packages installed on the system create large amounts of ignorable temporary data.

Maybe: Back up OS files

Depending on the situation, backing up the operating system files might or might not be advisable. If the machine is a standard installation of Red Hat Enterprise Linux without any customizations or extra packages installed, the system files can be restored by reinstalling Enterprise Linux. The trade-off is that reinstalling and reconfiguring a system probably takes more time and attention than restoring the file system from backup. However, this trade-off can be worthwhile because of the amount of backup media that can be saved.

In the particular case that a single Red Hat Enterprise Linux installation is copied verbatim onto many machines, backing up the system files of just one of the machines might be appropriate. If the system files are identical across machines, a single backup should restore them all. In any case, backing up at least the /etc directory of each machine is probably wise. Most likely, the machines have at least some differing configuration information, such as network and hostname settings.

Do: Back up database files and user files

One thing definitely needs to be backed up, and indeed, needs to be backed up via a special method: database files. Doing a straight tar from database files won't save you from a database crash because the database files will all be in different states, having been written to backup when open. Oracle, Informix, Sybase, and other database programs all allow the administrator to put the database table spaces in backup mode. In *backup mode,* the data to be written goes to a memory cache rather than the file, and transaction logs are updated only when the cache is flushed. This procedure slows things down but makes certain that the database will survive a crash.

Another part of the file system that need to be backed up — other than the system files — is the user files. All user files are stored in subdirectories of the /home directory. You should find it easy, therefore, to back up all user files at once.

Even when the entire file system — both system and user files — is being backed up, you should still back them up separately. System and user files can have different relative priorities depending on the situation. The user files are important because they might be irreplaceable, whereas many of the system files generally can be replaced by reinstalling Red Hat Enterprise Linux. On the other hand, restoration of the system files is necessary for the machine to function and provide services, whereas the machine can be totally functional without restoration of the user files. Such priority considerations must be made when designing a backup strategy.

Give special thought to resources that do not easily fall into the system and user categories. Information stored in SQL (Structured Query Language) databases, for instance, is often technically owned by root or by a special system user but also often contains irreplaceable content entered by users. This kind of data can often be the most important to back up. You might find it beneficial to investigate which of the installed packages use this kind of data. Other examples besides databases are Web servers and mailing list archivers.

Selecting Your Backup Media

A variety of backup media are available on the market today. Which backup media you use depends on a number of factors and the particular needs of the situation. You should consider how often files are backed up, how long the backups need to last, how redundant the backups need to be, and how much money can be allocated to purchasing backup media. Table 19-1 provides a comparison of backup media.

Table 19-1		Comparison of Backup Media		
Medium	*Capacity*	*Reliability*	*Cost*	*Speed*
Magnetic tape	High	High	Cheap	Slow
Writeable CD	Medium	Medium	Cheap	Fast
Hard drive	High	High	Expensive	Fast
Floppy disk	Low	Low	Cheap	Slow
DVD	High	High	Cheap	Slow
Zip disk	Medium	Low	Medium	Slow
Flash ROM	Medium	High	Expensive	Fast
Removable hard drive (FireWire)	High	High	Expensive	Fast
Removable hard drive (USB)	High	High	Expensive	Medium

Determining Your Backup Method

In order to save time and money when creating backups and restoring corrupted file systems and purchasing backup media, institute a methodology for creating scheduled backups. The number of different backup methodologies is unlimited. How you should perform backups depends on the particular needs of your institution and computing infrastructure. The scheduling and type of backups depends on the type of backup media being used, the importance of the data, and the amount of downtime that you can tolerate.

When to use full backups and when to use incremental backups depends on the particular data stored on the machines, how the machines are used, and how much money can be allocated to buying backup media. After you decide on a backup methodology, you must configure your tools to use this methodology. Full and incremental backups can be implemented in scripts on top of the primitive backup tools such as `tar`. More advanced tools such as `dump` and `amanda` have built-in support for backup levels and scheduling of various kinds of backups. `amanda` even has a complex configuration language that lets you specify all kinds of details about the various types of backups you might want to do, the length of your backup cycle, and what files should be excluded from backup (such as private or temporary files).

Another thing to consider is the criticality of the system. If the system must be up at all times and downtime is a critical situation, full backups are necessary in order to minimize downtime. One strategy for backing up critical machines is to create a separate volume group on mirrored disks solely for backups and use it as an intermediate area to copy files to prior to writing them to tape. A compressed `tar` file can be created on disk and then be written to tape faster than a normal `tar` file. Also, because a backup exists on disk, the tape archive is used only as a last resort if the disk archive fails. This strategy is similar to the one that the `amanda` automated backup utility uses to take into account faulty backup devices or media. Even if the tape drive fails, the backup on disk can be written to tape when the problem has been solved.

The simplest backup methodology is to create a *full backup,* which copies the entire file system to the backup medium. This methodology can be good for: small systems in which there is not much data to back up; or systems in which the data is very important and changes rapidly, and thus historical snapshots of the system at different points in time are useful.

However, performing frequent full backups has several disadvantages:

- ✔ **Time-consuming:** Full backups take a long time to perform if there is a lot of data to back up or if the backup medium is slow.

- ✔ **Tolerable downtime:** In order to get a clear snapshot of the system, you might need to suspend the execution of processes that modify the file system while the backup process takes place. If backups take a long time, this downtime might be prohibitive.

✔ **Partial restoration hassle:** Full backups have no disadvantages when it comes to restoring an entire file system from backup. However, there is a disadvantage when restoring a partial file system from backup. If a sequential media such as magnetic tape is used, it must be searched sequentially in order to find the files that need to be restored. This process can cause a partial restoration to take as long as a full file system restoration in the worst case.

✔ **Space hogs:** Full backups also take significantly more space to archive than incremental backups. This situation is not too much of a disadvantage if you reuse the same backup media — you can just overwrite the old backup with the new one. However, keeping multiple generations of backups is often advisable because sometimes problems with the file system, such as corrupted or erased files, are not detected or reported immediately. If the file system is backed up once a day on the same backup tapes and an accidentally erased file is not found for two days, it cannot be recovered. On the other hand, if the file system is backed up once a week, any files lost between backups cannot be recovered.

Keeping multiple full backups also has this disadvantage: If a full backup is made every day, the amount of archive media necessary to store it quickly becomes prohibitive.

The alternative to doing a full backup is to do an *incremental backup,* which archives only the files that have changed or been added since the last backup. Incremental backups solve all the disadvantages of full backups:

✔ **Backup speed:** Incremental backups are fast. In fact, the more often you do them, the faster they are because you have less to back up.

✔ **Partial restoration speed:** Because the backups are smaller, searching from a given backup for a particular file is faster, thus making partial restorations faster if you need to restore from a particular known incremental backup archive. Because less is backed up each time, less media is used; thus, either less backup media needs to be bought or a longer history can be kept in the same amount of backup media. In the latter case, backups are more robust against lost or damaged files that are not discovered for a while.

However, using incremental backups does have disadvantages. Although incremental backups are faster for retrieving individual files, they are slower for restoring entire file systems. To explain this problem, imagine that you have a week-long backup cycle. On the first day of the week, you make a full backup. The rest of the week, you make an incremental backup. If a file system is erased accidentally on the last day of the week (right before a new full backup is to be made), you have to start at the last full backup and then load in a whole week of tapes in order to entirely restore the file system. If you made a full backup every day, you have to load only the full backup, and then you would be done restoring the file system.

Enterprise Linux Backup Tools

Red Hat Enterprise Linux provides numerous tools for doing file system back-ups. There are tools for interacting with backup media, such as `ftape` for manipulating tapes drives, `cdrecord` for writing to CD drives, and `mirrordir` for making backups to hard drives. Command line tools such as `tar` and `dump` allow for low-level control of file system backups and also easy automation through scripting. With only shell scripts and periodic scheduling through `cron` jobs, you can develop a robust automated backup solution for many situations. Graphical tools also exist to create a more user-friendly interface to performing manual backups. Finally, there are advanced backup tools that you can configure to fully automate backing up multiple machines.

Command line tools

Red Hat Enterprise Linux provides a number of command line tools for performing backups and restoring from backups. The tools for interacting directly with backup media are `ftape`, `cdrecord`, and `mirrordir`. The standard tools for creating archives are `dump` and `tar` for tape archives and `mkisofs` for CD archives. Each command provides a different interface and a number of options.

Managing tape drives with ftape

The `ftape` package is installed by default on the system. It's a collection of command line tools for accessing and managing magnetic tape drives. These utilities are useful if you are using tape drives to store your backups.

The `ftape` package's `mt` command is used to scan, rewind, and eject magnetic tapes if you have an IDE drive. If you have a SCSI tape drive, the `st` command performs the same functions.

You must be root in order to access the tape drives. As root, you can test a new magnetic tape by inserting it into the tape drive and then using the following command:

```
mt -f /dev/rft0 rewind
```

The preceding command rewinds the magnetic tape. You can also format the magnetic tape with the command

```
ftformat -f /dev/rft0
```

However, many tapes come preformatted, so it's usually unnecessary to format new tapes.

Making CD backups with the cdrecord package

In order to make backups on CDs under Red Hat Linux, you need the cdrecord package installed. It contains several commands such as cdrecord, devdump, isodump, isoinfo, isovfy, and readcd. These commands are useful utilities for creating and managing writable CDs.

The cdrecord package requires that you have a SCSI CD drive. If you have an IDE CD drive, you must configure it to use SCSI emulation in order to use the cdrecord package. A good source of information about writing to CDs is the CD-Writing How-to at

```
www.tldp.org/HOWTO/CD-Writing-HOWTO.html
```

The disadvantage to making backups on CD is that you must first create a CD image on the file system and then copy the CD image to the actual CD all in one step. This process requires that you have empty space on a single file system partition that is large enough to hold a CD image (up to 650MB). You create a CD image with the mkisofs command:

```
mkisofs -o /tmp/cd.image /home/terry
```

This command makes a CD image file in the /tmp directory called cd.image. The CD image file contains all the files in the /home/terry directory. You must have enough space to make the image file on the partition holding the /tmp directory. You can determine how much is free by using the df command. You can determine how much space the image file is going to take by using the command du /home/terry. By default, mkisofs preserves the ownership and permissions from the file system in the CD image.

In order to burn the image file to an actual CD, you must determine which SCSI device has the CD drive. If you don't actually have any SCSI drives and are using SCSI emulation with an IDE drive, the drive is probably on device scsi0. You can see what drives are on what SCSI devices with the following command:

```
dmesg | grep scsi
```

Next, you must determine which SCSI device ID the drive is using. You can find this with the following command:

```
cdrecord -scanbus
```

Then, determine the Logical Unit Number. If the device ID is 0 (zero), the Logical Unit Number should always be 0. You supply the SCSI device number, the device ID, and the logical unit number to the cdrecord command, in that order, as part of the dev option. A sample cdrecord command is as follows:

```
cdrecord -v dev=0,0,0 -data /tmp/cd.image
```

This command does not generally produce a bootable CD. In order for a CD to be bootable, the image file being recorded onto the CD needs to follow a specific format. Also, your BIOS must support booting from your particular CD-ROM. In order to produce a bootable image file, you need to follow several steps. First, you need to obtain a boot image. If you have a boot disc in the disc drive, the boot image can be written to a file with the following command:

```
dd if=/dev/fd0 of=boot.img bs=10k count=144
```

This command puts the boot image in the file boot.img. You must put this boot.img file into the directory that you are going to put on the CD. In the example provided, you could create a directory /home/blanu/boot and place the file there. You also need to give mkisofs some extra parameters in order to have it create a bootable image.

```
mkisofs -r -b /home/terry/boot/boot.img -c /home/terry/boot/
            boot.catalog -o  /tmp/cd.image /home/terry
```

The boot.catalog file does not need to already exist. It is generated by mkisofs. The command line option just tells mkisofs where in the image to store the generated file.

Backing up to a hard drive with mirrordir

The mirrordir command (in the mirrordir package) is a tool that enables you to easily back up a file system to an additional hard drive. In order to use mirrordir, you must first mount the additional hard drive:

```
mount /dev/hdb1 /mnt
```

Then you can back up a given directory to the mounted hard drive by using the mirrordir command:

```
mirrordir /home /mnt
```

The command backs up the /home directory, which contains all the users' personal files, to the backup hard drive. When executed, the mirrordir command makes the contents of the hard drive mounted on /mnt exactly identical to the contents of /home. All files are copied, and any files not present in /home are deleted. Subdirectories and their files are also copied.

You must get the order of the arguments correct. If the arguments were reversed, the /home directory is overwritten with the contents of the backup hard drive, thus erasing valuable data.

To recover lost files if the partition containing /home crashes, the arguments to the mirrordir command are simply reversed. The following command overwrites the contents of /home with the contents of /mnt:

```
mirrordir /mnt /home
```

Note that any files extant in /home that are not also in /mnt are erased. Therefore, mirrordir is not useful for recovering individual files but rather only when the entire directory, partition, or drive has been corrupted or erased.

If /home happens to be alone on a separate partition from the rest of the file system, you don't even need to restore the directory using mirrordir. The partition mounted on /mnt (in the example, /dev/hdb1) is an exact copy of the /home directory — and so, in this case, an exact copy of that partition. Thus, you can simply modify the /etc/fstab file and change the partition mounted under /home to be the partition where it is mirrored.

Backing up with dump

The dump package consists of several commands for doing backup and restoration of the file system. The dump command is used to do backups of either entire partitions or individual directories. The restore command is used to restore an entire partition, individual directories, or individual files.

The first argument to the dump command is a list of options. Following that are all the arguments required by the various options in the same order as the options were specified. The last argument is the file system to back up. Table 19-2 lists the available dump options.

Table 19-2	Dump Options	
Option	*Meaning*	*Type*
B	The number of records per volume	Number
b	The number of kilobytes per dump record	Number
h	The dump level at which to use nodump flags	Number
f	Name of file or device to write to	Filename
d	Tape density	Number
n	Tells dump to send a message when done	None
s	Length of dump tape	Number in feet
u	Records the date of this dump in /etc/dumpdates	None

(continued)

Table 19-2 *(continued)*

Option	Meaning	Type
T	Adds only files older than the given time	Time (`ctime`)
W	Lists the file systems that need be backed up	None
w	Lists individual files that need be backed up	None
0–9	Specifies a dump level of 0–9	None

The following command specifies that the file system on `/dev/hda3` should be backed up on the magnetic tape on device `/dev/rft0`. It specifies that the backup should use backup level 0 (full backup) and write the time of the backup to the `/etc/dumpdates` file.

```
dump 0uf /dev/rft0 /dev/hda3
```

Restoring dumped files

The `restore` command is used to retrieve files from the backups created with `dump`. You can use `restore` to restore an entire file system, or you can use it to interactively select which files you want to restore.

The syntax for the `restore` command is the same as for the `dump` command although it has different options. Table 19-3 lists the options.

Table 19-3   **Restore Options**

Option	Meaning	Type
r	Restores the entire dump archive	None
C	Compares the files on the file system to those in the dump archive	None
R	Starts the restore from a particular tape in a multivolume sequence	None
x	Extracts only specified files	List of files
t	Lists the contents of the dump archive	List of files
I	Restores files in interactive mode	None
b	Blocks size of the dump in kilobytes	Number
D	Name of the file system to be compared against	File system
f	Name of the dump archive to restore from	Filename

Option	Meaning	Type
h	Re-creates directories but do not restore their contents	None
m	Extracts files by inode number instead of name	None
N	Prints filenames rather than extracting them	None
s	Specifies the tape number to start on when using the R option	Number
T	Specifies where to write temporary files	Directory
v	Verbose mode	None
y	Does not prompt when bad blocks are encountered	None

Restoring the file system

In order to restore a damaged or erased file system, you must first re-create the directory or partition that has been lost. If, for instance, you want to re-create the /home directory, which existed by itself on the /dev/hdb1 partition, you could use the following command:

```
mkfs /dev/hdb1
```

and then you would mount the partition with this command:

```
mount /dev/hdb1 /home
```

Note that the first command (mkfs /dev/hdb1) erases all the data on the /dev/hdb1 partition. This method of restoration is useful only for restoring all the files previously archived with dump. If any files have been added, modified, or deleted since the last backup, those changes are lost. Restoring individual files is covered in the section "Restoring individual files using restore." Also, if mkfs is accidentally run on a different partition than the one you meant to restore, all the data on the partition on which it is mistakenly run are irrevocably erased.

restore must be run inside the directory that is going to be restored. So, restore can restore the /home directory with the following commands:

```
cd /home
restore rf /dev/rft0
```

The r flag tells restore to restore the entire archive rather than just some files. The f flag tells restore that the archive is located on the device /dev/rft0.

Restoring individual files using restore

The `restore` command, in addition to being used to restore an entire file system, can also be used in an interactive mode, which enables you to restore individual files. The interactive mode is invoked as follows:

```
restore if /dev/rft0
```

This command runs `restore` in interactive mode and specifies that it should restore from the archive on the device `/dev/rft0`. The interactive mode enables you to type options to `restore` in order to control its behavior. It includes the options shown in Table 19-4.

Table 19-4	restore Commands
Command	*Meaning*
add	Adds a file or directory to the list of files to be extracted. If a directory is specified, all contained files, subdirectories, and files contained in subdirectories are extracted. File paths are relative to the current directory being viewed in the dump archive.
cd	Changes which directory within the dump archive is being viewed.
delete	Removes a file or directory from the list of files to be extracted. If a directory is specified, all files in that directory, subdirectories, and files in subdirectories are removed from the list as well. Note that this does not affect what is stored in the dump archive, but rather which files are extracted during the restore.
extract	Extracts all files and directories currently in the list of files to extract and restore them in the file system.
help	Lists available commands.
ls	Lists the contents of the directory currently being viewed in the dump archive. If a directory is specified, the contents of the specified directory are listed rather than the contents of the current directory. Files and directories marked with * in the file listing are currently marked for extraction.
pwd	Prints the path within the dump archive of the directory currently being viewed.
quit	Exits the `restore` program. No other actions are taken by `restore`.
setmodes	Rather than extract the files, sets the permissions on the files in the file system so that they match the permissions of the files in the dump archive that are marked for extraction.
verbose	Switches verbose mode on or off.

Creating archives with tar

The `tar` program is a utility originally designed for making magnetic tape backups but is useful for any kind of archiving purpose. When making archives, it is important to specify a leading `. /` for files. This creates a relative path, which is necessary when restoring the files.

Red Hat Enterprise Linux includes the GNU version of `tar`. It includes some extensions to the older standard versions of `tar`, including multivolume archiving. *Multivolume archiving* is an automated process in which `tar` prompts for new media to be inserted whenever it runs out of space.

The `tar` command requires one command option followed by any number of optional options. Table 19-5 lists the command options.

Table 19-5	tar Options
Command	*Explanation*
A	Appends the contents of the given `tar` files to the specified tar archive.
c	Creates a new `tar` archive and add the given files to it.
d	Finds differences between what's in the `tar` archive and what's in the file system.
r	Appends the given files to the specified `tar` archive.
t	Lists the contents of the specified `tar` archive.
u	Appends the given files to the specified `tar` archive but only if they are newer than the files in the `tar` archive.
x	Extracts the given files from the specified `tar` archive.

In addition to specifying a command, you must specify a device or file to act as the destination of the `tar` archive. Take a look at an example of creating a `tar` archive.

Suppose you want to create a tar archive containing all files in your home directory ending with the extension `.doc`. First, be sure that you are in your home directory. Then, to create an archive containing individual files. you can use the following command:

```
tar -cf docfiles.tar *.doc
```

After running the command, a file named docfiles.tar is created and contains all the files ending with .doc that are in your home directory. If you want to create a tar archive of all files and subdirectories in a directory, you can use the same command as above — but instead of listing files, you list the directory, as follows:

```
tar -cf home.tar /home/terry/
```

This command creates a tar archive called home.tar that contains the contents of my home directory, including all files and subdirectories.

Advanced tools

This section discusses a number of advanced backup tools including amanda, the amdump test, and pax.

Backing up multiple systems using amanda

The AMANDA (Advanced Maryland Automatic Network Disk Archiver) package is a set of tools for doing backups of multiple machines over the network. With AMANDA, you can configure your Red Hat Enterprise Linux machine to be a backup server for the other machines in the network, including Windows systems. AMANDA is included with Red Hat Enterprise Linux. To use AMANDA, you should install the following packages:

✔ amanda

✔ amanda-client

✔ amanda-server

✔ gnuplot

You need to install the amanda-server and gnuplot packages only on the machine that is going to be the backup server. However, you must install amanda-client on any machine that you want to back up by using amanda. You must install the base amanda package on both the client and server machines. The amanda package contains several commands, shown in Table 19-6.

Table 19-6	amanda Commands
Command	**Use**
amdump	Normally executed periodically by a cron job, this utility is run on the amanda server. It requests backups from the various amanda clients.

Command	Use
amflush	If amdump has trouble writing backups to tape, they are kept in temporary storage space on disk until the problem is corrected. After the problem is fixed, this command is run to write the data in the temporary storage space to the tapes.
amcleanup	If the amanda server crashes during the running of amdump, this utility should be run to clean up after the interrupted amdump.
amrecover	Provides a way to select which tapes should be used to recover files.
amrestore	Used to restore individual files or directories or entire partitions from amanda backups.
amlabel	Used to write an amanda label onto a tape. You must use this command to label tapes before they can be written to with amdump.
amcheck	Should be run before amdump to verify that the correct tape is in the drive.
amadmin	Does various administrative tasks.
amtape	Used for low-level tape control, such as loading and ejecting disks.
amverify	Checks amanda tapes for errors.
amrmtape	Deletes a tape with a particular label from the amanda tape database.
amstatus	Reports on the current status of a running amdump program.

Installing amanda

After installing the necessary Red Hat Package Manager (RPM) files, some additional installation is required to get amanda running. You must create sub-directories in the /etc/amanda and /usr/admn/amanda directories for each backup schedule that you are going to run. For instance, if you plan to run a backup schedule called test, you must execute the following commands:

```
mkdir -p /etc/amanda/test
mkdir -p /usr/admn/amanda/normal
```

You also need to create some temporary space for amanda to keep files, which it is in the process of backing up. For instance, if you want to create this space as a directory on your root partition, you can use the following command to make an `amanda` directory:

```
mkdir /amanda
```

Configuring amanda

To configure `amanda`, you must create an `amanda.conf` file and put it in the subdirectory in `/etc/amanda` that you created. In this example, for instance, it is called `/etc/amanda/amanda.conf`. The `amanda.conf` file has many options, as shown in Table 19-7, but has defaults for most of them.

Table 19-7	amanda.conf Options	
Option	**Example**	**Meaning**
`org name`	`org Tristero`	Specifies the name used in reports generated by `amanda`.
`mailto accounts`	`mailto root example`	Specifies account names that `amanda` should put in charge of the backup process.
`dumpuser account`	`dumpuser amanda`	Specifies the user account that the `amanda` dump process should run as.
`inparallel number`	`inparallel 5`	Specifies the number of `amdump` processes that can run simultaneously.
`netusage num unit`	`netusage 1000 Kpbs`	Indicates the bandwidth that `amanda` is allowed to consume while doing backups. It should be set such that even if all the allocated bandwidth is consumed, there is still enough bandwidth for other tasks that might operate at the same time as the `amanda` backup process.
`dumpcycle num unit`	`dumpcycle 1 week`	Specifies the length of the backup cycle.

Option	Example	Meaning
runspercycle *num*	runspercycle 7	Specifies the number of backups that should be done during a single dump cycle. With a dump cycle of 1 week and 7 runs per cycle, amanda makes one full backup and 6 incremental backups every week.
tapespercycle *num unit*	tapespercycle 7 tapes	Specifies how many tapes are available for use in a single backup cycle.
runtapes *num*	runtapes 1	Specifies how many tapes are available for use in each backup.
tapedev *device*	tapedev /dev/rft0	Specifies the device name of the tape device.

The `amanda.conf` file also has some complex options, which consist of blocks with multiple subfields. The `holdingdisk` block defines a temporary storage space for holding data that is being backed up. You can define multiple `holdingdisk` blocks in a single file. The definition has the following format:

```
Holdingdisk name
{
     directory name
     use num unit
}
Example holdingdisk block:
Holdingdisk example
{
     directory /example
     use 4 Gb
}
```

The `tapetype` block defines a particular kind of magnetic tape that might be used in backups. It defines properties about the tape such as length and speed. The `tapetype` definition has the following format:

```
Define tapetype name
{
comment freeform string
length num unit
filemark num unit
speed num unit
}
```

Here is an example `tapetype` definition:

```
Define tapetype EXAMPLE
{
comment "These are fictional numbers."
Length 5000 mbytes
Filemark 100 kbytes
Speed 500 kbytes
}
```

The `interface` block defines a particular network interface that can be used for communication between an `amanda` server and client. The `interface` definition specifies how much bandwidth can be used on that particular network interface. The syntax of the definition is as follows:

```
Define interface name
{
comment "Freeform string"
use num unit
}
```

Here is an example `interface` definition:

```
Define interface eth0
{
comment "This sets the bandwidth usage of the Ethernet
         network interface"
use 500 kmps
}
```

The `dumptype` block defines a particular kind of dump. The entries in the `disklist` file refer to these definitions. A corresponding `dumptype` block must exist in the `amanda.conf` file for it to be referenced in the `disklist` file. The `dumptype` block specifies certain properties of the kind of dump, such as which program to use for dumping, whether to compress backups, and files that should not be backed up.

The `dumptype` block has many options, as shown in Table 19-8, which define how the dump works.

Table 19-8	dumptype Options
Option	**Explanation**
`auth`	Specifies which authorization method should be used between the client and the server. This option can be set to either `bsd` or `krb4` and defaults to `bsd`.
`comment`	Is a freeform string and is ignored.

Option	Explanation
comprate	Specifies the compression rates for backed up files in terms of how the size of the compressed file should compare with the size of the uncompressed file. Can be either a single value or two values separated by a comma. The first value specifies the compression rate for full backups. The second value specifies the compression rate for incremental backups and is assumed to be the same as the first value if omitted.
compress	Specifies the method to be used for compressing the data. The options are presented in Table 19-9. The default compression type is client fast.
dumpcycle	Specifies the number of days in the backup cycle. A full backup is performed at the beginning of each backup cycle.
exclude	Specifies which files should not be included in the backup. This option works only when the backup program being used is tar. When used with dump or samba, it is ignored. The possible values for exclude are either a quote wildcard pattern or the list keyword followed by a quoted filename. If the list keyword is used, the filename should refer to a file on the client machine, which contains a list of wildcard patterns to match. Wildcard patterns are listed one per line. Any files matched by either the quoted patterns or any of the patterns in the specified file are excluded from the amanda backups.
holdingdisk	Specifies whether the holding disk should be used for temporarily storing files that are going to be dumped. The default is yes.
ignore	Specifies that this dump type should not actually be backed up even if the disklist file specifies that it should.
index	Specifies whether to keep an index of files that have been backedup up. The default is no.
kencrypt	Specifies whether the connection between the client and the server should be encrypted. The default is n.
maxdumps	Specifies how many simultaneous instances of the amdump process can be run. The default is 1.
priority	Specifies the priority of the dump. When amanda runs out of tape or is otherwise unable to write backups for some reason, all the data that can be kept on the holding disk is put there in order of highest to lowest priority dump type. The possible values for the priority of a dump are high, medium, and low. The default is medium.

(continued)

Table 19-8 *(continued)*

Option	Explanation
program	Specifies which program should be used for making the backup dump. The possible values are DUMP and GNUTAR. The default is DUMP. You must change this to GNUTAR if you wish to use the exclude option.
record	Specifies whether the date of the dump should be written to the /etc/dumpdates file. The default is yes.
skip-full	Specifies that when amanda is scheduled to do a full backup, it should refrain from doing so. This option is useful if you want to use amanda for incremental backups or to use some other method for full backups.
skip-incr	Specifies that when amanda is scheduled to do an incremental backup, it should refrain from doing so. This option is useful if you want to use amanda for full backups but also use some other method for incremental backups or if you do not want to do incremental backups at all.
starttime	Specifies that the starting time of the dump should be delayed.
strategy	Specifies the dumping strategy that should be used for this kind of dump. The various available dump strategies are listed in Table 19-10. The default strategy is Standard.

Table 19-9   **amanda Compression Types**

Type	Explanation
none	Specifies that no compression should be used on amanda backups.
client best	Specifies that the client should use the compression algorithm that results in the highest compression levels.
client fast	Specifies that the client should use the fastest compression algorithm.
server best	Specifies that the server should use the compression algorithm that results in the highest compression levels.
server fast	Specifies that the server should use the fastest compression algorithm.

Table 19-10	amanda Dumping Strategies
Strategy	**Explanation**
Standard	Specifies that amanda should use the standard dumping strategy, which includes both full and incremental backups.
Nofull	Specifies that amanda should use level 1 incremental backups always and never do full backups. This is useful when a set of machines all have the same base installation and setup with only minor differences that do not change rapidly. amanda then saves space by backing up only the changes that occur over time.
Noinc	Specifies that incremental backups should never occur and that amanda should always do full backups. This is useful if it is important to make the restoration of a machine as swift and easy as possible. However, this makes backups much slower and requires much more storage space for the backups.
Skip	This option specifies that the dump type should never be backed up either with full backups or incremental backups. The dump type is ignored even if it occurs in the disklist file.

You need to adapt the amanda.conf file to your system. Most notably, you need to correctly specify the paths to the tape drive devices, the type of tape drives, and the path to the directory that amanda can use as temporary space.

You must also create a disklist file that specifies which partitions to back up. In the example setup, this file would be stored as /etc/amanda/test/disklist.

The format of the disklist file is a series of entries, one per line, in the following format:

```
Hostname device dumptype
```

The disklist file has the arguments shown in Table 19-11.

Table 19-11	disklist Arguments
Argument	**Explanation**
Hostname	Specifies the hostname of the amanda client to be backed up. For the amanda client to enable a connection from the amanda server, the hostname of the amanda server must be in that client's .amandahosts file.
Device	Specifies the name of the directory to be backed up.
Dumptype	Specifies the name of the dumptype definition in the amanda.conf file, which defines the properties associated with this type of dump.

amanda client configuration

In order to enable the amanda backup servers to connect to the clients to request backups, you must create on each client an .amandahosts file in the /root directory of the machine. The file consists simply of the names of the server machines that are allowed to connect to the client in order to request backups.

You are wise to set the permissions of this file to 600 by using chmod. That ensures that only root can modify the file and other users cannot add hosts to the file, thus bypassing the permission system and gaining access to the full file system.

Performing backups with amanda

In order to perform a backup, you simply run amdump with the name of the backup that you want to run. The configuration information and list of partitions to back up are read from the configuration files in the particular subdirectory in /etc/amanda that you created for this particular backup type.

amdump test

The amdump commands then go through the list of the partitions specified in amdump and back up each of them, in order, to the tape drives specified in the associated amanda.conf file. Specify, in order of importance, the partitions in the disklist file so that in case of problems, the most important files are more likely to have already been backed up. The results of the amdump operation, including any errors, are written to the /usr/adm/amanda/test directory.

Using pax

The pax (portable archive exchange) tool is used for reading and writing file archives and copying directory structures. The pax tool is also useful for converting between different archive formats. This capability is especially important in an environment where different operating systems and distributions are running in conjunction. Incompatibilities between the various tools and various versions of tools can be quite a hassle. pax solves this problem by knowing how to read many versions of several different archiving formats. Table 19-12 lists the options you can use with pax:

Table 19-12	pax Options
Option	**Meaning**
-r	Reads files from archive.
-w	Writes files to archive.

Option	Meaning
-a	Appends files to an existing archive.
-b blocksize	Specifies the size of a block of data in the archive. Block sizes must be a multiple of 512.
-c	Matches all files except those with the specified pattern.
-d	Matches wildcards against the filenames only rather than the complete path.
-f	Specifies the name of the archive file.
-I	Prompts to rename files when archiving.
-k	Does not overwrite existing files.
-l	Links files with hard links when in copying mode.
-n	Matches only the first file that matches the supplied pattern.
-o options	Specifies a list of additional options that are specific to the archiving format.
-p string	Specifies file characteristics that should be retained on the archived versions of the files.
-s string	Specifies that the names of the files should be modified using the regular expression given in the argument string before the files are archived.
-t	Specifies that the access time information associated with the files that are being archived should be retained in the archived copies of the files.
-u	Specifies that pax should not overwrite files in the archive even if the files in the archive are older than the files specified to be archived.
-v	Specifies that pax should produce verbose output.
-x format	Specifies which format the archive should be in. The possible values for the format are cpio, bcpio, sv4cpio, sv4rc, tar, and ustar. The default format is ustar. When reading an archive instead of writing one, pax automatically determines the type of the archive, so this option is needed only when writing an archive.
-B number	Specifies the number of bytes in each volume of the archive. It is useful for creating multivolume archives on volumes with a known size such as CD-ROMs or floppy disks.

(continued)

Table 19-12 *(continued)*

Option	Meaning
-D	Specifies that `pax` should not overwrite files in the tar archive with files supplied to be archived if the supplied files are older than the files already in the archive.
-E number	Specifies the number of times that `pax` should attempt to retry reading or writing an archive in the case of an error.
-G group	Specifies that only files in the given group should be written or read. The given group string is assumed to be a group name unless it starts with the # character, in which case it is assumed to be a group ID number.
-H	Specifies that only command line symbolic links should be followed.
-L	Specifies that all symbolic links should be followed.
-P	Specifies that no symbolic links should be followed.
-T time	Specifies that only files with the given modification time should be read or written.
-U user	Specifies that only files owned by the given user should be written or read. The given user string is assumed to be a user name unless it starts with a # character, in which case it is assumed to be a user ID number.
-X	Specifies that directories should not be entered if the directory is on a different partition or device than the parent directory.

Take a look at a few examples of using `pax`. To copy one directory hierarchy to another, use the following command:

```
pax -rw directory1 directory2
```

To copy the current directory to a tape drive, enter the following command:

```
pax -wf /dev/rmt0
```

To create an archive of your current directory by using `pax`, enter the following command:

```
pax -wf mydir.pax
```

In this example, `mydir.pax` is the name of the archive that is created. You should substitute your filename for `mydir.pax` in this example.

Part VI
The Part of Tens

The 5th Wave — By Rich Tennant

"This part of the test tells us whether you're personally suited to the job of network administrator."

In this part . . .

One part of every *For Dummies* book is its Part of Tens. Here you find two chapters that are full of useful tips and solutions to common problems. In Chapter 20, you find some configuration changes that you can make to optimize many of your system services. And the last chapter, Chapter 21, contains ten common problems frequently encountered by new users and their solutions.

Chapter 20

Ten Tips for Optimizing Your System

● ●

In This Chapter

▶ Optimizing the X Window System

▶ Optimizing NFS

▶ Optimizing Samba

▶ Optimizing DNS

▶ Optimizing Sendmail

▶ Optimizing FTP

▶ Optimizing your Web server

▶ Building a custom kernel

▶ Shutting down unused services

▶ Using Webmin for system configuration

● ●

*I*n this chapter, I offer you tips for optimizing your systems. Most of the tips here help you to provide better services to your users by configuring your servers for best performance. I also give you a few techniques to make your Desktop or Workstation version of Enterprise Linux run more smoothly.

Optimizing the X Window System

You can't do much to optimize the X Window System because it's already pretty well tuned. Of course, you can take some steps to improve the performance of the XFree86 system running on your Red Hat Enterprise Linux systems.

▶ **Beef up the hardware.** The biggest improvement that you can make for your X Window System is to beef up the hardware on which XFree86 runs. There is simply no way around the fact that a faster CPU, faster GPU (graphics processing unit) that supports hardware acceleration, more RAM, and more video RAM will do more than anything else to speed up XFree86. Of course, hardware upgrades are not always an option, but they are the best option that you have.

✔ **Use a lightweight window manager.** The eye candy and functionality provided by desktop environments such as GNOME and KDE carry a heavy price tag in terms of overall system performance. If, like me, you use XFree86 mostly as a platform for running XTerms, a Web browser, and other graphical applications, you might not even miss the integration between the applications and the window manager provided.

✔ **Consider reducing the color depth at which you run XFree86.** Obviously, if you need millions of colors (such as for heavy-duty image processing or watching videos), using 16-bit color results in poor quality images. However, an awful lot of computing that takes place on a Red Hat Enterprise Linux system is text processing, programming, and e-mail. Using 24-bit and 32-bit color is computationally intensive; 16-bit color is much less demanding.

✔ **Try not to use custom backgrounds.** A solid color background is much less memory intensive than a full-color wallpaper image. Transparent backgrounds in terminal emulators are cool but usually impose overhead on the windowing system to keep the background properly rendered and up-to-date. Shaped windows and borders are aesthetically pleasing but somewhat expensive in terms of resources.

✔ **Run a local font server.** Running a local font server makes the fonts that you want available locally, so they don't have to be sent across the network. Similarly, you can free memory and speed up the server's font handling by getting rid of fonts (that is, not loading them in /etc/X11/Xorg.conf) that you do not use.

✔ **Try to find lightweight XFree86-based applications.** I no longer use Mozilla, for example, because I found that Firefox (the browser-only replacement for Mozilla) provides everything I need in a Web browser.

✔ **Make sure that the X server is up-to-date.** The XFree86 project is working to separate drivers from the rest of the system, which enables you to download and install an updated driver for your video card without having to refresh the entire XFree86 installation. Drivers sometimes improve dramatically from release to release, so stay informed about the driver for your video card.

✔ **Unload modules that you don't use.** The standard XFree86 installation, for example, loads the RECORD and XTRAP extensions. Edit /etc/X11/Xorg.conf and comment out the lines that read

```
Load "record"
Load "xtrap"
```

Granted, these are only two modules with negligible memory and CPU impacts, but every little bit helps.

✔ **Run XFree86 at a lower** `nice` **value.** By increasing XFree86's priority over other processes, you will get a more responsive system. One way to do this is to start XFree86 by using the command `nice -n -10 X :0`. You need root access to use this command. If you run XFree86 from XDM, GDM, or KDM, modify the `Xservers` file (`/etc/X11/xdm/Xservers`). XDM is the X display manager, GDM is the GNOME display manager, and KDM is the KDE display manager. All three of these services provide a graphical login for the user.

Find the line that resembles the following:

```
:0 local /usr/X11R6/bin/X
```

Change it so that it looks like the following, and then exit and restart X.

```
:0 local nice -10 /usr/X11R6/bin/X
```

Restart X. If you run XFree86 for long periods of time, memory gets tied up as cache. Occasionally restarting X refreshes potentially stale caches and also frees up memory that might have been lost to leaks.

Optimizing NFS

Here are a few tips that you can use to increase the performance of a system's Network File System (NFS) server. Most of these tips apply to server systems, but they are also relevant on client systems as well.

✔ **Go for SCSI disks or fibre channel arrays.** Replace IDE disks with SCSI disks. And, if you have the budget for it, replace SCSI disks with fibre channel disk arrays. IDE disks, even the Ultra-DMA (UDMA) variety that operate at 66 Mhz, use the system CPU for I/O transfers whereas SCSI disks do not. This step prevents disk I/O from becoming CPU-bound and also takes advantage of SCSI's generally faster performance. Fibre channel, although markedly more expensive than SCSI, offers even faster performance.

✔ **Use RAID 1 or 0.** If your NFS server uses Redundant Array of Independent (or Inexpensive) Disks (RAID), use RAID 1 or 0 to maximize write speed and to provide redundancy in the event of a disk crash. RAID 5 seems compelling at first because it ensures good read speeds, which is important for NFS clients; however, write performance is lackluster, and good write speeds are important for NFS servers. Write performance is critical because NFS on Linux now (since about kernel version 2.4.7) defaults to synchronous mode, meaning that NFS operations do not complete until the data is actually synced to disk.

✔ **Spread NFS exported file systems.** Spread NFS exported file systems across multiple disks and, if possible, across multiple disk controllers. The purpose of this strategy is to avoid disk *hot spots,* which occur when I/O operations concentrate on a single disk or a single area of a disk.

Similarly, distribute disks containing NFS exported file systems across multiple disk controllers. This measure reduces the amount of I/O traffic on any single controller, which improves the overall performance of the I/O subsystem.

✔ **Replacing 10Mbit Ethernet cards with 100Mbit.** Consider replacing 10Mbit Ethernet cards with 100Mbit Ethernet cards throughout the network. Although only slightly more expensive than their 10Mbit cousins, 100Mbit cards offer considerably more throughput per dollar. The faster cards result in better network performance across the board, not just for NFS. Of course, to reap the benefit of 100Mbit cards, they need to be used on both clients and servers. Also, the gateways, routers, and switches must be capable of handling 100MB speeds.

✔ **Consider using Gigabit Ethernet.** In situations in which performance or availability is the paramount concern, Gigabit Ethernet (1000Mbit) is available albeit expensive. Other high performance network options, such as Myrinet and Synchronous Optical Networking (SONET), exist as well but are typically used as cluster interconnect networks.

✔ **Replace hubs with switches.** Network hubs, although less expensive than switches, route all network traffic across the same data channel. During periods of heavy activity, this single data channel can easily become saturated. Switches, on the other hand, transmit network packets across multiple data channels, thus reducing congestion and packet collisions and resulting in faster overall throughput.

✔ **Dedicate server(s).** If necessary, dedicate one or more servers specifically to NFS work. CPU- or memory-intensive processes, such as Web, database, or compute servers, can starve an NFS server for needed CPU cycles or memory pages.

✔ **Resegment the network.** In extreme cases, resegmenting the network might be the answer to NFS performance problems. The goal with this tip is to isolate NFS traffic on its own segment, reducing network saturation and congestion and allocating dedicated bandwidth to NFS traffic.

Optimizing Samba

Probably the most important consideration for optimizing Samba performance is file transfer speed between the Samba server and clients. The following options can be set in the `/etc/samba/smb.conf` file to increase file transfer performance between client and server. You can try them to determine whether your performance increases after implementing them:

✔ `socket options`: These are controls on the networking layer of the operating system that enable tuning of the connection. For a complete list of options, refer to the `smb.conf` man page. A good choice for getting better performance from your local network is to use `socket options = IPTOS_LOWDELAY TCP_NODELAY`.

✔ `dns proxy`: This option should be set to `no` unless your Samba server is acting as a Windows Internet Name Service (WINS) server. Setting this option to `no` prevents the server from doing unnecessary name lookups while increasing system performance.

✔ `debug level`: This option should be set to 2 or smaller. Setting the `debug level` higher than 2 causes the server to flush the `logfile` after each operation, which is a time-consuming process indeed.

✔ `Level2 oplocks`: This option provides for caching of downloaded files on the client machine. Setting this option to `true` can increase system performance.

Optimizing DNS

You can improve the performance of your master domain server by making some changes in the options section of the `/etc/named.custom` file. The first change that you can make is to allow only zone transfers between master and slave servers. By default, `BIND` allows zone transfers between all hosts. However, because zone transfers are required only between masters and slaves, you can specify the IP address of the slave server so that the master looks for this server only. Enter the following line in the options sections of `/etc/named.custom`:

```
allow-transfer { enter IP address of slave server; };
```

The next change to make is to configure your master server to respond to queries only from specified hosts, which are the other computers that are inside your firewall. Enter the following line into `/etc/named.conf`.

```
allow-query ( enter your internal network number here; localhost; };
```

If you have set up caching-only name servers, you can configure them to respond only to recursive requests from specific hosts. Again, the specified hosts are the other computers that are inside your firewall. Enter the following line into `/etc/named.conf` on your caching-only server:

```
Allow-recursion { enter your internal network number here; localhost; };
```

The last thing that you can do to tweak your Domain Name System (DNS) settings is to change the performance of your DNS log files. You can make two changes. One, you can disable logging for lame servers. *Lame servers* appear to be name servers for a domain but really are not. By excluding these servers, you reduce system resource use. Add the following lines to `/etc/named.conf`:

```
Logging {
 category lame-servers { null; };
};
```

Next, configure your logs to automatically *rotate* — that is, be deleted automatically — to keep log files from filling up your system.

When you installed BIND, there was a file created called /etc/logrotate.d/ named. A listing of this file is shown here:

```
/var/log/named.log {
    missingok
    create 0644 named named
    postrotate
        /sbin/service named reload  2> /dev/null > /dev/null || true
    endscript
}
```

Delete this line:

```
create 0644 named named
```

and change the line

```
/sbin/service named reload  2> /dev/null > /dev/null || true
```

to the following:

```
/bin/kill -HUP `cat /var/run/named.pid 2> /dev/null` 2> /dev/null || true
```

Save your changes and restart the named server.

Optimizing Sendmail

In this section, I give you a few tips that you can use to keep your Sendmail server running efficiently. All messages that Sendmail tries to send are first sent to the mail queue located at /var/spool/mqueue. The queued messages are then sent to their destination if possible. Sometimes messages are undeliverable for any number of reasons. These undelivered messages accumulate in the mail queue, and eventually they can cause your system performance to suffer. Periodically check the mail queue for undeliverable mail and force Sendmail to clear the queue.

To see the contents of the mail queue, you can use the mailq command as shown in Listing 20-1:

Listing 20-1:   Sample Output of Using mailq Command

```
[root@main root]#/usr/bin/mailq
              /var/spool/mqueue (51 requests)
----Q-ID---- --Size-- -----Q-Time----- ------------Sender/Recipient------------
iABCJiX10531*    193 Thu Nov 11 07:19 murphy
              (Deferred: Connection timed out with mail2.saveinternet.net.)
                             gaston.huang@allglobalnews.com
iAB8MDs00851    4086 Thu Nov 11 03:22 MAILER-DAEMON
              (Deferred: 451 4.3.0 Cannot connect to database)
                             <Nelsongbgot@venturalink.net>
iAB6E9628354    1822 Thu Nov 11 01:14 norr1634@muhlenberg.edu
              (Deferred: Connection refused by thebeach.net.)
                             aarontandy@thebeach.net
iAB3Qk714961   32995 Wed Nov 10 22:26 MAILER-DAEMON
              (host map: lookup (americaftp.com): deferred)
<output clipped here>
                             <alan@americaftp.com>
```

The output shows the message ID, the size of the file, the time it was sent, who sent it, whom it is going to, and the status of the message. You can see in this listing that the message status is *deferred,* meaning that the messages have not been delivered, with the reason shown.

Sendmail continues to attempt to send undeliverable messages until it reaches the default time-out setting, which is typically five days. After the timeout period is reached, Sendmail stops trying to send the undeliverable messages and drops them from the queue. You can, if you desire, remove the undeliver-able messages from your mail queue by listing them with the `mailq` command, changing to the `/var/spool/mqueue` directory, and then deleting the messages. For example, to remove the first message shown in the list, first change to the `/var/spool/mqueue` directory by entering the following command:

```
[root@main root]#cd /var/spool/mqueue
```

Then remove the message by entering the queue identification number of the message to delete:

```
[root@main root]#rm -f iABCJiX10531
```

You can remove as many messages as you like by using this method. You can even clear the entire queue by deleting the contents of the directory although you probably wouldn't want to do this because you delete messages that could still be delivered.

Optimizing FTP

The vsftpd FTP server is designed to be a lightweight file server that doesn't put too much strain on your system. There aren't too many ways to make it faster or less demanding on your system, but here are a few tips suggested by the vsftpd documentation.

✔ **Simultaneous connections:** You should limit the number of simultaneous connections that you allow to the server. Check this setting in the /etc/vsftpd/vsftpd.conf file.

✔ **Directory size:** You should limit the number of files contained in any one directory to no more than a few hundred. If necessary, create additional directories to spread the number of files across them.

✔ **Disable NIS and NIS+ lookups:** You can change the /etc/nsswitch.conf file to disable lookups for passwd, shadow, and groups. This prevents the unnecessary loading of runtime libraries into the vsftpd memory space.

Optimizing Your Web Server

The most important system resource used by Apache is RAM. Adding more RAM to your system improves the performance of Apache as well as other services. You can also use a dedicated Web server that doesn't need to share system resources with other services.

You can make many tweaks to change the performance of your Web server. I list a few of them here. All the tweaks involve making changes to the directives in the /etc/httpd/conf/httpd.conf file.

✔ TimeOut: This directive controls how long the server waits before it closes a connection. A longer value means that the server might be unavailable to other clients until the server times out. The default value is 300 seconds; experiment to find the correct value for your system.

✔ MaxRequestsPerChild: This directive controls how many requests a child process handles before a new child process starts. The default value is 100.

✔ HostnameLookups: Set this directive to Off to increase performance. By not having to look up hostnames, your Web server becomes faster.

✔ **IP addresses:** You can use IP addresses rather than hostnames in directives that allow them. This avoids having to do name resolution to determine the IP address.

✔ **NFS-mounted files:** Don't use NFS-mounted file systems to hold files served by Apache. NFS performance is slower than a local file system.

Building a Custom Kernel

At the core of any computer operating system is the kernel. The *kernel* contains the basic instructions for controlling the hardware and software devices on the computer. With many operating systems, the kernel is relatively static, and the user has no control over how the kernel functions. A great feature of Linux, though, is the ability to customize the kernel to match the specific devices on the computer.

Building a kernel is not particularly difficult, but it is a rather involved process. I can't go into all the gory details here; that could easily be a chapter all its own. I can give you some basic information, though, and point you in the direction of finding more information.

The two basic types of kernels in Enterprise Linux are monolithic and modular.

- ✔ **Monolithic kernel:** All the drivers necessary for your system are built into the kernel.

- ✔ **Modular kernel:** The device drivers are compiled as modules and are loaded into the kernel when they are required. The default kernel distributed with Enterprise Linux is a fully modular kernel.

In most instances, you won't need to build a custom kernel; the stock kernel supplied with the distribution should work well in most cases. Sometimes, though, you might need to build a custom kernel to support devices on your system.

You can use several tools to build your kernel: command line tools as well as a graphical based tool. Here I introduce you to the graphical tool xconfig.

1. **Before you can start to build your custom kernel, you need to be in the Linux directory created when you installed your system. Use the** cd **command to change to** /usr/src/linux -<kernel number>.

   In this section, *kernel number* refers to the kernel *version number.* You can find out your kernel version number by entering the following command:

   ```
   [root@main linux-2.4]# uname -r
   ```

   Here is my output:

   ```
   2.4.21-4.EL
   ```

2. **Type** xconfig **at a command prompt to start the graphical-based kernel configuration tool.**

   You see a screen similar to Figure 20-1.

Linux Kernel Configuration		
Code maturity level options	Fusion MPT device support	Sound
Loadable module support	IEEE 1394 (FireWire) support (EXPERIMENTAL)	USB support
Processor type and features	I2O device support	Additional device driver support
General setup	Network device support	Bluetooth support
Memory Technology Devices (MTD)	Amateur Radio support	Profiling support
Parallel port support	IrDA (infrared) support	Kernel hacking
Plug and Play configuration	ISDN subsystem	Cryptographic options
Block devices	Old CD-ROM drivers (not SCSI, not IDE)	Library routines
Multi-device support (RAID and LVM)	Input core support	
Networking options	Character devices	Save and Exit
Telephony Support	Multimedia devices	Quit Without Saving
ATA/IDE/MFM/RLL support	File systems	Load Configuration from File
SCSI support	Console drivers	Store Configuration to File

Figure 20-1:
Use the
`xconfig`
tool to build
a custom
kernel.

3. **Click each of the buttons in the main dialog box and enter the configuration choices to meet your needs. When you finish making your configuration choices, save your configuration to file.**

4. **Compile your new kernel and then install it.**

   a. Compile the new kernel by entering the following commands:

```
make dep
make bzimage
make modules
```

   b. Copy the newly created kernel into place so that it loads when the system boots.

   The newly created kernel is placed into

```
/usr/src/linux- <kernel number>/arch/i386/boot
```

   and is called `vmlinuz-<kernel number>`.

   You need to copy this file into the `/boot` directory.

A good place to look for information about the Linux kernel is `http://kernel.org`. A good book with complete instructions for building a custom kernel is *Red Hat Linux Networking and System Administration*, 2nd Edition, by Terry Collings and Kurt Wall (Wiley).

Shutting Down Unused Services

A typical Red Hat Enterprise system has many services running that are rarely (if ever) used in daily operations. You can stop these services from running, which speeds up your system and also makes your system more secure. To check for running services, you can use the `chconfig --list` command, as follows:

```
[root@terry root]# chkconfig --list
```

Listing 20-2 holds sample output from my system:

Listing 20-2: Sample Check for Running Services Output

ntpd	0:off	1:off	2:off	3:off	4:off	5:off	6:off
syslog	0:off	1:off	2:on	3:on	4:on	5:on	6:off
vmware	0:off	1:off	2:off	3:off	4:off	5:off	6:off
wine	0:off	1:off	2:on	3:on	4:on	5:on	6:off
netfs	0:off	1:off	2:off	3:on	4:on	5:on	6:off
network	0:off	1:off	2:on	3:on	4:on	5:on	6:off
random	0:off	1:off	2:on	3:on	4:on	5:on	6:off
rawdevices	0:off	1:off	2:off	3:on	4:on	5:on	6:off
saslauthd	0:off	1:off	2:off	3:on	4:on	5:on	6:off
xinetd	0:off	1:off	2:off	3:on	4:on	5:on	6:off
portmap	0:off	1:off	2:off	3:on	4:on	5:on	6:off
apmd	0:off	1:off	2:on	3:off	4:on	5:off	6:off
atd	0:off	1:off	2:off	3:on	4:on	5:on	6:off
gpm	0:off	1:off	2:off	3:on	4:on	5:on	6:off
autofs	0:off	1:off	2:off	3:on	4:on	5:on	6:off
irda	0:off	1:off	2:off	3:off	4:off	5:off	6:off
isdn	0:off	1:off	2:off	3:off	4:off	5:off	6:off
smartd	0:off	1:off	2:on	3:on	4:on	5:on	6:off
kudzu	0:off	1:off	2:off	3:on	4:on	5:on	6:off
nscd	0:off	1:off	2:off	3:off	4:off	5:off	6:off
sshd	0:off	1:off	2:on	3:on	4:on	5:on	6:off
snmpd	0:off	1:off	2:off	3:off	4:off	5:off	6:off
snmptrapd	0:off	1:off	2:off	3:off	4:off	5:off	6:off
sendmail	0:off	1:off	2:on	3:on	4:on	5:on	6:off
iptables	0:off	1:off	2:on	3:on	4:on	5:on	6:off
nfs	0:off	1:off	2:off	3:off	4:off	5:off	6:off
nfslock	0:off	1:off	2:off	3:on	4:on	5:on	6:off
rhnsd	0:off	1:off	2:off	3:on	4:on	5:on	6:off
pcmcia	0:off	1:off	2:off	3:off	4:on	5:off	6:off
crond	0:off	1:off	2:on	3:on	4:on	5:on	6:off
anacron	0:off	1:off	2:on	3:on	4:on	5:on	6:off
xfs	0:off	1:off	2:on	3:on	4:on	5:on	6:off
ypbind	0:off	1:off	2:off	3:off	4:off	5:off	6:off
named	0:off	1:off	2:off	3:off	4:off	5:off	6:off
lisa	0:off	1:off	2:off	3:off	4:off	5:off	6:off
firstboot	0:off	1:off	2:off	3:off	4:off	5:off	6:off
httpd	0:off	1:off	2:off	3:on	4:on	5:on	6:off
aep1000	0:off	1:off	2:off	3:off	4:off	5:off	6:off
bcm5820	0:off	1:off	2:off	3:off	4:off	5:off	6:off
winbind	0:off	1:off	2:off	3:off	4:off	5:off	6:off
smb	0:off	1:off	2:off	3:off	4:off	5:off	6:off
squid	0:off	1:off	2:off	3:off	4:off	5:off	6:off

(continued)

Listing 20-2 *(continued)*

```
tux              0:off   1:off   2:off   3:off   4:off   5:off   6:off
webmin           0:off   1:off   2:on    3:on    4:off   5:on    6:off
microcode_ctl    0:off   1:off   2:on    3:on    4:on    5:on    6:off
irqbalance       0:off   1:off   2:off   3:off   4:off   5:off   6:off
eloq6            0:off   1:off   2:on    3:on    4:on    5:on    6:off
messagebus       0:off   1:off   2:off   3:on    4:on    5:on    6:off
cups             0:off   1:off   2:on    3:on    4:on    5:on    6:off
vsftpd           0:off   1:off   2:off   3:off   4:off   5:off   6:off
mysqld           0:off   1:off   2:off   3:on    4:on    5:on    6:off
lircd            0:off   1:off   2:off   3:off   4:off   5:off   6:off
nagios           0:off   1:off   2:off   3:on    4:on    5:on    6:off
innd             0:off   1:off   2:off   3:off   4:off   5:off   6:off
yum              0:off   1:off   2:off   3:off   4:off   5:off   6:off
snortd           0:off   1:off   2:on    3:on    4:on    5:on    6:off
xinetd based services:
        chargen-udp:    off
        rsync:          on
        chargen:        off
        daytime-udp:    off
        daytime:        off
        echo-udp:       off
        echo:           off
        services:       on
        servers:        off
        time-udp:       off
        time:           off
        swat:           on
        rsh:            on
        cups-lpd:       off
        sgi_fam:        on
        ktalk:          off
        rexec:          on
        vsftpd:         on
```

Services listed at the top of the list are standalone services, and services listed under xinetd based services are controlled by the xinetd server. The numbers 0–6 indicate the runlevel of the system with levels 3, 4, and 5 being the levels for which you want to disable services.

For example, suppose that you want to disable the gpm standalone service. (This service provides for a mouse at the virtual console.) You can see from the output of the chkconfig --list command that gpm is enabled for run-levels 3, 4, and 5. To stop the service now and to prevent it from starting when the system boots, do the following:

1. **Stop the running service by issuing a command like the following:**

```
[root@terry root]# service gpm stop
```

You want to see the following response:

```
Shutting down console mouse services:                    [  OK  ]
```

2. **Disable** gpm **so it won't start when the system boots. You do this by entering the command**

```
chkconfig -level 345 gpm off
```

3. **Check sure that the service is disabled by entering**

```
[root@terry root]# chkconfig --list | grep gpm
```

You want to see the following response:

```
gpm              0:off   1:off   2:off   3:off   4:off   5:off   6:off
```

To disable a service that is controlled by the xinetd server, the procedure is a little different but just as easy. If you look at the list of xinetd-based services, you see that vsftpd is on. If you want to turn it off or disable it, do the following:

1. **Open the** /etc/xinetd.d/vsftpd **file, using your favorite text editor.**

2. **Find the line that reads**

```
Disable = NO
```

3. **Change the** NO **to a** Yes.

4. **Save and close the file.**

5. **Restart the** xinetd **server by issuing the command**

```
service xinetd restart
```

6. **After the** xinetd **server restarts, check to be sure the service is disabled by using the** chkconfig --list **command again.**

You should go through all your services and disable the ones that you know you will not use.

You can use the graphical services tool to disable the services if you desire. Just choose Applications⇨System Settings⇨Server Settings⇨Services. The graphical tool also provides a brief description of the services.

Administering Your System by Using Webmin

For a long time, the only way to administer a Linux system was by editing text configuration files and learning a lot of cryptic command line commands. Although Red Hat Enterprise Linux has come a long way from those early days and now that many graphical tools for doing system configuration are included with Enterprise Linux, I'd like to tell you about one of my favorite graphical system configuration tools.

That tool, Webmin, has been making the job of a Linux system administrator easier for quite awhile. With Webmin, you can configure your entire Enterprise Linux system by using a Web browser to access the Webmin program. I can't go into a lot of detail about Webmin here, but I can tell you where to get it and how to install it. I show you how to log in and then I leave you to explore Webmin on your own.

Before you can install Webmin, you first need to download it. You can find Webmin at

```
http://prdownloads.sourceforge.net/webadmin/webmin-1.160-1.noarch.rpm
```

After you download the file, use the `rpm` command to install the file, as shown here.

```
[root@main beta2]# rpm -Uvh webmin*
```

You see something like the following:

```
warning: webmin-1.160-1.noarch.rpm: V3 DSA signature: NOKEY, key ID 11f63c51
Preparing...                ########################################### [100%]
Operating system is Redhat Linux 3.0AS
   1:webmin                 ########################################### [100%]
Webmin install complete. You can now login to
            http://main.tactechnology.com:10000/
as root with your root password.
```

After the program is installed, you can follow the directions as shown to browse to the Webmin program on your system. Be sure to use the information relevant to your system instead of what is shown in this example output.

To log in to Webmin, open your Web browser of choice and enter your system domain name and the port 10000. For example, to open Webmin on my system, I enter **http://main.tactechnology.com:10000** into the browser location bar. You now see the Webmin login screen.

You need to enter root for the username and the system root password to log in to Webmin. If you successfully log in, you see a screen similar to Figure 20-2.

From the main Webmin page, you can click the icons near the top of the page to open a related detail dialog box, from which you can make configuration changes for the item that you select. I strongly encourage you to explore the entire Webmin program to familiarize yourself with the various dialog boxes and their purpose before you begin making any changes.

Figure 20-2:
The Webmin home page for my Enterprise Linux system.

Chapter 21

Ten Troubleshooting and Problem-Solving Tips

In This Chapter

▶ Unable to log in

▶ Lost or forgotten root password

▶ CD-ROM drive not detected during installation

▶ Sound does not work

▶ Unable to unmount a drive

▶ System hangs during boot

▶ Unable to access network hosts

▶ Making an emergency disk

▶ Shell commands don't work

▶ Sources of additional information

*I*n this chapter, I offer you tips for troubleshooting and solving problems that new users typically encounter with their systems. No matter how well your systems might be running, you will eventually run into a problem that gives you trouble or makes your systems unusable. I try to cover some of those problems here and tell you what to do to correct them.

Unable to Log In

A very common problem for a lot of users is not being able to log in. This problem can be caused by a number of reasons, but the most common reason is that the user has forgotten his password. Another reason why a user might not be able to log in is because she doesn't have an account on the system that she is trying to use. In either case, you can log in as the root user and reset a user's password, or you can create an account for a user who doesn't have one.

Resetting a user's password

To reset a user's password, you have to change it to a different password. Do this as follows:

1. **Log in as the root user, open a terminal window, and enter the following command:**

```
passwd <user name>
```

2. **Type a new password for the user and press Enter.**

3. **Type the same password again and press Enter.**

4. **Log out as root and try logging in as the user to be sure that the login now works.**

Creating a user account

Another reason why a user might not be able to log in is because the user does not have an account. This is easily remedied by creating an account for the user. To create a user account, do the following:

1. **Open a terminal window and log in as the root user.**

2. **At the command prompt, type** useradd *username* **and then press Enter.**

   Be sure to enter the correct username for the user.

3. **Type the command** passwd *username* **and then press Enter.**

4. **Type the password for the user when prompted and then press Enter.**

5. **Log out as root and try logging in as the user to be sure the login now works.**

Lost or forgotten root password

If a user forgets his password, you can always log in as root to change the user's password. But what can you do if you forget the root user's password? You won't be able to do a lot of administrative tasks if you can't become the root user when necessary. Fortunately, the procedure for resetting the root password is not difficult:

1. **Reboot your system.**

2. **When the GRUB boot prompt appears, highlight the kernel image that you want to boot and then press e.**

   This opens the GRUB edit window for this kernel.

3. **Place the cursor on the second line, which should look similar to the following:**

```
kernel /vmlinuz-2.4.22-1.2115.nptl ro root=LABEL=/1
```

4. **At the end of the line, insert a space and then type the word** single.

5. **Press Enter and then press b to boot the kernel.**

   After the system boots into single-user mode, it opens a terminal window with a root shell prompt of init-2.05b#.

6. **At the prompt, type** passwd root **and then press Enter.**

7. **Type the new password for root and then press Enter.**

8. **Type** exit **and then press Enter.**

   The system reboots, and you know the new root password. Try not to forget this one.

CD-ROM Drive Not Detected During Installation

Before beginning your installation, you should check the hardware compatibility list at the Red Hat Web site. This will ensure that your hardware is compatible with Enterprise Linux. But even if you check and find that your CD-ROM drive is supported, the drive might not be detected by Enterprise Linux although it is recognized by the system BIOS and you can boot from the drive.

In this case, you can specifically tell the system where to find the CD-ROM drive by following this procedure:

1. **Boot your system by using the first installation disk.**

2. **When you see the** boot **prompt, type** linux hdx=cdrom **and then press Enter.**

   This command specifically tells the kernel where to look for the CD-ROM drive. x should be one of the following:

   - a: First drive on primary IDE controller (master)
   - b: Second drive on primary IDE controller (slave)
   - c: First drive on secondary IDE controller (master)
   - d: Second drive on secondary IDE controller (slave)

   Your system should now see the CD-ROM drive, and you can install Enterprise Linux.

CD-ROM Drive Does Not Mount After Installation

On some systems, the CD-ROM drive will not mount after the installation. If you encounter this problem, try this solution:

1. **Boot your system from a backup boot disk.**

   Read how in the upcoming section, "Making an Emergency Boot Disk."

2. **At a terminal command line, type the command** depmod -ae **and then press Enter.**

   This command creates a dependency file of the system modules. When the system boots, this file is used by the modprobe command to automatically load the proper modules.

Sound Does Not Work After Installation

The Enterprise Linux installation program does a good job of detecting the hardware on your system and attempting to configure it properly. Most of the time, your sound card will be detected and the proper modules loaded so that it works. Sometimes, though, the installation program might not be able to detect your sound card. Or your sound card might be detected but not configured properly. Here are some suggestions that you can try to get your sound to work:

- ✔ **Try running the automatic configuration program again.** Sometimes running it again after logging in as root can correct the problem.

- ✔ **Choose Applications⇨System Settings⇨Soundcard Detection.** If your sound card is detected, you are given the option to test the configuration. If your sound works during the test, that's great: You're finished.

- ✔ **Edit the** /etc/modprobe.conf **file.** If the sound doesn't work or if your sound card isn't even detected, you can manually try some settings by editing the /etc/modprobe.conf file. The /etc/modprobe.conf file from my system is shown in Listing 21-1.

Listing 21-1:   Sound Module and Configuration Information of the /etc/modprobe.conf File

```
[terry@terry terry]$ cat /etc/modprobe.conf
alias parport_lowlevel parport_pc
alias eth0 e100
alias usb-controller usb-uhci
```

```
alias sound-slot-0 snd-cs4232
options sound dmabuf=1
alias synth0 opl3
options opl3 io=0x388
options cs4232 isapnp=1
```

A good source of information about configuring sound cards in Linux is the Advanced Linux Sound Architecture Web site at www.alsa-project.org.

When I installed Enterprise Linux on one of my older systems, it could not detect my sound card during installation. After I logged in, running the sound card detection tool still did not detect my sound card. I had to manually edit the /etc/modprobe.conf file to configure my sound card, as shown in Listing 21-1. The sound configuration information begins with the line alias sound-slot-0 snd-cs4232. The lines following it are options for the cs4232 sound card.

To configure sound on your system, you need to know the type of sound card installed in your system as well as the configuration options for the sound card. The best place to get specific information for your card and configuring it under Enterprise Linux is the ALSA Web site. You can find information about nearly every sound card there as well as specific instructions to configure the card. With a little effort on your part and some reading at the ALSA site, you can get your sound working.

Unable to Unmount a Drive

Whenever you work with a floppy disk or CD-ROM, you have to mount the disk before you can read or write to it. After you finish, you no longer need the drive mounted. In fact, if you want to remove the CD from the drive, you must unmount the disk, or the CD-ROM drive won't let you eject the disk. Look at an example. You finish using the CD-ROM drive, and you try to unmount the drive by using the umount command, as follows:

```
[root@terry cdrom]# umount /mnt/cdrom
```

The system returns a message telling you that the drive is busy.

```
umount: /mnt/cdrom: device is busy
```

Although this is a really easy problem to solve, it is a real source of frustration for a new user. You can see from the example prompt that the current working directory is cdrom. If you use the pwd command

```
[root@terry cdrom]# pwd
```

you see that you are in the directory that you're trying to unmount.

```
/mnt/cdrom
```

All you need to do is to change to a different directory and then run the `umount` command again. Now you can successfully unmount the drive.

I have also noticed a similar problem that isn't related to the current working directory. Sometimes when trying to unmount a drive, I receive the `Drive Busy` error message even though I'm not in the directory that I'm trying to unmount. No matter what I try, I can't get the `umount` command to unmount the drive.

After some thought one day, I decided to try logging out of the desktop and then logging back in. I thought that perhaps there was some glitch in the GNOME or KDE desktop that was not allowing the drive to unmount. Sure enough, this method did work because when I logged back in, the drive was no longer mounted. If you experience a similar situation when trying to unmount a drive, give this method a try.

System Hangs During Boot

Sometimes your system might seem to hang during the boot process when starting many of your network services. If your system hangs when starting Sendmail, the Sendmail daemon (`httpd`), the Apache Web server, or the Samba daemon (`smb`), this could indicate that your system is unable to resolve the hostname to an IP address.

The system hang is actually the kernel waiting for the name resolver to time out. After the name resolver times out, the boot process continues.

If your network has a working Domain Name System (DNS) server, try the following to correct this problem:

1. **Log in as root and check the contents of your** `/etc/resolv.conf` **file.**

   Your file should look similar to the file shown here.

   ```
   [root@terry root]# cat /etc/resolv.conf
   ; generated by /sbin/dhclient-script
   search muhlenberg.edu
   nameserver 192.104.181.5
   ```

2. **If your** `/etc/resolv.conf` **file does not have the proper values for your system in the search and nameserver lines, make corrections as necessary and save the file.**

If you don't have a DNS server on your network, or if your system is the DNS server, you can try the following to correct your system hang.

1. **Log in as root and check the contents of your** `/etc/hosts` **file.**

   Your file should look similar to the file shown here:

   ```
   cat /etc/hosts
   127.0.0.1        localhost.localdomain    localhost
   192.168.9.110    terry.muhlenberg.edu     terry
   ```

2. **You want to be sure that your system's IP address and hostname are listed in the file. Make changes as required and save the file.**

Unable to Access Network Hosts

If you can't get to hosts on a network, check that you have at least one name server listed in the `/etc/resolv.conf` file. This file contains the IP address or domain name of name servers used for DNS name resolution. Your `/etc/resolv.conf` file should be similar to the listing shown here:

```
[root@terry root]# cat /etc/resolv.conf
; generated by /sbin/dhclient-script
search muhlenberg.edu
nameserver 192.104.181.5
```

If you use static IP addresses for your system, be sure that you specify a default gateway. Without a default gateway, your system doesn't know what to do with requests for connections to external networks. You can check your gateway setting by using the `route` command. In the following, you can see the default gateway shown on the last line.

```
[root@terry root]# route
Kernel IP routing table
Destination    Gateway       Genmask          Flags Metric Ref    Use Iface
192.168.9.0    *             255.255.255.0    U     0      0        0 eth0
127.0.0.0      *             255.0.0.0        U     0      0        0 lo
default        192.168.9.1   0.0.0.0          UG    0      0        0 eth0
```

If a system can't connect to your system, check the `/etc/hosts.allow` and the `/etc/hosts.deny` files. The system will first check the `/etc/hosts.allow` file and then the `/etc/hosts.deny` file. Rules found in the `/etc/hosts.allow` file are applied first; the rules in `/etc/hosts.deny` are then applied, superseding the rules in `/etc/hosts.allow`. Consequently, if you have the other systems listed in your `/etc/hosts.deny` file, they will be denied access.

If you upgraded from a previous version of Red Hat, your networking configuration files are saved with the extension `.rpmsave`. This makes it appear that your networking configuration files were not saved when in fact they have been in the network service's directory. You might need to copy your configuration from the saved file to the new file if you encounter networking problems after upgrading.

Making an Emergency Boot Disk

Sometimes you might have a problem with your system that prevents it from booting properly. Maybe you made some configuration changes and then shut down your system. When you tried to boot up again, the system wouldn't start because you changed the boot loader configuration files. This is just the time when you could use an emergency rescue disk. In this section, I show you how to make one.

Making a boot disk is very easy. Follow this procedure:

1. **From a terminal command line, find your kernel version by entering the command**

   ```
   [root@main root]#uname -r
   ```

   which gives the following output. (Your output might be different.)

   ```
   2.6.9-5.EL
   ```

2. **Type the command** mkbootdisk 2.6.9-5.EL.

3. **Insert a floppy disk into the disk drive when prompted and then press Enter.**

   When the command prompt returns, the boot disk has been created.

Shell Commands Don't Work

This is a common problem encountered by new users who log in as a regular user and then execute the substitute user command to become the root user. The problem is that after entering the su command and becoming root, commands issued return the message Command Not Found.

This problem is caused because even though the su command lets a regular user become the root user with all of root's permissions, it does not give root an actual login shell. So in this case, the user has root's permissions but does not have root's search path for directories. For example, when I use su to

become root on my system and then run a command (chkconfig, for example), I receive the following:

```
[terry@terry terry]$ su
Password:
[root@terry terry]# chkconfig --list
bash: chkconfig: command not found
[root@terry terry]#
```

To solve this problem, you can do two things:

✔ **Enter the complete path to the command.**

✔ **Use the su command with the - (hyphen) option as shown here:**

```
[terry@terry terry]$ su -
Password:
[root@terry root]# chkconfig --list
ntpd            0:off  1:off  2:off  3:off  4:off  5:off  6:off
syslog          0:off  1:off  2:on   3:on   4:on   5:on   6:off
<output clipped>
```

Another instance of shell commands not working is also related to the search
path. Users who are familiar with DOS know that DOS looks in the current
directory for executable files as well as the search path. Linux, on the other
hand, does not search the current directory but only the search path. Thus,
an executable file in the same directory as the directory which the user is in
will not be found.

You need to explicitly tell the shell to look in the current directory by using
./(executable file name). The period and forward slash tells the shell to
look in the current directory.

Sources of Additional Information

If you are new to Enterprise Linux, don't worry about obtaining more information. You can find many sources of information about all aspects of running Linux. A good place to start is the Internet, where you can search for the
topics in which you're interested.

Here are some links that you can start with to begin your exploring.

✔ **The Linux Documentation Project,** www.tldp.org/tldp-redirect.
php?url=/. This is a good place to look for HOWTO documents on
many Linux topics.

✔ **Linux Journal,** www.linuxjournal.com. Available online, the Linux
Journal was the first magazine devoted entirely to Linux.

✔ **Usenet.** There are many Usenet news groups about Linux. Do a search on your favorite search engine for these groups.

✔ **Linux Online,** www.linux.org. This is a great source for Linux news and information.

✔ **The Linux Kernel Archives,** http://kernel.org. Information about the Linux kernel can be obtained from this Web site.

✔ **Red Hat,** www.redhat.com. Of course, I must mention the Red Hat Web site, which is a good place to get information specific to your distribution.

✔ **Mailing lists.** Hundreds of mailing lists are on the Internet. These mailing lists typically focus on specific topics and are great sources for really helpful people.

✔ **Linux users groups.** Many Linux user groups are located throughout the country. There is probably one in your area (or not too far from you) that you can join, or at least attend a meeting or two. Here you can find people who share the same interest as you, at least about Linux, and are more than willing to help new users.

Part VII

Appendixes

"I guess you could say this is the hub of our network."

In this part . . .

The appendixes contain some useful information that you should know about but didn't seem to fit too well in the main part of the book. Appendix A has instructions and illustrations of a basic system installation, using the installation CDs. In Appendix B, you find a description of the rescue CD and instructions on how to use it. You can use the rescue CD if you have trouble booting your system.

Appendix A

Installing Red Hat Enterprise Linux

In This Chapter

▶ Exploring your PC's components

▶ Checking for supported hardware

▶ Starting the installation

▶ Partitioning your hard disk

▶ Configuring Red Hat Enterprise Linux installation

▶ Selecting packages to install

*T*his chapter explains the steps necessary to install Red Hat Enterprise Linux on a single system. Regardless of the version of Enterprise Linux that you are installing, the installation procedure is the same. You begin by making a list of your PC's hardware. You use this hardware inventory later when you begin the installation.

Exploring Your PC's Components

Before installing Red Hat Enterprise Linux, you should compile a list of the hardware components in your computer. Linux supports different types of hardware through device drivers, similar to other operating systems. A driver is required for each type of peripheral device; depending on the age of your hardware, a driver might not be available. If your hardware is current — meaning less than two years old — the drivers that you need are probably available and included with the distribution. If you need a driver that is not included with the distribution, searching the Internet usually provides you with a solution.

Whenever I need a driver, I usually do a Google search for it. For example, if I needed a driver for an NVIDIA video card, I search for *NVIDIA Linux driver,* or I could search for *Crystal Audio Linux driver* for my sound card driver.

You can install and run Red Hat Enterprise Linux even if no Linux drivers are available for certain devices, such as your video card or soundcard. Of course, these devices might not function or perhaps function in a limited capacity, but this might not be a problem for you, depending on the device. To be able to install Red Hat Enterprise Linux, though, you must have compatibility in the following:

- Processor
- Bus type
- Video card
- Monitor
- Hard disk
- Floppy disk drive
- Keyboard
- Mouse
- CD-ROM drive

If you plan to use a graphical user interface (GUI) such as GNOME or KDE, you must ensure that XFree86 (the X Window System for Linux) supports the mouse, the video card, and the monitor. Nearly all devices made within the last two years are supported. Read how to check for this compatibility in the upcoming section, "Checking for Supported Hardware."

The following sections briefly describe the PC hardware supported by Red Hat Enterprise Linux. Your hardware list should contain information about the hardware described here before you begin to install Red Hat Enterprise Linux on your PC.

Processor

The *central processing unit* (CPU; or just *the processor*) is an integrated circuit chip that performs nearly all the control and processing functions in the PC. Red Hat Enterprise Linux runs on an Intel 80386 processor or newer as well as compatibles made by AMD or Cyrix. However, you probably don't want to use any processor older than a Pentium-class processor. Red Hat Enterprise Linux also supports motherboards with multiple processors with the symmetric multiprocessing (SMP) Linux kernel.

Bus type

The *bus* provides the electrical connection between the processor and its peripherals. Several types of PC buses exist. The most recent is the Peripheral

Component Interconnect (PCI) bus, which is found on all current production motherboards. Another is the Industry Standard Architecture (ISA) bus, formerly called the *AT bus* because IBM introduced it in the IBM PC-AT computer in 1984. Other buses include Extended Industry Standard Architecture (EISA), VESA local (VL-bus), and Micro Channel Architecture (MCA). Red Hat Enterprise Linux supports all these buses.

Memory

If you are buying a new PC, it probably comes with 128MB or more RAM. If you can afford it, buy as much RAM as you can because the more RAM a system has, the more efficiently it runs multiple programs (because the programs can all fit in memory). Red Hat Enterprise Linux can use a part of the hard disk as virtual memory. Such disk-based memory, called *swap space,* is much slower than physical memory.

Video card and monitor

If you don't plan to use the X Window System, any video card works. Red Hat Enterprise Linux supports all video cards in text mode. If you are planning to use the X Window System, be sure to find a video card that is supported by XFree86 so you can take full advantage of its graphical interface. You can save yourself a lot of aggravation if your video card is supported by XFree86.

Your choice of monitors depends on your use of the X Window System. For text mode displays, which are typically used on servers, any monitor will do. However, if you're setting up a workstation or if you're using the X Window System on your server, choose a monitor that supports the display resolution that you use. *Resolution* is expressed in terms of the number of picture elements (pixels) horizontally and vertically (such as 1024 x 768).

XFree86's support for a video card depends on the *video chipset* — the integrated circuit that controls the monitor and causes the monitor to display output. You can find out the name of the video chipset used in a video card from the card's documentation. Then you can look for the name of the video chipsets listed at the Red Hat site.

Your video card's name might not be in the list at the Red Hat site. The important thing to note is the name of the video chipset because many popular video cards made by different manufacturers use the same video chipsets. In nearly all cases, the Red Hat Enterprise Linux installation program automatically detects the video chipset as it sets up the X Window System.

Hard drive

Red Hat Enterprise Linux supports any hard drive that your PC's basic input/output system (BIOS) supports as long as the system BIOS supports the hard drive without any additional drivers. To be able to boot Red Hat Enterprise Linux from a large hard drive (any drive with more than 1,024 cylinders), the Linux Loader (LILO), the Linux kernel, and the LILO configuration files must be located in the first 1,024 cylinders of the drive. This is because the Linux Loader uses the BIOS to load the kernel, and the BIOS cannot access cylinders beyond the first 1,024.

For hard drives connected to your PC through a Small Computer System Interface (SCSI) controller card, Red Hat Enterprise Linux must have a driver that enables the SCSI controller to access and use the hard drive.

As for the size (storage capacity) of the drive, most new systems seem to have 8–10GB of capacity. You should buy the highest capacity drive that you can afford.

Floppy disk drive

Linux drivers use the PC's BIOS to access the floppy disk drive, so any floppy disk drive is compatible with Red Hat Enterprise Linux. The Red Hat Enterprise Linux installation program can be started from the CD-ROM if your PC has one and can boot from it. If not, you have to boot Red Hat Enterprise Linux from a floppy disk drive during the installation, so you need a high-density 3.5-inch (1.44MB capacity) floppy disk drive. You can also avoid booting from a floppy if you can boot your PC under MS-DOS (not an MS-DOS window under Windows 95/98/NT/Me/2000/XP), and you can access the CD-ROM from the DOS command prompt.

Keyboard and mouse

Red Hat Enterprise Linux supports any keyboard that already works with your PC. The mouse, however, needs explicit support in Red Hat Enterprise Linux. You need a mouse if you want to configure and run XFree86, the X Window System for Linux. Red Hat Enterprise Linux supports most popular mice, including the commonly found PS/2-style mouse. Red Hat Enterprise Linux also supports touchpad devices, such as the ALPS GlidePoint, as long as they are compatible with one of the supported mice.

SCSI controller

The Small Computer System Interface is a standard way of connecting many types of peripheral devices to a computer. SCSI is used in many kinds of computers, from high-end Unix workstations to PCs. Typically, you connect hard drives and CD-ROM drives through a SCSI controller. To use a SCSI device on your PC, you need a SCSI controller card that plugs into one of the connector slots on your PC's bus.

A single SCSI controller supports device addresses 0–7, with 7 usually assigned to the controller itself. This means that you can connect up to seven SCSI devices to your PC. (With SCSI 2, you can connect up to 14 devices.) If you want to access and use a SCSI device under Linux, you have to make sure that Red Hat Enterprise Linux supports your SCSI controller card.

CD-ROM drive

CD-ROM drives are popular because each CD can hold up to 650MB of data, which is a relatively large amount of storage compared with a floppy disk. CDs are reliable and inexpensive to manufacture. Vendors can use a CD to distribute a large amount of information at a reasonable cost.

Sound card

If you are configuring a server, you probably aren't too interested in playing sounds. However, with Red Hat Enterprise Linux, you can play sound on a sound card to enjoy multimedia programs and games. If you have a sound card, you can also play audio CDs. Nearly all sound cards available today are supported.

Network card

A network interface card (NIC) is necessary if you connect your Red Hat Enterprise Linux PC to a local area network (LAN), which is usually an Ethernet network. If you are configuring a server, you certainly want to configure a network card. Red Hat Enterprise Linux supports a variety of Ethernet network cards. ARCNet and IBM's token ring network are also supported. Check the hardware list on the Red Hat site to see whether your NIC is supported. Nearly all NICs currently in use are supported.

For any Red Hat Enterprise Linux PC connected to a network, you need the following information:

- The PC's hostname
- Domain name of the network
- Internet Protocol (IP) address of the PC (or, if the IP address is provided by a DHCP server, the server's address)
- Gateway address
- IP address of name servers

Checking for Supported Hardware

To check whether Red Hat Enterprise Linux supports the hardware in your PC, follow these steps:

1. **Make a list of the make, model, and other technical details of all hardware installed in your PC.**

   Most of this information is in the manuals that came with your hardware. If you don't have the manuals and you already have an operating system on the PC, you might be able to obtain this information from that operating system.

2. **Go to the Red Hat Web site at** `www.redhat.com/hardware` **to compare your hardware list against the list of hardware that the latest version of Red Hat Enterprise Linux supports.**

   If the components listed earlier are supported, you can prepare to install Red Hat.

Starting the Red Hat Enterprise Linux Installation

Enterprise Linux is only available by purchasing from Red Hat; it is not available as a free download. To start the Red Hat Enterprise Linux installation, put the first Red Hat Installation CD in your PC's CD drive and restart your PC. The PC loads Red Hat Enterprise Linux from the CD-ROM and begins running the Red Hat installation program. The Red Hat installation program controls the installation of the operating system.

A few moments after you start the boot process, an initial screen appears. The screen displays a welcome message and ends with a `boot:` prompt. The welcome message tells you that more information is available by pressing one of the function keys F1 through F5.

If you want to read the help screens, press the function key corresponding to the help that you want. If you don't press any keys after a minute, the boot process proceeds with the loading of the Linux kernel into the PC's memory. To start booting Red Hat Enterprise Linux immediately, press Enter. After the Linux kernel loads, it automatically starts the Red Hat Enterprise Linux installation program. This, in turn, starts the X Window System, which provides a graphical user interface for the installation.

You should have all the configuration information explained earlier in this chapter before you begin. If the installation program detects your hardware, installing Red Hat Enterprise Linux from the CD-ROM on a fast (200 MHz or better) Pentium PC should take 30–40 minutes.

During the installation, the Red Hat installation program tries to determine the hardware in your PC and alters the installation steps as required. For example, if the installation program detects a network card, the program displays the appropriate network configuration screens. If a network card is not detected, the network configuration screens are not displayed. Depending on your specific hardware, the screens that you see during installation might differ from those shown in this section.

You go through the following steps before moving on to disk setup and installation:

1. **After the installation program starts the X Window System and displays a list of languages in a graphical installation screen, use your mouse to select the language you want and then click Next to proceed to the next step.**

In the graphical installation, each screen has online help available on the left side. You can read the help message to learn more about what you are supposed to select in a specific screen.

2. **Make your keyboard selections:**

   a. **When the installation program displays a list of keyboard types, select a keyboard model that closely matches your PC's keyboard.**

   If you don't see your keyboard model listed, select one of the generic models: Generic 101-key PC or Generic 104-key PC. (Newer keyboards with the Windows keys match this model.)

b. **Select a keyboard layout that depends on your language's character set (for example, English, in the United States).**

c. **Select the Enable Dead Keys option if the language that you select has special characters that must be composed by pressing multiple keys in sequence.**

For the English language, you can safely select the Disable Dead Keys option.

d. **Click Next to go to the next screen where you will configure your mouse.**

3. **Configure the mouse for your system from the installation program screen.**

The various mouse types are listed in a tree structure organized alphabetically by manufacturer. You need to know your mouse type and whether it is connected to the PC's serial port or the PS/2 port.

a. **If your mouse type appears in the list, select it.**

b. **If your mouse type does not appear in the list, select a generic mouse type.**

Most new PCs have a PS/2 or USB mouse.

c. **For a two-button mouse, you should select the Emulate 3 Buttons option.**

Because many X applications assume that you use a three-button mouse, you should select this option. On a typical two-button mouse, you can simulate a middle-button click by pressing both buttons simultaneously. On a Microsoft IntelliMouse, the wheel acts as the middle button.

If you select a mouse with a serial interface, you are asked to specify the serial port where the mouse is connected.

• **For COM1,** specify /dev/ttyS0 as the device.

• **For COM2,** the device name is /dev/ttyS1.

4. **After the installation program displays a welcome message that provides some helpful information, including a suggestion that you access the online manuals at** www.redhat.com, **click Next.**

The installation program displays a screen asking whether you want to install a new system or upgrade an older Red Hat installation if one is found.

The next major phase of installation involves partitioning the hard disk for use in Red Hat Enterprise Linux.

Partitioning the Hard Disk for Red Hat Enterprise Linux

Red Hat Enterprise Linux requires you to partition and prepare a hard disk before you can install Red Hat Enterprise Linux. For a new PC, you usually do not perform this step because the vendor normally takes care of preparing the hard disk and installing Windows and all other applications on the hard disk. Because you are installing Red Hat Enterprise Linux from scratch, however, you have to perform this crucial step yourself. As you see in the following sections, this task is just a matter of following instructions.

The Red Hat Enterprise Linux installation program offers you two choices for partitioning your hard drive, as shown in Figure A-1.

You can choose to have the installation program automatically partition your disk, or you can choose to use Disk Druid to manually partition your disk. For this installation, you will choose to have the disk partitions set up automatically by following these steps.

1. **Be sure that the Automatically Partition radio button is selected and then click Next.**

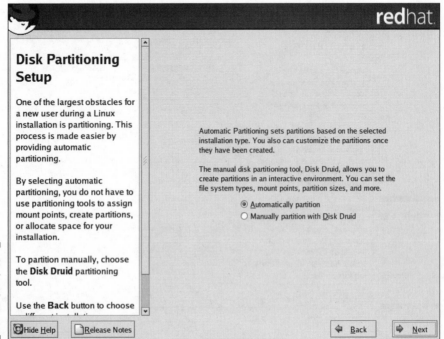

Figure A-1: Choose your disk partitioning method.

The Automatic Partitioning dialog box, as shown in Figure A-2, appears. From this dialog box, you select which areas of your hard drive are partitioned.

The default choice on the Automatic Partitioning dialog box is to remove all partitions on the system. You should accept the default unless you have data on the drive that you wish to retain.

2. After making your selection, click Next to continue.

If you accept the default choice to remove all partitions, you see a warning message.

3. Click Yes to continue.

You now see the Disk Setup dialog box, as shown in Figure A-3.

4. Because you are using automatic partitioning, you can accept these choices by clicking Next to continue.

This completes the disk preparation phase of the installation. The installation program performs the actual formatting of the partitions after it asks for some more configuration information, including the packages that you want to install.

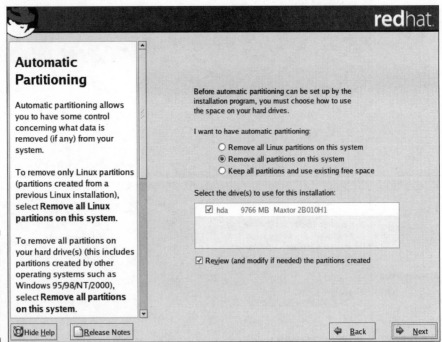

Figure A-2: Select the data to remove during partitioning.

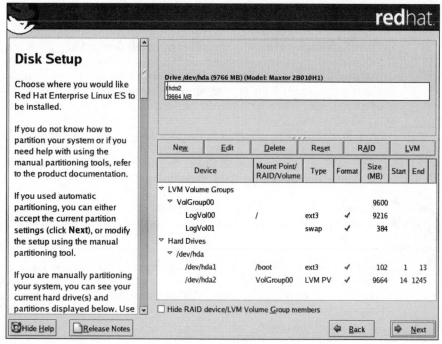

Figure A-3:
The Disk
Setup dialog
box shows
your disk
partitioning
choices.

Configuring Red Hat Enterprise Linux Installation

After you prepare the disk partitions, the installation program moves on to some configuration steps. The typical configuration steps are

- Configure the boot loader
- Configure the network
- Configure the firewall
- Set the time zone
- Set the root password
- Select the packages to install

The following sections guide you through each of these configuration steps.

Configuring the boot loader

The Red Hat Enterprise installation program displays the Boot Loader Configuration screen, as shown in Figure A-4, which asks you where you want to install the boot loader. A *boot loader* is a program that resides on your disk and starts Red Hat Enterprise Linux from the hard disk. Red Hat Enterprise Linux uses GRUB, which stands for Grand Unified Bootloader.

GRUB is installed by default in the master boot record (MBR) of the first hard disk in your system. However, if you desire, you can choose a different location or choose not to install GRUB by clicking the Change Boot Loader button and entering the appropriate information in the pop-up box.

If you choose not to install the boot loader, you should definitely create a boot disk. Otherwise, you can't start Red Hat Enterprise Linux when you reboot the PC.

In the center of the Boot Loader Configuration screen, you have the option to select the disk partition from which you want to boot the PC. A table then lists the Linux partition and any other partitions that might contain another operating system. Each entry in that table is an operating system that the boot loader can boot.

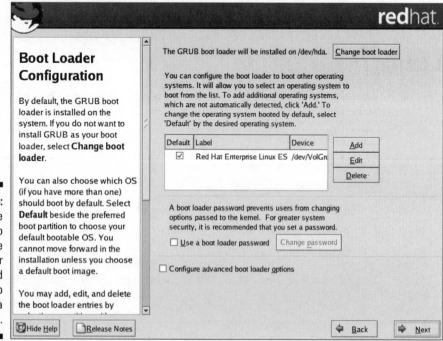

Figure A-4: Specify here where to install the boot loader and whether to create a boot disk.

All the instructions in this section are for your information if you choose to change any of the default settings. You can essentially accept the default selections on this screen and then click Next to proceed to the next configuration step.

Configuring the network

If the Linux kernel detects a network card, the Red Hat installation program displays the Network Configuration screen, as shown in Figure A-5, which enables you to configure the LAN parameters for your Enterprise Linux system.

This step is not for configuring dialup networking. You need to perform this step if your Linux system is connected to a TCP/IP LAN through an Ethernet card.

The Network Configuration screen displays each network card installed on your system and detected by the Linux kernel. If your system has only one Ethernet card, you see only one card, identified as eth0, listed in the table.

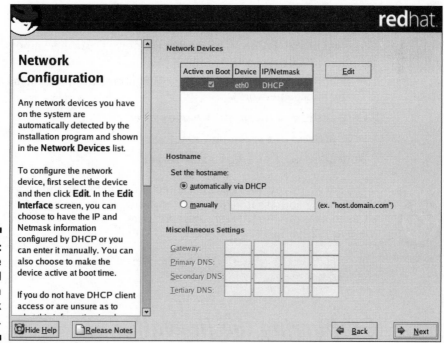

Figure A-5:
Configure
the local
area
network
here.

The default setting for the card is to use Dynamic Host Configuration Protocol (DHCP) to obtain IP information. You should select DHCP only if a DHCP server is running on your LAN. If you choose DHCP, your network configuration is set automatically, and you can skip the rest of this section. You should leave the Activate on Boot check box selected so that the network is configured whenever you boot the system.

If you do not want to use DHCP but want to set a static IP address and other network information, you have to enter certain parameters for TCP/IP configuration. You can do this as follows:

1. **Click the Edit button next to the Network Devices table to open a properties window for the network interface.**

2. **Deselect the Configure Using DHCP option.**

3. **Enter the IP address and netmask for the Ethernet card.**

4. **Mark the Activate on Boot check box to have the Ethernet card started when the system boots.**

5. **Click OK to return to the Network Configuration dialog box.**

If you enter a static IP address, you need to enter the following information in the Network Configuration dialog box:

✔ **Hostname for your Linux system**

For a private LAN, you can assign your own hostname without worrying about conflicting with any other existing systems on the Internet.

✔ **IP address of the *gateway*** (the system through which you might go to any outside network)

✔ **IP address of the primary name server**

✔ **IP address of a secondary name server**

✔ **IP address of a tertiary name server**

If you have a private LAN (one not directly connected to the Internet), you can use an IP address from a range designated for private use. Common IP addresses for private LANs are the addresses in the range 192.168.1.1 through 192.168.1.254.

After you enter the requested parameters, click Next to proceed to the next configuration step.

Configuring the firewall

In this part of the installation process, you can choose the firewall settings for your system security. Look at Figure A-6 as you go through this section's configuration steps.

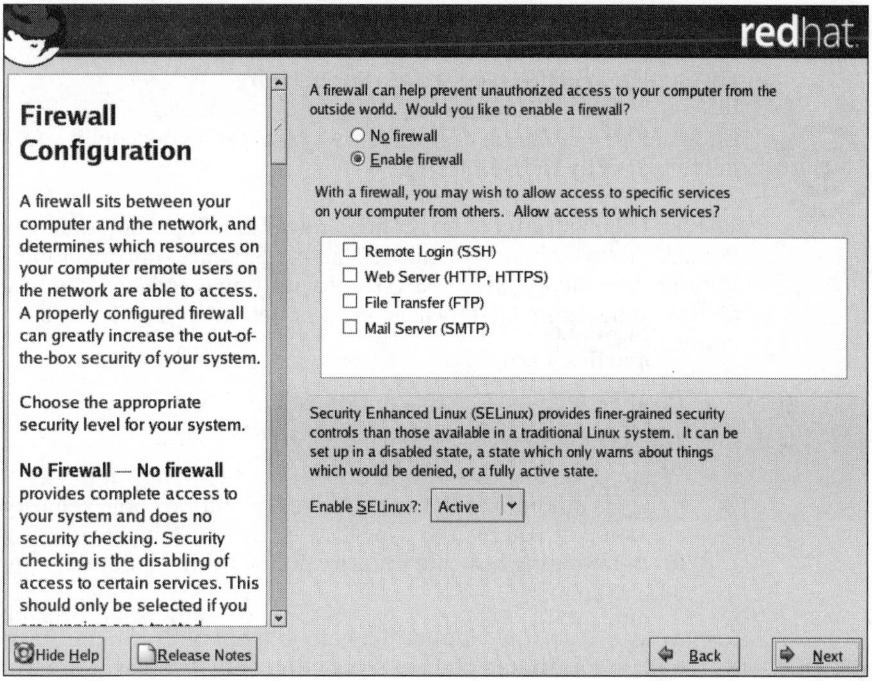

Firewall Configuration

A firewall sits between your computer and the network, and determines which resources on your computer remote users on the network are able to access. A properly configured firewall can greatly increase the out-of-the-box security of your system.

Choose the appropriate security level for your system.

No Firewall — No firewall provides complete access to your system and does no security checking. Security checking is the disabling of access to certain services. This should only be selected if you

A firewall can help prevent unauthorized access to your computer from the outside world. Would you like to enable a firewall?

- ○ No firewall
- ● Enable firewall

With a firewall, you may wish to allow access to specific services on your computer from others. Allow access to which services?

- ☐ Remote Login (SSH)
- ☐ Web Server (HTTP, HTTPS)
- ☐ File Transfer (FTP)
- ☐ Mail Server (SMTP)

Security Enhanced Linux (SELinux) provides finer-grained security controls than those available in a traditional Linux system. It can be set up in a disabled state, a state which only warns about things which would be denied, or a fully active state.

Enable SELinux?: [Active ▾]

⊙Hide Help   ▢Release Notes   ⇦ Back   ⇨ Next

Figure A-6: Set firewall parameters here.

The first choice that you make from this dialog box is whether you want to enable the firewall or to choose no firewall. By default, the installation program selects to enable the firewall for you. If you choose to enable the firewall, only connections that are in response to outbound requests are accepted. You can also select individual services that are allowed through the firewall. The services that you can allow are

- ✔ **Remote Login (SSH):** If you allow remote access to your server through the ssh protocol, you should enable this option.

- ✔ **Web Server (HTTP, HTTPS):** If you plan to run a Web server, you should choose this option. You do not need to choose this option to use a browser to view Web sites.

- ✔ **File Transfer (FTP):** If you plan to run an FTP server, you should enable this option. You do not need to choose this option to retrieve files from FTP sites.

- ✔ **Mail Server (SMTP):** If you are going to run an e-mail server, you should enable this option. You do not need to enable this option to retrieve mail from an ISP.

If you choose the No Firewall option, all connections are allowed and no security checking is done on your system. Select No Firewall only if you have absolute faith in the security of your network.

Choosing to enable the firewall is always safest, especially if you will be connecting directly to the Internet.

The final configuration step on the Firewall Configuration dialog box concerns Security-Enhanced Linux (SELinux). SELinux was developed by the National Security Agency (NSA) to provide enhanced security based on access control specified by a security policy. You can choose one of three states for SELinux:

- ✔ **Disable:** If you select this option, SELinux is not enabled on your system and there is no enforcement of a security policy.

- ✔ **Warn:** Choosing this option puts a security policy in place, but the policy is not enforced. Only warnings about possible security violations are noted. If you plan to use SELinux, this option provides a good basis for determining how the security policy would affect the operation of your system.

- ✔ **Active:** This state applies full enforcement of the SELinux security policy. You should choose this option only if you are sure that the policy will not affect your system operation.

You can read more about SELinux by visiting the NSA Web site at `www.nsa.gov/selinux`.

After you make your configuration choices, click Next to continue.

Configuring additional languages

Next you can choose additional languages to install on your system. Simply mark the box in front of any other languages you want to install and then click Next to continue.

Setting the time zone

Select the time zone for your system. The installation program shows you the Time Zone Selection screen from which you can select the time zone, either in terms of a geographic location or as an offset from the Coordinated Universal Time (UTC).

You select your location from a long list of countries and regions. If you live on the East Coast of the United States, for example, select USA/Eastern.

Setting the root password

After completing time zone selection, the installation program displays the Account Configuration screen, in which you set the root password.

The root user is the *superuser* in Enterprise Linux. Because the superuser can do anything in the system, you should assign a password that you can remember but that others cannot guess easily. Typically, make the password at least eight characters long, include a mix of letters and numbers, and (for good measure) throw in some special characters such as + or *. Remember the password is also case-sensitive.

Type the password on the first line and then reenter the password on the next line. Each character in the password appears as an asterisk (*) on the screen for security reasons. Both entries must match before the installation program accepts the password. The installation program displays a message when it accepts the root password.

Selecting the package groups to install

After you complete the key configuration steps, the installation program displays a screen from which you can choose to install the default Red Hat Enterprise Linux packages or choose to select additional groups that you want to install. After you select the package groups, you can take a coffee break while the Red Hat installation program formats the disk partitions and copies all selected files to those partitions.

Figure A-7 shows the Package Group Selection screen with the list of package groups that you can elect to install. An icon, a descriptive label, and a check box for enabling or disabling identify each package group.

Some of the components are already selected, as indicated by the check marks in front of the package name. This is the minimal set of packages that Red Hat recommends for installation for the version of Enterprise Linux (Desktop, WS, ES, or AS) that you are installing. You can, however, choose to install any or all of the components. Use the mouse to move up and down in the scrolling list and then click an entry to select or deselect that package group.

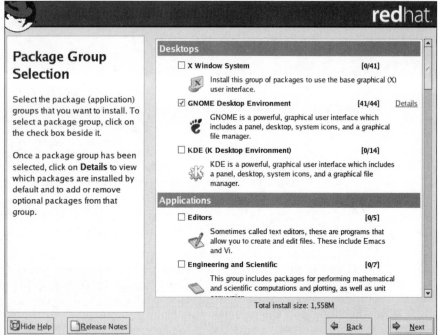

In an actual Red Hat Enterprise Linux installation, you install exactly those package groups that you need. Each package group requires specific packages to run. The Red Hat installation program automatically checks for any package dependencies and shows you a list of packages that are required but that you have not selected. In this case, you should install the required packages. You should install only those packages that you think you will need immediately after starting the system. Installing too many packages could expose your system to security risks. You can always add packages later.

Because each package group is a collection of many different Red Hat packages, the installation program also gives you the option to select individual packages. If you select the Select Individual Packages item (that appears below the list in Figure A-7) and then click Next, the installation program takes you to other screens where you can select individual packages. If you are installing Red Hat Enterprise Linux for the first time, you really don't need to go down to this level of detail to install specific packages. Simply pick the components that you think you need from the screen shown in Figure A-7. After you select the components you want, click Next to continue with the rest of the installation.

Completing the Installation

After you complete the key configuration steps and select the components to install, the installation program presents you with the About to Install dialog box, as shown in Figure A-8.

This dialog box tells you that the installation begins when you click Next. You still have the opportunity to abort the installation at this point because nothing has been written to the drives in your system yet. If you're sure of all your configuration choices and want to continue with the installation, click Next.

Depending on the packages that you selected for installation and the speed of your system, the installation can take 20 minutes or longer. You can take a break during the installation, but be sure to check the progress occasionally because you will need to change CDs when prompted.

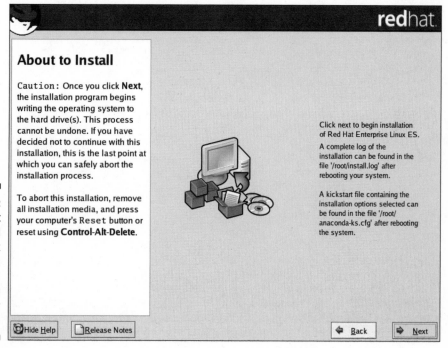

Figure A-8:
The About to Install dialog box gives you one more chance to change your mind.

Appendix B

What's on the CD-ROM?

*T*he CD included with this book is a rescue CD that you can use if you can't get your system to boot normally. The CD was created by Kent Robotti, and I would like to thank him for doing such a good job putting it together. Nice work, Kent!

Using the rescue CD is really easy. Just follow these simple instructions:

1. **Be sure that you are able to boot from your CD drive and then insert the rescue CD into the CD drive of your PC and boot your system.**

   After a short delay, you see the R.I.P. menu as shown in Figure B-1. There are several choices on the menu, but to save time and get you into your system as soon as possible, these steps use the quickest method. Later, when you have more time, you can experiment with the other options on the CD to discover what they do.

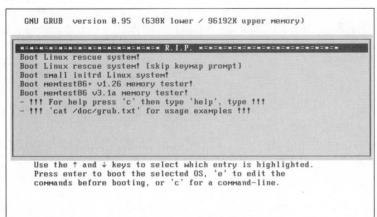

```
GNU GRUB  version 0.95  (638K lower / 96192K upper memory)

***********************  R.I.P.  ***********************
Boot Linux rescue system!
Boot Linux rescue system! [skip keymap prompt]
Boot small initrd Linux system!
Boot memtest86+ v1.26 memory tester!
Boot memtest86 v3.1a memory tester!
- !!! For help press 'c' then type 'help', type !!!
- !!! 'cat /doc/grub.txt' for usage examples !!!




    Use the ↑ and ↓ keys to select which entry is highlighted.
    Press enter to boot the selected OS, 'e' to edit the
    commands before booting, or 'c' for a command-line.
```

Figure B-1:
The R.I.P.
Main menu.

2. **Use your cursor keys to highlight the second choice and press Enter.**

3. **When the system login prompt appears, enter** `root` **and press Enter.**

4. Start logical volume management by entering the following commands:

```
sh /etc/rc.d/rc.lvm2 start
vgmknode -v
```

5. Mount your volumes to access your file system.

I can't give you the exact command to mount your volumes because I can't know how your system is set up. Be sure to enter the appropriate device and path information for your system. You can get volume information about your system by using the commands available in the Logical Volume Manager. You use the `vgscan` command to scan your system for volume groups. On my system, the result of running `vgscan` shows that I have `VolGrp00` and `VolGrp01` on my system. To mount the volume at the `/mnt` directory on my system, I enter the following command:

```
mount /dev/VolGroup00/LogVol00 /mnt
```

6. After you have mounted your file system, change into the directory you mounted to access your file system to make the changes necessary so your system will boot.

7. When you are finished, remove the CD from the drive and enter `reboot` **at the command prompt and press Enter.**

The rescue CD has been tested and found to work on the vast majority of computer hardware. We did discover in our testing that the CD would not boot on two older Pentium II class PCs. If you are trying to use the rescue CD and your system will not boot from it, you will have to get a rescue image that will fit on a floppy disk. Go to http://www.tux.org/pub/people/ kent-robotti/looplinux/rip/ and find the link labeled Floppy Version (RIP-3.1-1440.bin). Click the link to download the floppy rescue image. Be sure to read the README file for important information about using the floppy rescue disk.

GNU GENERAL PUBLIC LICENSE

Version 2, June 1991
Copyright (C) 1989, 1991 Free Software Foundation, Inc.
59 Temple Place - Suite 330, Boston, MA 02111-1307, USA

Preamble

The licenses for most software are designed to take away your freedom to share and change it. By contrast, the GNU General Public License is intended to guarantee your freedom to share and change free software–to make sure the software is free for all its users. This General Public License applies to most of the Free Software Foundation's software and to any other program whose authors commit to using it. (Some other Free Software Foundation software is covered by the GNU Library General Public License instead.) You can apply it to your programs, too.

When we speak of free software, we are referring to freedom, not price. Our General Public Licenses are designed to make sure that you have the freedom to distribute copies of free software (and charge for this service if you wish), that you receive source code or can get it if you want it, that you can change the software or use pieces of it in new free programs; and that you know you can do these things.

To protect your rights, we need to make restrictions that forbid anyone to deny you these rights or to ask you to surrender the rights. These restrictions translate to certain responsibilities for you if you distribute copies of the software, or if you modify it.

For example, if you distribute copies of such a program, whether gratis or for a fee, you must give the recipients all the rights that you have. You must make sure that they, too, receive or can get the source code. And you must show them these terms so they know their rights.

We protect your rights with two steps: (1) copyright the software, and (2) offer you this license which gives you legal permission to copy, distribute and/or modify the software.

Also, for each author's protection and ours, we want to make certain that everyone understands that there is no warranty for this free software. If the software is modified by someone else and passed on, we want its recipients to know that what they have is not the original, so that any problems introduced by others will not reflect on the original authors' reputations.

Finally, any free program is threatened constantly by software patents. We wish to avoid the danger that redistributors of a free program will individually obtain patent licenses, in effect making the program proprietary. To prevent this, we have made it clear that any patent must be licensed for everyone's free use or not licensed at all.

The precise terms and conditions for copying, distribution and modification follow.

Terms and Conditions for Copying, Distribution and Modification

0. This License applies to any program or other work which contains a notice placed by the copyright holder saying it may be distributed under the terms of this General Public License. The "Program", below, refers to any such program or work, and a "work based on the Program" means either the Program or any derivative work under copyright law: that is to say, a work containing the Program or a portion of it, either verbatim or with modifications and/or translated into another language. (Hereinafter, translation is included without limitation in the term "modification".) Each licensee is addressed as "you".

Activities other than copying, distribution and modification are not covered by this License; they are outside its scope. The act of running the Program is not restricted, and the output from the Program is covered only if its contents constitute a work based on the Program (independent of having been made by running the Program). Whether that is true depends on what the Program does.

1. You may copy and distribute verbatim copies of the Program's source code as you receive it, in any medium, provided that you conspicuously and appropriately publish on each copy an appropriate copyright notice and disclaimer of warranty; keep intact all the notices that refer to this License and to the absence of any warranty; and give any other recipients of the Program a copy of this License along with the Program.

You may charge a fee for the physical act of transferring a copy, and you may at your option offer warranty protection in exchange for a fee.

2. You may modify your copy or copies of the Program or any portion of it, thus forming a work based on the Program, and copy and distribute such modifications or work under the terms of Section 1 above, provided that you also meet all of these conditions:

    a) You must cause the modified files to carry prominent notices stating that you changed the files and the date of any change.

    b) You must cause any work that you distribute or publish, that in whole or in part contains or is derived from the Program or any part thereof, to be licensed as a whole at no charge to all third parties under the terms of this License.

    c) If the modified program normally reads commands interactively when run, you must cause it, when started running for such interactive use in the most ordinary way, to print or display an announcement including an appropriate copyright notice and a notice that there is no warranty (or else, saying that you provide a warranty) and that users may redistribute the program under these conditions, and telling the user how to view a copy of this License. (Exception: if the Program itself is interactive but does not normally print such an announcement, your work based on the Program is not required to print an announcement.)

These requirements apply to the modified work as a whole. If identifiable sections of that work are not derived from the Program, and can be reasonably considered independent and separate works in themselves, then this License, and its terms, do not apply to those sections when you distribute them as separate works. But when you distribute the same sections as part of a whole which is a work based on the Program, the distribution of the whole must be on the terms of this License, whose permissions for other licensees extend to the entire whole, and thus to each and every part regardless of who wrote it.

Thus, it is not the intent of this section to claim rights or contest your rights to work written entirely by you; rather, the intent is to exercise the right to control the distribution of derivative or collective works based on the Program.

In addition, mere aggregation of another work not based on the Program with the Program (or with a work based on the Program) on a volume of a storage or distribution medium does not bring the other work under the scope of this License.

3. You may copy and distribute the Program (or a work based on it, under Section 2) in object code or executable form under the terms of Sections 1 and 2 above provided that you also do one of the following:

    a) Accompany it with the complete corresponding machine-readable source code, which must be distributed under the terms of Sections 1 and 2 above on a medium customarily used for software interchange; or,

    b) Accompany it with a written offer, valid for at least three years, to give any third party, for a charge no more than your cost of physically performing source distribution, a complete machine-readable copy of the corresponding source code, to be distributed under the terms of Sections 1 and 2 above on a medium customarily used for software interchange; or,

    c) Accompany it with the information you received as to the offer to distribute corresponding source code. (This alternative is allowed only for noncommercial distribution and only if you received the program in object code or executable form with such an offer, in accord with Subsection b above.)

The source code for a work means the preferred form of the work for making modifications to it. For an executable work, complete source code means all the source code for all modules it contains, plus any associated interface definition files, plus the scripts used to control compilation and installation of the executable. However, as a special exception, the source code distributed need not include anything that is normally distributed (in either source or binary form) with the major components (compiler, kernel, and so on) of the operating system on which the executable runs, unless that component itself accompanies the executable.

If distribution of executable or object code is made by offering access to copy from a designated place, then offering equivalent access to copy the source code from the same place counts as distribution of the source code, even though third parties are not compelled to copy the source along with the object code.

4. You may not copy, modify, sublicense, or distribute the Program except as expressly provided under this License. Any attempt otherwise to copy, modify, sublicense or distribute the Program is void, and will automatically terminate your rights under this License. However, parties who have received copies, or rights, from you under this License will not have their licenses terminated so long as such parties remain in full compliance.

5. You are not required to accept this License, since you have not signed it. However, nothing else grants you permission to modify or distribute the Program or its derivative works. These actions are prohibited by law if you do not accept this License. Therefore, by modifying or distributing the Program (or any work based on the Program), you indicate your acceptance of this License to do so, and all its terms and conditions for copying, distributing or modifying the Program or works based on it.

6. Each time you redistribute the Program (or any work based on the Program), the recipient automatically receives a license from the original licensor to copy, distribute or modify the Program subject to these terms and conditions. You may not impose any further restrictions on the recipients' exercise of the rights granted herein. You are not responsible for enforcing compliance by third parties to this License.

7. If, as a consequence of a court judgment or allegation of patent infringement or for any other reason (not limited to patent issues), conditions are imposed on you (whether by court order, agreement or otherwise) that contradict the conditions of this License, they do not excuse you from the conditions of this License. If you cannot distribute so as to satisfy simultaneously your obligations under this License and any other pertinent obligations, then as a consequence you may not distribute the Program at all. For example, if a patent license would not permit royalty-free redistribution of the Program by all those who receive copies directly or indirectly through you, then the only way you could satisfy both it and this License would be to refrain entirely from distribution of the Program.

   If any portion of this section is held invalid or unenforceable under any particular circumstance, the balance of the section is intended to apply and the section as a whole is intended to apply in other circumstances.

   It is not the purpose of this section to induce you to infringe any patents or other property right claims or to contest validity of any such claims; this section has the sole purpose of protecting the integrity of the free software distribution system, which is implemented by public license practices. Many people have made generous contributions to the wide range of software distributed through that system in reliance on consistent application of that system; it is up to the author/donor to decide if he or she is willing to distribute software through any other system and a licensee cannot impose that choice.

   This section is intended to make thoroughly clear what is believed to be a consequence of the rest of this License.

8. If the distribution and/or use of the Program is restricted in certain countries either by patents or by copyrighted interfaces, the original copyright holder who places the Program under this License may add an explicit geographical distribution limitation excluding those countries, so that distribution is permitted only in or among countries not thus excluded. In such case, this License incorporates the limitation as if written in the body of this License.

9. The Free Software Foundation may publish revised and/or new versions of the General Public License from time to time. Such new versions will be similar in spirit to the present version, but may differ in detail to address new problems or concerns.

   Each version is given a distinguishing version number. If the Program specifies a version number of this License which applies to it and "any later version", you have the option of following the terms and conditions either of that version or of any later version published by the Free Software Foundation. If the Program does not specify a version number of this License, you may choose any version ever published by the Free Software Foundation.

10. If you wish to incorporate parts of the Program into other free programs whose distribution conditions are different, write to the author to ask for permission. For software which is copyrighted by the Free Software Foundation, write to the Free Software Foundation; we sometimes make exceptions for this. Our decision will be guided by the two goals of preserving the free status of all derivatives of our free software and of promoting the sharing and reuse of software generally.

NO WARRANTY

11. BECAUSE THE PROGRAM IS LICENSED FREE OF CHARGE, THERE IS NO WARRANTY FOR THE PROGRAM, TO THE EXTENT PERMITTED BY APPLICABLE LAW. EXCEPT WHEN OTHERWISE STATED IN WRITING THE COPYRIGHT HOLDERS AND/OR OTHER PARTIES PROVIDE THE PROGRAM "AS IS" WITHOUT WARRANTY OF ANY KIND, EITHER EXPRESSED OR IMPLIED, INCLUDING, BUT NOT LIMITED TO, THE IMPLIED WARRANTIES OF MERCHANTABILITY AND FITNESS FOR A PARTICULAR PURPOSE. THE ENTIRE RISK AS TO THE QUALITY AND PERFORMANCE OF THE PROGRAM IS WITH YOU. SHOULD THE PROGRAM PROVE DEFECTIVE, YOU ASSUME THE COST OF ALL NECESSARY SERVICING, REPAIR OR CORRECTION.

12. IN NO EVENT UNLESS REQUIRED BY APPLICABLE LAW OR AGREED TO IN WRITING WILL ANY COPYRIGHT HOLDER, OR ANY OTHER PARTY WHO MAY MODIFY AND/OR REDISTRIBUTE THE PROGRAM AS PERMITTED ABOVE, BE LIABLE TO YOU FOR DAMAGES, INCLUDING ANY GENERAL, SPECIAL, INCIDENTAL OR CONSEQUENTIAL DAMAGES ARISING OUT OF THE USE OR INABILITY TO USE THE PROGRAM (INCLUDING BUT NOT LIMITED TO LOSS OF DATA OR DATA BEING RENDERED INACCURATE OR LOSSES SUSTAINED BY YOU OR THIRD PARTIES OR A FAILURE OF THE PROGRAM TO OPERATE WITH ANY OTHER PROGRAMS), EVEN IF SUCH HOLDER OR OTHER PARTY HAS BEEN ADVISED OF THE POSSIBILITY OF SUCH DAMAGES.

END OF TERMS AND CONDITIONS

Index

• Symbols & Numbers •

* (asterisk
 following file name, 71
 wildcard, 67
@ (at sign), following file name, 71
[] (brackets), wildcards, 68
: (colon), in device alias, 119
$ (dollar sign), ending shell prompt, 65
= (equal sign), assigning permissions, 74
> (greater-than), output redirection, 67
- (hyphen) file type, 73
< (less-than), input redirection, 67
- (minus sign), removing permissions, 74
.. (periods, two), move up a directory
 level, 70
+ (plus sign), adding permissions, 74
# (pound sign)
 in configuration file, 226
 ending shell prompt, 65
? (question mark)
 in Alert icon, 259
 wildcard, 68
/ (slash)
 following directory name, 71
 root directory, 63
| (vertical bar), pipe symbol, 66
3-D hardware acceleration, 92

• A •

a (all) permissions, 74
access control list
 firewall using, 157
 specifying, 189
Accessories item, Applications menu,
 24, 39
Account Info tab, User Properties, 272
accounts
 e-mail, configuring, 45–48
 user, creating, 148, 268, 270, 330
 user, removing, 273–274

ACK Stealth Scan, 165
acl statement, named.conf file, 189
Actions menu, GNOME desktop, 21, 24–25
active intrusion detection, 162
add command, in restore, 298
Add Group icon, Red Hat User Manager,
 268–270
Add User icon, Red Hat User Manager,
 268–269
administration tools. See also specific tools
 accessing, 23, 38–39
 Webmin tool, 325–327
Advanced Linux Sound Architecture Web
 site, 333
Advanced Maryland Automatic Network
 Disk Archiver. See AMANDA
Advanced tab, GNOME Screensave
 Preferences, 34
Alert icon, Red Hat Network, 259
alias command, 81
aliases
 for commands, 81
 for devices, 119
 for e-mail, 216–217
aliases file, 216–217
all (a) permissions, 74
ALPS GlidePoint touchpad, 344
amadmin command, in AMANDA, 301
AMANDA (Advanced Maryland Automatic
 Network Disk Archiver)
 commands in, 300–301
 configuring, 302–308
 definition of, 300–301
 installing, 301–302
 packages in, 300
 performing backups with, 308
amanda package, 300
amanda-client package, 300
amanda.conf file, 302–308
amanda-server package, 300
amcheck command, in AMANDA, 301
amcleanup command, in AMANDA, 301

AMD processors, 342

amdump command, in AMANDA, 300

amflush command, in AMANDA, 301

amlabel command, in AMANDA, 301

amrecover command, in AMANDA, 301

amrestore command, in AMANDA, 301

amrmtape command, in AMANDA, 301

amstatus command, in AMANDA, 301

amtape command, in AMANDA, 301

amverify command, in AMANDA, 301

anonymous FTP, 226, 233

Apache Web server. *See* Web server

applets

  on GNOME desktop, 21–22

  on KDE desktop, 36–37

applications. *See also* executable files;

    packages; *specific applications*

  on GNOME desktop, 22–24, 41

  installing from RPM format, 14

  on KDE desktop, 37–39

  not installed for AS and ES version, 42

  starting, 24

  third-party, included with Enterprise

    Linux, 12

  third-party, installing, 282–284

  third-party, removing, 285

Applications menu

  GNOME desktop, 21–24

  KDE desktop, 36–39

archives (backups)

  AMANDA tool for, 300–308

  cdrecord package for, 293–294

  dump package for, 295–298

  ftape package for, 292

  media for, 289

  methods of, 289–291

  mirrordir package for, 294–295

  pax tool for, 308–310

  tar command for, 299–300

  which files to back up, 287–289

arrows, green, in Alert icon, 259

AS version of Red Hat Enterprise Linux

  applications not installed by default, 42

  definition of, 11

  topics covered in this book for, 1

asterisk (*)

  following file name, 71

  wildcard, 67

AT bus, 343

at sign (@), following file name, 71

audio files, playing, 56–57

Automatic Partitioning, 349–351

● *B* ●

b file type, 72

Back button, Firefox Web browser, 43

background

  for Nautilus File Manager, 32–33

  optimization and, 314

backup mode, for database files, 288

backups

  AMANDA tool for, 300–308

  cdrecord package for, 293–294

  dump package for, 295–298

  ftape package for, 292

  media for, 289

  methods of, 289–291

  mirrordir package for, 294–295

  pax tool for, 308–310

  tar command for, 299–300

  which files to back up, 287–289

badges, identification, 144

bash shell (Bourne again shell), 65. *See*

    also shell

Basic tab, Add NFS Share, 124

Behavior tab, Nautilus File Management

    Preferences, 31

bin directory, 63

binary rpm files, installing, 283–284

blue check mark, Alert icon, 259

bombing, e-mail, 218

bookmarks

  in Firefox Web browser, 43

  in Nautilus File Manager, 28–29

Bookmarks menu

  Firefox Web browser, 43

  Nautilus File Manager, 28–29

boot directory, 63

boot disk

  creating, 336

  included with this book, 361–362

boot loader, configuring, 352–353

boot: prompt, 347

Bourne again shell (bash shell), 65. *See*

    also shell

brackets ([]), wildcards, 68
browseable option, Samba configuration
    file, 135
Bus ID option, X configuration files, 92
bus type, requirements for, 342–343
bye command, FTP, 233

• C •

c file type, 72
cache files, not backing up, 287
caching server
    configuration files for, list of, 183–184
    configuring, 195–196
    definition of, 183
    host.conf file for, 196
    named.conf file for, 185–193, 195
    named.local file for, 195
    nsswitch file for, 196
    resolv.conf file for, 196
    starting, 196
Calc (OpenOffice.org), 52–53
calculator, 24, 39
cameras, security, 144
case sensitivity of file system, 63
cat command, 136
CD
    for backups, 289, 293–294
    included with this book, contents of,
        361–362
cd command
    in FTP, 233
    in restore, 298
    in shell, 69–70
CD-R Drive icon, GNOME desktop, 20
cdrecord package, 293–294
CD-ROM drive
    does not mount after installation, 332
    not detected during installation, 331
    requirements for, 345
central processing unit (CPU)
    optimizing, 313–314
    requirements for, 342
CERT (Computer Emergency Response
    Team), 219
CGI scripts, environment variables for,
    243–244
chains, for iptables command, 159

Channels tab, Red Hat Network, 263
check mark, blue, in Alert icon, 259
chgrp command, 77
chkconfig command, 158, 168–170,
    228–229, 323–324
chmod command
  in FTP, 233
  in shell, 74–75
chown command, 77
clean desk policy, 144
close command, FTP, 233
Close Window icon, GNOME desktop, 21
Collings, Terry (*Red Hat Linux Networking
    and System Administration*), 322
colon (:), in device alias, 119
color depth
  display settings for, changing, 87
  reducing for optimization, 314
colors of directory and file listings, 70
command shell
  bash shell, 65
  command syntax, 66–68
  default shell, 65
  definition of, 64
  prompt for, 65
  terminal window for, 64–65
commands, AMANDA, 300–301
commands, FTP, 232–233
commands, restore, 298
commands, shell
  alias command, 81
  aliases for, 81
  cat command, 136
  cd command, 69–70
  chgrp command, 77
  chkconfig command, 158, 168–170,
    228–229, 323–324
  chmod command, 74–75
  chown command, 77
  combining, 66
  command completion, 67
  configure command, 286
  cp command, 75–76
  dd command, 294
  df command, 80–81
  dmesg command, 293
  du command, 81
  dump command, 290, 295–296

commands, shell *(continued)*
  `echo` command, 78
  `edquota` command, 276–277
  `export` command, 78
  `find` command, 76
  `ftformat` command, 292
  help for, 66
  `history` command, 68
  `info` command, 69
  input for, redirecting, 66–67
  `kill` command, 80
  `less` command, 77
  list of, displaying, 68
  `ls` command, 70–74
  `mailq` command, 318–319
  `man` command, 66, 68–69
  `mkbootdisk` command, 336
  `mkdir` command, 69
  `mkfs` command, 297
  `mkisofs` command, 293–294
  `more` command, 76–77
  `mount` command, 79, 129, 276
  `mt` command, 292
  `mv` command, 76
  `newaliases` command, 217
  not working, 336–337
  output for, redirecting, 66–67
  `passwd` command, 330–331
  `ps` command, 80
  `pwd` command, 70
  `quotacheck` command, 275, 277
  repeating, 68
  `repquota` command, 277–278
  `rm` command, 76
  `route` command, 335
  `rpm` command, 14, 131, 283–285
  `sendmail` command, 212
  `service` command, 136–137
  `st` command, 292
  `startx` command, 96
  `su` command, 78, 336–337
  syntax for, 66–68
  `tar` command, 285–286, 290, 299–300
  `testparm` command, 136
  `umount` command, 79, 275, 333–334
  `useradd` command, 330
  `whatis` command, 69
  wildcards in, 67–68

`comment` option, Samba configuration file, 135
comments
  in FTP configuration file, 226
  in Samba configuration file, 135
Common profile, 121
compressed zip files, installing packages from, 285–286
Computer Emergency Response Team (CERT), 219
Computer icon, GNOME desktop, 20
`configure` command, 286
Connect Scan, 165
console (terminal window), 64–65
contextual menus, KDE desktop, 37
Control Center item, Applications menu, 38
`cp` command, 75–76
CPU (central processing unit)
  optimizing, 313–314
  requirements for, 342
`create mode` option, Samba configuration file, 135
CUPS (IPP) print queue, 100
Cyrix processors, 342

• D •

d file type, 72
daemon, 103, 221
database
  backing up files for, 288–289
  for RPM, 215, 284
  for Tripwire, 171–174
`dd` command, 294
`debug level` option, Samba configuration file, 317
debugging programs, 24, 39
`DefaultDepth` option, X configuration files, 94
`delete` command, in `restore`, 298
Delete icon, Red Hat User Manager, 268
demilitarized zone (DMZ) firewall, 157
`Depth` option, X configuration files, 95
desktop (GUI), switching between, 18. *See also* GNOME desktop; KDE (K Desktop Environment)

Desktop version of Red Hat Enterprise Linux
  definition of, 12
  topics covered in this book for, 1
dev directory, 63
device aliases, 119
Device option, X configuration files, 94
Device section, X configuration files, 91–92
devices. *See also specific devices*
  compatibility with Red Hat Enterprise Linux, 342, 346
  compatibility with XFree86, 342–343
  configuring, 91–92, 93
  directory for, 63
  Ethernet, adding to network, 110–113
  mounting and unmounting, 79
  optimizing, 313–314
  requirements, 341–346
Devices tab, Network Configuration Tool, 110
df command, 80–81
DHCP (Dynamic Host Configuration Protocol), 354
dig program, 199–201
Direct Rendering Infrastructure (DRI), 92
directories. *See also* files; folders
  accessing from NFS server, 129–130
  changing, 69–70
  colors of, 70
  creating, 69
  determining working directory, 70
  in file system, list of, 63–64
  listing contents of, 70–71
  permissions for, 149–151
  sharing from NFS server, 123–128
  in system path, 78
directory mode option, Samba configuration file, 135
Disk Druid partitioning, 349
disk quotas
  configuring, 274–277
  statistics on, 277–278
disk space, checking, 80–81
display. *See also* monitor
  capturing, 24
  color depth, changing, 87
  resolution, changing, 86–87

Display subsection, X configuration files, 95
Display tab, Nautilus File Management Preferences, 31
distribution, Linux, 9
dmesg command, 293
DMZ (demilitarized zone) firewall, 157
DNS (Domain Name System) server
  configuration files for, list of, 183–185
  configuring caching server, 195–196
  configuring primary master server, 197–199
  configuring secondary master (slave) server, 196–197
  definition of, 181–182
  named.conf file, 185–193
  optimizing, 317–318
  testing configuration of, 199–201
  types of, 183
  zone files, 193–195
dns proxy option, Samba configuration file, 135, 317
DNS tab, Network Configuration Tool, 110, 119–120
documents. *See also* files
  opening with OpenOffice.org Writer, 50–51
  recent, viewing, 24
  saving with OpenOffice.org Writer, 51–52
  security for, 144–145
dollar sign ($), ending shell prompt, 65
domain name
  finding IP address for, 199
  searching for, 200–201
Domain Name System (DNS) server
  configuration files for, list of, 183–185
  definition of, 181–182
  optimizing, 317–318
  types of, 183
domains, top-level, list of, 182
door locks, 144
download preferences, Firefox Web browser, 45
DRI (Direct Rendering Infrastructure), 92
DRI section, X configuration files, 92
Driver option, X configuration files, 92–93
Driver Options tab, Edit a print queue, 106–107

drivers, finding, 341–342

drives. *See also* CD-ROM drive; hard drive
mounting and unmounting, 79
will not unmount, 333–334

du command, 81

Dual Head tab, Display settings, 90

dual monitors, configuring, 90–91

dump command, 290, 295–296

dump package, 295–298

DVDs, for backups, 289

Dynamic Host Configuration Protocol
(DHCP), 354

• E •

eavesdropping, e-mail, 218

echo command, 78

Edit menu, Firefox Web browser, 42, 44

edquota command, 276–277

EISA (Extended Industry Standard
Architecture) bus, 343

e-mail. *See also* Evolution e-mail client
account, configuring, 45–48
bombing, 218
components of, 203–204
eavesdropping of, 218
IMAP4 (Internet Mail Access Protocol),
211, 216
LDA (Local Delivery Agent), 204, 209–210
mail aliases, 216–217
mail notifier for, 209–210
MTA (Mail Transfer Agent), 204, 209–210,
211–217
MUA (Mail User Agent), 204–208
POP3 (Post Office Protocol), 210–211, 215
receiving, 48, 207
security for, 217–219
sending, 48, 207–208
Sendmail, 211–217
SMTP (Simple Mail Transfer Protocol),
153, 210, 219, 355
spamming, 219
spoofing, 219

emblems
for files and folders, 30
for icons, 30, 32–33

emergency boot disk
creating, 336
included with this book, 361–362

encrypted option, Samba configuration
file, 134

encryption. *See also* security
of documents, 145
of e-mail, 218

Enterprise Linux. *See* Red Hat Enterprise
Linux (RHEL)

environment variables for CGI scripts,
243–244

equal sign (=), assigning permissions, 74

Errata tab, Red Hat Network, 263

errors. *See* troubleshooting

ES version of Red Hat Enterprise Linux
applications not installed by default, 42
definition of, 11–12
topics covered in this book for, 1

etc directory, 63, 288

Ethernet cards, optimization and, 316

Ethernet device, adding to network,
110–113

Evolution e-mail client
accessing, 41, 45
address book, 208
configuring, 204–207
configuring e-mail account for, 45–48
receiving e-mail, 48, 207
scheduling features, 48–49, 208
sending e-mail, 48, 207–208

exclamation point (!), in Alert icon, 259

executable files
indicated in directory listing, 70–71
preferences for handling by Nautilus File
Manager, 31
running from bash shell, 65
running from Nautilus File Manager,
24, 27, 31
setting permissions for, 82, 151

execute (x) permission, 73

export command, 78

exports file, 128

Extended Industry Standard Architecture
(EISA) bus, 343

external attacks, 15

extract command, in restore, 298

• F •

FBI (Federal Bureau of Investigation), 218
Fedora Project, 10
FHS (Filesystem Hierarchy Standard),
62–64
FHS Web site, 62
fibre channel disk arrays, 315
File Browser item, Applications menu,
23, 25
file integrity software, 171. *See also*
Tripwire program
File Management Preferences dialog box,
31–32
file manager. *See* Konqueror File Manager;
Nautilus File Manager
File menu
Firefox Web browser, 42
Red Hat User Manager, 267
file sharing
features for, 13–14
with NFS, 123–130
with Samba, 132
shareable and unshareable files, 62
file system. *See also* NFS (Network File
System)
case sensitivity of, 63
definition of, 61
directories in, list of, 63–64
FHS (Filesystem Hierarchy Standard),
62–64
mounting, 63
searching with wildcards, 67–68
File Transfer Protocol (FTP). *See* FTP
server; FTP site
files. *See also* backups; directories; *specific
files*
accessing from NFS server, 129–130
audio, playing, 56–57
bookmarking, 28–29
cache files, not backing up, 287
colors of, 70
copying, 75–76
deleting, 30, 76
display preferences for, 31
displaying contents of, 76–77
displaying in Konqueror File Manager, 40
displaying in Nautilus File Manager, 26–27

documents, opening with OpenOffice.org
Writer, 50–51
documents, recent, viewing, 24
documents, saving with OpenOffice.org
Writer, 51–52
documents, security for, 144–145
emblems for, 30, 32–33
executable files, indicated in directory
listing, 70–71
executable files, preferences for handling
by Nautilus File Manager, 31
executable files, running from `bash`
shell, 65
executable files, running from Nautilus
File Manager, 24, 27, 31
executable files, setting permissions for,
82, 151
graphics, opening, 28, 58–59
group for, changing, 77
linking to, 29
listing for a directory, 70–71
managing, 29–30
moving, 76
opening from Nautilus File Manager,
27–28
owner of, changing, 77
permissions for, assigning, 149–151
permissions for, changing, 30, 74–75
permissions for, listing, 71–74
searching for, 24, 76
static, 62
symbols following, 71
transferring with FTP, 231, 233
types of, 72–73
variable, 62
X configuration files, 91–95
zip files, compressed, installing packages
from, 285–286
zone files, 183
Files section, X configuration files, 92–93
Filesystem Hierarchy Standard (FHS),
62–64
Filesystem icon, GNOME desktop, 20
FIN | ACK Stealth Scan, 165
FIN Stealth Scan, 166
`find` command, 76
Finkelstein, Ellen (*OpenOffice.org
For Dummies*), 49

Firefox icon, Firefox Web browser, 43
Firefox Web browser
  accessing, 41, 42
  customizing, 44–45
  menu bar, 42–43
  navigation toolbar, 43
  personal toolbar, 44
Firefox Web site, 43
firewall
  configuring during installation, 354–356
  configuring with `iptables` command,
    158–160
  configuring with Security Level
    Configuration tool, 157–158
  definition of, 156
  for e-mail, 218
  features for, 14–15
  types of, 157
FireWire drive, for backups, 289
flash ROM, for backups, 289
floppy disk
  for backups, 289
  requirements for, 344
Floppy Drive icon, GNOME desktop, 20
folders. *See also* directories
  bookmarking, 28–29
  creating, 30
  deleting, 30
  displaying in Konqueror File Manager, 40
  displaying in Nautilus File Manager, 26–27
  emblems for, 30, 32–33
  linking to, 29
  managing, 29–30
  permissions for, changing, 30
font server
  location of files for, 92–93
  optimization and, 314
`Fontpath` option, X configuration files,
    92–93
fonts used in this book, 5
Forward button, Firefox Web browser, 43
forward slash (/), root directory, 63
`fstab` file, 129–130, 274–275
`ftape` package, 292
`ftformat` command, 292
FTP Bounce Attack scan, 166

`ftp` command, 232–233
`ftp` directory, 223, 233
FTP (File Transfer Protocol) server
  anonymous user, logging in as, 226, 233
  commands for, 232–233
  configuring, 222–228
  configuring firewall for, 355
  definition of, 16
  installing, 221–222
  logging in to, 229–233
  optimizing, 320
  security and, 153
  starting, 228–229
  testing, 229
  transferring files with, 231, 233
FTP site
  accessing from Nautilus File Manager, 28
  bookmarking, 28–29
full backups, 290–291

• **G** •

g (group) permissions, 73, 74
General Options tab, Add NFS Share,
    125–126
General tab
  Ethernet Device, 118–119
  Up2date Agent Configuration tool, 256
`generic-linux.mc` file, 213–214
`get` command, FTP, 233
gFTP program, 230–231
GIMP (Gnu Image Manipulation Program),
    58–59
`global` section, Samba configuration file,
    134–135
GNOME desktop. *See also* Nautilus File
    Manager
  applets on, 21–22
  configuring, 33–34
  definition of, 13, 17
  description of, 19–21
  icons on, 20–21
  locking, 24
  logging in to, 19
  logging out, 24, 34
  optimization and, 314
  top and bottom panels of, 20–21

Gnu Image Manipulation Program (GIMP), 58–59
GNU Network Object Model Environment. *See* GNOME desktop
gnuplot package, 300
Go menu
  Firefox Web browser, 42
  Nautilus File Manager, 27
GPU (graphics processing unit), optimizing, 313–314
Grand Unified Bootloader (GRUB), 352
graphical programs, 24, 39
graphics
  opening and manipulating with GIMP, 58–59
  opening from Nautilus File Manager, 28
Graphics item, Applications menu, 24, 39
graphics processing unit (GPU), optimizing, 313–314
gray question mark, Alert icon, 259
greater-than (>), output redirection, 67
green double arrows, Alert icon, 259
group (g) permissions, 73–74
groups
  adding, 268, 270–271
  displaying, 269
  private group for user, 270
  properties for, changing, 272–273
Groups tab
  Red Hat User Manager, 269
  User Properties, 272
grpquota option, 274
GRUB (Grand Unified Bootloader), 352
GUI (desktop), switching between, 18. *See also* GNOME desktop; KDE (K Desktop Environment)

• *H* •

hard drive
  for backups, 289, 294–295
  partitioning for installation, 349–351
  requirements for, 344
hard limit for disk quotas, 276
hardware. *See also* devices
  optimizing, 313–314
  requirements, 341–346

Hardware Device tab, Ethernet Device, 119
Hardware tab
  Display settings, 88–89
  Network Configuration Tool, 110
help command
  in FTP, 233
  in restore, 298
help for commands, 68–69
Help icon, Red Hat User Manager, 268
Help item, Applications menu, 23, 38
Help menu
  Firefox Web browser, 43
  Red Hat User Manager, 268
Help tab, Red Hat Network, 264
history command, 68
history of Red Hat Enterprise Linux, 9–10
Home button, Firefox Web browser, 43
home directory
  accessing from Applications menu, 38
  accessing from GNOME, 20
  accessing from Nautilus File Manager, 27
  accessing from Samba, 135
  backing up, 288
  definition of, 63
  disk quotas for, 274–277
  for new users, 270
Home directory icon, GNOME desktop, 20
Home icon, Nautilus File Manager, 27
Home item, Applications menu, 38
homes section, Samba configuration file, 135
HorizSync option, X configuration files, 94
Host List scan, 166
host program, 199
host.conf file, 196
hosts
  configuring, 110, 120
  scanning for host names, 166
  security for, 144
  unable to access, 335–336
hosts file, 120
Hosts tab, Network Configuration Tool, 110, 120
hosts.allow file, 335
hosts.deny file, 335
HP JetDirect print queue, 103–104

HTTP configuration tool
general information, configuring, 240
performance tuning, configuring, 249–250
SSL, configuring, 247–248
starting, 239–240
virtual hosts, configuring, 240–248
Web server, configuring, 248–249
HTTP (HyperText Transfer Protocol)
configuring firewall for, 355
security and, 153
httpd (Apache Web) server, 16
httpd directory and files, 238–239
httpd.conf file, 320
HTTPS, configuring firewall for, 355
hubs, optimization and, 316
HyperText Transfer Protocol (HTTP), 153
hyphen (-) file type, 73

• *I* •

icons. *See also* toolbars
emblems for, 30, 32–33
on GNOME desktop, 20–21, 41
on KDE desktop, 36
identification badges, 144
Identifier option, X configuration files,
92–95
Identity page, Evolution e-mail client, 45–46
Idle Scan, 166
images
opening and manipulating with GIMP,
58–59
opening from Nautilus File Manager, 28
IMAP4 (Internet Mail Access Protocol),
211, 216
imapconf file, 216
Impress (OpenOffice.org), 53–54
include statement, named.conf file, 189
incremental backups, 290–291
Industry Standard Architecture (ISA)
bus, 343
info command, 69
input devices, configuring, 93
input redirection for commands, 66–67
InputDevice section, X configuration
files, 93
INSTALL file, 286

installation. *See also* Red Hat
Network (RHN)
AMANDA (Advanced Maryland Automatic
Network Disk Archiver), 301–302
applications, from RPM format, 14
binary rpm files, 283–284
CD-ROM drive does not mount after, 332
CD-ROM drive not detected during, 331
compressed zip files, 285–286
FTP server, 221–222
KDE (K Desktop Environment), 35
nmap tool, 163
partitioning hard drive for, 349–351
Red Hat Enterprise Linux, 346–348, 359
Samba, 131–132
sound does not work after, 332–333
system packages, 280–282
third-party applications, 282–284
Tripwire program, 171–172
vsftpd (Very Secure FTP daemon)
server, 221–222
Web server (Apache), 235–236
internal attacks, 15
Internet item, Applications menu, 24, 39
Internet Mail Access Protocol (IMAP4), 211
Internet Printing Protocol (IPP) print
queue, 100
Internet services
accessing, 24, 39
features for, 16
security for, 152–153
servers supported, 16
Internet superserver (xinetd),
155–156, 325
intrusion detection
closing ports for unused services,
167–171
definition of, 161
nmap tool for, 163
port scanning with nmap tool, 164–167
Tripwire program for, 171–178
types of, 161–162
IP address
for Ethernet device, configuring, 112
searching for, 200
translating Web names to, 181–182
IP Protocol Scan, 166
ipop3 file, 215

IPP (Internet Printing Protocol) print queue, 100
IPSec tab, Network Configuration Tool, 110
`iptables` command, 158–160
ISA (Industry Standard Architecture) bus, 343

• *J* •

JetDirect print queue, 103–104

• *K* •

KDE (K Desktop Environment)
  applets on, 36–37
  configuring, 38
  definition of, 13, 17
  description of, 35–36
  installing, 35
  Konqueror File Manager, 39–40
  locking, 38
  logging in, 35
  logging out, 38, 40
  optimization and, 314
kernel, Linux
  custom, building, 321–322
  definition of, 9
  location of, 63
keyboard
  configuring, 93
  requirements for, 344
  selecting during installation, 347–348
`kill` command, 80
Konqueror File Manager, 39–40

• *L* •

`l` file type, 73
lame servers, 317
LAN (local area network). *See* network
Language option, login window, 18
languages, configuring, 18, 356
`lcd` command, FTP, 233
LDA (Local Delivery Agent), 204, 209–210
Leete, Gurdy (*OpenOffice.org For Dummies*), 49
Leete, Mary (*OpenOffice.org For Dummies*), 49

`less` command, 77
less-than (<), input redirection, 67
`Level2 oplocks` option, Samba configuration file, 317
`lib` directory, 63
LILO (Linux Loader), 344
links to files and folders, 29
Linux command shell
  `bash` shell, 65
  command syntax, 66–68
  default shell, 65
  definition of, 64
  prompt for, 65
  terminal window for, 64–65
Linux distribution, 9
The Linux Documentation Project Web site, 337
Linux file system. *See also* NFS (Network File System)
  case sensitivity of, 63
  definition of, 61
  directories in, list of, 63–64
  FHS (Filesystem Hierarchy Standard), 62–64
  mounting, 63
  searching with wildcards, 67–68
Linux Journal Web site, 337
Linux kernel
  custom, building, 321–322
  definition of, 9
  location of, 63
The Linux Kernel Archives Web site, 338
Linux Loader (LILO), 344
Linux Online Web site, 338
Linux users groups, 338
List Columns tab, Nautilus File Management Preferences, 31
local area network (LAN). *See* network
Local Delivery Agent (LDA), 204, 209–210
Locally-Connected print queue, 100
location bar
  Konqueror File Manager, 40
  Nautilus File Manager, 26
Location field, Firefox Web browser, 43
Lock Screen item, Actions menu, 24
Lock Session item, Applications menu, 38
locks, door, 144
`log file` option, Samba configuration file, 134

Log Out item, Actions menu, 24, 34
logging for Web server, 242–243
logging in
  FTP (File Transfer Protocol) server, 226,
    229–233
  GNOME desktop, 19
  KDE (K Desktop Environment), 35
  Red Hat Enterprise Linux, 17–19
  unable to, 329–331
logging, options for, 189–191
logging out
  GNOME, 24, 34
  KDE, 38, 40
logging statement, named.conf file,
    189–191
login window, 17–19
Logout item, Applications menu, 38, 40
logrotate file, 238
LPD print queue, 100
LPR printing protocol, 101
ls command
  in FTP, 233
  in restore, 298
  in shell, 70–74

• *M* •

m4 macro processor, 213–214
macro, 213
macro file for Sendmail, 213–214
magnetic tape, for backups, 289, 292
mail. *See* e-mail
mail aliases, 216–217
mail notifier, 209–210
mail queue
  managing, 214–215
  removing messages from, 318–319
Mail Transfer Agent (MTA)
  definition of, 204, 209
  Sendmail, 211–217
  SMTP used for, 210
Mail User Agent (MUA)
  definition of, 204
  Evolution e-mail client, 204–208
  types of, 204
mailing lists, 338
mailq command, 318–319
Main tab, HTTP configuration tool, 240

maintenance. *See* backups; optimization;
    updates
man command, 66, 68–69
master server
  configuration files for, 183–184
  definition of, 183
  named.conf file for, 185–193
  primary, configuring, 197–199
  restarting, 198–199
  secondary, configuring, 196–197
  zone files for, 193–195
max connections option, Samba
    configuration file, 135
max log size option, Samba
    configuration file, 134
MCA (Micro Channel Architecture)
    bus, 343
mdelete command, FTP, 233
media directory, 63
media for backups, 289
memory
  increasing, 313–314
  requirements for, 343
menu bar
  Firefox Web browser, 42–43
  Konqueror File Manager, 39
  Nautilus File Manager, 25
mget command, FTP, 233
Micro Channel Architecture (MCA)
    bus, 343
MIME (Multipurpose Internet Mail
    Extensions), 210
minus sign (-), removing permissions, 74
mirrordir package, 294–295
mkbootdisk command, 336
mkdir command
  in FTP, 233
  in shell, 69
mkfs command, 297
mkisofs command, 293–294
mnt directory, 63
Mode option, X configuration files, 95
Modeline option, X configuration files, 94
ModelName option, X configuration files, 94
modems
  adding to network, 115–117
  security of, 145
modular kernel, 321

`Module` section, X configuration files, 93
`Modulepath` option, X configuration files, 93
monitor. *See also* display
  configuring, 93–95
  dual, configuring, 90–91
  requirements for, 343
  type settings, changing, 88–89
`Monitor` option, X configuration files, 95
`Monitor` section, X configuration files, 93–94
monolithic kernel, 321
`more` command, 76–77
`mount` command, 79, 129, 276
mouse
  configuring, 93
  requirements for, 344
  selecting during installation, 348
movies, playing, 57–58
MP3 files, 56
MPlayer movie player, 58
MPlayer Web site, 58
`mput` command, FTP, 233
`mt` command, 292
MTA (Mail Transfer Agent)
  definition of, 204, 209
  Sendmail, 211–217
  SMTP used for, 210
MUA (Mail User Agent)
  definition of, 204
  Evolution e-mail client, 204–208
  types of, 204
Multipurpose Internet Mail Extensions (MIME), 210
multivolume archiving, with `tar` command, 299
`mv` command, 76

• N •

name address resolution, 181–182. *See also* DNS (Domain Name System) server
`named.conf` file
  `acl` statement, 189
  caching server, 195
  definition of, 184–185
  `include` statement, 189

`logging` statement, 189–191
`options` statement, 185–189
  primary master server, 197–198
  secondary master server, 196–197
`server` statement, 191–192
`zone` statements, 192–193
`named.custom` file, 317–318
`named.local` file, 195
nameserver, root, 183
nameservers, 119–120, 183. *See also* DNS (Domain Name System) server
Nautilus File Manager
  accessing, 23
  background for, 32–33
  bookmarks in, 28–29
  customizing, 30–33
  description of, 25–26
  display preferences, 31–32
  files, managing, 29–30
  files, opening, 27–28
  folders, displaying, 26–27
  folders, managing, 29–30
  FTP sites, accessing, 28
  starting, 25
  views, showing and hiding, 33
NCP print queue, 102
`netbios name` option, Samba configuration file, 134
network. *See also* NFS (Network File System); Red Hat Network (RHN); Samba
  configuring during installation, 353–354
  DNS settings, configuring, 119–120
  Ethernet device, adding, 110–113
  features for, 13–14
  hosts, configuring, 110, 120
  hosts, scanning for host names, 166
  hosts, security for, 144
  hosts, unable to access, 335–336
  information required for installation, 346
  modem connection, adding, 115–117
  NIC, changing configuration of, 118–119
  NIC, removing, 117–118
  NIC, requirements for, 345–346
  NIC, wired, adding to network, 110–113
  NIC, wireless, adding to network, 113–115
  profiles, configuring, 120–121

network *(continued)*
 security for, 145, 152–156
 system hanging when starting network
  services, 334–335
 wireless NIC, adding, 113–115
Network Configuration tool
 accessing, 109
 description of, 110
 DNS settings, configuring, 119–120
 Ethernet device, adding, 110–113
 hosts, configuring, 120
 modem connection, adding, 115–117
 NIC, changing configuration of, 118–119
 NIC, removing, 117–118
 profiles, configuring, 120–121
 wireless NIC, adding, 113–115
Network File System (NFS)
 client, configuring, 129–130
 definition of, 13, 123
 exporting (sharing) directories, 123–128
 mounting (accessing) shared directories,
  129–130
 optimizing, 315–316
 server, configuring, 123–128
 server, restarting, 128
Network icon, GNOME desktop, 20
Network Information System (NIS), 14
network interface card (NIC)
 changing configuration of, 118–119
 removing from network, 117–118
 requirements for, 345–346
 wired, adding to network, 110–113
 wireless, adding to network, 113–115
Network Servers item, Applications
  menu, 23
Networked CUPS (IPP) print queue, 100
Networked JetDirect print queue, 103–104
Networked Novell (NCP) print queue, 102
Networked UNIX (LPD) print queue, 100
Networked Windows (SMB) print queue,
  101–102
New button, Evolution e-mail client, 48
newaliases command, 217
NFS (Network File System)
 client, configuring, 129–130
 definition of, 13, 123

 exporting (sharing) directories, 123–128
 mounting (accessing) shared directories,
  129–130
 optimizing, 315–316
 server, configuring, 123–128
 server, restarting, 128
nfs restart command, 128
NFS Server Configuration tool
 adding shares to export, 124–127
 deleting shares, 127
 editing shares, 127
NIC (network interface card)
 changing configuration of, 118–119
 removing from network, 117–118
 requirements for, 345–346
 wired, adding to network, 110–113
 wireless, adding to network, 113–115
nice value, reducing for optimization, 315
NIS (Network Information System), 14
nmap tool
 definition of, 162
 installing, 163
 port scanning, 164–167, 170–171
 starting, 163–164
nmapfe command, 163
Novell (NCP) print queue, 102
nsswitch file, 196
NULL Stealth Scan, 166

• *O* •

o (others) permissions, 73–74
office application suite. *See* OpenOffice.org
Office item, Applications menu, 24, 39
OpenOffice.org
 accessing, 24, 39, 41
 book about, 49
 Calc (spreadsheet program), 52–53
 configuring, 54–55
 definition of, 42, 49
 Impress (presentation program), 53–54
 Writer (word processor), 50–52
OpenOffice.org For Dummies (Leete,
  Finkelstein, and Leete), 49
operating system files, backing up, 288
opt directory, 64

optimization
  administering system using Webmin,
    325–327
  of Apache Web server, 249–250
  building custom kernel for, 321–322
  of DNS, 317–318
  of FTP, 320
  of NFS, 315–316
  of Samba, 316–317
  of sendmail server, 318–319
  shutting down unused services, 322–325
  of Web server, 320
  of X Window System, 313–315
options statement, named.conf file,
    185–189
OSTYPE macro, 214
others (o) permissions, 73–74
output redirection for commands, 66–67

• *P* •

Package Exceptions tab, Up2date Agent
    Configuration tool, 258
Package Manager. *See* Red Hat Package
    Manager (RPM)
packages
  installed, finding, 284
  installing from compressed zip files,
    285–286
  installing system packages, 280–282
  installing third-party packages, 282–284
  removing system packages, 282
  removing third-party packages, 285
  selecting during installation, 357–358
  updating, configuring up2date agent for,
    256–258
  updating, registering for, 253–255
  updating, using up2date agent for,
    259–261
packet filtering firewall, 157–160
panels on GNOME desktop
  applets on, 21–22
  applications on, 22–24
  icons on, 20–21, 41
panels on KDE desktop, 36
panes
  Konqueror File Manager, 40
  Nautilus File Manager, 26, 28

passive intrusion detection, 162
passwd command, 330, 331
Password Info tab, User Properties, 272
passwords
  resetting, 330
  root, resetting, 330–331
  root, setting, 357
  security of, 144, 148–149
$PATH, changing, 78
path option, Samba configuration file, 135
pax (portable archive exchange) tool,
    308–310
PC network, connecting to. *See* Samba
PCI (Peripheral Component Interconnect)
    bus, 342–343
Pentium processors, 342
performance. *See* optimization
Performance Tuning tab, HTTP
    configuration tool, 249–250
periods, two (..), move up a directory
    level, 70
Peripheral Component Interconnect (PCI)
    bus, 342–343
permissions
  assigning, 82, 149–151
  changing, 30, 74–75
  listing, 71–74
Permissions tab, Permissions, 150–151
physical security, 144
Ping Sweep scan, 166
pipe symbol (|), 66
plus sign (+), adding permissions, 74
POP3 (Post Office Protocol), 210–211, 215
port scanning
  considered an attack, 164
  with nmap tool, 164–167, 170–171
portable archive exchange (pax) tool,
    308–310
ports
  closing, 167–171
  list of, 164–165
Post Office Protocol (POP3), 210–211
pound sign (#)
  in configuration file, 226
  ending shell prompt, 65
Preferences item, Applications menu,
    24, 39

Preferences menu, Red Hat User
    Manager, 267
presentation program, 53–54
Preview tab, Nautilus File Management
    Preferences, 31
primary master server, configuring,
    197–199
print driver
  options for, 106–107
  selecting, 104–105, 106
print queue, configuring, 100–104, 105–106
printable option, Samba configuration
    file, 135
printer daemon
  definition of, 103
  restarting, 105
Printer Driver tab, Edit a print queue, 106
printers
  configuring for Samba, 135–136
  configuring with Printing Configuration
    tool, 98–105
  default, setting, 107
  deleting, 107
  editing configuration of, 105–107
  print driver for, 104–105
  security for, 103–104
  support for, 13
printers section, Samba configuration
    file, 135–136
Printing Configuration tool
  default printer, setting, 107
  deleting a printer, 107
  print driver, options for, 106–107
  print driver, selecting, 104–106
  print queue, configuring, 100–104,
    105–106
  starting, 98–99
privacy preferences, Firefox Web
    browser, 44
private group, 270
problems. See troubleshooting
proc directory, 64
processes, viewing and stopping, 80
processor (CPU)
  optimizing, 313–314
  requirements for, 342

procmail program, 209
Products link, Firefox Web browser, 44
profiles, configuring, 120–121
Programming item, Applications menu,
    24, 39
programs. See applications; packages
Properties icon, Red Hat User Manager, 268
protocol switching firewall, 157
ps command, 80
PS/2-style mouse, 344
pub directory, 233
put command, FTP, 233
pwd command
  in FTP, 233
  in restore, 298
  in shell, 70

• Q •

question mark (?)
  in Alert icon, 259
  wildcard, 68
Queue Name tab, Edit a print queue, 105
Queue Options tab, Edit a print queue, 106
Queue Type tab, Edit a print queue,
    105–106
quit command
  in FTP, 233
  in restore, 298
quotacheck command, 275, 277

• R •

r (read) permission, 73
RAID (Redundant Array of Independent
    Disks), optimization and, 315
RAM
  increasing, 313–314
  requirements for, 343
read (r) permission, 73
README file, 286
Reboot option, login window, 18
Receiving Mail dialog box, Evolution e-mail
    client, 47
Recent Documents item, Actions menu, 24
red exclamation point, Alert icon, 259

Red Hat Enterprise Linux (RHEL). *See also*
      specific versions
   configuring, 351–358
   features of, 13–16
   history of, 9–10
   installing, 346–348, 359
   partitioning hard disk for, 349–351
   rebooting, 18
   release cycle for, 10–11
   shutting down, 18
   support for, 11, 44
   third-party applications included with, 12
   updating, 11, 279–282
   versions of, 1, 10–12
Red Hat Global Learning Services, 44
Red Hat icon
   GNOME desktop, 21–22
   KDE desktop, 36
Red Hat, Inc. link, Firefox Web browser, 44
*Red Hat Linux Networking and System
      Administration* (Collings, Wall), 322
Red Hat Network link, Firefox Web
      browser, 44
Red Hat Network (RHN)
   accessing from Web browser, 262–266
   Alert icon, 259
   configuring up2date agent, 256–258
   registering with, 253–255
   searching for updates with up2date
      agent, 259–261
Red Hat Network Web site, 44
Red Hat Package Manager (RPM). *See also*
      .rpm files
   definition of, 14
   description of, 279–280
   installing system packages, 280–282
   removing system packages, 282
Red Hat Store Web site, 44
Red Hat User Manager
   description of, 267–269
   group properties, changing, 272–273
   groups, adding, 270–271
   user properties, changing, 271–272
   users, adding, 269–270
   users, removing, 273–274
Red Hat Web site, 44, 262, 338
redhat-config-network-cmd
      command, 121

Redundant Array of Independent Disks
      (RAID), optimization and, 315
Refresh icon, Red Hat User Manager, 268
release cycle, 10–11
Reload button, Firefox Web browser, 43
remote logins, 16
remote server, properties for, 191–192
repquota command, 277–278
rescue CD
   creating, 336
   included with this book, 361–362
resize handle, Nautilus File Manager, 26
resolution of display
   changing, 86–87
   definition of, 343
resolv.conf file, 196, 335
resources, 337–338. *See also* Web sites
restore command, 296–298
Retrieval/Installation tab, Up2date Agent
      Configuration tool, 256–258
reverse zone file, 195
RGBpath option, X configuration files, 93
RHEL. *See* Red Hat Enterprise Linux
RHN (Red Hat Network)
   accessing from Web browser, 262–266
   Alert icon, 259
   configuring up2date agent, 256–258
   registering with, 253–255
   searching for updates with up2date
      agent, 259–261
Rhythmbox audio player, 56–57
Rhythmbox Web site, 56
right-pointing arrows on menu items, 22
rm command, 76
root directory (/), 63
root directory, 64
root nameserver, 183
root user
   password for, resetting, 330–331
   password for, setting, 357
   privileges for, 78
route command, 335
Route tab, Ethernet Device, 119
rpm command, 14, 131, 283–285
.rpm files (RPM format)
   binary, installing, 283–284
   definition of, 14, 283

RPM (Red Hat Package Manager)
    definition of, 14
    description of, 279–280
    installing system packages, 280–282
    removing system packages, 282
`.rpmsave` files, 335–336
Run Application item, Actions menu, 24
Run Command item, Applications menu, 38

• S •

Samba
    client, connecting to, 138–139
    client, definition of, 131
    installing, 131–132
    optimizing, 316–317
    server, configuring, 132–136
    server, connecting to, 137–138
    server, definition of, 131
    server, starting, 136–137
    system hanging when starting, 334–335
    users, creating, 136
SANE (Scanner Access Now Easy)-
        compliant scanner, 59
`sbin` directory, 64
Schedule tab, Red Hat Network, 264
scheduling features, Evolution e-mail
        client, 48–49
SCP (Secure Copy), 152
screen. *See* display; monitor
`Screen` option, X configuration files, 92
`Screen` section, X configuration files, 94–95
screensaver
    configuring, 33–34
    starting, 24, 38
Screensaver Preferences dialog box, 33–34
screenshot, capturing, 24
SCSI controllers, requirements for, 345
SCSI disks
    optimization and, 315
    requirements for, 344
Search button, Firefox Web browser, 43
Search Filter field, Red Hat User Manager,
        268–269
Search for Files item, Actions menu, 24, 27
secondary master (slave) server
    configuration files for, 183–184
    configuring, 196–197

    definition of, 183
    `named.conf` file for, 185–193, 196–197
Secure Copy (SCP), 152
Secure File Transfer Protocol (SFTP), 153
Secure Multi-Purpose Internet Mail
        Extensions (S/MIME), 218
Secure Shell (SSH)
    configuring firewall for, 355
    security and, 152
security. *See also* intrusion detection
    of documents, 144–145
    of e-mail, 217–219
    features for, 14–15
    file and directory permissions, 149–151
    firewall for, 156–160
    of FTP, 153
    of hosts, 144, 147–152
    of HTTP, 153
    of Internet services, 152–153
    of modems, 145
    of network, 145, 152–156
    passwords, 144, 148–149
    physical security, 144
    of printers, 103–104
    SELinux (Security-Enhanced Linux), 356
    of servers, 144, 153–155
    of SMTP, 153, 219
    of SSH, 152
    system updates for, 152
    updates for, 152
security cameras, 144
Security Level Configuration tool, 157–158
`security` option, Samba configuration
        file, 134
security policy
    consequences for breaking, 145–146
    definition of, 143–144
    document security, 144–145
    network security, 145
    physical security, 144
    responsibility for, 146
SELinux (Security-Enhanced Linux), 356
Sendmail
    configuring, 212–213
    configuring IMAP4 for, 216
    configuring POP3 for, 215
    definition of, 16, 211
    macro file for, 213–214

mail aliases for, 216–217

mail queue, managing, 214–215

optimizing, 318–319

starting, 211–212

system hanging when starting, 334–335

`sendmail` command, 212

`sendmail.cf` file, 212–213

Send/Receive button, Evolution e-mail client, 48

Server Message Block (SMB) print queue, 101–102

`server` statement, `named.conf` file, 191–192

`server string` option, Samba configuration file, 134

Server tab, HTTP configuration tool, 248–249

servers. *See also* DNS server; FTP server; Web server; X Server

font server, 92–93, 314

nameservers, 119–120, 183

NFS (Network File System) server, 123–128

Samba server, 131–138

security for, 144, 153–155

standalone, disabling, 153–154

stopping services for, 155, 322–325

`xinetd` servers, 155–156, 325

`service` command, 136–137

services

closing ports for, 167–171

Internet, 16, 24, 39, 152–153

listing, 323–324

standalone, disabling, 153–154

stopping, 155, 322–325

`xinetd`, disabling, 155–156, 325

Session option, login window, 18

`setmodes` command, in `restore`, 298

SFTP (Secure File Transfer Protocol), 153

shareable files, 62

shares (in NFS)

choosing for export, 124–128

definition of, 123

deleting, 127

editing, 127

mounting (accessing), 129–130

shares (in Samba configuration file), 132

sharing files

features for, 13–14

with NFS, 123–130

with Samba, 132

shareable and unshareable files, 62

shell

`bash` shell, 65

command syntax, 66–68

default shell, 65

definition of, 64

prompt for, 65

terminal window for, 64–65

shell commands. *See* commands, shell

shell scripts, 82

Shop link, Firefox Web browser, 44

shortcuts (applets)

on GNOME desktop, 21–22

on KDE desktop, 36–37

Shut Down option, login window, 18

Simple Mail Transfer Protocol (SMTP), 153

slash (/)

following directory name, 71

root directory, 63

slave (secondary master) server

configuration files for, 183–184

configuring, 196–197

definition of, 183

`named.conf` file for, 185–193, 196–197

`smb passwd file` option, Samba configuration file, 134

`smb` protocol, 138

SMB (Server Message Block) print queue, 101–102

`smbclient` utility, 138

`smb.conf` file, 132–136, 316–317

`smbmount` command, 138–139

`smbpasswd` command, 136

`smbumount` command, 139

S/MIME (Secure Multi-Purpose Internet Mail Extensions), 218

SMTP (Simple Mail Transfer Protocol)

configuring firewall for, 355

definition of, 153, 210

security of, 153, 219

spoofing and, 219

SOA (Start of Authority), 193–194

socket options option, Samba
    configuration file, 135, 316
soft limit for disk quotas, 276
software detection tools. *See* nmap tool;
    Tripwire program
sound
  does not work after installation, 332–333
  utilities for, 23, 39
sound card
  configuring, 55–56
  requirements for, 345
sound files, playing, 56–57
Sound & Video item, Applications menu,
    23, 39
spamming, 219
spoofing, e-mail, 219
spreadsheet program, 52–53
SQL (Structured Query Language)
    databases, backing up, 289
.src.rpm files, 283
ssh program, 16
SSH (Secure Shell)
  configuring firewall for, 355
  security and, 152
SSL for Web server, 247–248
st command, 292
standalone servers, disabling, 153–154
Start of Authority (SOA), 193–194
startx command, 96
static files, 62
status bar
  Konqueror File Manager, 40
  Nautilus File Manager, 26
stdin (standard input), 66–67
stdout (standard output), 66–67
Stop button, Firefox Web browser, 43
Structured Query Language (SQL)
    databases, backing up, 289
su command, 78, 336–337
subscription service. *See* Red Hat Network
    (RHN)
superuser (root user)
  password for, resetting, 330–331
  password for, setting, 357
  privileges for, 78
support, 11, 44. *See also* troubleshooting
Support icon, Firefox Web browser, 44

swap space, 343
switches, optimization and, 316
symbolic links, 245
SYN Stealth Scan, 165
sysadmin user name, 148
sysconfig directory, 63
system administration tools
  accessing, 23, 38–39
  Webmin tool, 325–327
system hanging when starting network
    services, 334–335
system kernel
  custom, building, 321–322
  definition of, 9
  location of, 63
system path, changing, 78
system performance. *See* optimization
system preferences, 24
System Settings item, Applications menu,
    23, 39
System Tools item, Applications menu,
    23, 38
Systems tab, Red Hat Network, 263

• *T* •

tac.rev file, 198
tactech.com file, 198
Take Screenshot item, Actions menu, 24
tape, magnetic, for backups, 289, 292
tar command, 285–286, 290, 299–300
tarballs, 285
.tar.gz files, 285
TCP Window Scan, 166
TCP/IP (Transmission Control/Internet
    Protocol)
  definition of, 16
  e-mail using, 204
  Internet services using, 152–153
Telnet, 16, 153
temporary files, not backing up, 287
terminal window, 64–65
testparm command, 136
text editors, 24, 39
text files, opening from Nautilus File
    Manager, 28

third-party applications
  included with Enterprise Linux, 12
  installing, 282–284
  removing, 285
3-D hardware acceleration, 92
time zone, setting, 356–357
tmp directory, 64
toolbars
  Firefox Web browser, 43–44
  Konqueror File Manager, 39
  Nautilus File Manager, 26
Tools menu, Firefox Web browser, 43
top-level domains, list of, 182
Torvalds, Linus (Linux developer), 9
touchpads, requirements for, 344
Training link, Firefox Web browser, 44
Transmission Control/Internet Protocol
    (TCP/IP)
  definition of, 16
  e-mail using, 204
  Internet services using, 152–153
trash
  displaying items in, 30
  emptying, 30
  moving files or folders to, 30
  restoring items in, 30
Trash icon, GNOME desktop, 20
Tree view, Nautilus File Manager, 26–27
tripwire command, 173, 177
Tripwire program
  configuring, 172–176
  definition of, 162
  documentation for, 172
  installing, 171–172
  integrity check, running, 173–176
  policy file for, editing, 176–177
  reports, viewing, 177–178
troubleshooting. *See also* optimization
  CD-ROM drive does not mount after
      installation, 332
  CD-ROM drive not detected during
      installation, 331
  drive will not unmount, 333–334
  emergency boot disk, creating, 336
  emergency boot disk, included with this
      book, 362
  logging in, unable to, 329–331

network hosts, unable to access, 335–336
  password, resetting, 330–331
  resources for, 337–338
  shell commands not working, 336–337
  sound does not work after installation,
      332–333
  system hanging when starting network
      services, 334–335
twadmin command, 177
two periods (..), move up a directory
    level, 70
twprint command, 178

• *U* •

u (user) permissions, 73–74
UDP Port Scan, 166
UID (user ID), 270
umount command, 79, 275, 333–334
UNIX (LPD) print queue, 100
unsharable files, 62
up2date agent
  configuring, 256–258
  definition of, 14
  registering with, 254–255
  searching for updates with, 259–261
Up2date Agent Configuration tool, 256–258
up2date-config command, 256
updates. *See also* Red Hat Network (RHN);
      Red Hat Package Manager (RPM)
  features for, 11, 14
  for security, 152
USB drive, for backups, 289
Usenet news groups about Linux, 338
User Access tab, Add NFS Share, 126
User Data tab, User Properties, 272
user ID (UID), 270
User Manager
  description of, 267–269
  group properties, changing, 272–273
  groups, adding, 270–271
  user properties, changing, 271–272
  users, adding, 269–270
  users, removing, 273–274
user (u) permissions, 73–74
useradd command, 330

users
  adding, 148, 268–270, 330
  backing up files for, 288–289
  directories for, 63
  disk quotas for, 274–277
  displaying, 269
  home directory for, 63, 270
  password, resetting, 330
  private group for, 270
  properties for, changing, 271–272
  removing, 273–274
  Samba, creating, 136
  UID for, 270
users groups for Linux, 338
Users tab
  Red Hat Network, 264
  Red Hat User Manager, 269
usr directory, 64
usrquota option, 274–275

• V •

var directory, 64
variable files, 62
VendorName option, X configuration
    files, 94
verbose command, in restore, 298
vertical bar (|), pipe symbol, 66
VertRefresh option, X configuration
    files, 94
VESA local bus (VL-bus), 343
video card
  configuring, 91–92
  requirements for, 343
  type, changing, 89–90
video chipset, 343
video files, playing, 57–58
video, utilities for, 23, 39
Videoram option, X configuration files, 92
View menu, Firefox Web browser, 42
Views tab, Nautilus File Management
    Preferences, 31
Virtual Hosts tab, HTTP configuration tool,
    240–248
VL-bus (VESA local bus), 343
vsftpd file, 223

vsftpd (Very Secure FTP daemon) server
  configuring, 222–228
  definition of, 16
  installing, 221–222
  logging in to, 229–233
  optimizing, 320
  starting, 228–229
  testing, 229
  transferring files with, 231, 233
vsftpd.conf file, 223–227
vsftpd.ftpusers file, 223, 227
vsftpd.user_list file, 223, 228

• W •

w (write) permission, 73
Wall, Kurt (*Red Hat Linux Networking and
    System Administration*), 322
Web browsers. *See also* Firefox Web
    browser
  accessing, 24
  accessing Red Hat Network from, 262–266
  Konqueror File Manager as, 39
  optimization and, 314
Web server (Apache)
  configuring, general information, 239–240
  configuring, performance tuning, 249–250
  configuring, server, 248–249
  configuring, SSL, 247–248
  configuring, virtual hosts, 240–248
  definition of, 16
  directories used by, 244–247
  environment variables for CGI scripts,
      243–244
  files and directories for, list of, 238–239
  installing, 235–236
  logging for, 242–243
  optimizing, 320
  restarting after configuration, 250
  starting, 236–237
  system hanging when starting, 334–335
  testing, 237–238
Web sites
  Advanced Linux Sound Architecture, 333
  Apache Web server, 235
  CD-Writing How-to, 293

CERT (Computer Emergency Response Team), 219
FHS (Filesystem Hierarchy Standard), 62
Firefox, 43
The Linux Documentation Project Web site, 337
Linux Journal Web site, 337
The Linux Kernel Archives Web site, 338
Linux Online Web site, 338
MPlayer, 58
ports, list of, 164–165
Red Hat, 44, 262, 338
Red Hat Network, 44, 254
Red Hat Store, 44
Red Hat supported hardware, 346
Rhythmbox, 56
SELinux (Security-Enhanced Linux), 356
S/MIME, 218
Tripwire program, 171
Usenet news groups about Linux, 338
users groups for Linux, 338
Xine, 57
Webmin tool, 325–327
whatis command, 69
wildcards in commands, 67–68
window manager. *See* GNOME desktop; KDE (K Desktop Environment)
window panes
  Konqueror File Manager, 40
  Nautilus File Manager, 26, 28
Windows network, connecting to. *See* Samba
Windows (SMB) print queue, 101–102
wireless NIC, adding to network, 113–115
word processor, 50–52
workgroup option, Samba configuration file, 134
Workspace Switcher
  GNOME desktop, 21
  KDE desktop, 36
world permissions
  all (a) permissions, 74
  others (o) permissions, 73–74
write (w) permission, 73
writeable option, Samba configuration file, 135

Writer (OpenOffice.org), 50–52
WS version of Red Hat Enterprise Linux
  definition of, 12
  topics covered in this book for, 1

X client, 85–86
X configuration files
  Device section, 91–92
  DRI section, 92
  Files section, 92–93
  InputDevice section, 93
  location of, 91
  Module section, 93
  Monitor section, 93–94
  Screen section, 94–95
  structure of, 91
X Configuration tool
  display color depth, changing, 87
  display resolution, changing, 86–87
  dual monitors, configuring, 90–91
  monitor type settings, changing, 88–89
  video card type, changing, 89–90
x (execute) permission, 73
X Server
  configuring manually from configuration files, 91–95
  configuring with X Configuration tool, 86–91
  definition of, 85–86
  disabling, 96
  restarting, 95
  starting manually, 96
X Window System. *See also* X Server
  desktops provided for, 13
  optimizing, 313–315
  X client, 85–86
  XFree86, compatibility with devices, 342–343
  XFree86, optimization and, 313–315
xconfig tool, 321–322
XFree86. *See also* X Server
  compatibility with devices, 342–343
  optimization and, 313–315
  X client, 85–86

xfs font server, 92
Ximian Evolution e-mail client. *See*
  Evolution e-mail client
Xine movie player, 57–58
Xine Web site, 57
xinetd servers, disabling, 155–156, 325
Xmas Tree Stealth Scan, 166

• Y •

Your RHN tab, Red Hat Network, 262–263

• Z •

zip disks, for backups, 289
zip files, compressed, installing packages
  from, 285–286
zone files, 183, 193–195
zone statements, named.conf file, 192–193